Date Due

DEC 16			
NOV 28			
JAN -6			

Man, Economy, and State

A TREATISE ON ECONOMIC PRINCIPLES

The William Volker Fund Series in the Humane Studies

Man, Economy, and State

A TREATISE ON ECONOMIC PRINCIPLES

by

MURRAY N. ROTHBARD

VOLUME I

D. VAN NOSTRAND COMPANY, INC.

PRINCETON, NEW JERSEY

TORONTO   LONDON

NEW YORK

D. VAN NOSTRAND COMPANY, INC.
120 Alexander St., Princeton, New Jersey (*Principal office*)
24 West 40 Street, New York 18, New York

D. VAN NOSTRAND COMPANY, LTD.
358, Kensington High Street, London, W.14, England

D. VAN NOSTRAND COMPANY (Canada), LTD.
25 Hollinger Road, Toronto 16, Canada

PRINTED IN THE UNITED STATES OF AMERICA

TO
LUDWIG VON MISES

Preface

One of the unhappy casualties of World War I, it seems, was the old-fashioned treatise on economic "principles." Before World War I, the standard method, both of presenting and advancing economic thought, was to write a disquisition setting forth one's vision of the corpus of economic science. A work of this kind had many virtues wholly missing from the modern world. On the one hand, the intelligent layman, with little or no previous acquaintance with economics, could read it. On the other hand, the author did not limit himself, textbook-fashion, to choppy and oversimplified compilations of currently fashionable doctrine. For better or worse, he carved out of economic theory an architectonic—an edifice. Sometimes the edifice was an original and noble one, sometimes it was faulty; but at least there *was* an edifice, for beginners to see, for colleagues to adopt or criticize. Hyperrefinements of detail were generally omitted as impediments to viewing economic science as a whole, and they were consigned to the journals. The university student, too, learned his economics from the treatise on its "principles"; it was not assumed that special works were needed with chapter lengths fitting course requirements and devoid of original doctrine. These works, then, were read by students, intelligent laymen, and leading economists, all of whom profited from them.

Their spirit is best illustrated by a prefatory passage from one of the last of the species:

I have tried in this book to state the principles of economics in such form that they shall be comprehensible to an educated and intelligent person who has not before made any systematic study of the subject. Though designed in this sense for beginners, the book does not gloss over difficulties or avoid severe reasoning. No one can understand economic phenomena or prepare himself to deal with economic problems who is unwilling to follow trains of reasoning which call for sustained attention. I have done my best to be clear, and to state with care the grounds on which my conclusions rest, as well as the conclusions themselves, but have made no vain pretense of simplifying all things." [1]

Since the brilliant burst that gave us the works of Wicksteed (1910), Taussig (1911), and Fetter (1915), this type of treatise has disappeared from economic thought, and economics has become appallingly fragmented, dissociated to such a degree that there hardly *is* an *economics* any more; instead, we find myriad bits and pieces of uncoordinated analysis. Economics has, first, been fragmented into "applied" fields—"urban land economics," "agricultural economics," "labor economics," "public finance economics," etc., each division largely heedless of the others. More grievous still has been the disintegration of what has been confined to the category of "economic theory." Utility theory, monopoly theory, international trade theory, etc., down to linear programming and games theory—each moves in its sharply isolated compartment, with its own hyperrefined literature. Recently, growing awareness of this fragmentation has led to vague "interdisciplinary" admixtures with all the other "social sciences." Confusion has been worse confounded, with resulting invasive forays of numerous other disciplines into economics, rather than the diffusion of economics elsewhere. At any rate, it is somewhat foolhardy to attempt to integrate economics with everything else before economics has *itself* been made whole. Only then will the proper place of economics among the other disciplines become manifest.

I think it fair to say that, with only a single exception (Ludwig von Mises' *Human Action*) *not one* general treatise on economic principles has appeared since World War I. Perhaps the closest approach was Frank H. Knight's *Risk, Uncertainty, and Profit,* and *that* was published far back in 1921. Since then there has been no book of remotely as broad a scope.

[1] Frank W. Taussig, *Principles of Economics* (New York: Macmillan, 1911), p. vii.

The only place where we can find economics treated with any degree of breadth is in the elementary textbooks. These textbooks, however, are sorry substitutes for a genuine Principles. Since they must, by their nature, present only currently received doctrine, their work is uninteresting to the established economist. Furthermore, since they may only boil down the existing literature, they must of necessity present to the student a hodgepodge of fragmented chapters, each with little or no relation to the other.

Many economists see no loss in all this; in fact, they herald these developments as signs of the enormous progress the science has made on all fronts. Knowledge has grown so vast that no man can encompass it all. Yet economists should at least be responsible for knowing *economics*—the essentials of the body of their discipline. Certainly, then, these essentials could have been presented by this time. The plain fact is that economics is fragmented precisely *because* it is no longer regarded as an edifice; since it is considered a congeries of isolated splinters, it is treated as such.

Perhaps the key to this change is that formerly economics was regarded as a logical structure. Fundamentally, whatever the differences of degree, or even of proclaimed methodology, economics was considered a deductive science using verbal logic. Grounded on a few axioms, the edifice of economic thought was deduced step by step. Even when the analysis was primitive or the announced methodology far more inductive, this was the essence of economics during the nineteenth century. Hence, the treatise on economic "principles"—for if economics proceeds by deductive logic grounded on a few simple and evident axioms, then the corpus of economics can be presented as an interrelated whole to the intelligent layman with no loss of ultimate rigor. The layman is taken step by step from simple and evident truths to more complex and less evident ones.

The "Austrian" economists best perceived this method and used it most fully and cogently. They were the classic employers, in short, of the "praxeologic" method. In the present day, however, the prevailing epistemology has thrown over praxeology for methods at once too empirical and too "theoretical." Empiricism has disintegrated economics to such an extent that no one thinks to look for a complete edifice; and, paradoxically, it has falsified economics by making economists eager to introduce admittedly false and short-cut assumptions in order to make their theories more readily "testable." Alfred Marshall's distrust of "long chains of deduction," as well as the whole Cambridge impetus toward such short cuts, has contributed a great deal to this breakdown. On the other hand, verbal logic in economic theory has been replaced by mathematics, seemingly more precise and basking in the reflected glory of the physical sciences. The dominant econometric wing of mathematical economists also looks for empirical verifications and thereby compounds the errors of both methods. Even on the level of pure theoretical integration, mathematics is completely inappropriate for any sciences of human action. Mathematics has, in fact, contributed to the compartmentalization of economics—to specialized monographs featuring a hyperrefined maze of matrices, equations, and geometric diagrams. But the really important thing is *not* that nonmathematicians cannot understand them; the crucial point is that mathematics cannot contribute to economic knowledge. In fact, the recent conquest of mathematical economics by econometrics is a sign of recognition that pure mathematical theory in economics is sterile.

This book, then, is an attempt to fill part of the enormous gap of forty years' time. Since the last treatise on economic "principles," economics has proceeded a long way in many areas, and its methodology has been immeasurably improved and strengthened by those continuing to work in the praxeological tradition. Furthermore, there are still great gaps in the praxeological corpus, since so few economists have worked at shaping it. Hence, the attempt in this book to develop the edifice of economic science in the manner of the old-fashioned works on its "principles"— slowly and logically to build on the basic axioms an integrated and coherent edifice of economic truth. Hyperrefinements have been shunned as much as possible. In short, Professor Taussig's quoted statement of intention has been mine also, with the addition that I have felt it necessary to include, at pertinent points, refutation of some of the main opposing doctrines. This was especially needed because economic fallacy prevails far more widely than in Taussig's time.

I have indicated briefly that there has been *one* general treatise since World War I. Professor Paul Samuelson has written rhapsodically of the joy of being under thirty at the time of publication of Keynes' *General Theory*. I can say the same for the publication of Ludwig von Mises' *Human Action* in 1949. For here at last was economics *whole* once more, once again an edifice. Not only that—here was a structure of economics with many of the components newly contributed by Professor Mises himself. There is no space here to present or expound Mises' great contributions to economic science. That will have to be done elsewhere. Suffice it to say that from now on, little constructive work can be done in economics unless it starts from *Human Action*.

Human Action is a general treatise, but not an old-style Principles. Instead, it assumes considerable previous economic knowledge and includes within its spacious confines numerous philosophic and historical insights. In one sense, the present work attempts to isolate the economic, fill in the interstices, and spell out the detailed implications, as I see them, of the Misesian structure. It must not be thought, however, that Professor Mises is in any way responsible for these pages. Indeed, he may well differ strongly with many sections of this volume. Yet it is my hope that this work may succeed in adding a few bricks to the noble structure of economic science that has reached its most modern and developed form in the pages of *Human Action*.

The present work deduces the entire corpus of economics from a few simple and apodictically true axioms: the Fundamental Axiom of *action*—that men employ means to achieve ends, and two subsidiary postulates: that there is a *variety* of human and natural resources, and that leisure is a consumers' good. Chapter 1 begins with the action axiom and deduces its immediate implications; and these conclusions are applied to "Crusoe economics" —that much maligned but highly useful analysis that sets individual man starkly against Nature and analyzes his resulting actions. Chapter 2 introduces other men and, consequently, social relations. Various types of interpersonal relations are analyzed, and the economics of *direct exchange* (barter) is set forth. Exchange cannot be adequately analyzed until property rights are fully defined—so chapter 2 analyzes property in a free society. Chapter 2, in fact, marks the beginning of the body of the book—an analysis of the economics of voluntary exchange. Chapter 2 discusses the free market of barter, and the subsequent chapters treat the economics of *indirect*—or monetary—exchange. Thus, analytically, the book deals fully with the economics of the free market, from its property relations to the economics of money.

Chapter 3 introduces money and traces the patterns of indirect exchange on the market. Chapter 4 treats the economics of consumption and the pricing of consumers' goods. Chapters 5–9 analyze production on the free market. One of the features of this consumption and production theory is the resurrection of Professor Frank A. Fetter's brilliant and completely neglected theory of *rent*—i.e., the concept of rent as the hire price of a unit service. *Capitalization* then becomes the process of determining the present values of the expected future rents of a good. The Fetter-Mises pure time-preference theory of interest is synthesized with the Fetter rent theory, with the Austrian theory of the structure of production, and with separation of *original* from *produced* factors of production. One "radical" feature of our analysis of production is a complete break with the currently fashionable "short-run" theory of the firm, substituting for this a general theory of marginal value productivity and capitalization. It is a "general equilibrium" analysis in the dynamic Austrian, and not in the static, currently popular Walrasian sense.

Chapter 10 expounds a completely new theory of monopoly—that monopoly can be meaningfully defined only as a grant of privilege by the State, and that a monopoly price can be attained only from such a grant. In short, there can be no monopoly or monopoly price on the free market. The theory of monopolistic competition is also discussed. And chapter 11 sets forth the theory of money on the free market, along with an extensive discussion of the Keynesian theories.

Having completed the theory of the purely free market, I then turn, in the final chapter, to applying praxeological analysis to a systematic discussion of various forms and degrees of coercive intervention and their consequences. The effects of coercive intervention can be studied only after fully analyzing the construct of a purely free market. Chapter 12 presents a typology of intervention, discusses its direct and indirect consequences and the effects on utility, and sets forth a necessarily brief analysis of the various major types of intervention, including price control, monopoly grants, taxation, inflation, and government enterprise and expenditures. The chapter and the book conclude with a brief summary assessment of the free market, as contrasted to interventionist and other coercive systems.

Divisions into volumes are always more or less arbitrary in works of this kind; but, in general, Volume I (chapters 1 through 7) sets forth the basic theory of the workings of the free-market economy, while Volume II (chapters 8 through 12) builds on that foundation by discussing the complex problems of dynamic change, of particular factors, of monopoly, and of money, as well as the economics of intervention in that market.

Apart from my intellectual debt to Professor Ludwig von Mises, I can never fully express my personal debt. His wisdom, insight, kindness, enthusiasm, and unflagging encouragement of even the slightest signs of productivity among his students have been a continuous inspiration to all who know him. He is one of the great teachers of economics, as well as one of the great economists, and I am grateful to have had the opportunity of studying for many years at his Seminar in Advanced Economic Theory at New York University.

I am also grateful to Mr. Herbert C. Cornuelle, of the Dole Pineapple Company, for introducing me to the Misesian approach and for first igniting my interest in this project. I owe a great debt to Mr. Richard C. Cornuelle, both for the days of discovery when we first learned economics and political philosophy together, and for his keen insight and encouragement in the writing of this work. I would also like to thank Dr. Ivan R. Bierly for his help in seeing the book through to publication, and Mr. Arthur Goddard for his patience and great editorial competence. And I am profoundly grateful to the directors of the foundation that is publishing this series of studies.

Finally, I must express my gratitude for the inspiration provided by that legion of friends and acquaintances who are fearlessly reaching out for truth in political philosophy and political economy, and who have widened the knowledge of all of us on the nature of coercion and of freedom.

Needless to say, the responsibility for this work is wholly my own.

MURRAY N. ROTHBARD

Table of Contents

1

Fundamentals of Human Action[1]

1. *The Concept of Action*

The distinctive and crucial feature in the study of man is the concept of *action. Human action is defined simply as purposeful behavior.* It is therefore sharply distinguishable from those observed movements which, from the point of view of man, are not purposeful. These include all the observed movements of inorganic matter and those types of human behavior that are purely reflex, that are simply involuntary responses to certain stimuli. *Human action,* on the other hand, can be *meaningfully interpreted* by other men, for it is governed by a certain *purpose* that the actor has in view.[2] The purpose of a man's act is his *end;* the desire to achieve this end is the man's *motive* for instituting the action.

All human beings *act* by virtue of their existence and their nature as human beings.[3] We could not conceive of human beings who do not act purposefully, who have no ends in view that they desire and attempt to attain. Things that did not *act,* that did not behave purposefully, would no longer be classified as human.

It is this fundamental truth—this axiom of human action—that forms the key to our study. The entire realm of praxeology and its best developed subdivision, economics, is based on an analysis of the necessary logical implications of this concept.[4] The fact that men act by virtue of their being human is indisputable and incontrovertible. To assume the contrary would be an ab-

1

surdity. The contrary—the absence of motivated behavior—would apply only to plants and inorganic matter.[5]

2. First Implications of the Concept

The first truth to be discovered about human action is that *it can be undertaken only by individual "actors."* Only individuals have ends, and can act to attain them. There are no such things as ends of or actions by "groups," "collectives," or "States," which do not take place as actions by various specific individuals. "Societies" or "groups" have no independent existence aside from the actions of their individual members. Thus, to say that "governments" act is merely a metaphor; actually, certain individuals are in a certain relationship with other individuals and act in a way that they and the other individuals recognize as "governmental."[6] The metaphor must not be taken to mean that the collective institution itself has any reality apart from the acts of various individuals. Similarly, an individual may contract to act as an agent in representing another individual or on behalf of his family. Still, only individuals can desire and act. The existence of an institution such as government becomes meaningful only through influencing the actions of those individuals who are and those who are not considered as members.[7]

In order to institute action, it is not sufficient that the individual man have unachieved ends that he would like to fulfill. *He must also expect that certain modes of behavior will enable him to attain his ends.* A man may have a desire for sunshine, but if he realizes that he can do nothing to achieve it, he does not act on this desire. He must have certain *ideas* about how to achieve his ends. Action thus consists of the behavior of individuals directed towards ends in ways that they believe will accomplish their purpose. Action requires an image of a desired end and "technological ideas" or plans on how to arrive at this end.

Men find themselves in a certain *environment*, or *situation*. It is this situation that the individual decides to change in some way in order to achieve his ends. But man can work only with the numerous elements that he finds in his environment, by rearranging them in order to bring about the satisfaction of his ends. With reference to any given act, the environment external to the individual may be divided into two parts: those elements which he believes he cannot control and must leave unchanged, and those which he can alter (or rather, thinks he can alter) to arrive at his ends. The former may be termed the *general conditions* of the action; the latter the *means* used. Thus, the individual actor is faced with an environment that he would like to change in order to attain his ends. To act, he must have technological ideas about how to use some of the elements of the environment as *means*, as pathways, to arrive at his ends. Every act must therefore involve the employment of means by individual actors to attempt to arrive at certain desired ends. In the external environment, the general conditions cannot be the objects of any human action; only the means can be employed in action.[8]

All human life must take place *in time*. Human reason cannot even conceive of an existence or of action that does not take place through time. At a time when a human being decides to act in order to attain an end, his goal, or end, can be finally and completely attained only at some point *in the future*. If the desired ends could all be attained instantaneously in the present, then man's ends would all be attained, and there would be no reason for him to act; and we have seen that action is necessary to the nature of man. Therefore, an actor chooses means from his environment, in accordance with his ideas, to arrive at an expected end, completely attainable only at some point in the future. For any given action, we can distinguish among three periods of time involved: the period before the action, the time absorbed by the action, and the period after the action has been completed. All action aims at rendering conditions at some time in the future more satisfactory for the actor than they would have been without the intervention of the action.

A man's *time* is always scarce. He is not immortal; his time on earth is limited. Each day of his life has only twenty-four hours in which he can attain his ends. Furthermore, all actions must take place through time. Therefore time is a *means* that man must use to arrive at his ends. It is a means that is omnipresent in all human action.

Action takes place by *choosing* which ends shall be satisfied by the employment of means. Time is *scarce* for man only because whichever ends he chooses to satisfy, there are others that must remain unsatisfied. When we must use a means so that some ends remain unsatisfied, the necessity for a *choice among ends* arises. For example, Jones is engaged in watching a baseball game on television. He is faced with the choice of spending the next hour in: (*a*) continuing to watch the baseball game, (*b*) playing bridge, or (*c*) going for a drive. He would like to do all three of these things, but his means (time) is insufficient. As a result, he must *choose;* one end can be satisfied, but the others must go unfulfilled. Suppose that he decides on course A. This is a clear indication that he has *ranked* the satisfaction of end A higher than the satisfaction of ends B or C.

From this example of action, many implications can be deduced. In the first place, *all means are scarce,* i.e., limited with respect to the ends that they could possibly serve. If the means are in unlimited abundance, then they need not serve as the object of attention of any human action. For example, air in most situations is in unlimited abundance. It is therefore not a means and is not employed as a means to the fulfillment of ends. It need not be allocated, as time is, to the satisfaction of the more important ends, since it is sufficiently abundant for all human requirements. Air, then, though indispensable, is not a means, but a *general condition* of human action and human welfare.

Secondly, these scarce means must be allocated by the actor to serve certain ends and leave other ends unsatisfied. This act of *choice* may be called *economizing* the means to serve the most desired ends. Time, for example, must be economized by the actor to serve the most desired ends. The actor may be interpreted as ranking his alternative ends in accordance with their *value* to him. This scaling of ends may be described as assigning ranks of *value* to the ends by the actor, or as a process of *valuation.* Thus, suppose that Jones ranked his alternative ends for the use of an hour of time as follows:

(First)   1. Continuing to watch the baseball game
(Second)   2. Going for a drive
(Third)   3. Playing bridge

This was his *scale of values* or *scale of preferences*. The supply of means (time) available was sufficient for the attainment of only one of these ends, and the fact that he chose the baseball game shows that he ranked that highest (or first). Suppose now that he is allocating two hours of his time and can spend an hour on each pursuit. If he spends one hour on the game and then a second hour on the drive, this indicates that his ranking of preferences is as above. The lowest-ranking end—playing bridge—goes unfulfilled. Thus, the larger the supply of means available, the more ends can be satisfied and the lower the rank of the ends that must remain unsatisfied.

Another lesson to be derived is that *action* does not necessarily mean that the individual is "active," as opposed to "passive," in the colloquial sense. Action does not necessarily mean that an individual must stop doing what he has been doing and do something else. He also acts, as in the above case, who chooses to continue in his previous course, even though the opportunity to change was open to him. Continuing to watch the game is just as much *action* as going for a drive.

Furthermore, action does not at all mean that the individual must take a great deal of time in deliberating on a decision to act. The individual may take a decision to act hastily, or after great deliberation, according to his desired choice. He may decide on an action coolly or heatedly; none of these courses affects the fact that action is being taken.[9]

Another fundamental implication derived from the existence of human action is the *uncertainty of the future*. This must be true because the contrary would completely negate the possibility of action. If man knew future events completely, he would never act, since no act of his could change the situation. Thus, the fact of action signifies that the future is uncertain to the actors. This uncertainty about future events stems from two basic sources: the unpredictability of human acts of choice and insufficient knowledge about natural phenomena. Man does not know enough about natural phenomena to predict all their future developments, and he cannot know the content of future human choices. All human choices are continually changing as a result of changing valuations and changing ideas about the most appropriate means of arriving at ends. This does not mean, of course, that people do not try their best to estimate future developments. Indeed, any actor, when employing means, estimates that he will thus arrive at his desired goal. But he never has certain knowledge of the future. All his actions are of necessity *speculations* based on his *judgment* of the course of future events. The omnipresence of uncertainty introduces the ever-present possibility of *error* in human action. The actor may find, after he has completed his action, that the means have been *inappropriate* to the attainment of his end.

To sum up what we have learned thus far about human action: The distinguishing characteristic of human beings is that all humans *act*. Action is purposeful behavior directed toward the attainment of ends in some future period which will involve the fulfillment of wants otherwise remaining unsatisfied. Action involves the expectation of a less imperfectly satisfied state as a result of the action. The individual actor chooses to employ elements in his environment as means to the expected achievement of his ends, *economizing* them by directing them toward his most valued ends (leaving his least valued ones unsatisfied), and in the ways that his reason tells him are most appropriate to attain these ends. His method—his chosen means—may or may not turn out to be inappropriate.

3. *Further Implications: The Means*

The *means* to satisfy man's wants are called *goods*. These goods are all the objects of economizing action.[10] Such goods may all be classified in either of two categories: (*a*) they are immediately and *directly serviceable* in the satisfaction of the actor's wants, or (*b*) they may be transformable into directly serviceable goods only at some point in the future—i.e., are *indirectly serviceable*

means. The former are called *consumption goods* or *consumers'
goods* or *goods of the first order.* The latter are called *producers'
goods* or *factors of production* or *goods of higher order.*

Let us trace the relations among these goods by considering a
typical human end: *the eating of a ham sandwich.* Having a desire
for a ham sandwich, a man decides that this is a want that should
be satisfied and proceeds to act upon his judgment of the methods by which a ham sandwich can be assembled. *The consumers'
good* is the ham sandwich at the point of being eaten. It is obvious
that there is a scarcity of this consumers' good as there is for all
direct means; otherwise it would always be available, like air, and
would not be the object of action. But if the consumers' good is
scarce and not obviously available, how can it be made available?
The answer is that man must rearrange various elements of his
environment in order to *produce* the ham sandwich at the desired
place—the consumers' good. In other words, man must use various
indirect means as co-operating factors of production to arrive at
the direct means. This necessary process involved in all action is
called *production;* it is the use by man of available elements of his
environment as indirect means—as co-operating factors—to arrive
eventually at a consumers' good which he can use directly to arrive
at his end.

Let us consider the pattern of some of the numerous co-operating factors that are involved in a modern developed economy to
produce one ham sandwich as a consumers' good for the use of one
consumer. Typically, in order to produce a ham sandwich for
Jones in his armchair, it is necessary for his wife to expend energy
in unwrapping the bread, slicing the ham, placing the ham between bread slices, and carrying it to Jones. All this work may be
called the *labor* of the housewife. The co-operating factors that
are directly necessary to arrive at the consumers' good are, then:
the housewife's labor, bread in the kitchen, ham in the kitchen,
and a knife to slice the ham. Also needed is the land on which to
have room to live and carry on these activities. Furthermore, this
process must, of course, take *time,* which is another indispensable
co-operating factor. The above factors may be called *first-order
producers' goods,* since, in this case, these co-operate in the produc-

tion of the consumers' good. Many of the first-order producers' goods, however, are also unavailable in nature and must be *produced* themselves, with the help of other producers' goods. Thus, bread in the kitchen must be produced with the co-operation of the following factors: *bread-in-retail-shop* and *housewife's labor* in carrying it (plus the ever-present land-as-standing-room, and time). In this procedure, these factors are second-order producers' goods, since they co-operate in producing first-order goods. Higher-order factors are those co-operating in the production of factors of lower order.

Thus, any process (or *structure*) of production may be analyzed as occurring in different *stages*. In the *earlier* or "higher" stages, producers' goods must be produced that will later co-operate in producing other producers' goods that will finally co-operate in producing the desired consumers' good. Hence, in a developed economy, the structure of production of a given consumers' good might be a very complex one and involve numerous stages.

Important general conclusions can, however, be drawn that apply to all processes of production. In the first place, each stage of production takes *time*. Secondly, the factors of production may all be divided into two classes: *those that are themselves produced,* and *those that are found already available in nature—in man's environment.* The latter may be used as indirect means without having been previously produced; the former must first be produced with the aid of factors in order to aid in the *later* (or "lower") stages of production. The former are the *produced factors of production;* the latter are the *original factors of production.* The original factors may, in turn, be divided into two classes: *the expenditure of human energy,* and *the use of nonhuman elements provided by nature.* The first is called *Labor;* the latter is Nature or *Land.*[11] Thus, the classes of factors of production are Labor, Land, and the produced factors which are termed *Capital Goods.*

Labor and Land, in one form or another, enter into each stage of production. Labor helps to transform seeds into wheat, wheat into flour, pigs into ham, flour into bread, etc. Not only is Labor present at every stage of production, but so also is Nature. Land must be available to provide room at every stage of the process, and time, as has been stated above, is required for each stage. Furthermore, if we wish to trace each stage of production far enough back to original sources, we must arrive at a point where only labor and nature existed and there were no capital goods. This must be true by logical implication, since all capital goods must have been produced at earlier stages with the aid of labor. If we could trace each production process far enough back in time, we must be able to arrive at the point—the earliest stage—where man combined his forces with nature unaided by produced factors of production. Fortunately, it is not necessary for human actors to perform this task, since action uses materials available in the present to arrive at desired goals in the *future,* and there is no need to be concerned with development in the *past.*

There is another unique type of factor of production that is indispensable in every stage of every production process. This is the "technological idea" of how to proceed from one stage to another and finally to arrive at the desired consumers' good. This is but an application of the analysis above, namely, that for any action, there must be some *plan* or idea of the actor about how to use things as means, as definite pathways, to desired ends. Without such plans or ideas, there would be no action. These plans may be called *recipes;* they are ideas of recipes that the actor uses to arrive at his goal. A *recipe* must be present at each stage of each production process from which the actor proceeds to a later stage. The actor must have a recipe for transforming iron into steel, wheat into flour, bread and ham into sandwiches, etc.

The distinguishing feature of a recipe is that, *once learned,* it generally does not have to be learned again. It can be noted and remembered. Remembered, it no longer has to be produced; it remains with the actor as an *unlimited* factor of production that never wears out or needs to be economized by human action. It becomes a general condition of human welfare in the same way as air.[12]

It should be clear that the end of the production process—the consumers' good—is valued because it is a direct means of satisfying man's ends. The consumers' good is *consumed,* and this act of *consumption* constitutes the satisfying of human wants. This

consumers' good may be a material object like bread or an immaterial one like friendship. Its important quality is not whether
it is material or not, but whether it is valued by man as a means of
satisfying his wants. This function of a consumers' good is called
its *service* in ministering to human wants. Thus, the material
bread is valued not for itself, but for its service in satisfying wants;
just as an immaterial thing, such as music or medical care, is
obviously valued for such service. All these services are "consumed" to satisfy wants. "Economic" is by no means equivalent to
"material."

It is also clear that the factors of production—the various higher-
order producers' goods—*are valued solely because of their anticipated usefulness in helping to produce future consumers' goods or
to produce lower-order producers' goods that will help to bring
about consumers' goods.* The valuation of factors of production is
derived from actors' evaluation of their products (lower stages),
all of which eventually derive their valuation from the end
result—the consumers' good.[13]

Furthermore, the omnipresent fact of the scarcity of consumers'
goods must be reflected back in the sphere of the factors of production. The scarcity of consumers' goods must imply a scarcity of
their factors. If the factors were unlimited, then the consumers'
goods would also be unlimited, which cannot be the case. This
does not exclude the possiblity that *some* factors, such as recipes,
may be unlimited and therefore general conditions of welfare
rather than scarce indirect means. But other factors at each stage
of production must be in scarce supply, and this must account for
the scarcity of the end product. Man's endless search for ways to
satisfy his wants—i.e., to *increase his production of consumers'
goods*—takes two forms: increasing his available supply of factors
of production and improving his recipes.

Although it has seemed evident that there are several co-operating factors at each stage of production, it is important to realize
that for each consumers' good *there must always be more than one
scarce factor of production.* This is implied in the very existence
of human action. It is impossible to conceive of a situation where
only one factor of production produces a consumers' good or even

advances a consumers' good from its previous stage of production. Thus, if the sandwich in the armchair did not require the co-operating factors at the previous stage (labor of preparation, carrying, bread, ham, time, etc.), then it would always be in the status of a consumers' good—sandwich-in-the-armchair. To simplify the example, let us suppose the sandwich already prepared and in the kitchen. Then, to produce a consumers' good from this stage forward requires the following factors: 1) the sandwich; 2) carrying it to the armchair; 3) time; 4) the land available. If we assume that it required only one factor—the sandwich—then we would have to assume that the sandwich was magically and instantaneously moved from kitchen to armchair without effort. But in this case, the consumers' good would not have to be produced at all, and we would be in the impossible assumption of Paradise. Similarly, at each stage of the productive process, the good must have been produced by at least *more than one* (higher-order) scarce co-operating factor; otherwise this stage of production could not exist at all.

4. *Further Implications: Time*

Time is omnipresent in human action as a means that must be economized. Every action is related to time as follows:

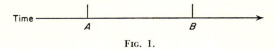

FIG. 1.

. . . *A* is the period before the beginning of the action; *A* is the point in time at which the action begins; *AB* is the period during which the action occurs; *B* is the point at which the action ends; *B* . . . is the period after the end of the action.

AB is defined as the *period of production*—the period from the beginning of the action to the time when the consumers' good is available. This period may be divided into various stages, each itself taking a period of time. The time expended during the period of production consists of the time during which *labor energy* is expended (*or working time*) and *maturing time,* i.e., time required without the necessity of concurrent expenditure of labor. An obvious example is the case of agriculture. There might be six months between the time the soil is tilled and the time the harvest is reaped. The total time during which labor must be expended may be three weeks, while the remaining time of over five months consists of the time during which the crop must mature and ripen by the processes of nature. Another example of a lengthy maturing time is the aging of wine to improve its quality.

Clearly, each consumers' good has its own period of production. The differences between the time involved in the periods of production of the various goods may be, and are, innumerable.

One important point that must be emphasized when considering action and the period of production is that acting man does *not* trace back past production processes to their original sources. In the previous section, we traced back consumers' goods and producers' goods to their original sources, demonstrating that all capital goods were *originally* produced solely by labor and nature. Acting man, however, is not interested in past processes, but only in using *presently available means* to achieve anticipated future ends. At any point in time, when he begins the action (say *A*), he has available to him: labor, nature-given elements, and *previously produced capital goods*. He begins the action at *A* expecting to reach his end at *B*. For *him,* the period of production is *AB,* since he is not concerned with the amount of time spent in past production of his capital goods or in the methods by which they were produced.[14] Thus, the farmer about to use his soil to grow crops for the coming season does not worry about whether or to what extent his soil is an original, nature-given factor or is the result of the improvements of previous land-clearers and farmers. He is not concerned about the previous time spent by these past improvers. He is concerned only with the capital (and other) goods in the present and the future. This is the necessary result of the fact that action occurs in the present and is aimed at the future. Thus, acting man considers and values the factors of production available in the present in accordance with their anticipated services in the future production of consumers' goods, and never in accordance with what has happened to the factors in the past.

A fundamental and constant truth about human action is that *man prefers his end to be achieved in the shortest possible time.* Given the specific satisfaction, the sooner it arrives, the better. This results from the fact that time is always scarce, and a means to be economized. The sooner any end is attained, the better. Thus, with any *given end* to be attained, the shorter the period of action, i.e., production, the more preferable for the actor. *This is the universal fact of time preference.* At any point of time, and for any action, the actor most prefers to have his end attained in the immediate present. Next best for him is the immediate future, and the further in the future the attainment of the end appears to be, the less preferable it is. *The less waiting time,* the more preferable it is for him.[15]

Time enters into human action not only in relation to the wait-ing time in production, but also in *the length of time in which the consumers' good will satisfy the wants of the consumer.* Some consumers' goods will satisfy his wants, i.e., attain his ends, for a short period of time, others for a longer period. They can be con-sumed for shorter or longer periods. This may be included in the diagram of any action as shown in Fig. 2. This length of time, *BC,*

FIG. 2. PERIOD OF PRODUCTION AND CONSUMPTION

is the *duration of serviceableness* of the consumers' good. It is the length of the time the *end* served by the consumers' good con-tinues to be attained. This duration of serviceableness differs for each consumers' good. It may be four hours for the ham sand-wich, after which period of time the actor desires other food or another sandwich. The builder of a house may expect to use it to serve his wants for ten years. Obviously, the expected durative power of the consumers' good to serve his end will enter into the actor's plans.[16]

Clearly, all other things being equal, the actor will prefer a consumers' good of greater durability to one of lesser, since the

former will render more total service. On the other hand, if the
actor values the total service rendered by two consumers' goods
equally, he will, because of time preference, choose the less durable
good since he will acquire its total services sooner than the other.
He will have to wait less for the total services of the less durable
good.

The concepts of period of production and duration of serviceableness are present in all human action. There is also a third
time-period that enters into action. Each person has a general
time-horizon, stretching from the present into the future, for
which he plans various types of action. Whereas period of production and duration of serviceableness refer to specific consumers'
goods and differ with each consumers' good, the *period of provision*
(the time-horizon) is the length of future time for which each
actor plans to satisfy his wants. The period of provision, therefore, includes planned action for a considerable variety of consumers' goods, each with its own period of production and duration. This period of provision differs from actor to actor in accordance with his choice. Some people live from day to day, taking
no heed of later periods of time; others plan not only for the
duration of their own lives, but for their children as well.

5. *Further Implications*

A. ENDS AND VALUES

All action involves the employment of scarce means to attain
the most valued ends. Man has the choice of using the scarce means
for various alternative ends, and the ends that he chooses are the
ones he values most highly. The less urgent wants are those that
remain unsatisfied. Actors can be interpreted as *ranking* their
ends along a scale of values, or scale of preferences. These scales
differ for each person, both in their content and in their orders
of preference. Furthermore, they differ for the same individual at
different times. Thus, at some other point in time, the actor
mentioned in section 2 above might choose to go for a drive, or
to go for a drive and then to play bridge, rather than to continue

watching the game. In that case, the ranking on his preference scale shifts to this order:

(First)   1. Going for a drive
(Second) 2. Playing bridge
(Third)   3. Continuing to watch the baseball game

Moreover, a new end might have been introduced in the meantime, so that the actor might enjoy going to a concert, and this may change his value scale to the following:

(First)   1. Going for a drive
(Second) 2. Going to a concert
(Third)   3. Playing bridge
(Fourth) 4. Continuing to watch the baseball game

The choice of which ends to include in the actor's value scale and the assignment of rank to the various ends constitute the process of *value judgment*. Each time the actor ranks and chooses between various ends, he is making a judgment of their value to him.

It is highly useful to assign a *name* to this value scale held by all human actors. We are not at all concerned with the specific *content* of men's ends, but only with the fact that various ends are ranked in the order of their importance. These scales of preference may be called *happiness* or *welfare* or *utility* or *satisfaction* or *contentment*. Which name we choose for value scales is not important. At any rate, it permits us to say, whenever an actor has attained a certain end, that he has *increased* his state of satisfaction, or his contentment, happiness, etc. Conversely, when someone considers himself worse off, and fewer of his ends are being attained, his satisfaction, happiness, welfare, etc., have *decreased*.

It is important to realize that there is never any possibility of *measuring* increases or decreases in happiness or satisfaction. Not only is it impossible to measure or compare changes in the satisfaction of different people; it is not possible to measure changes in the happiness of any given person. In order for any measurement to be possible, there must be an eternally fixed and objectively given unit with which other units may be compared. There is no such objective unit in the field of human valuation. The individual must determine subjectively for himself whether he is better or worse off as a result of any change. His preference can only be expressed in terms of simple choice, or *rank*. Thus, he can say, "I am better off" or "I am happier" because he went to a concert instead of playing bridge (or "I will be better off" for going to the concert), but it would be completely meaningless for him to try to assign units to his preference and say: "I am two and a half times happier because of this choice than I would have been playing bridge." Two and a half times *what?* There is no possible unit of happiness that can be used for purposes of comparison, and hence of addition or multiplication. Thus, values cannot be measured; values or utilities cannot be added, subtracted, or multiplied. They can only be ranked as better or worse. A man may know that he is or will be happier or less happy, but not by "how much," not by a measurable quantity.[17]

All action is an attempt to exchange a less satisfactory state of affairs for a more satisfactory one. The actor finds himself (or expects to find himself) in a nonperfect state, and, by attempting to attain his most urgently desired ends, expects to be in a better state. He cannot measure the gain in satisfaction, but he does know which of his wants are more urgent than others, and he does know when his condition has improved. Therefore, *all action involves exchange*—an exchange of one state of affairs, X, for Y, which the actor anticipates will be a more satisfactory one (and therefore higher on his value scale). If his expectation turns out to be correct, the value of Y on his preference scale will be higher than the value of X, and he has made a *net gain* in his state of satisfaction or utility. If he has been in error, and the value of the state that he has given up—X—is higher than the value of Y, he has suffered a *net loss*. This psychic gain (or *profit*) and loss cannot be measured in terms of units, but the actor always knows whether he has experienced psychic profit or psychic loss as a result of an action-exchange.[18]

Human actors value *means* strictly in accordance with their valuation of the ends that they believe the means can serve. Obviously, consumers' goods are graded in value in accordance with the ends that men expect them to satisfy. Thus, the value placed on the enjoyment contributed by a ham sandwich or a house will determine the value a man will place on the ham sandwich or the house themselves. Similarily, producers' goods are valued in accordance with their expected contribution in producing consumers' goods. Higher-order producers' goods are valued in accordance with their anticipated service in forming lower-order producers' goods. Hence, those consumers' goods serving to attain more highly valued ends will be valued more highly than those serving less highly valued ends, and those producers' goods serving to produce more highly valued consumers' goods will themselves be valued more highly than other producers' goods. Thus, the *process of imputing values to goods* takes place in the opposite direction to that of the process of production. Value proceeds from the ends to the consumers' good to the various first-order producers' goods, to the second-order producers' goods, etc.[19] The original source of value is the ranking of ends by human actors, who then impute value to consumers' goods, and so on to the orders of producers' goods, in accordance with their expected ability to contribute toward serving the various ends.[20]

B. THE LAW OF MARGINAL UTILITY

It is evident that things are valued as means in accordance with their ability to attain ends valued as more or less urgent. *Each physical unit of a means* (direct or indirect) that enters into human action is valued separately. Thus, the actor is interested in evaluating only those units of means that enter, or that he considers will enter, into his concrete action. Actors choose between, and evaluate, not "coal" or "butter" in general, but specific units of coal or butter. In choosing between acquiring cows or horses, the actor does not choose between the class of cows and the class of horses, but between specific units of them—e.g., two cows vs. three horses. Each unit that enters into concrete action is graded and evaluated separately. Only when several units together enter into human action are all of them evaluated together.

The processes that enter into valuation of specific units of different goods may be illustrated in this example: [21] An individual possessing two cows and three horses might have to choose between giving up one cow or one horse. He may decide in this case to keep the horse, indicating that in this state of his stock, a horse is more valuable to him than a cow. On the other hand, he might be presented with the choice of keeping either his entire stock of cows or his stock of horses. Thus, his stable and cowshed might catch fire, and he is presented with the choice of saving the inhabitants of one or of the other building. In this case, two cows might be more valuable to him than three horses, so that he will prefer to save the cows. When deciding between units of his stock, the actor may therefore prefer good *X* to good *Y*, while he may choose good *Y* if he must act upon his *whole stock of each good.*

This process of valuation according to the specific units involved provides the solution for the famous "value paradox" which puzzled writers for centuries. The question was: How can men value bread less than platinum, when "bread" is obviously more useful than "platinum"? The answer is that acting man does not evaluate the goods open to him by abstract classes, but in terms of the specific units available. He does not wonder whether "bread-in-general" is more or less valuable to him than "platinum-in-general," but whether, given the present available stock of bread and platinum, a "loaf of bread" is more or less valuable to him than "an ounce of platinum." That, in most cases, men prefer the latter is no longer surprising.[22]

As has been explained above, value, or utility, cannot be measured, and therefore cannot be added, subtracted, or multiplied. This holds for specific units of the same good in the same way as it holds for all other comparisons of value. Thus, if butter is an object serving human ends, we know that two pounds of butter will be valued more highly than one pound. This will be true until a point is reached when the butter is available in unlimited quantities to satisfy human wants and will then be transferred from the status of a means to that of a general condition of human welfare. However, we *cannot* say that two pounds of butter are "twice as useful or valuable" as one pound.

What has been involved in this key concept of "specific units of a good"? In these examples, the units of the good have been *inter-*

changeable from the point of view of the actor. Thus, any concrete pound of butter was evaluated in this case perfectly equally with any other pound of butter. Cow A and cow B were valued equally by the individual, and it made no difference to him which cow he was faced with the choice of saving. Similarly, horse A was valued equally with horse B and with horse C, and the actor was not concerned which particular horse he had to choose. When a commodity is in such a way available in *specific homogeneous units equally capable of rendering the same service to the actor,* this available stock is called a *supply*. A *supply of a good* is available in specific units each perfectly substitutable for every other. The individual above had an available supply of two cows and three horses, and a supply of pounds of butter.

What if one pound of butter was considered by the actor as of better quality than another pound of butter? In that case, the two "butters" are really *different goods* from the point of view of the actor and will be evaluated differently. The two pounds of butter are now two different goods and are no longer two units of a supply of one good. Similarly, the actor must have valued each horse or each cow identically. If he preferred one horse to each of the others, or one cow to the other, then they are no longer units of the supply of the same good. No longer are his horses interchangeable for one another. If he grades horse A above the others and regards horses B and C indifferently, then he has supplies of two different goods (omitting the cows): say, "Grade A horses—1 unit"; and "Grade B horses—2 units." If a specific unit is differently evaluated from all other units, then the supply of that good is only one unit.

Here again, it is very important to recognize that what is significant for human action is *not* the physical property of a good, but the evaluation of the good by the actor. Thus, physically there may be no discernible difference between one pound of butter and another, or one cow and another. But if the actor chooses to evaluate them differently, they are no longer part of the supply of the same good.

The interchangeability of units in the supply of a good does not mean that the concrete units are actually valued equally. They may and will be valued differently whenever their *position in the supply* is different. Thus, suppose that the isolated individual successively finds one horse, then a second, then a third. Each horse may be identical and interchangeable with the others. The first horse will fulfill the most urgent wants that a horse can serve; this follows from the universal fact that action uses scarce means to satisfy the most urgent of the not yet satisfied wants. When the second horse is found, he will be put to work satisfying the most urgent of the wants remaining. These wants, however, must be ranked lower than the wants that the previous horse has satisfied. Similarly, the third horse acquired might be capable of performing the same service as the others, but he will be put to work fulfilling the highest of the remaining wants—which, however, will yet be lower in value than the others.

The important consideration is the *relation between the unit to be acquired or given up and the quantity of supply (stock) already available to the actor.* Thus, if no units of a good (whatever the good may be) are available, the first unit will satisfy the most urgent wants that such a good is capable of satisfying. If to this supply of one unit is added a second unit, the latter will fulfill the most urgent wants remaining, but these will be less urgent than the ones the first fulfilled. Therefore, the value of the second unit to the actor will be less than the value of the first unit. Similarly, the value of the third unit of the supply (added to a stock of two units) will be less than the value of the second unit. It may not matter to the individual *which* horse is chosen first and which second, or *which* pounds of butter he consumes, but those units which he does use first will be the ones that he values more highly. *Thus, for all human actions, as the quantity of the supply (stock) of a good increases, the utility (or value) of each additional unit decreases.*

Let us now consider a supply from the point of view of a possible *decrease,* rather than an increase. Assume that a man has a supply of six (interchangeable) horses. They are engaged in fulfilling his wants. Suppose that he is now faced with the necessity of giving up one horse. It now follows that this smaller stock of means is not capable of rendering as much service to him as the larger supply. This stems from the very existence of the good as a means.[23] Therefore, *the utility of X units of a good is always greater than the utility of X − 1 units*. Because of the impossibility of measurement, it is impossible to determine *by how much greater* one value is than the other. Now, the question arises: Which utility, which end, does the actor give up because he is deprived of one unit? Obviously, he gives up the *least urgent of the wants which the larger stock would have satisfied*. Thus, if the individual was using one horse for pleasure riding, and he considers this the least important of his wants that were fulfilled by the six horses, the loss of a horse will cause him to give up pleasure riding.

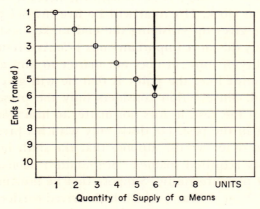

Fig. 3.   Value-Scale Diagram

The principles involved in the utility of a supply may be illustrated in the accompanying value-scale diagram (Fig. 3). We are considering any given means, which is divisible into homogeneous units of a supply, each interchangeable and capable of giving service equal to that of the other units. The supply must be scarce in relation to the ends that it is capable of fulfilling; otherwise it would not be a good, but a condition of human welfare. We assume for simplicity that there are 10 ends which the means could fulfill, and that each unit of means is capable of serving one of the ends. If the supply of the good is 6 units, then the first 6 ends, ranked in order of importance by the valuing individual, are the ones that are being satisfied. Ends ranked 7–10 remain unsatisfied. If we assume that the stock arrived in successive units, then the first unit went to satisfy end 1, the second unit was used to serve end 2, etc. The sixth unit was used to serve end 6. The dots indicate how the units were used for the different ends, and the arrow indicates the direction the process took, i.e., that the most important ends were served first; the next, second, etc. The diagram illustrates the aforementioned laws that the utility (value) of more units is greater than the utility of fewer units and that the utility of each successive unit is less as the quantity of the supply increases.

Now, suppose the actor is faced with the necessity of giving up one unit of his stock. His total will be five instead of six units. Obviously, he gives up satisfying the end ranked sixth, and continues to satisfy the more important ends 1–5. As a result of the interchangeability of units, it does not matter to him *which* of the six units he must lose; the point is that he will give up serving this sixth end. Since action considers only the present and the future and not the past, it does not matter to him *which* units he acquired first in the past. He deals only with his presently available stock. In other words, suppose that the sixth horse that he had previously acquired (named "Seabiscuit") he had placed in the service of pleasure riding. Suppose that he now must lose another horse ("Man o' War") which had arrived earlier, and which was engaged in the more important duty (to him) of leading a wagon. He will still give up end 6 by simply transferring Seabiscuit from this function to the wagon-leading end. This consequence follows from the defined interchangeability of units and from disregard of past events which are of no consequence for the present and the future.

Thus, the actor gives up the lowest-ranking want that the original stock (in this case, six units) was capable of satisfying. This one unit that he must consider giving up is called *the marginal unit*. It is the unit "at the margin." This least important end fulfilled by the stock is known as the *satisfaction provided by the marginal unit,* or the *utility of the marginal unit*—in short: the marginal satisfaction, or *marginal utility*. If the marginal unit is one unit, then the *marginal utility of the supply* is the end that must be given up as the result of a loss of the unit. In the diagram above, the marginal utility is ranked sixth among the ends. If the supply consisted of four units, and the actor were faced with the necessity of giving up one unit, then the value of the marginal unit, or the *marginal utility,* would have a rank of 4. If the stock consisted of one unit, and this had to be given up, the value of the marginal unit would be 1—the value of the highest-ranked end.

We are now in a position to complete an important law indicated above, but with different phraseology: *The greater the supply of a good, the lower the marginal utility; the smaller the supply, the higher the marginal utility.* This fundamental law of economics has been derived from the fundamental axiom of human action; it is the *law of marginal utility,* sometimes known as the *law of diminishing marginal utility.* Here again, it must be emphasized that "utility" is not a cardinal quantity subject to the processes of measurement, such as addition, multiplication, etc. It is a *ranked number* expressible only in terms of higher or lower order in the preferences of men.

This law of marginal utility holds for all goods, regardless of the size of the unit considered. The size of the unit will be the one that enters into concrete human action, but whatever it is, the same principle applies. Thus, if in certain situations, the actor must consider only *pairs of horses* as the units to add or subtract from his stock, instead of the individual horses, he will construct a new and shorter scale of ends with fewer units of supply to consider. He will then go through a similar process of assigning means to serve ends and will give up the least valued end should he lose a unit of supply. The ends will simply be ranked in terms of the alternative uses of pairs of horses, instead of single horses.

What if a good cannot be divided into homogeneous units for purposes of action? There are cases where the good must be treated as a whole in human action. Does the law of marginal utility apply in such a case? The law does apply, since we then treat the supply as consisting of *one unit.* In this case, the marginal unit is equal in size to the total supply possessed or desired by the actor. The value of the marginal unit is equal to the *first rank of the ends which the total good could serve.* Thus, if an individual must dispose of his whole stock of six horses, or acquire a stock of six horses together, the six horses are treated as one unit. The marginal utility of his supply would then be equal to the first-ranking end that the unit of *six horses* could supply.

If, as above, we consider the case of *additions* instead of decreases to stock, we recall that the law derived for this situation was that as the quantity of supply increases, the utility of each additional unit decreases. Yet this additional unit is precisely the *marginal unit.* Thus, if instead of decreasing the supply from six to five horses, we *increase* it from five to six, the value of the additional horse is equal to the value of the sixth-ranking end—say, pleasure riding. This is the same marginal unit, with the same utility, as in the case of decreasing the stock from six to five. Thus, the law derived previously was simply another form of the law of marginal utility. The greater the supply of a good, the lower the marginal utility; the smaller the supply, the higher the marginal utility. This is true whether or not the marginal unit is the unit of decrease of stock or the unit of addition to stock, when these are considered by the actor. If a man's supply of a good equals X units, and he is considering the addition of one unit, this is the marginal unit. If his supply is $X + 1$ units, and he is considering the loss of one unit, this too is his marginal unit, and its value is identical with the former (provided that his ends and their ranking are the same in both cases).

We have dealt with the laws of utility as they apply to each good treated in human action. Now we must indicate the relationship among various goods. It is obvious that more than one good exists in human action. This has already been definitely proven, since it was demonstrated that more than one factor of production, hence more than one good, must exist. Fig. 4 below demonstrates the relationship between the various goods in human action. Here the value scales of two goods are considered—X and Y. For each good, the law of marginal utility holds, and the relation between supply and value is revealed in the diagram for each good. For simplicity, let us assume that X is horses and Y cows, and that the value scales representing those held by the individual are as follows (horizontal lines are drawn through each end to demonstrate the relationship in the ranking of the ends of the two goods): End *Y*-1 is ranked highest (say, cow 1); then ends *X*-1, *X*-2, and *X*-3 (horses 1, 2, and 3); *Y*-2; *Y*-3; *X*-4; *Y*-4; *X*-5; *Y*-5; *X*-6; *X*-7; *Y*-6; *Y*-7.

Now, the man's value scales will reveal his choices involving alternatives of action in regard to these two goods. Suppose that his

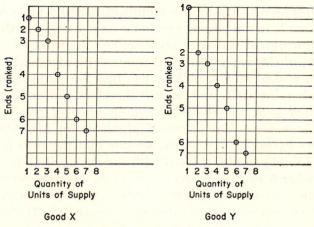

FIG. 4. VALUE SCALES

stock is: 3*Y* (cows) and 4*X* (horses). He is faced with the alternative of giving up: *either one cow or one horse.* He will choose the alternative which will deprive him of the least valued end possible. Since the marginal utility of each good is equal to the value of the least important end of which he would be deprived, *he compares the marginal utility of X with the marginal utility of Y.* In this case, the marginal unit of *X* has a rank of *X*-4, and the marginal unit of *Y* has a rank of *Y*-3. But the end *Y*-3 is ranked higher on his value scale than *X*-4. Hence the marginal utility of *Y* is in this case higher than (or greater than) the marginal utility of *X*. Since he will give up the lowest possible utility, he will give up one unit of *X*. *Thus, presented with a choice of units of goods to give up, he will give up the good with units of lowest marginal utility on his value scale.* Suppose another example: that his stock is three horses and two cows. He has the alternative of giving up 1X or 1Y. In this case, the marginal utility of Y is ranked at Y-2, and that of X is ranked at X-3. But X-3 occupies a higher position on his value scale than Y-2, and therefore the marginal utility of Y is at this point lower than the marginal utility of X. He gives up a unit of Y.

The converse occurs if the man must choose between the alternative of *increasing* his stock by either one unit of X or a unit of Y. Thus, suppose that his stock is 4 units of X and 4 units of Y. He must choose between adding one horse or one cow. He then compares the marginal utility of increase, i.e., the value of the most important of the not yet satisfied wants. The marginal utility of X is then ranked at X-5; of Y at Y-5. But X-5 ranks higher than Y-5 on his value scale, and he will therefore choose the former. *Thus, faced with the choice of adding units of goods, he will choose the unit of highest marginal utility on his value scale.*

Another example: Previously, we saw that the man in a position of (4X, 3Y) would, if faced with the choice of giving up one unit of either X or Y, give up the unit of X, with a lower marginal utility. In other words, he would prefer a position of (3X, 3Y) to (4X, 2Y). Now suppose he is in a position of (3X, 3Y) and faced with the choice of adding 1 unit of X or 1 unit of Y. Since the marginal utility of the increased X is greater than that of Y, he will choose to add the unit of X and to arrive at a position of (4X, 3Y) rather than (3X, 4Y). The reader can work out the hypothetical choices for all the possible combinations of the actor's stock.

It is evident that in the act of choosing between giving up or adding units of either X or Y, the actor must have, in effect, placed both goods on a *single, unitary value scale*. Unless he could place X and Y on *one* value scale for comparison, he could not have determined that the marginal utility of the fourth unit of X was higher than that of the fourth unit of Y. The very fact of action in choosing between more than one good implies that the units of these goods must have been ranked for comparison on one value scale of the actor. The actor may not and cannot *measure* differences in utility, but he must be engaged in ranking all the goods considered on one value scale. Thus, we should actually consider the ends served by the two means as ranked on one value scale as follows:

Ends (Ranked)

1—*Y*-1
2—*X*-1
3—*X*-2
4—*X*-3
5—*Y*-2
6—*Y*-3
7—*X*-4
8—*Y*-4
9—*X*-5
10—*Y*-5
11—*X*-6
12—*X*-7
13—*Y*-6
14—*Y*-7

These principles permit of being extended from two to any number of goods. Regardless of the number of goods, any man will always have a certain combination of units of them in his stock. He may be faced with the choice of giving up one unit of any good that he might choose. By ranking the various goods and the ends served by the relevant units, the actor will give up the unit of that good of which the marginal utility to him is the lowest. Similarly, with any given combination of goods in his stock, and faced with the choice of adding one unit of any of the goods available, the actor will choose that good whose marginal utility of increase will be highest. In other words, all the goods are ranked on one value scale in accordance with the ends they serve.

If the actor has no units of some goods in his possession, this does not affect the principle. Thus, if he has no units of *X* or *Y* in his possession, and he must choose between adding a unit of *X* or one unit of *Y*, he will choose the marginal unit of greatest utility, in this case, *Y*. The principle is easily extended to the case of *n* goods.

It must be reiterated here that value scales do not exist in a void apart from the concrete choices of action. Thus, if the actor has a stock of (3*X*, 4*Y*, 2*Z*, etc.), his choices for adding and subtracting from stock take place in this region, and there is no need for him to formulate hypothetical value scales to determine what his choices would have been if his stock were (6X, 8Y, 5Z, etc.). No one can predict with certainty the course of his choices except that they will follow the law of marginal utility, which was deduced from the axiom of action.

The solution of the value paradox mentioned above is now fully clear. If a man prefers one ounce of platinum to five loaves of bread, he is choosing between units of the two goods based on the supply available. On the basis of the available supply of platinum and of bread, the marginal utility of a unit of platinum is greater than the marginal utility of a unit of bread.[24]

6. *Factors of Production: The Law of Returns*

We have concluded that the value of each unit of any good is equal to its marginal utility at any point in time, and that this value is determined by the relation between the actor's scale of wants and the stock of goods available. We know that there are two types of goods: consumers' goods, which directly serve human wants, and producers' goods, which aid in the process of production eventually to produce consumers' goods. It is clear that the utility of a consumers' good is the end directly served. The utility of a producers' good is its contribution in producing consumers' goods. With value imputed backward from ends to consumers' goods through the various orders of producers' goods, the utility of any producers' good is its contribution to its product—the lower-stage producers' good or the consumers' good.

As has been discussed above, the very fact of the necessity of producing consumers' goods implies a scarcity of factors of production. If factors of production at each stage were not scarce, then there would be unlimited quantities available of factors of the next lower stage. Similarly, it was concluded that at each stage of production, the product must be produced by *more than one* scarce higher-order factor of production. If only one factor were necessary for the process, then the process itself would not be necessary, and consumers' goods would be available in un-

limited abundance. Thus, at each stage of production, the produced goods must have been produced with the aid of more than
one factor. These factors *co-operate* in the production process
and are termed *complementary factors*.

Factors of production are available as units of a homogeneous
supply, just as are consumers' goods. On what principles will an
actor evaluate a unit of a factor of production? He will evaluate a unit of supply on the basis of the least importantly valued
product which he would have to forgo were he deprived of the
unit factor. In other words, he will evaluate each unit of a factor
as equal to the satisfactions provided by its marginal unit—in this
case, *the utility of its marginal product*. The marginal product
is the product forgone by a loss of the marginal unit, and its
value is determined either by *its* marginal product in the next
stage of production, or, if it is a consumers' good, by the utility
of the end it satisfies. Thus, the value assigned to a unit of a
factor of production is equal to the *value of its marginal product*, or its *marginal productivity*.

Since man wishes to satisfy as many of his ends as possible,
and in the shortest possible time (see above), it follows that he
will strive for the *maximum product from given units of factors
at each stage of production*. As long as the goods are composed
of homogeneous units, their quantity can be measured in terms
of these units, and the actor can know when they are in greater
or lesser supply. Thus, whereas value and utility cannot be measured or subject to addition, subtraction, etc., quantities of homogeneous units of a supply can be measured. A man knows how
many horses or cows he has, and he knows that four horses are
twice the quantity of two horses.

Assume that a product P (which can be a producers' good or
a consumers' good) is produced by three complementary factors,
X, Y, and Z. These are all higher-order producers' goods. Since
supplies of goods are quantitatively definable, and since in nature quantitative causes lead to quantitatively observable effects,
we are always in a position to say that: a quantities of X, combined with b quantities of Y, and c quantities of Z, lead to p
quantities of the product P.

Now let us assume that we hold the quantitative amounts b and c unchanged. The amounts a and therefore p are free to vary. The value of a yielding the maximum p/a, i.e., the maximum average return of product to the factor, is called the *optimum* amount of X. The *law of returns states that with the quantity of complementary factors held constant, there always exists some optimum amount of the varying factor.* As the amount of the varying factor decreases or increases from the optimum, p/a, the *average unit product* declines. The quantitative extent of that decline depends on the concrete conditions of each case. As the supply of the varying factor increases, just below this optimum the average return of product to the varying factor is increasing; after the optimum, it is decreasing. These may be called states of *increasing returns* and *decreasing returns* to the factor, with the maximum return at the optimum point.

The law that such an optimum must exist can be proved by contemplating the implications of the contrary. If there were no optimum, the average product would increase indefinitely as the quantity of the factor X increased. (It could not increase indefinitely as the quantity *decreases*, since the product will be zero when the quantity of the factor is zero.) But if p/a can always be increased merely by increasing a, this means that any desired quantity of P could be secured by merely increasing the supply of X. This would mean that the proportionate supply of factors Y and Z can be ever so small; any decrease in their supply can always be compensated to increase production by increasing the supply of X. This would signify that factor X is perfectly substitutable for factors Y and Z and that the scarcity of the latter factors would not be a matter of concern to the actor so long as factor X was available in abundance. But a lack of concern for their scarcity means that Y and Z would *no longer be scarce factors.* Only one scarce factor, X, would remain. But we have seen that there must be more than one factor at each stage of production. Accordingly, the very existence of various factors of production implies that the average return of product to each factor must have some maximum, or optimum, value.

In some cases, the optimum amount of a factor may be the

only amount that can effectively co-operate in the production process. Thus, by a known chemical formula, it may require precisely two parts of hydrogen and one part of oxygen to produce one unit of water. If the supply of oxygen is fixed at one unit, then anv supply of hydrogen under two parts will produce no product at all, and all parts beyond two of hydrogen will be quite useless. Not only will the combination of two hydrogen and one oxygen be the optimum combination, but it will be the only amount of hydrogen that will be at all useful in the production process.

The relationship between *average product* and *marginal product* to a varying factor may be seen in the following hypothetical example:

TABLE 1

FACTOR Y b UNITS	FACTOR X a UNITS	TOTAL PRODUCT p UNITS	AVERAGE UNIT PRODUCT p/a	MARGINAL PRODUCT $\Delta p/\Delta a$
3	0	0	0	. . .
3	1	4	4	4
3	2	10	5	6
3	3	18	6	8
3	4	30	7.5	12
3	5	40	8	10
3	6	45	7.5	5
3	7	49	7	4

Here is a hypothetical picture of the returns to a varying factor, with other factors fixed. The average unit product increases until it reaches a peak of 8 at 5 units of X. This is the optimum point for the varying factor. The *marginal product is the increase in total product provided by the marginal unit*. At any given supply of units of factor X, a loss of one unit will entail a loss of total product equal to the marginal product. Thus, if the supply of X is increased from 3 units to 4 units, total product is increased from 18 to 30 units, and this increase is the mar-

ginal product of X with a supply of 4 units. Similarly, if the
supply is cut from 4 units to 3 units, the total product must be
cut from 30 to 18 units, and thus the marginal product is 12.

It is evident that the amount of X that will yield the optimum
of average product is not necessarily the amount that maximizes
the marginal product of the factor. Often the marginal product
reaches its peak before the average product. The relationship that
always holds mathematically between the average and the marginal product of a factor is that *as the average product increases
(increasing returns), the marginal product is greater than the average product. Conversely, as the average product declines (diminishing returns), the marginal product is less than the average
product.*[25]

It follows that when the average product is at a maximum, it
equals the marginal product.

It is clear that, with one varying factor, it is easy for the actor
to set the proportion of factors to yield the optimum return for
the factor. But how can the actor set an optimum combination
of factors if all of them can be varied in their supply? If one
combination of quantities of X, Y, and Z yields an optimum return for X, and another combination yields an optimum return
for Y, etc., how is the actor to determine which combination to
choose? Since he cannot quantitatively compare units of X with
units of Y or Z, how can he determine the optimum proportion
of factors? This is a fundamental problem for human action, and
its methods of solution will be treated in subsequent chapters.

7. *Factors of Production: Convertibility and Valuation*

Factors of production are valued in accordance with their
anticipated contribution in the eventual production of consumers'
goods. Factors, however, differ in the *degree of their specificity,*
i.e., the variety of consumers' goods in the production of which
they can be of service. Certain goods are *completely specific*—are
useful in producing only one consumers' good. Thus, when, in
past ages, extracts from the mandrake weed were considered useful in healing ills, the mandrake weed was a completely specific

factor of production—it was useful purely for this purpose. When the ideas of people changed, and the mandrake was considered worthless, the weed lost its value completely. Other producers' goods may be relatively nonspecific and capable of being used in a wide variety of employments. They could never be perfectly nonspecific—equally useful in all production of consumers' goods —for in that case they would be general conditions of welfare available in unlimited abundance for all purposes. There would be no need to economize them. Scarce factors, however, including the relatively nonspecific ones, must be employed in their most urgent uses. Just as a supply of consumers' goods will go first toward satisfying the most urgent wants, then to the next most urgent wants, etc., so a supply of factors will be allocated by actors first to the most urgent uses in producing consumers' goods, then to the next most urgent uses, etc. The loss of a unit of a supply of a factor will entail the loss of the least urgent of the presently satisfied uses.

The less specific a factor is, the more *convertible* it is from one use to another. The mandrake weed lost its value because it could not be converted to other uses. Factors such as iron or wood, however, are convertible into a wide variety of uses. If one type of consumers' good falls into disuse, iron output can be shifted from that to another line of production. On the other hand, once the iron ore has been transformed into a machine, it becomes less easily convertible and often completely specific to the product. When factors lose a large part of their value as a result of a decline in the value of the consumers' good, they will, if possible, be converted to another use of greater value. If, despite the decline in the value of the product, there is no better use to which the factor can be converted, it will stay in that line of product or cease being used altogether if the consumers' good no longer has value.

For example, suppose that cigars suddenly lose their value as consumers' goods; they are no longer desired. Those cigar machines which are not usable in any other capacity will become valueless. Tobacco leaves, however, will lose some of their value, but may be convertible to uses such as cigarette production with little loss of value. (A loss of all desire for tobacco, however, will result in a far wider loss in the value of the factors, although part of the land may be salvaged by shifting from tobacco to the production of cotton.)

Suppose, on the other hand, that some time after cigars lose their value this commodity returns to public favor and regains its former value. The cigar machines, which had been rendered valueless, now recoup their great loss in value. On the other hand, the tobacco leaves, land, etc., which had shifted from cigars to other uses will reshift into the production of cigars. These factors will gain in value, but their gain, as was their previous loss, will be less than the gain of the completely specific factor. These are examples of a general law that *a change in the value of the product causes a greater change in the value of the specific factors than in that of the relatively nonspecific factors.*

To further illustrate the relation between convertibility and valuation, let us assume that complementary factors 10X, 5Y, and 8Z produce a supply of 20P. First, suppose that each of these factors is completely specific and that none of the supply of the factors can be replaced by other units. Then, if the supply of one of the factors is lost (say 10X), the entire product is lost, and the other factors become valueless. In that case, the supply of that factor which must be given up or lost equals in value the value of the entire product—20P, while the other factors have a zero value. An example of production with purely specific factors is a pair of shoes; the prospect of a loss of one shoe is valued at the value of the entire pair, while the other shoe becomes valueless in case of a loss. Thus, *jointly,* factors 10X, 5Y, and 8Z produce a product that is valued, say, as rank 11 on the actor's value scale. Lose the supply of one of the factors, and the other complementary factors become completely valueless.

Now, let us assume, secondly, that each of the factors is nonspecific: that 10X can be used in another line of production that will yield a product, say, ranked 21st on the value scale; that 5Y in another use will yield a product ranked 15th on the actor's value scale; and that 8Z can be used to yield a product ranked 30th. In that case, the loss of 10X would mean that instead of satisfying a want of rank 11, the units of Y and Z would be shifted to their next most valuable use, and wants ranked 15th and 30th would be satisfied instead. We know that the actor preferred the satisfaction of a want ranked 11th to the satisfaction of wants ranked 15th and 30th; otherwise the factors would not have been engaged in producing P in the first place. But now the loss of value is far from total, since the other factors can still yield a return in other uses.

Convertible factors will be allocated among different lines of production according to the same principles as consumers' goods are allocated among the ends they can serve. Each unit of supply will be allocated to satisfy the most urgent of the not yet satisfied wants, i.e., where the value of its marginal product is the highest. A loss of a unit of the factor will deprive the actor of only the least important of the presently satisfied uses, i.e., that use in which the value of the marginal product is the lowest. This choice is analogous to that involved in previous examples comparing the marginal utility of one good with the marginal utility of another. This lowest-ranked marginal product may be considered the value of the marginal product of any unit of the factor, with all uses taken into account. Thus, in the above case, suppose that X is a convertible factor in a myriad of different uses. If one unit of X has a marginal product of say, $3P$, a marginal product in another use of $2Q$, $5R$, etc., the actor ranks the values of these marginal products of X on his value scale. Suppose that he ranks them in this order: $4S$, $3P$, $2Q$, $5R$. In that case, suppose he is faced with the loss of 1 unit of X. He will give up the use of a unit of X in production of R, where the marginal product is ranked lowest. Even if the loss takes place in the production of P, he will not give up $3P$, but shift a unit of X from the less valuable use R and give up $5R$. Thus, just as the actor gave up the use of a horse in pleasure riding and not in wagon-pulling by shifting from the former to the latter use, so the actor who (for example) loses a cord of wood intended for building a house will give up a cord intended for a service less valuable to him—say, building a sled. Thus, the value of the marginal product of a unit of a factor will be equal to its value in its marginal use, i.e., that use served by the stock of the factor whose marginal product is ranked lowest on his value scale.

We can now see further why, in cases where products are made with specific *and* convertible factors, the general law holds that the value of convertible factors changes less than that of specific factors in response to a change in the value of P or in the conditions of its production. The value of a unit of a convertible factor is set, not by the conditions of its employment in *one* type of product, but by the value of its marginal product when *all* its uses are taken into consideration. Since a specific factor is usable in only one line of production, its unit value is set as equal to the value of the marginal product in that line of production alone. Hence, in the process of valuation, the specific factors are far more responsive to conditions in *any given process of production* than are the nonspecific factors.[26]

As with the problem of optimum proportions, the process of value imputation from consumers' good to factors raises a great many problems which will be discussed in later chapters. Since one product cannot be measured against other products, and units of different factors cannot be compared with one another, how can value be imputed when, as in a modern economy, the structure of production is very complex, with myriads of products and with convertible and inconvertible factors? It will be seen that value imputation is easy for isolated Crusoe-type actors, but that special conditions are needed to enable the value-imputing process, as well as the factor-allocating process, to take place in a complex economy. In particular, the various units of products and factors (*not* the values, of course) must be made commensurable and comparable.

8. *Factors of Production: Labor vs. Leisure*

Setting aside the problem of allocating production along the most desired lines and of measuring one product as against another, it is evident that every man desires *to maximize his production of consumers' goods per unit of time.* He tries to satisfy as many of his important ends as possible, and at the earliest possible time. But in order to increase the production of his consumers' goods, he must relieve the scarcity of the scarce factors of production; he must increase the available supply of these scarce factors. The *nature-given* factors are limited by his environment and therefore cannot be increased. This leaves him with the choice of increasing his supply of *capital goods* or of increasing his *expenditure of labor.*

It might be asserted that another way of increasing his production is to improve his technical knowledge of how to produce the desired goods—to improve his recipes. A recipe, however, can only set *outer limits* on his increases in production; the actual increases can be accomplished solely by an increase in the supply of productive factors. Thus, suppose that Robinson Crusoe lands, without equipment, on a desert island. He may be a competent engineer and have full knowledge of the necessary processes involved in constructing a mansion for himself. But without the necessary supply of factors available, this knowledge could not suffice to construct the mansion.

One method, then, by which man may increase his production per unit of time is by increasing his expenditure of labor. In the first place, however, the possibilities for this expansion are strictly limited—by the number of people in existence at any time and by the number of hours in the day. Secondly, it is limited by the ability of each laborer, and this ability tends to vary. And, finally, there is a third limitation on the supply of labor: whether or not the work is directly satisfying in itself, labor always involves the forgoing of *leisure,* a desirable good.[27]

We can conceive of a world in which leisure is not desired and labor is merely a useful scarce factor to be economized. In such a world, the total supply of available labor would be equal to the total quantity of labor that men would be capable of expending. Everyone would be eager to work to the maximum of capacity, since increased work would lead to increased production of desired consumers' goods. All time not required for maintaining and preserving the capacity to work would be spent in labor.[28] Such a situation could conceivably exist, and an economic analysis could be worked out on that basis. We know from empirical observation, however, that such a situation is very rare for human action. For almost all actors, *leisure is a consumers' good,* to be weighed in the balance against the prospect of acquiring other consumers' goods, including possible satisfaction from the effort itself. The more a man labors, the less leisure he can enjoy. Increased labor therefore reduces the available supply of leisure and the utility that it affords. Consequently, "people work only when they value the return of labor higher than the decrease in satisfaction brought about by the curtailment of leisure." [29] It is possible that included in this "return" of satisfaction yielded by labor may be satisfaction in the labor itself, in the voluntary expenditure of energy on a productive task. When such satisfactions from labor do not exist, then simply the expected value of the product yielded by the effort will be weighed against the *disutility* involved in giving up leisure—the utility of the leisure forgone. Where labor does provide intrinsic satisfactions, the utility of the product yielded will include the utility provided by the effort itself. As the quantity of effort increases, however, the utility of the satisfactions provided by labor itself declines, and the utility of the successive units of the final product declines as well. Both the marginal utility of the final product and the marginal utility of labor-satisfaction decline with an increase in their quantity, because both goods follow the universal law of marginal utility.

In considering an expenditure of his labor, man not only takes into account which are the most valuable ends it can serve (as he does with all other factors), these ends possibly including the satisfaction derived from productive labor itself, but he *also* weighs the prospect of abstaining from the expenditure of labor *in order* to obtain the consumers' good, leisure. Leisure, like any other good, is subject to the law of marginal utility. The first unit of leisure satisfies a most urgently felt desire; the next unit serves a less highly valued end; the third unit a still less highly valued end, etc. The marginal utility of leisure decreases as the supply increases, and this utility is equal to the value of the end that would have to be forgone with the loss of the unit of leisure. But in that case, the marginal disutility of work (in terms of leisure forgone) *increases* with every increase in the amount of labor performed.

In some cases, labor itself may be positively disagreeable, not only because of the leisure forgone, but also because of specific conditions attached to the particular labor that the actor finds disagreeable. In these cases, the marginal disutility of labor includes both the disutility due to these conditions and the disutility due to leisure forgone. The painful aspects of labor, like the forgoing of leisure, are endured for the sake of the yield of the final product. The addition of the element of disagreeableness in certain types of labor may reinforce and certainly does not counteract the increasing marginal disutility imposed by the cumulation of leisure forgone as the time spent in labor increases.

Thus, for each person and type of labor performed, the balancing of the marginal utility of the product of prospective units of effort as against the marginal disutility of effort will include the satisfaction or dissatisfaction with the work itself, in addition to the evaluation of the final product and of the leisure forgone. The labor itself may provide positive satisfaction, positive pain or dissatisfaction, or it may be neutral. In cases where the labor itself provides positive satisfactions, however, *these are intertwined with and cannot be separated from the prospect of obtaining the final product.* Deprived of the final product, man will consider his labor senseless and useless, and the labor itself will no longer bring positive satisfactions. Those activities which are engaged in *purely* for their own sake are not labor but pure *play,* consumers' goods in themselves. Play, as a consumers' good, is subject to the law of marginal utility as are all goods, and the time spent in play will be balanced against the utility to be derived from other obtainable goods.[30]

In the expenditure of any hour of labor, therefore, man weighs the disutility of the labor involved (including the leisure forgone plus any dissatisfaction stemming from the work itself) against the utility of the contribution he will make in that hour to the production of desired goods (including future goods and any pleasure in the work itself), i.e., with the *value of his marginal product.*

In each hour he will expend his effort toward producing *that* good whose marginal product is highest on his value scale. If he must give up an hour of labor, he will give up a unit of that good whose marginal utility is lowest on his value scale. At each point he will balance the utility of the product on his value scale against the disutility of further work. We know that a man's marginal utility of goods provided by effort will decline as his expenditure of effort increases. On the other hand, with each new expenditure of effort, the marginal disutility of the effort continues to increase. Therefore, a man will expend his labor as long as the marginal utility of the return *exceeds* the marginal disutility of the labor effort. A man will stop work when the marginal disutility of labor is greater than the marginal utility of the increased goods provided by the effort.[31]

Then, as his consumption of leisure increases, the marginal utility of leisure will decline, while the marginal utility of the goods forgone increases, until finally the utility of the marginal products forgone becomes greater than the marginal utility of leisure, and the actor will resume labor again.

This analysis of the laws of labor effort has been deduced from the implications of the action axiom and the assumption of leisure as a consumers' good.

9. *The Formation of Capital*

With the nature-given elements limited by his environment, and his labor restricted both by its available supply and its disutility, there is only one way by which man can increase his production of consumers' goods per unit of time—by increasing the quantity of capital goods. Beginning with unaided labor and nature, he must, to increase his productivity, mix his labor energy with the elements of nature to form capital goods. These goods are not immediately serviceable in satisfying his wants, but must be transformed by further labor into lower-order capital goods, and finally into the desired consumers' goods.

In order to illuminate clearly the nature of capital formation and the position of capital in production, let us start with the hypothetical example of Robinson Crusoe stranded on a desert island. Robinson, on landing, we assume, finds himself without the aid of capital goods of any kind. All that is available is his own labor and the elements given him by nature. It is obvious that without capital he will be able to satisfy only a few wants, of which he will choose the most urgent. Let us say that the only goods available without the aid of capital are berries and leisure. Say that he finds that he can pick twenty edible berries an hour, and, on this basis, works ten hours in berry-picking and enjoys fourteen hours a day of leisure. It is evident that, without the aid of capital, the only goods open to him for consumption are goods with the *shortest period of production*. Leisure is the one good that is produced almost instantaneously, while berries have a very short production period. Twenty berries have a production period of one hour. Goods with longer periods of production are not available to him unless he acquires capital goods.

There are two ways in which longer processes of production through the use of capital may increase productivity: (1) they may provide a greater production of the *same* good per unit of time; or (2) they may allow the actor to consume goods that are *not available at all* with shorter processes of production.

As an example of the first type of increase in productivity: Robinson may decide that if he had the use of a long stick, he could shake many berries off the trees instead of picking them by hand. In that way he might be able to step up his production to fifty berries an hour. How might he go about acquiring the stick? Obviously, he must expend labor in getting the materials, transporting them, shaping them into a stick, etc. Let us say that ten hours would be necessary for this task. This means that to obtain the stick, Crusoe must *forgo* ten hours' production of consumers' goods. He must either sacrifice ten hours of leisure or ten hours of berries at twenty per hour (two hundred berries), or some combination of the two. He must sacrifice, for ten hours, the enjoyment of consumers' goods, and expend his labor on producing a *capital good*—the stick—which will be of no *immediate* use to him. He will be able to begin using the capital good as an indirect aid to future production only after the ten hours are up. In the meantime, he must forgo the satisfaction of his wants. He must *restrict his consumption* for ten hours and *transfer his labor* for that period from producing immediately satisfying consumers' goods into the production of capital goods, which will prove their usefulness only *in the future.* The restriction of consumption is called *saving,* and the transfer of labor and land to the formation of capital goods is called *investment.*

We see now what is involved in the process of capital formation. The actor must decide whether or not to restrict his consumption and invest in the production of capital goods, by weighing the following factors: Does the utility yielded by the increased productivity of the longer process of production outweigh the sacrifice that I must make of *present* goods to acquire consumers' goods in the *future?* We have already seen above the universal fact of *time preference*—that a man will always prefer obtaining a given satisfaction earlier than later. Here, the actor must balance his desire to acquire *more satisfactions per unit of time* as against the fact that, to do so, he must give up satisfactions in the *present* to increase his production in the *future.* His time preference for present over future accounts for his *disutility of waiting,* which must be balanced against the utility that will be eventually provided by the capital good and the longer process of production. How he chooses depends on his scale of values. It is possible, for example, that if he thought the stick would provide him with only thirty berries an hour and would take twenty hours to make, he would not make the saving-investment decision. On the other hand, if the stick took five hours to make and could provide him with one hundred berries an hour, he might make the decision readily.

If he decides to invest ten hours in adding to his capital goods, there are many ways in which he might restrict his consumption. As mentioned above, he can restrict any combination of berries or leisure. Setting aside leisure for purposes of simplification, he may decide to take a whole day off at once and produce no berries at all, completing the stick in one day. Or, he may decide to pick berries for eight hours instead of ten, and devote the other two hours a day to making the stick, in which case the completion of the stick will take five days. Which method he will choose depends on the nature of his value scale. In any case, he must restrict his consumption by ten hours' worth of labor—two hundred berries. The *rate* of his restriction will depend on how urgently he wants the increased production, as compared with the urgency with which he desires to maintain his present supply of berries.

Analytically, there is little difference between working on consumers' goods, accumulating a stock of them, and *then* working full time on the capital good, and working on the capital good and consumer goods simultaneously. Other things being equal, however, it is possible that one of the methods will prove more productive; thus, it may be that the actor can complete the task in less time if he works on it continuously. In that case, he will tend to choose the former method. On the other hand, the berries might tend to spoil if accumulated, and this would lead him to choose the latter route. A balance of the various factors on his value scale will result in his decision.

Let us assume that Robinson has made his decision, and, after five days, begins to use the stick. On the sixth day and thereafter, then, five hundred berries a day will begin to pour forth, and he will harvest the fruits of his investment in capital goods.

Crusoe can use his increased productivity to *increase his hours of leisure* as well as to increase his output of berries. Thus, he might decide to cut his daily labor from ten hours to eight. His output of berries will then be increased, because of the stick, from two hundred to four hundred berries per day, while Crusoe is able to increase his hours of leisure from fourteen to sixteen per day. Obviously, Crusoe can choose to take his increased productivity in various combinations of increased output of the good itself and of increased leisure.[32]

Even more important than its use in increasing output per unit of time is the function of capital in enabling man to acquire goods which he could not *at all* obtain otherwise. A very short period of production enables Crusoe to produce leisure and at least some berries, but without the aid of capital he cannot

attain *any* of his other wants at all. To acquire meat he must
have a bow and arrows, to acquire fish he must have a pole or
net, to acquire shelter he must have logs of wood, or canvas, and
an axe to cut the wood. To satisfy any such wants, he must restrict his consumption and invest his labor in the production of
capital goods. In other words, he must embark on lengthier processes of production than had been involved in culling berries;
he must take time out to produce the capital goods themselves
before he can use them to enjoy consumers' goods. In each case,
the decisions that he makes in embarking on capital formation
will be a result of weighing on his value scale the utility of the
expected increased productivity as against the disutility of his
time preference for present as compared to future satisfactions.

It is obvious that the factor which holds every man back from
investing more and more of his land and labor in capital goods
is his time preference for present goods. If man, other things being equal, did not prefer satisfaction in the present to satisfaction in the future, he would never consume; he would invest all
his time and labor in increasing the production of future goods.
But "never consuming" is an absurdity, since consuming is the
end of all production. Therefore, at any given point in time,
all men will have invested in all the *shorter* periods of production to satisfy the most urgently felt wants that their knowledge
of recipes allows; *any further formation of capital will go into
longer processes of production.* Other things being equal (i.e., the
relative urgency of wants to be satisfied, and the actor's knowledge of recipes), any further investment will be in a longer process
of production than is now under way.

Here it is important to realize that "a period of production"
does not involve only the amount of time spent on making the
actual capital good, but refers to the amount of waiting-time
from the start of producing the capital good until the *consumers'
good* is produced. In the case of the stick and the berries, the
two times are identical, but this was so only because the stick
was a first-order capital good, i.e., it was but one stage removed
from the output of consumers' goods. Let us take, for example,
a more complex case—the building by Crusoe of an axe in order

to chop wood to produce a house for himself. Crusoe must decide whether or not the house he will gain will be worth the consumers' goods forgone in the meantime. Let us say it will take Crusoe fifty hours to produce the axe, and then a further two hundred hours, with the help of the axe, to chop and transport wood in order to build a house. The longer process of production which Crusoe must decide upon is now a three-stage one, totaling two hundred fifty hours. First, labor and nature produce the axe, a second-order capital good; second, labor, plus the axe, plus nature-given elements, produces logs-of-wood, a first-order capital good; finally, labor and the logs of wood combine to yield the desired consumers' good—a house. The length of the process of production is the entire length of time from the point at which an actor must begin his labor to the point at which the consumers' good is yielded.

Again, it must be observed that, in considering the length of a process of production, the actor is not interested in past history as such. The length of a process of production for an actor is the *waiting-time from the point at which his action begins.* Thus, if Crusoe were lucky enough to find an axe in good condition left by some previous inhabitant, he would reckon his period of production at two hundred hours instead of two hundred fifty. The axe would be given to him by his environment.

This example illustrates a fundamental truth about capital goods. Capital is a way station along the road to the enjoyment of consumers' goods. He who possesses capital is that much *further advanced in time* on the road to the desired consumers' good. Crusoe without the axe is two hundred fifty hours away from his desired house; Crusoe with the axe is only two hundred hours away. If the logs of wood had been piled up ready-made on his arrival, he would be that much closer to his objective; and if the house were there to begin with, he would achieve his desire immediately. He would be further advanced toward his goal without the necessity of further restriction of consumption. Thus, the role of capital is to advance men in time toward their objective in producing consumers' goods. This is true for both the case where *new* consumers' goods are being produced and the case where *more old goods* are being produced. Thus, in the previous case, without the stick, Crusoe was twenty-five hours away from an output of five hundred berries; with the stick, he is only ten hours away. In those cases where capital enables the acquisition of new goods—of goods which could not be obtained otherwise —it is an *absolutely indispensable,* as well as a convenient, way station toward the desired consumers' good.

It is evident that, for any formation of capital, there must be *saving*—a restriction of the enjoyment of consumers' goods in the present—and the investment of the equivalent resources in the production of capital goods. This enjoyment of consumers' goods —the satisfaction of wants—is called *consumption.* The saving might come about as a result of an increase in the available supply of consumers' goods, which the actor decides to save in part rather than consume fully. At any rate, consumption must always be less than the amount that could be secured. Thus, if the harvest on the desert island improves, and Crusoe finds that he can pick two hundred forty berries in ten hours without the aid of a stick, he may now save forty berries a day for five days, enabling him to invest his labor in a stick, without cutting back his berry consumption from the original two hundred berries. Saving involves the restriction of consumption compared to the amount that *could* be consumed; it does not always involve an actual reduction in the amount consumed over the previous level of consumption.

All capital goods are perishable. Those few products that are not perishable but permanent become, to all intents and purposes, part of the *land.* Otherwise, all capital goods are perishable, used up during the processes of production. We can therefore say that capital goods, during production, are *transformed* into their products. With some capital goods, this is physically quite evident. Thus, it is obvious, for example, that when a hundred pounds of bread-at-wholesale are combined with other factors to produce a hundred pounds of bread at retail, the former factor is immediately and completely transformed into the latter factor. The using up of capital goods is here dramatically clear. The whole of the capital good is used up in each production-event. The other capital goods, however, are also used up, but not as suddenly. A truck transporting bread may have a life of fifteen years, amounting to, say, three thousand of such conversions of bread from the wholesale to the retail stage. In this case we may say that 1/3,000 of the truck is used up each time the production process occurs. Similarly, a mill converting wheat into flour may have a useful life of twenty years, in which case we could say that ½₀ of the mill was used up in each year's production of flour. Each particular capital good has a different useful life and therefore a different rate of being used up, or, as it is called, of *depreciation*. Capital goods vary in the duration of their serviceableness.

Let us now return to Crusoe and the stick. Let us assume that the stick will have a useful life of ten days, and is so estimated by Crusoe, after which it wears out, and Crusoe's output reverts to its previous level of twenty berries per hour. He is back where he started from.

Crusoe is therefore faced with a choice, after his stick comes into use. His "standard of living" (now, say, at five hundred berries a day plus fourteen hours of leisure) has improved, and he will not like the prospect of a reduction to two hundred when the stick gives out. If he wishes to maintain his standard of living intact, therefore, he must, during the ten days, work on building another stick, which can be used to replace the old one when it wears out. This act of building another stick involves a *further act of saving*. In order to invest in a replacement for the stick, he must again save—restrict his consumption as compared to the production that might be available. Thus, he will again have to save ten hours' worth of labor in berries (or leisure) and devote them to investing in a good that is only indirectly serviceable for future production. Suppose that he does this by shifting one hour a day from his berry production to the labor of producing another stick. By doing so, he restricts his berry consumption, for ten days, to four hundred fifty a day. He has restricted consumption from his maximum, although he is still much better off than in his original, unaided state.

Thus, the *capital structure* is renewed at the end of the ten days, by saving and investing in a replacement. After that, Crusoe is *again* faced with the choice of taking his maximum production of five hundred berries per day and finding himself back to a two-hundred-per-day level at the end of ten more days, or of making a *third* act of saving in order to provide for replacement of the second stick when it wears out.[33]

If Crusoe decides *not* to replace the first or the second stick, and accepts a later drop in output to avoid undergoing present saving, he is *consuming capital*. In other words, he is electing to consume instead of to save and maintain his capital structure and future rate of output. Consuming his capital enables Crusoe to increase his consumption *now* from four hundred fifty to five hundred berries per day, but at some point in the future (here in ten days), he will be forced to cut his consumption back to two hundred berries. It is clear that what has led Crusoe to consume capital is his *time preference,* which in this case has led him to prefer more present consumption to greater losses in future consumption.

Thus, any actor, at any point in time, has the choice of: (*a*) adding to his capital structure, (*b*) maintaining his capital intact, or (*c*) consuming his capital. Choices (*a*) and (*b*) involve acts of saving. The course adopted will depend on the actor's weighing his disutility of waiting, as determined by his time preference, against the utility to be provided in the future by the increase in his intake of consumers' goods.

At this point in the discussion of the wearing out and replacement of capital goods we may observe that a capital good rarely retains its full "powers" to aid in production and then suddenly loses all its serviceability. In the words of Professor Benham, "capital goods do not usually remain in perfect technical condition and then suddenly collapse, like the wonderful 'one-hoss shay.' "[34] Crusoe's berry output, instead of remaining five hundred for ten days and then falling back to two hundred on the eleventh day, is likely to decline at some rate before the stick becomes completely useless.

Another method of maintaining capital may now prove available. Thus, Crusoe may find that, by spending a little time repairing the stick, breaking off weaker parts, etc., he may be able to prolong its life and maintain his output of berries longer. In short, he may be able to add to his capital structure via *repairs*.

Here again he will balance the added increase in future output of consumers' goods against the *present* loss in consumers' goods which he must endure by expending his labor on repairs. Making repairs therefore requires an independent act of saving and a choice to save. It is entirely possible, for example, that Crusoe will decide to replace the stick, and spend his labor on that purpose, but will not consider it worthwhile to repair it. Which course he decides to take depends on his valuation of the various alternative outputs and his rate of time preference.

An actor's decision on what objects to invest in will depend on the expected utility of the forthcoming consumers' good, its durability, and the length of his waiting-time. Thus, he may first invest in a stick and then decide it would not be worthwhile to invest in a second stick; instead, it would be better to begin building the axe in order to obtain a house. Or he may first make a bow and arrows with which to hunt game, and after that begin working on a house. Since the marginal utility of the stock of a good declines as the stock increases, the more he has of the stock of *one* consumers' good, the more likely he will be to expend his new savings on a different consumers' good, since the second good will now have a higher marginal utility of product to his invested labor and waiting, and the marginal utility of the first will be lower.

If two consumers' goods have the same expected marginal utility in daily serviceability and have the same period of waiting time, but one is more durable than the other, then the actor will choose to invest in production of the former. On the other hand, if the total serviceableness of two expected consumers' goods is the same, and their length of period of production is the same, the *less* durable good will be invested in, since its total satisfactions arrive earlier than the other. Also, in choosing between investing in one or the other of two consumers' goods, the actor will, other things being equal, choose that good with the shorter period of production, as has been discussed above.

Any actor will continue to save and invest his resources in various expected future consumers' goods as long as the utility, considered in the present, of the marginal product of each unit saved and invested is greater than the utility of present consumers' goods which he could obtain by not performing that saving. The latter utility—of present consumers' goods forgone—is the "disutility of waiting." Once the latter becomes greater than the utility of obtaining more goods in the future through saving, the actor will cease to save.

Allowing for the relative urgency of wants, man, as has been demonstrated above, tends to invest first in those consumers' goods with the shortest processes of production. Therefore, any given saving will be invested either in maintaining the present capital structure or in adding to it capital in *more and more remote* stages of production, i.e., in longer processes of production. Thus, any new saving (beyond maintaining the structure) will tend to lengthen production processes and invest in *higher and higher orders* of capital goods.

In a modern economy, the capital structure contains goods of almost infinite remoteness from the eventual consumers' goods. We saw above some of the stages involved in the production of a comparatively very simple good like a ham sandwich. The laborer in an iron mine is far removed indeed from the ham sandwich in Jones' armchair.

It is evident that the problems of measurement that arose in previous sections would be likely to pose a grave difficulty in saving and investing. How do actors know when their capital structure is being added to or consumed, when the types of capital goods and consumers' goods are numerous? Obviously, Crusoe knows when he has more or fewer berries, but how can a modern complex economy, with innumerable capital goods and consumers' goods, make such decisions? The answer to this problem, which also rests on the commensurability of different goods, will be discussed in later chapters.

In observing the increased output made possible by the use of capital goods, one may very easily come to attribute some sort of independent productive power to capital and to say that three types of productive forces enter into the production of consumers' goods: labor, nature, and capital. It would be easy to draw this conclusion, but completely fallacious. Capital goods have no independent productive power of their own; in the last analysis they are completely reducible to labor and land, which produced them, and time. Capital goods are "stored-up" labor, land, and time; they are intermediate way stations on the road to the eventual attainment of the consumers' goods into which they are transformed. At every step of the way they must be worked on by labor, in conjunction with nature, in order to continue the process of production. Capital is not an independent productive factor like the other two. An excellent illustration of this truth has been provided by Böhm-Bawerk:

The following analogy will make it perfectly clear. A man throws a stone at another man and kills him. Has the stone killed the man? If the question is put without laying any special emphasis it may be answered without hesitation in the affirmative. But how if the murderer, on his trial, were to defend himself by saying that it was not he but the stone that had killed the man? Taking the words in this sense, should we still say that the stone had killed the man, and acquit the murderer? Now it is with an emphasis like this that economists inquire as to the independent productivity of capital . . . We are not asking about dependent intermediate causes, but about ultimate independent elements. The question is not whether capital plays a part in the bringing about of a productive result—such as the stone does in the killing of the man—but whether, granted the productive result, some part of it is due to capital so entirely and peculiarly that it simply cannot be put to the credit of the two other recognized elementary factors, nature and labour.

Böhm-Bawerk replies in the negative, pointing out that capital goods are purely way stations in the process of production, worked on at every possible stage by the forces of labor and land:

If, today, by allying my labor with natural powers, I make bricks out of clay, and tomorrow, by allying my labor with natural gifts, I obtain lime, and the day after that make mortar and so construct a wall, can it be said of any part of the wall that I and the natural powers have *not* made it? Again, before a lengthy piece of work, such as the building of a house, is quite finished, it naturally must be at one time a fourth finished, then a half finished, then three-quarters finished. What now would be said if one were to describe these inevitable stages of the work as independent requisites of house-building, and maintain that, for the building of a house, we require, besides building materials and labor, a quarter-finished house, a half-finished house, a three-quarters finished house? In form perhaps it is less striking, but in effect it is not a whit more correct, to elevate those intermediate steps in the progress of the work, which outwardly take the shape of capital, into an independent agent of production by the side of nature and labor.[35]

And this holds true regardless of how many stages are involved or how remote the capital good is from the ultimate consumers' good.

Since investment in capital goods involves looking toward the future, one of the risks that an actor must always cope with is the *uncertainty* of future conditions. Producing consumers' goods directly involves a very short period of production, so that the uncertainty incurred is not nearly as great as the uncertainty of longer processes of production, an uncertainty that becomes more and more important as the period of production lengthens.[36]

Suppose that Crusoe, while deciding on his investment in the stick, believes that there is a good possibility of his finding a grove where berries are in abundance, giving him an output of fifty or more berries per hour without the aid of a stick, and also where the berries would be so close as to render the stick useless. In that case, the more likely he thinks are the chances of finding the grove, the less likely he is to make the decision to invest in the stick, which would then be of no help to him. The greater the doubt about the usefulness the stick will have after it is ready, the less likelihood of investing in it, and the more likelihood of either investing in another good or of consuming instead of saving. We can consider that there is a sort of "uncertainty discount" on the expected future utility of the investment that may be so large as to induce the actor not to make the investment. The uncertainty factor in this case works with the time-preference factor to the disadvantage of the investment, against which the actor balances the expected utility of future output.

On the other hand, uncertainty may work as an added spur to making the investment. Thus, suppose that Crusoe believes that a blight may strike the berries very shortly and that if this happens, his unaided berry-output would dangerously decline. If the blight struck, Crusoe would be in great need of the stick even to maintain his output at the present low level. Thus, the possibility that the stick may be of even greater use to him than he anticipates will add to the expected utility of his investment, and the greater the chance of this possibility in Crusoe's view, the more likely he will be to invest in the stick. Thus, the un-certainty factor may work in either direction, depending on the specific situation involved.

We may explain the entire act of deciding whether or not to perform an act of capital formation as the balancing of relative utilities, "discounted" by the actor's rate of time preference and also by the uncertainty factor. Thus, first let us assume, for pur-poses of simplification, that Crusoe, in making the stick, forgoes 10 hours' worth of present goods, i.e., 200 berries, and has ac-quired 1,500 berries three days later as a result of the investment decision. If the 1,500 berries had been immediately available, there would be no doubt that he would have given up 200 berries to acquire 1,500. Thus, 1,500 berries in the present might have a rank of 4 on his value scale, while 200 berries have a rank of 11:

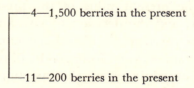

4—1,500 berries in the present

11—200 berries in the present

Now, how will Crusoe decide between 200 berries in the present and 1,500 three days from now? Since all choices have to be made on one value scale, Crusoe must grade the utility of 1,500 berries three days from now as against the utility of 200 berries now. If the former is greater (higher on his value scale) he will make the decision to save and invest in the stick. If the latter is greater, and his 200 berries forgone have a greater value than the expectation of 1,500 berries three days from now, then his time preference has conquered the increased utility of stock, and he will not make the saving-investment decision. Thus, the actor's value scale may be:

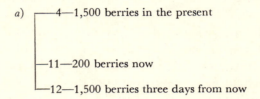

a) ┌──4—1,500 berries in the present

├─11—200 berries now

└─12—1,500 berries three days from now

or it may be:

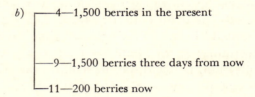

b) ┌──4—1,500 berries in the present

├──9—1,500 berries three days from now

└─11—200 berries now

In case (*b*) he will make the decision to invest; in case (*a*) he will not. We can say that the value of 1,500 berries three days from now is the *present value of the future good*. The expected future good is discounted by the actor according to his *rate of time preference*. The present value of his expected future good is compared to the present value of the present good on the actor's value scale, and the decision to save and invest is made accordingly. It is clear that the higher the rate of discount, the lower the present value of the future good will be, and the greater the likelihood of abstaining from the investment. On the other hand, the lower the rate of discount, the higher the present value of future goods will be on the actor's value scale, and the greater the likelihood of its being greater than the value of present goods forgone, and hence of his making the investment.

Thus, the investment decision will be determined by which is greater: the present value of the future good or the present value of present goods forgone. The present value of the future good, in turn, is determined by the value that the future good would have if immediately present (say, the "expected future value of the future good"); and by the rate of time preference. The greater the former, the greater will be the present value of the future good; the greater the latter (the rate of discount of future compared to present goods), the lower will be the present value.

At any point in time, an actor has a range of investment decisions open to him of varying potential utilities for the products that will be provided.[37] He also has a certain rate of time preference by which he will discount these expected future utilities to their present value. How much he will save and invest in any period will be determined by comparing these present values with the value of the consumers' goods forgone in making the investment decision. As he makes one investment decision after another, he will choose to allocate his resources first to investments of highest present value, then to those of next highest, etc. As he continues investing (at any given time), the present value of the future utilities will decline. On the other hand, since he is giving up a larger and larger supply of consumers' goods in the present, the utility of the consumers' goods that he forgoes (leisure and others) will increase—on the basis of the law of marginal utility. He will cease saving and investing at the point at which the value of goods forgone exceeds the present value of the future utilities to be derived. This will determine an actor's *rate* of saving and investing at any time.

It is evident that the problem again arises: How can actors decide and compare time-preference rates for innumerable possible goods and in a complex, modern economy? And here too, the answer for a complex economy lies in establishing commensurability among all the various commodities, present and future, as will be discussed in later chapters.

Now, the uncertainty factors enter into the actor's decision in one way or the other. The delicate procedure of weighing all the various factors in the situation is a complex process that takes place in the mind of every actor according to his understanding of the situation. It is a decision depending purely on the individual judgment, the subjective estimates, of each actor. The "best" decision cannot be exactly, or quantitatively, decided upon in advance by objective methods. This process of *forecasting* the future conditions that will occur during the course of his action is one that must be engaged in by every actor. This necessity of guessing the course of the relevant conditions and their possible change during the forthcoming action is called the *act of entrepreneurship*. Thus, to some extent at least, every man is an entrepreneur. Every actor makes his estimate of the uncertainty situation with regard to his forthcoming action.

The concepts of *success* or *failure* in entrepreneurship are thus deducible from the existence of action. The relatively successful entrepreneur is the one who has guessed correctly the changes in conditions to take place during the action, and has invested accordingly. He is the Crusoe who has decided not to build the stick because his judgment tells him that he will soon find a new grove of berries, which he then finds. On the other hand, the relatively unsuccessful entrepreneur is the one who has been badly mistaken in his forecast of the relevant changes in conditions taking place during the course of his action. He is the Crusoe who has failed to provide himself with a stick against the blight. The successful actor, the successful entrepreneur, makes correct estimates; the unsuccessful entrepreneur is the one who makes erroneous estimates.

Suppose now that an investment has already been made, and capital goods have already been built with a goal in view, when changing conditions reveal that an error has been made. The actor is then faced with the problem of determining what to do with the capital good. The answer depends on the *convertibility* of the capital good. If the good becomes worthless in the use for which it is intended, the actor, though having made an error in investing in it in the first place, now has it on his hands and has to make the best of it. If there is another use to which the actor can conveniently transfer the capital good, he will do so. Thus, if Crusoe finds that a new grove has rendered his stick useless for berry-picking, he may use it as a walking stick. He would not have invested in it originally if he had known it would be useless for berry-picking, but now that he has it, he turns it to its most urgent available use. On the other hand, he may feel that it is hardly worthwhile to spend time replacing the stick, now that it is usable only for walking purposes. Or, after working fifty hours and building an axe, he may find a house left by some previous inhabitant. The axe, however, may be convertible to use in something just a bit lower in value—say, building a bow and arrows for hunting or building a boat for fishing. The axe may be so valuable in these uses that Crusoe will still work to replace and maintain it in operation.

It is clear that the accumulated stock of capital goods (or, for that matter, durable consumers' goods) imposes a conservative force on present-day action. The actor in the present is influenced by his (or someone else's) actions in the past, even if the latter were to some extent in error. Thus, Crusoe might find an axe already available, built by a previous inhabitant. It might not be the sort of axe that Crusoe would consider the best available. However, he may decide, if it is a serviceable axe, to use it as a capital good and to wait until it wears out before replacing it with one of his choosing. On the other hand, he may feel that it is so blunt as to be of little use, and begin immediately to work on an axe of his own.

The conservatism of the past exercises a similar influence on the question of *location,* another aspect of the same problem. Thus, Crusoe may already have built his house, cleared a field, etc., in one portion of the island. Then, one day, in walking around the island, he might find a section at the other end with far greater advantages in fishing, fruits, etc. If he had not invested in any capital goods or durable consumers' goods, he would immediately shift his location to this more abundant area. However, he has already invested in certain capital goods: some, such as the axe, are easily convertible to the new location; others, such as the cleared field and house, cannot be converted in their location. Therefore, he has to decide on his value scale between the advantages and disadvantages of moving: the more abundant fish and fruits vs. the necessity of working to build a new house, new clearing, etc. He might decide, for example, to stay in the house and clearing until they have worn down to a certain point, without working on a replacement, and then shift to the new location.

If an actor decides to abandon nonconvertible capital, such as the stick or the cleared field, in favor of producing other capital and consumers' goods, he is *not,* as some may think, wasting his resources by allowing the emergence of "unused capacity" of his resources. When Crusoe abandons his clearing or stick or house (which may be considered in this connection as equivalent to capital), he is abandoning nonconvertible capital for the sake of using his labor in combination with natural elements or capital goods which he believes will yield him a greater utility. Similarly, if he refuses to go deep into a jungle for berries, he is not "wasting" his nonconvertible supply of land-and-berries, for he judges doing so of far less utility than other uses that he could make of his labor and time. The existence of a capital good not in use reveals an error made by this or by some previous actor *in the past,* but indicates that the actor expects to acquire a greater utility from other uses of his labor than he could obtain by continuing the capital good in its originally intended use or by converting it to some other use.[38]

This discussion provides the clue to an analysis of how actors will employ the original nature-given factors of production. In many cases, actors have their choice among the varying elements provided by nature. Thus, suppose that Crusoe, in his explorations of the island, finds that among the possible locations where he can settle, some are abundant in their output of berries (setting aside their production of other consumers' goods), some less so, and some useless and barren. Clearly, other considerations being equal, he will settle on the most fertile—the "best" land—and employ this factor as far as is determined by the utility of its product, the possibility of investing in useful capital goods on the land, the value he places on leisure, etc. The poorer areas of land will remain unused. As stated above, this development is to be expected; there is no reason to be surprised at such evidence of "unused resources." On the other hand, if the better areas are used up, then Crusoe will go on to utilize some of the next best areas, until the utility of the supply produced fails to exceed the utility of his leisure forgone. ("Next best" includes all the relevant factors, such as productivity, convenient access to the best land, etc.)

Areas of potential use, but which the actor chooses *not* to bring into use because it would not "pay" in terms of utilities forgone, are called submarginal areas. They are not objects of action at the moment, but the actor has them in mind for possible future use.

On the other hand, Crusoe's island may be so small or so barren that all his available useful land or water areas must be pressed into use. Thus, Crusoe might have to explore the whole island for his daily output of two hundred berries. In that case, if his resources are such that he must always employ all the possibly useful nature-given factors, it is obvious that the actor is pretty close to the bare survival level.

In those cases where nature-given factors are worked on, "improved," and maintained by human labor, these are, in effect, thereby changed into capital goods. Thus, land that has been cleared, tilled, ploughed, etc., by human labor has become a capital good. This land is a produced good, and not an originally given good. Decisions concerning whether and how much to improve the soil, or whether to maintain it or extract the maximum present consumers' goods at the expense of future losses ("erosion"), are on exactly the same footing as all capital-formation decisions. They depend on a comparison of the expected utility of future production as against the utility of present consumers' goods forgone.

It is clear that capital formation and the concomitant lengthening of the period of production prolong the *period of provision* of the actor. Capital formation lengthens the period in the future for which he is providing for the satisfaction of wants. *Action* involves the anticipation of wants that will be felt in the future, an estimate of their relative urgency, and the setting about to satisfy them. The more capital men invest, the longer their period of provision will tend to be. Goods being directly and presently consumed are *present goods*. A *future good* is the present expectation of enjoying a consumers' good at some point in the future. A future good may be a claim on future consumers' goods, or it may be a capital good, which will be transformed into a consumers' good in the future. Since a capital good is a way station (and nature-given factors are original stations) on the route to consumers' goods, capital goods and nature-given factors are both future goods.

Similarly, the period of provision can be prolonged by lengthening the duration of serviceableness of the consumers' goods being produced. A house has a longer durability than a crop of berries, for example, and Crusoe's investment in a house considerably lengthens his period of provision. A durable consumers' good is consumed only partially from day to day, so that each day's consumption is that of a present good, while the stock of the remainder is a future good. Thus, if a house is built and will last 3,000 days, one day's use will consume 1/3,000 of it, while the remainder will be consumed in the future. 1/3,000 of the house is a present good, while the remaining part is a future good.[39]

It may be added that another method of lengthening the period of production is the simple accumulation of stocks of consumers' goods to be consumed in the future instead of the present. For example, Crusoe might save a stock of one hundred berries to be consumed a few days or a week later. This is often called *plain saving,* as distinguished from *capitalist saving,* in which saving enters into the process of capital formation.[40] We shall see, however, that there is no essential difference between the two types of saving and that plain saving is also capitalist saving in that it too results in capital formation. We must keep in mind the vital fact that the concept of a "good" refers to a thing the units of which the actor believes afford equal serviceability. It does not refer to the physical or chemical characteristics of the good. We remember our critique of the popular fallacious objection to the universal fact of time preference—that, in any given winter, ice the next summer is preferred to ice now.[41] This was not a case of preferring the consumption of the *same* good in the future to its consumption in the present. If Crusoe has a stock of ice in the winter and decides to "save" some until next summer, this means that "ice-in-the-summer" is a *different* good, with a different intensity of satisfaction, from "ice-in-the-winter," despite their physical similarities. The case of berries or of any other good is similar. If Crusoe decides to postpone consuming a portion of his stock of berries, this must mean that this portion will have a greater intensity of satisfaction if consumed later than now—enough greater, in fact, to overcome his time preference for the present. The reasons for such difference may be numerous, involving anticipated tastes and conditions of supply on that future date. At any rate, "berries-eaten-a-week-from-now" become a more highly valued good than "berries-eaten-now," and the number of berries that will be shifted from today's to next week's consumption will be determined by the behavior of the diminishing marginal utility of next week's berries (as the supply increases), the increasing marginal utility of today's berries (as the supply decreases), and the rate of time preference. Suppose that as a resultant of these factors, Crusoe decides to shift one hundred berries for this purpose. In that case, these hundred berries are removed from the category of consumers' goods and shifted to that of capital goods. These are the sort of capital goods, however, which, like wine, needs only *maturing time* to be transferred into consumers' goods, without the expenditure of labor (except the possible extra labor of storing and unstoring the berries).

It is clear, therefore, that the accumulation of a stock of consumers' goods is also saving that goes into capital formation.[42] The saved goods immediately become capital goods, which later mature into more highly valued consumers' goods. There is no essential difference between the two types of saving.

10. *Action as an Exchange*

We have stated that all action involves an exchange—a giving up of a state of affairs for what the actor expects will be a more satisfactory state.[43] We may now elaborate on the implications of this truth, in the light of the numerous examples that have been given in this chapter. Every aspect of action has involved a *choice* among alternatives—a giving up of some goods for the sake of acquiring others. Wherever the choice occurred—whether among uses of durable consumers' goods, or of capital goods; saving vs. consumption; labor vs. leisure; etc.—such choices among alternatives, such renouncing of one thing in favor of another, were always present. In each case, the actor adopted the course that he believed would afford him the highest utility on his value scale; and in each case, the actor gave up what he believed would turn out to be a lesser utility.

Before analyzing the range of alternative choices further, it is necessary to emphasize that *man must always act.* Since he is always in a position to improve his lot, even "doing nothing" is a form of acting. "Doing nothing"—or spending all of his time in leisure—is a choice that will affect his supply of consumers' goods. Therefore, man must always be engaged in choosing and in action.

Since man is always acting, he must always be engaged in trying to attain the *greatest height on his value scale,* whatever the type of choice under consideration. There must *always* be room for improvement in his value scale; otherwise all of man's wants would be perfectly satisfied, and action would disappear. Since this cannot be the case, it means that there is always open to each actor the prospect of improving his lot, of attaining a value higher than he is giving up, i.e., of *making a psychic profit.* What he is giving up may be called his *costs,* i.e., the utilities that he is forgoing in order to attain a better position. Thus, an actor's costs are his forgone opportunities to enjoy consumers' goods. Similarly, the (greater) utility that he expects to acquire because of the action may be considered his *psychic income,* or *psychic revenue,* which in turn will be equal to the utility of the goods he will consume as a result of the action. Hence, at the inauguration of any action, the actor will believe that this course of action will, among the alternatives, *maximize his psychic income or psychic revenue,* i.e., attain the greatest height on his value scale.

APPENDIX A: PRAXEOLOGY AND ECONOMICS

This chapter has been an exposition of part of *praxeological analysis*—the analysis which forms the body of economic theory. This analysis takes as its fundamental premise the existence of human action. Once it is demonstrated that human action is a necessary attribute of the existence of human beings, the rest of praxeology (and its subdivision, economic theory) consists of the elaboration of the logical implications of the concept of action. Economic analysis is of the form:

1) Assert *A*—action axiom.
2) If *A,* then *B;* if *B,* then *C;* if *C,* then *D,* etc.—by rules of logic.
3) Therefore, we assert (the truth of) *B, C, D,* etc.

It is important to realize that economics does not propound any laws about the *content* of man's ends. The examples that we have given, such as ham sandwich, berries, etc., are simply illustrative instances, and are not meant to assert anything about the content of a man's goals at any given time. The concept of action involves the use of scarce means for satisfying the most urgent wants at some point in the future, and the truths of economic theory involve the formal relations between ends and means, and not their specific contents. A man's ends may be "egoistic" or "altruistic," "refined" or "vulgar." They may emphasize the enjoyment of "material goods" and comforts, or they may stress the ascetic life. Economics is not concerned with their content, and its laws apply regardless of the nature of these ends.

Praxeology, therefore, differs from *psychology* or from the *philosophy of ethics.* Since all these disciplines deal with the subjective decisions of individual human minds, many observers have believed that they are fundamentally identical. This is not the case at all. Psychology and ethics deal with the content of human ends; they ask, *why* does the man choose such and such ends, or *what* ends *should* men value? Praxeology and economics deal with *any* given ends and with the formal implications of the fact that men have ends and employ means to attain them. Praxeology and economics are therefore disciplines separate and distinct from the others.

Thus, all explanations of the law of marginal utility on psychological or physiological grounds are erroneous. For example, many writers have based the law of marginal utility on an alleged "law of the satiation of wants," according to which a man can eat so many scoops of ice cream at one time, etc., and then becomes satiated. Whether or not this is true in psychology is completely irrelevant to economics. These writers erroneously concluded that, at the beginning of the supply, a second unit may be more enjoyable than the first, and therefore that marginal utility may increase at first before declining. This is completely fallacious. The law of marginal utility depends on no physiological or psychological assumptions, but is based on the praxeological truth that the first unit of a good will be used to satisfy the most urgent want, the second unit the next most urgent want, etc. It must be remembered that these "units" must be of equal potential serviceability.

For example, it is erroneous to argue as follows: Eggs are the good in question. It is possible that a man needs four eggs to bake a cake. In that case, the second egg may be used for a less urgent use than the first egg, and the third egg for a less urgent use than the second. However, since the fourth egg allows a cake to be produced that would not otherwise be available, the marginal utility of the fourth egg is greater than that of the third egg.

This argument neglects the fact that a "good" is not the physical material, but any material whatever of which the units will constitute an equally serviceable supply. Since the fourth egg is not equally serviceable and interchangeable with the first egg, the two eggs are *not* units of the same supply, and therefore the law of marginal utility does not apply to this case at all. To treat eggs in this case as homogeneous units of one good, it would be necessary to consider *each set of four eggs* as a unit.

To sum up the relationship and the distinctions between praxeology and each of the other disciplines, we may describe them as follows:

Why man chooses various ends: *psychology*.
What men's ends should be: *philosophy of ethics*.
                        also: *philosophy of aesthetics*.
How to use means to arrive at ends: *technology*.
What man's ends are and have been, and how man has used means
    in order to attain them: *history*.
The formal implications of the fact that men use means to attain
    various chosen ends: *praxeology*.

What is the relationship between praxeology and economic analysis? Economics is a subdivision of praxeology—so far the only fully elaborated subdivision. With praxeology as the general, formal theory of human action, economics includes the analysis of the action of an isolated individual (Crusoe economics) and, especially elaborate, the analysis of interpersonal exchange (catallactics). The rest of praxeology is an unexplored area. Attempts have been made to formulate a logical theory of war and violent action, and violence in the form of government has been treated by political philosophy and by praxeology in tracing the effects of violent intervention in the free market. A theory of games has been elaborated, and interesting beginnings have been made in a logical analysis of voting.

The suggestion has been made that, since praxeology and economics are logical chains of reasoning based on a few universally known premises, to be really scientific it should be elaborated according to the symbolic notations of mathematical logic.[44] This represents a curious misconception of the role of mathematical logic, or "logistics." In the first place, it is the great quality of verbal propositions that *each one* is meaningful. On the other hand, algebraic and logical symbols, as used in logistics, are not in themselves meaningful. Praxeology asserts the action axiom as true, and from this (together with a few empirical axioms—such as the existence of a variety of resources and individuals) are deduced, by the rules of logical inference, all the propositions of economics, each one of which is verbal and meaningful. If the logistic array of symbols were used, each proposition would not be meaningful. Logistics, therefore, is far more suited to the physical sciences, where, in contrast to the science of human action, the conclusions rather than the axioms are known. In the physical sciences, the premises are only hypothetical, and logical deductions are made from them. In these cases, there is no purpose in having meaningful propositions at each step of the way, and therefore symbolic and mathematical language is more useful.

Simply to develop economics verbally, then to translate into logistic symbols, and finally to retranslate the propositons back into English, makes no sense and violates the fundamental scientific principle of Occam's razor, which calls for the greatest possible simplicity in science and the avoidance of unnecessary multiplication of entities or processes.

Contrary to what might be believed, the use of verbal logic is not inferior to logistics. On the contrary, the latter is merely an auxiliary device based on the former. For formal logic deals with the necessary and fundamental laws of thought, which must be verbally expressed, and logistics is only a symbolic system that uses this formal verbal logic as its foundation. Therefore, praxeology and economics need not be apologetic in the slightest for the use of verbal logic—the fundamental basis of symbolic logic, and meaningful at each step of the route.[45]

APPENDIX B: ON MEANS AND ENDS

It is often charged that any theory grounded on a logical separation of *means* and *ends* is unrealistic because the two are often amalgamated or fused into one. Yet if man acts purposively, he therefore drives toward *ends,* and whatever route he takes, he must, *ipso facto,* employ *means* to achieve them. The distinction between means and ends is a necessary logical distinction rooted in all human—indeed, all purposive—action. It is difficult to see the sense in any denial of this primordial truth. The only sense to the charge concerns those cases where certain *objects,* or rather certain *routes of action,* become ends in themselves as well as means to other ends. This, of course, can often happen. There is no difficulty, however, in incorporating them into an analysis, as has been done above. Thus, a man may work at a certain job not only for the pay, but also because he enjoys the work or the location. Moreover, any desire for money is a desire for a means to other ends. The critics of praxeology confuse the necessary and eternal separation of ends and means as *categories* with their frequent coincidence in a particular concrete resource or course of action.

2

Direct Exchange

1. *Types of Interpersonal Action: Violence*

The analysis in chapter 1 was based on the logical implications of the assumption of action, and its results hold true for all human action. The *application* of these principles was confined, however, to "Crusoe economics," where the actions of isolated individuals are considered by themselves. In these situations there are no interactions between persons. Thus, the analysis could easily and directly be applied to n number of isolated Crusoes on n islands or other isolated areas. The next task is to apply and extend the analysis to consider interactions between individual human beings.

Let us suppose that Crusoe eventually finds that another individual, say Jackson, has also been living an isolated existence at the other end of the island. What types of interaction may now take place between them? One type of action is *violence*. Thus, Crusoe may entertain a vigorous hatred toward Jackson and decide to murder or otherwise injure him. In that case, Crusoe would gain his end—murder of Jackson—by committing violence. Or Crusoe may decide that he would like to expropriate Jackson's house and collection of furs and murder Jackson as a means to that end. In either case, the result is that Crusoe gains in satisfaction at the expense of Jackson, who, to say the least, suffers great psychic loss. Fundamentally similar is action based on a *threat of violence,* or *intimidation*. Thus, Crusoe may hold up Jackson at the point of a knife and rob him of his accumulated furs and provisions. Both examples are cases of *violent action* and involve gain for one at the expense of another.

The following factors, singly or in combination, might work to induce Crusoe (or Jackson) to *refrain* from any violent action against the other:

1) He may feel that the use of violence against any other human being is *immoral,* i.e., that refraining from violence against another person is an end in itself, whose rank in his value scale is higher that that of any advantages in the form of capital or consumers' goods that he might gain from such action.

2) He may decide that instituting violent action might well establish an unwelcome precedent, causing the other person to take up arms against him, so that he may end by being the victim instead of the victor. If he begins a type of action where one must gain at the expense of another, then he must face the fact that *he* might turn out to be the loser as a result of the action.

3) Even if he feels that his violent action will eventually result in victory over the other, he may conclude that the "costs of the war" would exceed his net gain from the victory. Thus, the disutility of time and labor-energy spent in *fighting the war* (war may be defined as violent action used by two or more opponents), in accumulating *weapons* for the war (capital goods for war uses), etc., might, in prospect, outweigh the spoils of conquest.

4) Even if Crusoe feels reasonably certain of victory and believes that the costs of fighting will be far less than the utility of his spoils of victory, this short-run gain may well be outweighed in his decision by long-run losses. Thus, his conquest of Jackson's furs and house may add to his satisfaction for a while after the "period of production" (= preparing for the war + the length of time of the war itself), but, after a time, his house will decay and his furs become worthless. He may then conclude that, by his murder of Jackson, he has lost permanently many services which Jackson's continued existence might have furnished. This might be companionship or other types of consumers' or capital goods. *How* Jackson might have served Crusoe without resort to violence will be indicated below, but, at any rate, Crusoe may

be detained from using violence by estimating the disutility of the long-run consequences more highly than the utility of the expected short-run gains. On the other hand, his time preference may be so high as to cause his short-run gains to override the long-run losses in his decision.

It is possible that Crusoe may institute violent action without taking into consideration the costs of the war or the long-run consequences, in which case his actions will turn out to be erroneous, i.e., the means he used were not the appropriate ones to maximize his psychic revenue.

Instead of murdering his opponent, Crusoe might find it more useful to *enslave* him, and, under continual threat of violence, to force Jackson to agree to expend his labor for the satisfaction of Crusoe's wants rather than his own.[1] Under *slavery,* the master treats the slave as he does his livestock, horses, and other animals, using them as factors of production to gratify his wants, and feeding, housing them, etc., just enough to enable them to continue in the master's service. It is true that the slave agrees to this arrangement, but this agreement is the result of a choice between working for the master and injury through violence. Labor under these conditions is qualitatively different from labor not under the threat of violence, and may be called *compulsory labor* as compared to *free labor* or *voluntary labor.* If Jackson agrees to continue working as a slave under Crusoe's dictates, it does *not* mean that Jackson is an enthusiastic advocate of his own slavery. It simply means that Jackson does not believe that *revolt* against his master will better his condition, because of the *costs* of the revolt in terms of possible violence inflicted on him, the labor of preparing and fighting, etc.

The argument that the slave might be an enthusiastic supporter of the system because of the food, etc., provided by his master ignores the fact that, in that case, violence and the threat of violence by the master would not be necessary. Jackson would simply voluntarily place himself in Crusoe's service, and this arrangement would not be slavery, but another type considered in the next section.[2,3] It is clear that the slave is always worse off than he would be without the threat of violence by the master, and therefore, that the master always gains at the expense of the slave.

The interpersonal relation under slavery is known as *hegemonic*.[4] The relationship is one of command and obedience, the commands being enforced by threats of violence. The master uses the slaves as instruments, as factors of production, for gratifying his wants. Thus, slavery, or hegemony, is defined as a system in which one must labor under the orders of another under the threat of violence. Under hegemony, the man who does the obeying—the "slave," "serf," "ward," or "subject"—makes only one choice among two alternatives: (1) to subject himself to the master or "dictator"; or (2) to revolt against the regime of violence by use of his own violence or by refusing to obey orders. If he chooses the first course, he submits himself to the hegemonic ruler, and all the other decisions and actions are made by that ruler. The subject chooses *once* in choosing to obey the ruler; the other choices are made by the ruler. The subject acts as a passive factor of production for use by the master. After that one act of (continual) choice made by the slave, he engages in coerced or compulsory labor, and the dictator alone is free to choose and act.

Violent action may result in the following developments: (*a*) inconclusive fighting, with neither opponent the victor, in which case the war may continue intermittently for a long period of time, or violent action may cease, and *peace* be established (the absence of war); (*b*) the victor may kill the victim, in which case there is no further interpersonal action between the two; (*c*) the victor may simply rob the victim and leave, to return to isolation, or perhaps with intermittent violent forays; or (*d*) the victor may establish a continuing hegemonic tyranny over the victim by threats of violence.

In course (*a*), the violent action has proved abortive and erroneous; in (*b*), there is no further interpersonal interaction; in (*c*), there is an alternation between robbery and isolation; and in (*d*), a continuing hegemonic bond is established.

Of these results, only in (*d*) has a continuing pattern of interpersonal relationship been constituted. These relations are compulsory, involving the following coerced "exchanges": the slaves are treated as factors of production in exchange for food and other provisions; the masters acquire factors of production in exchange for supplying the provisions. Any continuing pattern of interpersonal exchanges is called a *society,* and it is clear that a society has been established only in case (*d*).[5] In the case of Crusoe's enslavement of Jackson, the society established is a totally hegemonic one.

The term "society," then, denotes a pattern of interpersonal exchanges among human beings. It is obviously absurd to treat "society" as "real," with some independent force of its own. There is no reality to society apart from the individuals who compose it and whose actions determine the type of social pattern that will be established.

We have seen in chapter 1 that all action is an exchange, and we may now divide exchanges into two categories. One is *autistic exchange.* Autistic exchange consists of any exchange that does not involve some form of interpersonal exchange of services. Thus, all of isolated Crusoe's exchanges were autistic. On the other hand, the case of slavery did involve *interpersonal exchange,* in which each gives up some goods in order to acquire other goods from the other. In this form of compulsory exchange, however, only the ruler benefits from the exchange, since he is the only one who makes it of his own free choice. Since he must impose the threat of violence in order to induce the subject to make the exchange, it is clear that the latter loses by the exchange. The master uses the subject as a factor of production for his own profit at the latter's expense, and this hegemonic relationship may be called *exploitation.* Under hegemonic exchange, the ruler exploits the subject for the ruler's benefit.[6]

2. *Types of Interpersonal Action: Voluntary Exchange and the Contractual Society* [7]

From this point on, we shall develop an analysis of the workings of a society based purely on voluntary action, entirely *unhampered* by violence or threats of violence. We shall examine

interpersonal actions that are purely voluntary, and have no
trace of hegemonic relations. Then, after working out the laws
of the *unhampered market,* we shall trace the nature and results
of hegemonic relations—of actions based on violence or the threat
of violence. We shall note the various effects of violent interference with voluntary actions and shall consider the consequences
of approaches to a regime of total hegemony, of pure slavery
or subjection. At present, we shall confine our discussion to an
analysis of actions unhampered by the existence of violence of
man against man.

The major form of voluntary interaction is voluntary interpersonal exchange. A gives up a good to B in exchange for a good
that B gives up to A. The essence of the exchange is that *both
people make it because they expect that it will benefit them;
otherwise they would not have agreed to the exchange.* A necessary condition for an exchange to take place is that the *two goods
have reverse valuations on the respective value scales of the two
parties to the exchange.* Thus, suppose A and B are the two exchangers, and A gives B good *X* in exchange for good *Y.* In order
for this exchange to take place, the following must have been
their value scales before making the exchange:

A	*B*
1—(Good *Y*)	1—(Good *X*)
2—Good *X*	2—Good *Y*

(Parentheses around the good indicate that the party does not have
it in his stock; absence of parentheses indicates that he has.) A
possesses good *X,* and B possesses good *Y,* and each evaluates the
good of the other more highly than his own. After the exchange
is made, both A and B have shifted to a higher position on their
respective value scales.

Thus, the conditions for an exchange to take place are that
the goods are valued in reverse order by the two parties and that
each of the parties *knows* of the existence of the other and the
goods that he possesses. Without knowledge of the other person's
assets, no exchange of these assets could take place.

It is clear that the things that must be exchanged are *goods,* which will be useful to the receiving party. The goods may be present or future goods (or claims to future goods, which may be considered as equivalent to future goods), they may be capital goods or consumers' goods, labor or nature-given factors. At any rate, the objects of an exchange must be *scarce means* to human ends, since, if they were available in abundance for all, they would be general conditions of human welfare and not objects of human action. If something were a general condition of human welfare, there would be no need to give something up to acquire it, and it would not become the object of exchange.

If the goods in question are unique goods with a supply of one unit, then the problem of when exchanges will or will not be made is a simple one. If A has a vase and B a typewriter, if each knows of the other's asset, and if A values the typewriter more highly, and B values the vase more highly, there will be an exchange. If, on the other hand, *either* A or B values whatever he has more highly than what the other has, then an exchange will not take place. Similarly, an exchange will not take place if either party has no knowledge that the other party has a vase or a typewriter.

On the other hand, if the goods are available in *supplies* of homogeneous units, the problem becomes more complex. Here, in determining how far exchanges of the two goods will go, the law of marginal utility becomes the decisive factor.[8] If Jones and Smith have certain quantities of units of goods X and Y in their possession, then in order for Jones to trade *one unit* of X for *one unit* of Y, the following conditions have to be met: To Jones, the marginal utility of the added unit of Y must be greater than the marginal utility of the unit of X given up; and to Smith, the marginal utility of the added unit of X must be greater than the marginal utility of the unit of Y given up. Thus:

Jones 1 Unit of X Smith

■ ⟶ ← ■ occurs if:

1 Unit of Y

to Jones, M.U. of Addition of Y > M.U. of X.

to Smith, M.U. of Addition of X > M.U. of Y.

(The marginal utilities of the goods to Jones and to Smith are, of course, not comparable, since they cannot be measured, and the two value scales cannot be reduced to one measure or scale.)

However, as Jones continues to exchange with Smith units of X for units of Y, the marginal utility of X to Jones increases, because of the law of marginal utility. Furthermore, the marginal utility of the added unit of Y continues to decrease as Jones' stock of Y increases, because of the operation of this law. Eventually, therefore, Jones will reach a point where, in any further exchange of X for Y, the marginal utility of X will be greater than the marginal utility of the added unit of Y, so that he will make no further exchange. Furthermore, Smith is in a similar position. As he continues to exchange Y for X, for him the marginal utility of Y increases, and the marginal utility of the added unit of X decreases, with the operation of the law of marginal utility. He too will eventually reach a point where a further exchange will lower rather than raise his position on his value scale, so that he will decline to make any further exchange. Since it takes two to make a bargain, Jones and Smith will exchange units of X for units of Y *until one of them* reaches a point beyond which further exchange will lead to loss rather than profit.

Thus, suppose that Jones begins with a position where his *assets (stock of goods)* consist of a supply of 5 horses and 0 cows, while Smith begins with assets of 5 cows and 0 horses. How much, if any, exchanges of one cow for one horse will be effected is reflected in the value scales of the two people. Thus, suppose that Jones' value diagram is as shown in Fig. 5. The dots represent the value of the marginal utility of each additional cow, as Jones makes exchanges of one horse for one cow. The crosses represent the increasing marginal utility of each horse given up as Jones makes exchanges. Jones will stop trading after the third exchange, when his assets consist of 2 horses and 3 cows, since a further such exchange will make him worse off.

On the other hand, suppose that Smith's value diagram appears as in Fig. 6. The dots represent the marginal utility to Smith of each additional horse, while the crosses represent the marginal utility of each cow given up. Smith will stop trading after two exchanges, and therefore Jones will have to stop after two exchanges also. They will end with Jones having a stock of 3 horses and 2 cows, and Smith with a stock of 3 cows and 2 horses.

It is almost impossible to overestimate the importance of exchange in a developed economic system. Interpersonal exchanges have an enormous influence on productive activities. Their existence means that goods and units of goods have not only *direct use-value* for the producer, but also *exchange-value*. In other

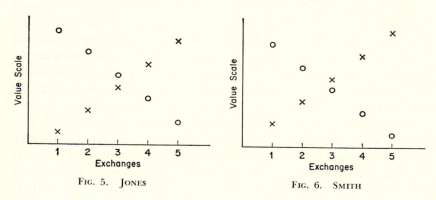

FIG. 5. JONES   FIG. 6. SMITH

words, goods may now be exchanged for other goods of greater usefulness to the actor. A man will exchange a unit of a good so long as the goods that it can command in exchange have greater value to him than the value it had in direct use, i.e., so long as its exchange-value is greater than its direct use-value. In the example above, the first two horses that Jones exchanged and the first two cows surrendered by Smith had a greater exchange value than direct use-value to their owners. On the other hand, from then on, their respective assets had greater use-value to their owners than exchange-value.[9]

The existence and possibilities of exchange open up for producers the avenue of producing for a "market" rather than for themselves. Instead of attempting to maximize his product in isolation by producing goods solely for his own use, each person can now produce goods in anticipation of their exchange-value, and exchange these goods for others that are more valuable to him. It is evident that since this opens a new avenue for the utility of goods, it becomes possible for each person to increase his productivity. Through praxeology, therefore, we know that only gains can come to every participant in exchange and that each must benefit by the transaction; otherwise he would not engage in it. Empirically we know that the exchange economy has made possible an enormous increase in productivity and satisfactions for all the participants.

Thus, any person can produce goods either for his own direct use or for purposes of exchange with others for goods that he desires. In the former case, *he* is the *consumer* of his own product; in the latter case, he produces in the service of *other consumers,* i.e., he "produces for a market." In either case, it is clear that, on the unhampered "market," it is the consumers who dictate the course of production.

At any time, a good or a unit of a good may have for its possessor either direct use-value or exchange-value or a mixture of both, and whichever is the greater is the determinant of his action. Examples of goods with only direct use-value to their owner are those in an isolated economy or such goods as eyeglasses ground to an individual prescription. On the other hand, producers of such eyeglasses or of surgical instruments find no direct use-value in these products, but only exchange-value. Many goods, as in the foregoing example of exchange, have both direct and exchange-value for their owners. For the latter goods, changing conditions may cause direct use-value to replace exchange-value in the actor's hierarchy of values, or vice versa. Thus, if a person with a stock of wine happens to lose his taste for wine, the previous greater use-value that wine had for him will change, and the wine's exchange-value will take precedence over its use-value, which has now become almost nil. Similarly, a grown person may exchange the toys that he had used as a child, now that their use-value has greatly declined.

On the other hand, the exchange-value of goods may decline, causing their possessors to use them directly rather than exchange them. Thus, a milliner might make a hat for purposes of exchange, but some minor defect might cause its expected exchange-value to dwindle, so that the milliner decides to wear the hat herself.

One of the most important factors causing a change in the relationship between direct use-value and exchange-value is an increase in the number of units of a supply available. From the law of marginal utility we know that an increase in the supply of a good available decreases the marginal utility of the supply for direct use. Therefore, the more units of supply are available, the more likely will the exchange-value of the marginal unit be greater than its value in direct use, and the more likely will its owner be to exchange it. The more horses that Jones had in his stock, and the more cows Smith had, the more eager would they be to exchange them. Conversely, a decrease in supply will increase the likelihood that direct use-value will predominate.

The network of voluntary interpersonal exchanges forms a society; it also forms a pattern of interrelations known as *the market.* A society formed solely by the market has an *unhampered market,* or a *free market,* a market not burdened by the interference of violent action. A society based on voluntary exchanges is called a *contractual society.* In contrast to the hegemonic society based on the rule of violence, the contractual type of society is based on freely entered contractual relations between individuals. Agreements by individuals to make exchanges are called *contracts,* and a society based on voluntary contractual agreements is a contractual society. It is the society of the unhampered market.

In a contractual society, each individual benefits by the exchange-contract that he makes. Each individual is an actor free to make his own decisions at every step of the way. Thus, the relations among people in an unhampered market are "symmetrical"; there is equality in the sense that each person has equal power to make his own exchange-decisions. This is in contrast to a hegemonic relationship, where power is asymmetrical—where the dictator makes all the decisions for his subjects except the one decision to obey, as it were, at bayonet point.

Thus, the distinguishing features of the contractual society, of the unhampered market, are self-responsibility, freedom from violence, full power to make one's own decisions (except the decision to institute violence against another), and benefits for all participating individuals. The distinguishing features of a hegemonic society are the rule of violence, the surrender of the power to make one's own decisions to a dictator, and exploitation of subjects for the benefit of the masters. It will be seen below that existing societies may be totally hegemonic, totally contractual, or various mixtures of different degrees of the two, and the nature and consequences of these various "mixed economies" and totally hegemonic societies will be analyzed.

Before we examine the exchange process further, it must be considered that, in order for a person to exchange anything, he must first possess it, or *own* it. He gives up the *ownership* of good X in order to obtain the *ownership* of good Y. Ownership by one or more owners implies exclusive control and use of the goods owned, and the goods owned are known as *property*. Freedom from violence implies that no one may seize the property of another by means of violence or the threat of violence and that each person's property is safe, or "secure," from such aggression.

What goods become property? Obviously, only *scarce means* are property. General conditions of welfare, since they are abundant to all, are not the objects of any action, and therefore cannot be owned or become property. On the free market, it is nonsense to say that someone "owns" the air. Only if a good is scarce is it necessary for anyone to obtain it, or ownership of it, for his use. The only way that a man could assume ownership of the air is to use violence to enforce this claim. Such action could not occur on the unhampered market.

On the free, unhampered market, a man can acquire property in scarce goods as follows: (1) In the first place, *each man has ownership over his own self*, over his will and actions, and the manner in which he will exert his own labor. (2) He acquires scarce nature-given factors either by appropriating hitherto unused factors for his own use or by receiving them as a gift from someone else, who in the last analysis must have appropriated them as hitherto unused factors.[10] (3) He acquires capital goods or consumers' goods either by mixing his own labor with nature-given factors to produce them or by receiving them as a gift from someone else. As in the previous case, gifts must eventually resolve themselves into some actor's production of the goods by the use of his own labor. Clearly, it will be nature-given factors, capital goods, and *durable* consumers' goods that are likely to be handed down through gifts, since nondurable consumers' goods will probably be quickly consumed. (4) He may *exchange* any type of factor (labor service, nature-given factor, capital good, consumers' good) for any type of factor. It is clear that gifts and exchanges as a source of property must eventually be resolved into: *self-ownership, appropriation of unused nature-given factors,* and *production of capital and consumers' goods,* as the ultimate sources of acquiring property in a free economic system. In order for the giving or exchanging of goods to take place, they must first be obtained by individual actors in one of these ways. The logical sequence of events is therefore: A man owns himself; he appropriates unused nature-given factors for his ownership; he uses these factors to produce capital goods and consumers' goods which become his own; he uses up the consumers' goods and/or gives them and the capital goods away to others; he exchanges some of these goods for other goods that had come to be owned in the same way by others.[11,12] These are the methods of acquiring goods that obtain on the free market, and they include all but the method of violent or other *invasive* expropriation of the property of others.[13]

In contrast to general conditions of welfare, which on the free market cannot be subject to appropriation as property, scarce goods in use in production must always be under *someone's* control, and therefore must always be *property*. On the free market, the goods will be owned by those who either produced them, first put them to use, or received them in gifts. Similarly, under a system of violence and hegemonic bonds, someone or some people must superintend and direct the operations of these goods. Whoever performs these functions in effect owns these goods as property, regardless of the legal definition of ownership. This applies to persons and their services as well as to material goods. On the free market, each person is a complete owner of himself, whereas under a system of full hegemonic bonds, he is subject to the ownership of others, with the exception of the one decision not to revolt against the authority of the owner. Thus, violent or hegemonic regimes do not and cannot *abolish* property, which derives from the fundamentals of human action, but can only transfer it from one person or set of people (the producers or natural self-owners) to another set.

We may now briefly sum up the various types of human action in the following table:

HUMAN ACTION

I. Isolation (Autistic Exchange)
II. Interpersonal Action

    A. Invasive Action   B. Noninvasive Action
        1. War   1. Gifts
        2. Murder, Assault   2. Voluntary Exchange
        3. Robbery
        4. Slavery

This and subsequent chapters are devoted to an analysis of a noninvasive society, particularly that constituted by voluntary interpersonal exchange.

3. *Exchange and the Division of Labor*

In describing the conditions that must obtain for interpersonal exchange to take place (such as reverse valuations), we implicitly assumed that it must be *two different goods* that are being exchanged. If Crusoe at his end of the island produced only berries, and Jackson at his end produced only the same kind of berries, then no basis for exchange between them would occur. If Jackson produced two hundred berries and Crusoe one hundred fifty, it would be nonsensical to assume that any exchange of berries would be made between them.[14] The only voluntary interpersonal action in relation to berries that could occur would be a gift from one to another.

If exchangers must exchange two different goods, this implies that each party must have a different proportion of assets of goods in relation to his wants. He must have relatively *specialized* in the acquisition of different goods from those the other party produced. This specialization by each individual may have occurred for any one of three different reasons or any combination of the three: (*a*) differences in suitability and yield of the nature-given factors; (*b*) differences in given capital and durable consumers' goods, and (*c*) differences in skill and in the desirability of different types of labor.[15] These factors, in addition to the potential exchange-value and use-value of the goods, will determine the line of production that the actor will pursue. If the production is directed toward exchange, then the exchange-value will play a major role in his decision. Thus, Crusoe may have found abundant crops on his side of the island. These resources, added to his greater skill in farming and the lower disutility of this occupation for him because of a liking for agriculture, might cause him to take up farming, while Jackson's greater skill in hunting and more abundant game supply induce him to specialize in hunting and trapping. Exchange, a productive process for both participants, implies specialization of production, or *division of labor*.

The extent to which division of labor is carried on in a society depends on the *extent of the market for the products*. The latter determines the exchange-value that the producer will be able to obtain for his goods. Thus, if Jackson knows that he will be able to exchange part of his catch of game for the grains and fruits of Crusoe, he may well expend all his labor on hunting. Then he will be able to devote all his labor-time to hunting, while Crusoe devotes his to farming, and their "surplus" stocks will be exchanged up to the limits analyzed in the previous section. On the other hand, if, for example, Crusoe has little use for meat, Jackson will not be able to exchange much meat, and he will be forced to be far more directly self-sufficient, producing his own grains and fruits as well as meat.

It is clear that, praxeologically, the very fact of exchange and the division of labor implies that it must be more productive for all concerned than isolated, autistic labor. Economic analysis alone, however, does not convey to us knowledge of the enor-

mous increase in productivity that the division of labor brings
to society. This is based on a further empirical insight, viz., the
enormous *variety* in human beings and in the world around them.
It is a fact that, superimposed on the basic unity of species and
objects in nature, there is a great diversity. Particularly is there
variety in the aforementioned factors that would give rise to specialization: in the locations and types of natural resources and
in the ability, skills, and tastes of human beings. In the words
of Professor von Mises:

One may as well consider these two facts as one and the same fact,
namely, the manifoldness of nature which makes the universe a complex of infinite varieties. If the earth's surface were such that the physical conditions of production were the same at every point and if one
man were . . . equal to all other men . . . division of labor would
not offer any advantages for acting man.[16]

It is clear that conditions for exchange, and therefore increased
productivity for the participants, will occur *where each party has
a superiority in productivity in regard to one of the goods exchanged*—a superiority that may be due either to better nature-
given factors or to the ability of the producer. If individuals
abandon attempts to satisfy their wants in isolation, and if each
devotes his working time to that specialty in which he excels, it
is clear that total productivity for each of the products is increased. If Crusoe can produce more berries per unit of time,
and Jackson can kill more game, it is clear that productivity in
both lines is increased if Crusoe devotes himself wholly to the
production of berries and Jackson to hunting game, after which
they can exchange some of the berries for some of the game.
In addition to this, full-time specialization in a line of production is likely to improve each person's productivity in that line
and intensify the relative superiority of each.

More puzzling is the case in which one individual is superior
to another in all lines of production. Suppose, for example, that
Crusoe is superior to Jackson both in the production of berries
and in the production of game. Are there any possibilities for
exchange in this situation? Superficially, it might be answered

that there are none, and that both will continue in isolation. Actually, it pays for Crusoe to specialize in that line of production in which he has the greatest *relative* superiority in production, and to exchange this product for the product in which Jackson specializes. It is clear that the inferior producer benefits by receiving some of the products of the superior one. The latter benefits also, however, by being free to devote himself to that product in which his productive superiority is the greatest. Thus, if Crusoe has a great superiority in berry production and a small one in game production, it will still benefit him to devote his full working time to berry production and then exchange some berries for Jackson's game products. In an example mentioned by Professor Boulding:

A doctor who is an excellent gardener may very well prefer to employ a hired man who as a gardener is inferior to himself, because thereby he can devote more time to his medical practice.[17]

This important principle—that exchange may beneficially take place even when one party is superior in both lines of production—is known as the *law of association,* the *law of comparative costs,* or the *law of comparative advantage.*

With all-pervasive variation offering possibilities for specialization, and favorable conditions of exchange occurring even when one party is superior in both pursuits, great opportunities abound for widespread division of labor and extension of the market. As more and more people are linked together in the exchange network, the more "extended" is the market for each of the products, and the more will exchange-value predominate, as compared to direct use-value, in the decisions of the producer. Thus, suppose that there are five people on the desert island, and each specializes in that line of product in which he has a comparative or absolute advantage. Suppose that each one concentrates on the following products:

A.............. berries
B.............. game
C.............. fish
D.............. eggs
E.............. milk.

With more people participating in the market process, the opportunities for exchange for each actor are now greatly increased. This is true even though each particular act of exchange takes place between just two people and involves two goods. Thus, as shown in Fig. 7, the following network of exchange may take place: Exchange-value now takes a far more dominant place in the decisions of the producers. Crusoe (if A is Crusoe) now knows that if he specializes in berries, he does not now have to rely solely

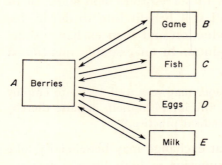

This diagram depicts the pattern of *A's exchanges*. He engages in exchange with each one of the other actors. For each of the other actors, the pattern would be similar.

FIG. 7.   PATTERN OF A'S EXCHANGES

on Jackson to accept them, but can exchange them for the products of several other people. A sudden loss of taste for berries by Jackson will not impoverish Crusoe and deprive him of all other necessities as it would have before. Furthermore, berries will now bring to Crusoe a wider variety of products, each in far greater abundance than before, some being available now that would not have been earlier. The greater productivity and the wider market and emphasis on exchange-value obtain for all participants in the market.

It is evident, as will be explained further in later sections on indirect exchange, that the contractual society of the market is a genuinely *co-operative society*. Each person specializes in the task for which he is best fitted, and each serves his fellow men in order to serve himself in exchange. Each person, by producing for exchange, co-operates with his fellow men voluntarily and without coercion. In contrast to the hegemonic form of society, in which one person or one group of persons exploits the others, a contractual society leaves each person free to benefit himself in the market and as a consequence to benefit others as well. An interesting aspect of this praxeological truth is that this benefit to others occurs regardless of the *motives* of those involved in exchange. Thus, Jackson may specialize in hunting and exchange the game for other products even though he may be indifferent to, or even cordially detest, his fellow participants. Yet regardless of his motives, the other participants are benefited by his actions as an indirect but necessary consequence of his own benefit. It is this almost marvelous process, whereby a man in pursuing his own benefit also benefits others, that caused Adam Smith to exclaim that it almost seemed that an "invisible hand" was directing the proceedings.[18]

Thus, in explaining the origins of society, there is no need to conjure up any mystic communion or "sense of belonging" among individuals. Individuals recognize, through the use of reason, the advantages of exchange resulting from the higher productivity of the division of labor, and they proceed to follow this advantageous course. In fact, it is far more likely that feelings of friendship and communion are the *effects* of a regime of (contractual) social co-operation rather than the cause. Suppose, for example, that the division of labor were not productive, or that men had failed to recognize its productivity. In that case, there would be little or no opportunity for exchange, and each man would try to obtain his goods in autistic independence. The result would undoubtedly be a fierce struggle to gain possession of the scarce goods, since, in such a world, each man's gain of useful goods would be some other man's loss. It would be almost inevitable for such an autistic world to be strongly marked by violence and perpetual war. Since each man could gain from his fellows only at their expense, violence would be prevalent, and it seems highly likely that feelings of mutual hostility would be dominant. As in the case of animals quarreling over bones, such a warring world could cause only hatred and hostility between man and man. Life would be a bitter "struggle for survival." On the other hand, in a world of voluntary social co-operation through mutually beneficial exchanges, where one man's gain is another man's *gain,* it is obvious that great scope is provided for the development of social sympathy and human friendships. It is the peaceful, co-operative society that creates favorable conditions for feelings of friendship among men.

The mutual benefits yielded by exchange provide a major incentive (as in the case of Crusoe above) to would-be *aggressors* (initiators of violent action against others) to restrain their aggression and co-operate peacefully with their fellows. Individuals then decide that the advantages of engaging in specialization and exchange outweigh the advantages that war might bring.

Another feature of the market society formed by the division of labor is its permanence. The wants of men are renewed for each period of time, and so they must try to obtain for themselves anew a supply of goods for each period. Crusoe wants to have a steady rate of supply of game, and Jackson would like to have a continuing supply of berries, etc. Therefore, the social relations formed by the division of labor tend to be permanent as individuals specialize in different tasks and continue to produce in those fields.

There is one, less important, type of exchange that does *not* involve the division of labor. This is an exchange of the *same types of labor* for certain tasks. Thus, suppose that Crusoe, Jackson, and Smith are trying to clear their fields of logs. If each one engaged solely in the work of clearing his own field, it would take a long period of time. However, if each put in some time in a joint effort to roll the other fellow's logs, the productivity of the log-rolling operations would be greatly increased. Each man could finish the task in a shorter period of time. This is particularly true for operations such as rolling heavy logs, which each man alone could not possibly accomplish at all and which they could perform only by agreed-upon joint action. In these cases, each man gives up his own labor in someone else's field in exchange for receiving the labor of the others in his field, the latter being worth more to him. Such an exchange involves a *combination* of the same type of labor, rather than a division of labor into different types, to perform tasks beyond the ready capacity of an isolated individual. This type of co-operative "log-rolling," however, would entail merely temporary alliances based on specific tasks, and, would not, as do specialization and division of labor, establish permanent exchange-ties and social relations.[19]

The great scope of the division of labor is not restricted to situations in which each individual makes all of one particular product, as was the case above. Division of labor may entail the specializing by individuals in the different *stages of production* necessary to produce a particular consumers' good. Thus, with a wider market permitting, different individuals specialize in the different stages, for example, involved in the production of the ham sandwich discussed in the previous chapter. General productivity is greatly increased as some people and some areas specialize in producing iron ore, some in producing different types of machines, some in baking bread, some in packaging meat, some in retailing, etc. The essence of developed market economies consists in the framework of co-operative exchange emerging with such specialization.[20]

4. *Terms of Exchange*

Before analyzing the problem of the terms of exchange, it is well to recall the reason for exchange—the fact that each individual values more highly the good he gets than the good he gives up. This fact is enough to elminate the fallacious notion that, if Crusoe and Jackson exchange five thousand berries for one cow, there is some sort of "equality of value" between the cow and the five thousand berries. Value exists in the valuing minds of individuals, and these individuals make the exchange precisely because for each of them there is an *inequality* of values between the cow and the berries. For Crusoe the cow is valued more than the five thousand berries; for Jackson it is valued less. Otherwise, the exchange could not be made. Therefore, for each exchange there is a *double inequality of values*, rather than an equality, and hence there are no "equal values" to be "measured" in any way.[21]

We have already seen what conditions are needed for exchange to occur and the extent to which exchange will take place on given terms. The question then arises: Are there any principles that decide the *terms* on which exchanges are made? Why does Crusoe exchange with Jackson at a rate of five thousand berries for one cow; or two thousand berries for one cow?

Let us take the hypothetical exchange of 5,000 berries for 1 cow. These are the terms, or the *rate of exchange* (5,000 berries for 1 cow). If we express one commodity in terms of the other, we obtain the *price* of the commodity. Thus, *the price of one good in terms of another is the amount of the other good divided by the amount of the first good in exchange.* If 2 cows exchange for 1,000 berries, then the *price* of cows in terms of berries ("the berry-price of cows") is 500 berries per cow. Conversely, the *price* of berries in terms of cows ("the cow-price of berries") is $\frac{1}{500}$ cow per berry. The *price* is the rate of exchange between two commodities expressed in terms of one of the commodities.

Other useful concepts in the analysis of exchange are those of "selling" and "buying." Thus, in the above exchange, we may say that Crusoe *sold* a thousand berries and *bought* two cows in exchange. On the other hand, Jackson *sold* two cows and *bought* a thousand berries. The *sale* is the good given up in exchange, while the *purchase* is the good received.

Let us again focus attention on the object of exchange. We remember from chapter 1 that the object of all action is to *maximize psychic revenue,* and to do this the actor tries to see to it that the psychic revenue from the action exceeds the psychic cost, so that he obtains a psychic profit. This is no less true of interpersonal exchange. The object in such an exchange for each party is to maximize revenue, to exchange so long as the expected psychic revenue exceeds the psychic cost. The psychic revenue from any exchange is the value of the goods received in the exchange. This is equal to the marginal utility to the purchaser of adding the goods to his stock. More complicated is the problem of the psychic costs of an exchange. *Psychic costs* include all that the actor gives up by making the exchange. This is equal to the *next best use* that he could have made of the resources that he has used.

Suppose, for example, that Jackson possesses five cows and is considering whether or not to sell one cow in exchange. He decides on his value scale that the following is the rank in value of the possible uses of the cow:

1. 5,000 berries offered by Crusoe
2. 100 bbls. of fish offered by Smith
3. 4,000 berries offered by Jones
4. Marginal utility of the cow in direct use.

In this case, the top three alternatives involve the exchange-value of the cow, and the fourth its value in direct use. Jackson will make the best use of his resource by making the exchange with Crusoe. The 5,000 berries of Crusoe will be his psychic revenue from the exchange, while the loss of the 100 barrels of fish constitutes his psychic cost. We saw above that, in order for exchange to take place, the marginal utility of the goods received must be greater than the marginal utility of the goods given up. We now see that for any *specific* exchange to occur, the marginal utility of the goods received must also be greater than the marginal utility forgone—that which could have been received in another type of exchange.

It is evident that Jackson will always prefer an offer of more units of one type of good to an offer of fewer units of the same good. In other words, the seller will always prefer *the highest possible selling price for his good.* Jackson will prefer the price of 5,000 berries per cow offered by Crusoe to the price of 4,000 berries per cow offered by Jones. It might be objected that this may not always be true and may be offset by other factors. Thus, the prospect of 4,000 berries from Jones may be evaluated higher than the prospect of 5,000 berries from Crusoe, if: (*a*) the psychic disutility of labor and time, etc., for delivery over a longer distance to the latter renders the prospect of sale to Crusoe less attractive despite the higher price in berries; or (*b*) special feelings of friendship for Crusoe or hatred for Jones serve to change the utilities on Jackson's value scale. On further analysis, however, these turn out *not* to be vitiating factors at all. The rule that the actor will prefer the highest selling price for his good in terms of the other good always holds. It must be reiterated that a *good* is not defined by its physical characteristics, but by the equal serviceability of its units to the actor. Now, clearly, a berry from a longer distance, since it must call forth the disutility of labor to move it, is *not* the same good as the berry from a shorter distance, even though it is physically the same berry. The very fact that the first is further away means that it is not as serviceable as the other berry, and hence not the same good. For one "price" to be comparable with another, the good must be the same. Thus, if Jackson prefers to sell his cow for 4,000 berries from Jones as compared to 5,000 berries from Crusoe, it does *not* mean that he chooses a *lower* price for his product in terms of the same good (berries), but that he chooses a price in terms of one good (berries from Jones) over a price in terms of an entirely different good (berries from Crusoe). Similarly, if, because of feelings of friendship or hostility, receiving berries from Crusoe takes on a different quality from that of receiving berries from Jones, the two packets of berries are no longer of equal serviceability to Jackson, and therefore they become for him *two different goods*. If these feelings cause him to sell to Jones for 4,000 berries rather than to Crusoe for 5,000 berries, this does not mean that he chooses a lower price for the same good; he chooses between two different goods—berries from Crusoe and berries from Jones. Thus, at all times, an actor will sell his product at the highest possible price in terms of the good received.

Clearly, the converse is true for the buyer. *The buyer will always purchase his good at the lowest possible price.* This truth can be traced in the example just discussed, since, at the point that Jackson was a seller of the cow, he was also a *buyer of the berries.* Where the good in question—berries—was comparable, he bought at the lowest possible price—say 1/5,000 cow per berry in preference to 1/4,000 cow per berry. In cases where Jackson chooses the latter price, the two berries are no longer the same, but different, goods. If, to buy berries, the purchaser has to range further afield or buy from someone he dislikes, then this good becomes a different one in kind from the good closer by or sold by a friend.

5. *Determination of Price: Equilibrium Price* [22]

One of the most important problems in economic analysis is the question: What principles determine the formation of prices on the free market? What can be said by logical derivation from the fundamental assumption of human action in order to explain the determination of all prices in interpersonal exchanges, past, present, and future?

It is most convenient to begin with a case of *isolated exchange,* a case where only two isolated parties are involved in the exchange of two goods. For example, Johnson and Smith are considering a possible exchange of a horse of the former for some barrels of fish possessed by the latter. The question is: What can economic analysis say about the determinants of the exchange rate established between the two goods in the exchange?

An individual will decide whether or not to make an exchange on the basis of the relative positions of the two goods on his value scale. Thus, suppose the value scale of Smith, the possessor of the fish, is as follows:

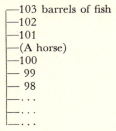

—103 barrels of fish
—102
—101
—(A horse)
—100
— 99
— 98
—· · ·
—· · ·
—· · ·

Fig. 8.   Smith's Value Scale

(Any desired numbers of rank could be assigned to the various quantities, but these are not necessary here.)

It is clear that Smith would be willing to acquire a horse from Johnson if he could give up *100 barrels of fish or less.* 100 barrels or less are less valuable to Smith than the horse. On the other hand, 101 or more barrels of fish are more valuable to him than the horse. Thus, if the *price* of the horse in terms of the fish offered by Smith is *100 barrels or less,* then Smith will make the exchange. If the price is 101 barrels or more, then the exchange will not be made.

Suppose Johnson's value scale looks like this:

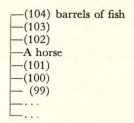

—(104) barrels of fish
—(103)
—(102)
—A horse
—(101)
—(100)
— (99)
— . . .
— . . .

FIG. 9. JOHNSON'S VALUE SCALE

Then, Johnson will not give up his horse for less than 102 barrels of fish. If the price offered for his horse is less than 102 barrels of fish, he will not make the exchange. Here, it is clear that *no exchange will be made;* for at Johnson's minimum selling price of 102 barrels of fish, it is more beneficial for Smith to keep the fish than to acquire the horse.

In order for an exchange to be made, then, the *minimum selling price of the seller must be lower than the maximum buying price of the buyer* for that good. In this case, it must be lower than the price of 100 barrels of fish per horse. Suppose that this condition is met, and Johnson's value scale is as follows:

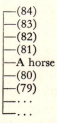

—(84)
—(83)
—(82)
—(81)
—A horse
—(80)
—(79)
— . . .
— . . .

FIG. 10. JOHNSON'S VALUE SCALE

Johnson will sell the horse for any amount of fish at or above 81 barrels. This, then, is his minimum selling price for the horse. With this as Johnson's value scale, and Smith's as pictured above, what price will they agree upon for the horse (and, conversely, for the fish)? All analysis can say about this problem is that, since the exchange must be for the mutual benefit of both parties, *the price of the good in isolated exchange will be established somewhere between the minimum buying price and the maximum selling price,* i.e., the price of the horse will be somewhere between 100 and 81 barrels of fish. (Similarly, the price of the fish will be set somewhere between $\frac{1}{81}$ and $\frac{1}{100}$ of a horse per barrel.) We cannot say at which point the price will be set. That depends on the data of each particular case, on the specific conditions prevailing. In particular, it will depend upon the *bargaining skill* of the two individuals. Clearly, Jackson will try to set the price of the horse as high as possible, while Smith will try to set the price as low as possible. This is based on the principle that the seller of the product tries to obtain the highest price, while the buyer tries to secure the lowest price. We cannot predict the point that the two will agree on, except that it will be somewhere in this range set by the two points.[23]

Now, let us gradually remove our assumption of isolated exchange. Let us first assume that Smith has a competitor, Brown, a rival in offering fish for the desired horse of Johnson's. We assume that the fish offered by Brown is of identical serviceability to Johnson as the fish offered by Smith. Suppose that Smith's value scale is the same as before, but that Brown's value scale is such that the horse is worth more than 90 barrels of fish to him, but less than 91 barrels. The value scales of the three individuals will then appear as follows:

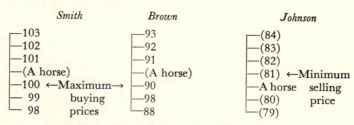

FIG. 11. VALUE SCALES OF THREE INDIVIDUALS

Brown and Smith are competing for the purchase of Johnson's horse. Clearly, only one of them can make the exchange for the horse, and since their goods are identical to Johnson, the latter's decision to exchange will be decided by the price offered for the horse. Obviously, Johnson will make the exchange with that potential buyer who will offer the highest price. Their value scales are such that Smith and Brown can continue to overbid each other as long as the price range is between 81 and 90 barrels of fish per horse. Thus, if Smith offers Johnson an exchange at 82 barrels per horse, Brown can compete by raising the bid to 84 barrels of fish per horse, etc. This can continue, however, only until Brown's maximum buying price has been exceeded. If Smith offers 91 barrels for the horse, it no longer pays for Brown to make the exchange, and he drops out of the competition. Thus, the price in the exchange will be high enough to exclude the "less capable" or "less urgent" buyer—the one whose value scale does not permit him to offer as high a price as the other, "more capable," buyer. We do not know exactly what the price will be, but we do know that it will be set by bargaining *somewhere at or below the maximum buying price of the most capable buyer and above the maximum buying price of the next most capable buyer.* It will be somewhere between 100 barrels and 91 barrels, and the exchange will be made with Smith. We see that the addition of another competing buyer for the product considerably narrows the zone of bargaining in determining the price that will be set.

This analysis can easily be extended to a case of one seller and *n* number of buyers (each offering the same commodity in exchange). Thus, suppose that there are five potential buyers for the horse, all offering fish, whose value scales are as follows:

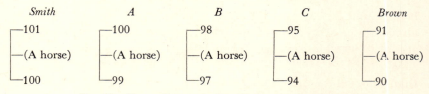

Fig. 12.   Value Scales of Five Potential Purchasers

With only one horse to be disposed of to one buyer, the buyers overbid each other until each must drop out of the competition.

Finally, Smith can outbid A, his next most capable competitor, only with a price of 100. We see that in this case, the price in the exchange is uniquely determined—once the various value scales are given—at 100, since at a lower price A is still in the bidding, and, at a higher price, no buyer will be willing to conclude the exchange. At any rate, even if the value scales are not such as to determine the price uniquely, the addition of more competitors greatly narrows the bargaining zone. The general rule still holds: The price will be between the maximum buying price of the most capable and that of the next most capable competitor, including the former and excluding the latter.[24]

It is also evident that the narrowing of the bargaining zone has taken place in an upward direction, and to the advantage of the seller of the product.

The case of one-sided competition of *many sellers with just one buyer* is the direct converse of the above and may be considered by merely reversing the example and considering the price of the fish instead of the price of the horse. As more sellers of the fish competed to conclude the exchange with the one buyer, the zone of determination of the price of fish narrowed, although this time in a downward direction and to the further advantage of the buyer. As more sellers were added, each tried to *underbid* his rival—to offer a lower price for the product than his competitors. The sellers continued to underbid each other until all but the one seller were excluded from the market. In a case of many sellers and one buyer, the price will be set at a *point between the minimum selling price of the second most capable and that of the most capable competitor*—strictly, at a point below the former and down to or including the latter. In the final example above, the point was pushed down to be uniquely determined at the latter point—$\frac{1}{100}$ horse per barrel.

We have so far considered the cases of one buyer and more than one seller, and of one seller and more than one buyer. We now come to the only case with great importance in a modern, complex economy based on an intricate network of exchanges: *two-sided competition of buyers and sellers.* Let us therefore consider a market with any number of competing buyers and sellers.

Any product could be considered, but our hypothetical example will continue to be the sale of horses in exchange for fish (with the horses as well as the fish considered by all parties as homogeneous units of the same good). The following is a list of the maximum buying prices of the various buyers, based on the valuations on their respective value scales:

Buyers of Horses	Maximum Buying Prices
$X1$	100 barrels of fish
$X2$	98
$X3$	95
$X4$	91
$X5$	89
$X6$	88
$X7$	86
$X8$	85
$X9$	83

The following is a list of the minimum selling prices of the various sellers on the market:

Sellers of Horses	Minimum Selling Prices
$Z1$	81 barrels of fish
$Z2$	83
$Z3$	85
$Z4$	88
$Z5$	89
$Z6$	90
$Z7$	92
$Z8$	96

The "most capable buyer" of fish we recognize as Smith, with a buying price of 100 barrels. Johnson is the "most capable seller"—the seller with the lowest minimum selling price—at 81 barrels. The problem is to find the principle by which the price, or prices, of the exchanges of horses will be determined.

Now, let us first take the case of $X1$—Smith. It is clear that it is to the advantage of Smith to make the exchange at a price of 100 barrels for the horse. Yet it is to Smith's greater advantage to buy the good at the lowest possible price. He is not engaged in overbidding his competitors merely for the sake of overbidding. He will try to obtain the good for the lowest price that he can. Therefore, Smith will prefer to begin bidding for a horse at the lowest prices offered by his competitors, and only raise the offered price if it becomes necessary to do so in order to avoid being shut out of the market. Similarly, Jackson would make an advantageous sale at a price of 81 barrels. However, he is interested in selling his product at the highest possible price. He will underbid his competitor only if it becomes necessary to do so in order to avoid being shut out of the market without making a sale.

It is evident that buyers will tend to start negotiations by offering as low prices as possible, while sellers will tend to start by asking for as high a price as they think they can obtain. Clearly, this preliminary "testing of the market" will tend to be more prolonged in a "new" market, where conditions are unfamiliar, while it will tend to be less prolonged in an "old" market, where the participants are relatively familiar with the results of the price-formation process in the past and can estimate more closely what the results will be.

Let us suppose that buyers begin by offering the low price of 82 barrels for a horse. Here is a price at which each of the buyers would be glad to make a purchase, but only one seller, $Z1$, would be willing to sell at 82. It is possible that $Z1$, through ignorance, might conclude the exchange with some one of the buyers at 82, without realizing that he could have obtained a higher price. It is also possible that the other buyers will, through ignorance, permit the buyer to get away with this windfall without overbidding him for this cheap horse. But such a result is not very likely. It seems most likely that $Z1$ will not sell at such a low price, and that the buyers would immediately overbid any attempt by one of their number to conclude an exchange at that price. Even if, by some chance, one exchange was concluded at 82, it is obvious that such a price could not last. Since no other seller would make an exchange at that price, the price of further exchanges would have to rise further, as a result of upbidding by buyers.

Let us assume at this point that no exchange will be made at this price because of the further upbidding of the buyers and the knowledge of this by the sellers. As the offering price rises, the least capable buyers, as in the previous case, begin to be excluded from the market. A price of 84 will bring two sellers into the market, but will exclude X9 from the buyer's side. As the offering price rises, the disproportion between the *amount offered for sale* and the *amount demanded for purchase* at the given price diminishes, but as long as the latter is greater than the former, mutual overbidding of buyers will continue to raise the price. The amount offered for sale at each price is called the *supply;* the amount demanded for purchase at each price is called the *demand.* Evidently, at the first price of 82, the supply of horses on the market is 1; the demand for horses on the market is 9. Only one seller would be willing to sell at this price, while all nine buyers would be willing to make their purchase. On the basis of the above tabulations of maximum buying prices and minimum selling prices, we are able to present a list of the quantities of the good that will be demanded and supplied at each hypothetical price.

TABLE 2

PRICE	SUPPLIED	DEMANDED	PRICE	SUPPLIED	DEMANDED
80........	0 horses	9 horses	91........	6 horses	4 horses
81........	1	9	92........	7	3
82........	1	9	93........	7	3
83........	2	9	94........	7	3
84........	2	8	95........	7	3
85........	3	8	96........	8	2
86........	3	7	97........	8	2
87........	3	6	98........	8	2
88........	4	6	99.	8	1
89........	5	5	100	8	1
90........	6	4	101	8	0

This table reflects the progressive entry into the market of the sellers as the price increases and the dropping out of the buyers as the price increases. As was seen above, as long as the demand exceeds the supply at any price, buyers will continue to overbid and the price will continue to rise.

The converse occurs if the price begins near its highest point. Thus, if sellers first demand a price of 101 barrels for the horse, there will be eight eager sellers and no buyers. At a price of 99, the sellers may find one eager buyer, but chances are that a sale will not be made. The buyer will realize that there is no point in paying such a high price, and the other sellers will eagerly underbid the one who tries to make the sale at the price of 99. Thus, when the price is so high that the *supply exceeds the demand* at that price, underbidding of suppliers will drive the price downwards. As the tentative price falls, more sellers are excluded from the market, and more buyers enter it.

If the overbidding of buyers will drive the price up whenever the quantity demanded is greater than the quantity supplied, and the underbidding of sellers drives the price down whenever supply is greater than demand, it is evident that the price of the good will find a resting point where the quantity demanded is equal to the quantity supplied, i.e., where supply equals demand. At this price and at this price only, *the market is cleared*, i.e., there is no incentive for buyers to bid prices up further or for sellers to bid prices down. In our example, this final, or *equilibrium price*, is 89, and at this price, five horses will be sold to five buyers. This equilibrium price is the price at which the good will tend to be set and sales to be made.[25]

Specifically, the sales will be made to the five most capable buyers at that price: $X1$, $X2$, $X3$, $X4$ and $X5$. The other less capable (or less urgent) buyers are excluded from the market, because their value scales do not permit them to buy horses at that price. Similarly, sellers $Z1-Z5$ are the ones that make the sale at 89; the other sellers are excluded from the market, because their value scales do not permit them to be in the market at that price.

In this horse-and-fish market, $Z5$ is the least capable of the sellers who have been able to stay in the market. $Z5$, whose minimum selling price is 89, is just able to make his sale at 89. He is the *marginal seller*—the seller at the margin, the one who would be excluded with a slight fall in price. On the other hand, X5 is the least capable of the buyers who have been able to stay in the market. He is the *marginal buyer*—the one who would be excluded by a slight rise in price. Since it would be foolish for the other buyers to pay more than they must to obtain their supply, they will also pay the same price as the marginal buyer, i.e., 89. Similarly, the other sellers will not sell for less than they could obtain; they will sell at the price permitting the marginal seller to stay in the market.

Evidently, the more capable or "more urgent" buyers (and sellers)—the *supramarginal* (which includes the marginal)—obtain a psychic surplus in this exchange, for they are better off than they would have been if the price had been higher (or lower). However, since goods can be ranked only on each individual's value scale, and no *measurement* of psychic gain can be made either for one individual or between different individuals, little of value can be said about this psychic gain except that it exists. (We cannot even make the statement, for example, that the psychic gain in exchange obtained by X1 is greater than that of X5.) The excluded buyers and sellers are termed *submarginal*.

The specific feature of the "clearing of the market" performed by the equilibrium price is that, at this price alone, all those buyers and sellers who are willing to make exchanges can do so. At this price five sellers with horses find five buyers for the horses; all who wish to buy and sell at this price can do so. At any other price, there are either frustrated buyers or frustrated sellers. Thus, at a price of 84, eight people would like to buy at this price, but only two horses are available. At this price, there is a great amount of "unsatisfied demand" or *excess demand*. Conversely, at a price of, say, 95, there are seven sellers eager to supply horses, but only three people willing to demand horses. Thus, at this price, there is "unsatisfied supply," or *excess supply*. Other terms for excess demand and excess supply are "shortage" and "surplus" of the good. Aside from the universal fact of the scarcity of all goods, a price that is below the equilibrium price creates an additional shortage of supply for demanders, while a price above equilibrium creates a surplus of goods for sale as compared to demands for purchase. We see that the market process always tends to eliminate such shortages and surpluses and establishes a price where demanders can find a supply, and suppliers a demand.

It is important to realize that this process of overbidding of buyers and underbidding of sellers always takes place in the market, even if the surface aspects of the specific case make it appear that only the sellers (or buyers) are setting the price. Thus, a good might be sold in retail shops, with prices simply "quoted" by the individual seller. But the same process of bidding goes on in such a market as in any other. If the sellers set their prices below the equilibrium price, buyers will rush to make their purchases, and the sellers will find that shortages develop, accompanied by queues of buyers eager to purchase goods that are unavailable. Realizing that they could obtain higher prices for their goods, the sellers raise their quoted prices accordingly. On the other hand, if they set their prices above the equilibrium price, surpluses of unsold stocks will appear, and they will have to lower their prices in order to "move" their accumulation of unwanted stocks and to clear the market.

The case where buyers quote prices and therefore appear to set them is similar. If the buyers quote prices below the equilibrium price, they will find that they cannot satisfy all their demands at that price. As a result, they will have to raise their quoted prices. On the other hand, if the buyers set the prices too high, they will find a stampede of sellers with unsalable stocks and will take advantage of the opportunity to lower the price and clear the market. Thus, regardless of the *form* of the market, the result of the market process is always to tend toward the establishment of the equilibrium price via the mutual bidding of buyers and sellers.

It is evident that, if we eliminate the assumption that no preliminary sales were made before the equilibrium price was established, this does not change the results of the analysis. Even if, through ignorance and error, a sale was made at a price of 81 or 99, these prices will still be ephemeral and temporary, and the final price for the good will tend to be the equilibrium price.

Once the market price is established, *it is clear that one price must rule over the entire market*. This has already been implied by the fact that all buyers and sellers will tend to exchange at the same price as their marginal competitors. There will always be a tendency on the market to establish one and only one price at any time for a good. Thus, suppose that the market price has been established at 89, and that one crafty seller tries to induce a buyer to buy at 92. It is evident that no buyer will buy at 92 when he knows that he can buy on the regular market at 89. Similarly, no seller will be willing to sell at a price below the market if he knows that he can readily make his sale at 89. If for example, an ignorant seller sells a horse at 87, the buyer is likely to enter the market as a seller to sell the horse at 89. Such drives for *arbitrage gains* (buying and selling to take advantage of discrepancies in the price of a good) act quickly to establish one price for one good over the entire market. Such market prices will tend to change only when changing supply and demand conditions alter the equilibrium price and establish a condition of excess supply or excess demand where before the market had been cleared.

A clearer picture of equilibrium prices as determined by supply and demand conditions will be derived from the graphical representation in Fig. 13.

It is evident that, as the price increases, new suppliers with higher minimum selling prices are brought into the market, while demanders with low maximum buying prices will begin to drop out. Therefore, as the price decreases, the quantity demanded must always either remain the same or increase, never decrease. Similarly, as the price decreases, the amount offered in supply must always decrease or remain the same, never increase. Therefore, the demand curve must always be vertical or rightward-sloping as the price decreases, while the supply curve must always be vertical or leftward-sloping as the price decreases. The curves will intersect at the equilibrium price, where supply and demand are equal.

Clearly, once the zone of intersection of the supply and demand curves has been determined, it is the buyers and sellers at the margin—in the area of the equilibrium point—that determine what the equilibrium price and the quantity exchanged will be.

The tabulation of supply offered at any given price is known as the *supply schedule,* while its graphical presentation, with the points connected here for the sake of clarity, is known as the

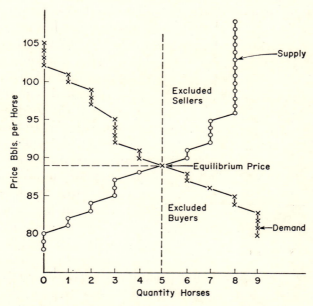

FIG. 13.   DETERMINATION OF EQUILIBRIUM PRICE

supply curve. Similarly, the tabulation of demand is the *demand schedule,* and its graphical representation the *demand curve,* for each product and market. Given the point of intersection, the demand and supply curves above and below that point could take many conceivable shapes without affecting the equilibrium price. The direct determinants of the price are therefore the marginal buyers and sellers, while the valuations of the supra-marginal people are important in determining *which* buyers and sellers will be at the margin. The valuations of the *excluded buyers and sellers* far beyond the margin have no direct influence on the price and will become important only if a change in the market demand and supply schedules brings them near the inter-section point.

Thus, given the intersection point, the pattern of supply and demand curves (represented by the solid and dotted lines) could be at least any one of the variants shown in Fig. 14.

Up to this point we have assumed, for the sake of simplicity and clarity, that each demander, as well as each supplier, was limited to one unit of the good the price of which we have been concentrating on—the horse. Now we can remove this restriction and complete our analysis of the real world of exchange by permitting sup-pliers and demanders to ex-change any number of horses that they may desire. It will be seen immediately that the re-moval of our implicit restric-tion makes no substantial change in the analysis. Thus, let us revert to the case of John-

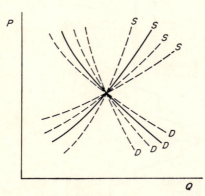

FIG. 14.   POSSIBLE PATTERNS OF SUPPLY
AND DEMAND CURVES

son, whose minimum selling price for a horse was 81 barrels of fish. Let us now assume that Johnson has a stock of several horses. He is willing to sell one horse—the first—for a minimum price of 81 barrels, since on his value scale, he places the horse between 81 and 80 barrels of fish. What will be Johnson's minimum sell-ing price to part with his second horse? We have seen earlier in this chapter that, according to the law of marginal utility, as a man's stock of goods declines, the value placed on each unit remaining increases; conversely, as a man's stock of goods in-creases, the marginal utility of each unit declines. Therefore, the marginal utility of the second horse (or, strictly, of each horse after the first horse is gone), will be greater than the marginal utility of the first horse. This will be true even though each horse is capable of the same service as every other. Similarly, the value of parting with a third horse will be still greater. On the other hand, while the marginal utility placed on each horse given up increases, the marginal utility of the additional fish acquired in exchange will decline. The result of these two factors is inevitably to raise the minimum selling price for each successive horse sold. Thus, suppose the minimum selling price for the first horse is 81 barrels of fish. When it comes to the second exchange, the value forgone of the second horse will be greater, and the value of the same barrels in exchange will decline. As a result, the minimum selling price below which Johnson will not sell the horse will increase, say, to 88. Thus, as the seller's stock dwindles, his minimum selling price increases. Johnson's value scale may appear as follows:

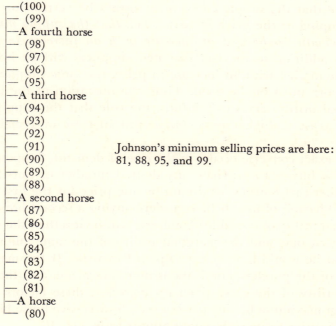

Johnson's minimum selling prices are here: 81, 88, 95, and 99.

Fig. 15. Johnson's Value Scale

On the basis of this value scale, Johnson's own individual supply schedule can be constructed. He will supply 0 horses up to a price of 80, 1 horse at a price between 81 and 87, 2 horses with the price between 88 and 94, 3 horses at a price of 95 to 98, and 4 horses at a price of 99 and above. The same can be done for each seller in the market. (Where the seller has only one horse to sell, the supply schedule is constructed as before.) It is clear that a market-supply schedule can be constructed simply by adding the supplies that will be offered by the various individual sellers in the market at any given price.

The essentials of the foregoing analysis of market supply remain unchanged. Thus, the effect of constructing the market-supply schedule in this case *is the same as if there were four sellers, each supplying one horse, and each with minimum selling prices of 81, 88, 95, and 99.* The fact that it is one man that is supplying the new units rather than different men does not change the results of the analysis. What it does is to reinforce the rule that the supply curve must always be vertical or rightward-sloping as the price increases, i.e., *that the supply must always remain unchanged or increase with an increase in price.* For, in addition to the fact that new suppliers will be brought into the market with an increase in price, the same supplier will offer more units of the good. Thus, the operation of the law of marginal utility serves to reinforce the rule that the supply cannot decrease at higher prices, but must increase or remain the same.

The exact converse occurs in the case of demand. Suppose that we allow buyers to purchase any desired number of horses. We remember that Smith's maximum buying price for the first horse was 100 barrels of fish. If he considers buying a second horse, the marginal utility of the additional horse will be less than the utility of the first one, and the marginal utility of the same amount of fish that he would have to give up will increase. If the marginal utility of the purchases declines as more are made, and the marginal utility of the good given up increases, these factors result in lower maximum buying prices for each successive horse bought. Thus, Smith's value scale might appear as in Fig. 16.

Such individual demand schedules can be made for each buyer on the market, and they can be added to form a resultant demand curve for all buyers on the market.

It is evident that, here again, there is no change in the essence of the market-demand curve. Smith's individual demand curve, with maximum buying prices as above, is analytically equivalent to four buyers with maximum buying prices of 83, 89, 94, and 100, respectively. The effect of allowing more than one unit to be demanded by each buyer brings in the law of marginal utility to reinforce the aforementioned rule that the demand curve is

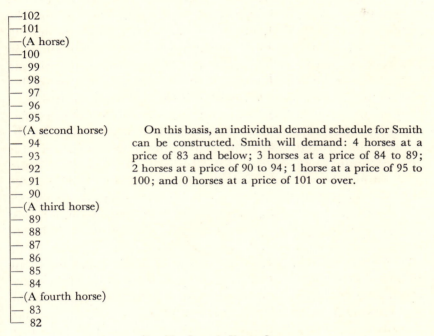

—102
—101
—(A horse)
—100
— 99
— 98
— 97
— 96
— 95
—(A second horse)
— 94
— 93
— 92
— 91
— 90
—(A third horse)
— 89
— 88
— 87
— 86
— 85
— 84
—(A fourth horse)
— 83
— 82

On this basis, an individual demand schedule for Smith can be constructed. Smith will demand: 4 horses at a price of 83 and below; 3 horses at a price of 84 to 89; 2 horses at a price of 90 to 94; 1 horse at a price of 95 to 100; and 0 horses at a price of 101 or over.

FIG. 16. SMITH'S VALUE SCALE

rightward-sloping as the price decreases, i.e., that *the demand must either increase or remain unchanged as the price decreases.* For, added to the fact that lower prices bring in previously excluded buyers, each individual will tend to demand more as the price declines, since the maximum buying prices will be lower with the purchase of more units, in accordance with the law of marginal utility.

Let us now sum up the factors determining prices in interpersonal exchange. One price will tend to be established for each good on the market, and that price will tend to be the equilibrium price, determined by the intersection of the market supply and demand schedules. Those making the exchanges at this price will be the supramarginal and marginal buyers and sellers, while the less capable, or submarginal, will be excluded from the sale, because their value scales do not permit them to make an exchange. Their maximum buying prices are too low, or their minimum selling prices too high. The market supply and demand schedules are themselves determined by the minimum selling prices and maximum buying prices of all the individuals in the market. The latter, in turn, are determined by the placing of the units to be bought and sold on the individuals' value scales, these rankings being influenced by the law of marginal utility.

In addition to the law of marginal utility, there is another factor influencing the rankings on each individual's value scale. It is obvious that the amount that Johnson will supply at any price is limited by the *stock* of goods that he has available. Thus, Jackson may be willing to supply a fourth horse at a price of 99, but if this exhausts his available stock of horses, no higher price will be able to call forth a larger supply from Jackson. At least this is true as long as Jackson has no further stock available to sell. Thus, at any given time, the total stock of the good available puts a maximum limit on the amount of the good that can be supplied in the market. Conversely, the total stock of the purchasing good will put a maximum limit on the total of the sale good that any one individual, or the market, can demand.

At the same time that the market supply and demand schedules are setting the equilibrium price, they are *also* clearly setting the equilibrium *quantity* of both goods that will be exchanged. In our previous example, the equilibrium quantities exchanged are 5 horses, and 5×89, or 445 fish, for the aggregate of the market.

6. *Elasticity of Demand* [26]

The demand schedule tells us how many units of the purchase good will be bought at each hypothetical price. From this schedule we may easily find the *total number of units of the sale good that will be expended at each price*. Thus, from Table 2, we find that at a price of 95, three horses will be demanded. If three horses are demanded at a price of 95 barrels of fish, then the total number of units of the sale good that will be offered in exchange will be 3 × 95, or 285 barrels of fish. This, then, is the *total outlay* of the sale good that will be offered on the market at that price.

The total outlay of the sale good at each hypothetical price is shown in Table 3.

TABLE 3

	BUYERS	
PRICE	DEMANDED	TOTAL OUTLAY SALE GOOD
80............	9 horses	720 barrels of fish
81............	9	729
82............	9	738
83............	9	747
84............	8	672
85............	8	680
86............	7	602
87............	6	522
88............	6	528
89............	5	445
90............	4	360
91............	4	364
92............	3	276
93............	3	279
94............	3	282
95............	3	285
96............	2	192
97............	2	194
98............	2	196
99............	1	99
100............	1	100
101............	0	0

Fig. 17 is a graphic presentation of the total outlay curve. It is evident that this is a logical derivation from the demand curve and that therefore it too is a curve of outlay by buyers at each hypothetical price.

A striking feature of the total outlay curve is that, in contrast to the other curves (such as the demand curve), it can slope in either direction as the price increases or decreases. The possi-

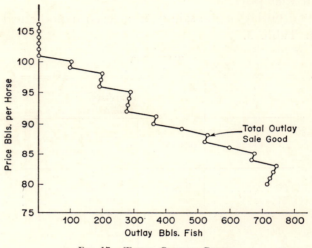

FIG. 17.   TOTAL OUTLAY CURVE

bility of a slope in either direction stems from the operation of the two factors determining the position of the curve. Outlay = Price × Quantity Demanded (of purchase good). But we know that as the price decreases, the demand must either increase or remain the same. Therefore, a decrease in price tends to be counteracted by an increase in quantity, and, as a result, the total outlay of the sale good may either increase or decrease as the price changes.

For any two prices, we may compare the total outlay of the sale good that will be expended by buyers. If the lower price yields a greater total outlay than the higher price, the total outlay curve is defined as being *elastic* over that range. If the lower price yields a lower total outlay than the higher price, then the curve is *inelastic* over that range. Alternatively, we may say that the former case is that of an *elasticity greater than unity,* the latter of an *elasticity less than unity,* and the case where the total outlay is the same for the two prices is one of *unit elasticity,* or elasticity equal to 1. Since numerical precision in the concept of elasticity is not important, we may simply use the terms "in-elastic," "elastic," and (for the last case) "neutral."

Some examples will clarify these concepts. Thus, suppose that we examine the total outlay schedule at prices of 96 and 95. At 96, the total outlay is 192 barrels; at 95, it is 285 barrels. The outlay is greater at the lower price, and hence the outlay schedule is *elastic* in this range. On the other hand, let us take the prices 95 and 94. At 94, the outlay is 282. Consequently, the schedule here is *inelastic.* It is evident that there is a simple geometrical device for deciding whether or not the demand curve is elastic or inelastic between two hypothetical prices: if the outlay curve is further to the right at the lower price, the demand curve is elastic; if further to the left, the latter is inelastic.

There is no reason why the concept of elasticity must be confined to two prices next to each other. Any two prices on the schedule may be compared. It is evident that an examination of the entire outlay curve demonstrates that the foregoing demand curve is basically elastic. It is elastic over most of its range, with the exception of a few small gaps. If we compare any two rather widely spaced prices, it is evident that the outlay is less at the higher price. If the price is high enough, the demand for any good will dwindle to zero, and therefore the outlay will dwindle to zero.

Of particular interest is the elasticity of the demand curve at the equilibrium price. Going up a step to the price of 90, the curve is clearly elastic—total outlay is less at the higher price. Going down a step to 88, the curve is also elastic. This particular demand curve is elastic in the neighborhood of the equilibrium price. Other demand curves, of course, could possibly be inelastic at their equilibrium price.

Contrary to what might be thought at first, the concept of "elasticity of supply" is not a meaningful one, as is "elasticity

of demand." If we multiply the quantity supplied at each price
by the price, we shall obtain the number of barrels of fish (the
sale good) which the sellers will demand in exchange. It will
easily be seen, however, that this quantity *always increases* as the
price increases, and *vice versa*. At 82 it is 82, at 84 it is 168, at
88 it is 352, etc. The reason is that its other determinant, quantity supplied, changes in the *same* direction as the price, not in
the inverse direction as does quantity demanded. As a result,
supply is always "elastic," and the concept is an uninteresting
one.[27]

7. *Speculation and Supply and Demand Schedules*

We have seen that market price is, in the final analysis, determined by the intersection of the supply and demand schedules.
It is now in order to consider further the determinants of these
particular schedules. Can we establish any other conclusions concerning the causes of the shape and position of the supply and
demand schedules themselves?

We remember that, at any given price, the amount of a good
that an individual will buy or sell is determined by the position
of the sale good and the purchase good on his value scale. He
will demand a good if the marginal utility of adding a unit of
the purchase good is greater than the marginal utility of the sale
good that he must give up. On the other hand, another individual will be a seller if his valuations of the units are in a reverse order. We have seen that, on this basis, and reinforced by
the law of marginal utility, the market demand curve will never
decrease when the price is lowered, and the supply curve will
never increase when the price decreases.

Let us further analyze the value scales of the buyers and sellers.
We have seen above that the two sources of value that a good
may have are direct use-value and exchange-value, and that the
higher value is the determinant for the actor. An individual,
therefore, can demand a horse in exchange for one of two reasons: its direct use-value to him or the value that he believes
it will be able to command in exchange. If the former, then he

will be a consumer of the horse's services; if the latter, then he purchases in order to make a more advantageous exchange later. Thus, suppose in the foregoing example, that the existing market price has not reached equilibrium—that it is now at 85 barrels per horse. Many demanders may realize that this price is below the equilibrium and that therefore they can attain an arbitrage profit by buying at 85 and reselling at the final, higher price.

We are now in a position to refine the analysis in the foregoing section, which did not probe the question whether or not sales took place before the equilibrium price was reached. We now assume explicitly that the demand schedule shown in Table 2 referred to demand for direct use by consumers. Smoothing out the steps in the demand curve represented in Fig. 13, we may, for purposes of simplicity and exposition, portray it as in Fig. 18. This, we may say, is the demand curve for direct use. For

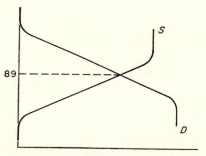

FIG. 18.   SIMPLIFIED DEMAND CURVE

this demand curve, then, the approach to equilibrium takes place through *actual* purchases at the various prices, and then the shortages or the surpluses reveal the overbidding or underbidding, until the equilibrium price is finally reached. To the extent that buyers foresee the final equilibrium price, however, they will not buy at a higher price (even though they would have done so if *that* were the final price), but will wait for the price to fall. Similarly, if the price is below the equilibrium price, to the extent that the buyers foresee the final price, they will tend to buy some of the good (e.g., horses) in order to resell at a profit at the final price. Thus, if exchange-value enters the picture, and a good number of buyers act on their anticipations, the demand curve might change as shown in Fig. 19. The old demand curve, based only on demand for use, is *DD,* and the new demand curve, including anticipatory forecasting of the equilibrium price, is *D'D'.* It is clear that such anticipations render the demand curve

far more *elastic*, since more will be bought at the lower price
and less at the higher.

Thus, the introduction of exchange-value can restrict demand
above the anticipated equilibrium price and increase it below that
price, although the final demand—to consume—at the equilibrium
price will remain the same.

Now, let us consider the situation of the seller of the commodity. The supply curve in Fig. 13 treats the amount supplied

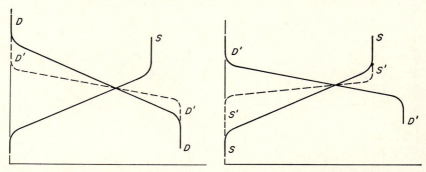

Fig. 19.   Demand Curve Modified by   Fig. 20.   Supply Curve Modified by
                   Speculation   Speculation

at any price without considering possible equilibrium price. Thus,
we may say that, with such a supply curve, sales will be made
en route to the equilibrium price, and shortages or surpluses will
finally reveal the path to the final price. On the other hand,
suppose that many sellers anticipate the final equilibrium price.
Clearly, they will refuse to make sales at a lower price, even
though they would have done so if *that* were the final price. On
the other hand, they will sell more above the equilibrium price,
since they will be able to make an arbitrage profit by selling
their horses above the equilibrium price and buying them back
at the equilibrium price. Thus, the supply curve, with such anticipations, may change as shown in Fig. 20. The supply curve
changes, as a result of anticipating the equilibrium price, from
SS to *S'S'*.

Let us suppose the highly unlikely event that *all* demanders
and suppliers are able to forecast *exactly* the final, equilibrium

price. What would be the pattern of supply and demand curves on the market in such an extreme case? It would be as follows: At a price above equilibrium (say 89) no one would demand the good, and suppliers would supply their entire stock. At a price below equilibrium, no one would supply the good, and everyone would demand as much as he could purchase, as shown in Fig. 21. Such unanimously correct forecasts are not likely to take place in human action, but this case points up the fact that, the

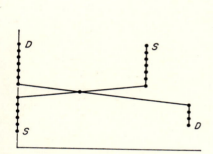

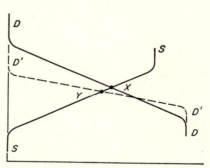

FIG. 21. UNANIMOUSLY CORRECT FORE-
CASTS OF FINAL PRICE

FIG. 22. DEMAND CURVE MODIFIED BY
ERRONEOUS ANTICIPATION

more this anticipatory, or *speculative,* element enters into supply and demand, the more quickly will the market price tend toward equilibrium. Obviously, the more the actors anticipate the final price, the further apart will be supply and demand at any price differing from equilibrium, the more drastic the shortages and surpluses will be, and the more quickly will the final price be established.

Up to now we have assumed that this *speculative* supply and demand, this anticipating of the equilibrium price, has been correct, and we have seen that these correct anticipations have hastened the establishment of equilibrium. Suppose, however, that most of these expectations are erroneous. Suppose, for example, that the demanders tend to assume that the equilibrium price will be lower than it actually is. Does this change the equilibrium price or obstruct the passage to that price? Suppose that the demand and supply schedules are as shown in Fig. 22. Suppose that

the basic demand curve is *DD*, but that the demanders anticipate lower equilibrium prices, thus changing and lowering the
demand curve to *D'D'*. With the supply curve given at *SS*, this
means that the intersection of the supply and demand schedules
will be at *Y* instead of *X*, say at 85 instead of 89. It is clear, however, that this will be only a provisional resting point for the
price. As soon as the price settles at 85, the demanders see that
shortages develop at this price, that they would like to buy more
than is available, and the overbidding of the demanders raises
the price again to the genuine equilibrium price.

The same process of revelation of error occurs in the case of
errors of anticipation by suppliers, and thus the forces of the
market tend inexorably toward the establishment of the genuine
equilibrium price, undistorted by speculative errors, which tend
to reveal themselves and be eliminated. As soon as suppliers or
demanders find that the price that their speculative errors have
set is not really an equilibrium and that shortages and/or surpluses develop, their actions tend once again to establish the
equilibrium position.

The actions of both buyers and sellers on the market may be
related to the concepts of psychic revenue, profit, and cost. We
remember that the aim of every actor is the highest position of
psychic revenue and thus the making of a psychic profit compared to his next best alternative—his cost. Whether or not an
individual *buys* depends on whether it is his best alternative with
his given resources—in this case, his fish. His expected revenue
in any action will be balanced against his expected cost—his next
best alternative. In this case, the revenue will be either (*a*) the
satisfaction of ends from the direct use of the horse or (*b*) expected resale of the horse at a higher price—whichever has the
highest utility to him. His cost will be either (*a*) the marginal
utility of the fish given up in direct use or (*b*) (possibly) the exchange-value of the fish for some other good or (*c*) the expected
future purchase of the horse at a lower price—whichever has the
highest utility. He will buy the horse if the expected revenue is
greater; he will fail to buy if the expected cost is greater. The
expected revenue is the marginal utility of the added horse for

the buyer; the expected cost is the marginal utility of the fish given up. For either revenue or cost, the higher value in direct use or in exchange will be chosen as the marginal utility of the good.

Now let us consider the seller. The seller, as well as the buyer, attempts to maximize his psychic revenue by trying to attain a revenue higher than his psychic cost—the utility of the next best alternative he will have to forgo in taking his action. The seller will weigh the marginal utility of the added sale-good (in this case, fish) against the marginal utility of the purchase-good given up (the horse), in deciding whether or not to make the sale at any particular price.

The psychic revenue for the seller will be the higher of the utilities stemming from one of the following sources: (*a*) the value in direct use of the sale-good (the fish) or (*b*) the speculative value of re-exchanging the fish for the horse at a lower price in the future. The cost of the seller's action will be the highest utility forgone among the following alternatives: (*a*) the value in direct use of the horse given up or (*b*) the speculative value of selling at a higher price in the future or (*c*) the exchange-value of acquiring some other good for the horse. He will sell the horse if the expected revenue is greater; he will fail to sell if the expected cost is greater. We thus see that the situations of the sellers and the buyers are comparable. Both act or fail to act in accordance with their estimate of the alternative that will yield them the highest utility. It is the position of the utilities on the two sets of value scales—of the individual buyers and sellers— that determines the market price and the amount that will be exchanged at that price. In other words, it is, for every good, *utility* and utility alone that determines the price and the quantity exchanged. Utility and utility alone determines the nature of the supply and demand schedules.

It is therefore clearly fallacious to believe, as has been the popular assumption, that utility and "costs" are equally and independently potent in determining price. "Cost" is simply the utility of the next best alternative that must be forgone in any action, and it is therefore part and parcel of utility on the individual's value scale. This cost is, of course, always a *present* consideration of a *future* event, even if this "future" is a very near one. Thus, the forgone utility in making the purchase might be the direct consumption of fish that the actor might have engaged in within a few hours. Or it might be the possibility of exchanging for a cow, whose utility would be enjoyed over a long period of time. It goes without saying, as has been indicated in the previous chapter, that the present consideration of revenue and of cost in any action is based on the present value of expected future revenues and costs. The point is that both the utilities derived and the utilities forgone in any action refer to some point in the future, even if a very near one, and that *past costs* play no role in human action, and hence in determining price. The importance of this fundamental truth will be made clear in later chapters.

8. *Stock and the Total Demand to Hold*

There is another way of treating supply and demand schedules, which, for some problems of analysis, is more useful than the schedules presented above. At any point on the market, suppliers are engaged in offering some of their stock of the good and withholding their offer of the remainder. Thus, at a price of 86, suppliers supply three horses on the market and withhold the other five in their stock. This withholding is caused by one of the factors mentioned above as possible costs of the exchange: either the direct use of the good (say the horse) has greater utility than the receipt of the fish in direct use; or else the horse could be exchanged for some other good; or, finally, the seller expects the final price to be higher, so that he can profitably delay the sale. The amount that sellers will withhold on the market is termed their *reservation demand*. This is not, like the demand studied above, a demand for a good *in exchange;* this is a demand to *hold stock.* Thus, the concept of a "demand to hold a stock of goods" will always include both demand-factors; it will include the demand for the good in exchange by nonpossessors, *plus* the demand to hold the stock by the possessors. The demand for the good in exchange is also a demand to hold, since, regardless of what the buyer intends to do with the good in the future, he must hold the good from the time when it comes into his ownership and possession by means of exchange. We therefore arrive at the concept of a "total demand to hold" for a good, differing from the previous concept of exchange-demand, although including the latter in addition to the reservation demand by the sellers.

If we know the total stock of the good in existence (here, 8 horses), we may, by inspecting the supply and demand schedules, arrive at a "total demand to hold"—or *total demand schedule* for the market. For example, at a price of 82, 9 horses are demanded by the buyers, in exchange, and 8 − 1 = 7 horses are withheld by the sellers, i.e., demanded to be held by the sellers. Therefore, the total demand to hold horses on the market is 9 + 7 = 16 horses. On the other hand, at the price of 97, no horses are withheld by sellers, whose reservation demand is therefore 0, while the demand by buyers is 2. Total demand to hold at this price is 0 + 2 = 2 horses.

Table 4 shows the total demand to hold derived from the sup-

TABLE 4

PRICE	TOTAL DEMAND TO HOLD	TOTAL STOCK	PRICE	TOTAL DEMAND TO HOLD	TOTAL STOCK
80	17 horses	8 horses	91	6 horses	8 horses
81	16	8	92	4	8
82	16	8	93	4	8
83	15	8	94	4	8
84	14	8	95	4	8
85	13	8	96	2	8
86	12	8	97	2	8
87	11	8	98	2	8
88	10	8	99	1	8
89	8	8	100	1	8
90	6	8	101	0	8

ply and demand schedule in Table 2, along with the total stock, which is, for the moment, considered as fixed. Figure 23 represents the total demand to hold and the stock.

It is clear that the rightward-sloping nature of the total demand curve is even more accentuated than that of the demand curve. For the demand schedule increases or remains the same as the price falls, while the reservation demand schedule of the

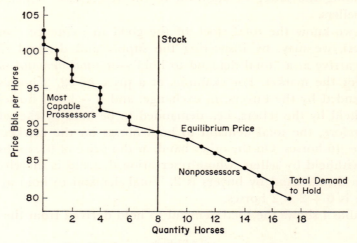

FIG. 23.   STOCK AND TOTAL DEMAND TO HOLD

sellers also tends to increase as the price falls. The total demand schedule is the result of adding the two schedules. Clearly, the reservation demand of the sellers increases as the price falls for the same reason as does the demand curve for buyers. With a lower price, the value of the purchase-good in direct use or in other and future exchanges relatively increases, and therefore the seller tends to withhold more of the good from exchange. In other words, the reservation demand curve is the obverse of the supply curve.

Another point of interest is that, at the equilibrium price of 89, the total demand to hold is 8, equal to the total stock in existence. Thus, the equilibrium price not only equates the supply and demand on the market; *it also equates the stock of a good to be held with the desire of people to hold it, buyers and sellers included.* The total stock is included in the foregoing diagram at a fixed figure of 8.

It is clear that the market always tends to set the price of a good so as to equate the stock with the total demand to hold the stock. Suppose that the price of a good is higher than this equilibrium price. Say that the price is 92, at which the stock is 8 and the total demand to hold is 4. This means that four horses exist which their possessors do not want to possess. It is clear that *someone* must possess this stock, since all goods must be property; otherwise they would not be objects of human action. Since all the stock must at all times be possessed by someone, the fact that the stock is greater than total demand means that there is an imbalance in the economy, that some of the possessors are unhappy with their possession of the stock. They tend to lower the price in order to sell the stock, and the price falls until finally the stock is equated with the demand to hold. Conversely, suppose that the price is below equilibrium, say at 85, where 13 horses are demanded compared to a stock of 8. The bids of the eager nonpossessors for the scarce stock push up the price until it reaches equilibrium.

In cases where individuals correctly anticipate the equilibrium price, the speculative element will tend to render the total demand curve even more "elastic" and flatter. At a higher-than-equilibrium price few will want to keep the stock—the buyers will demand very little, and the sellers will be eager to dispose of the good. On the other hand, at a lower price, the demand to hold will be far greater than the stock; buyers will demand heavily, and sellers will be reluctant to sell their stock. The discrepancies between total demand and stock will be far greater, and the underbidding and overbidding will more quickly bring about the equilibrium price.

We saw above that, at the equilibrium price, the most capable (or "most urgent") buyers made the exchanges with the most capable sellers. Here we see that the result of the exchange process is that the stock finally goes into the hands of the *most capable possessors*. We remember that in the sale of the eight horses, the most capable buyers, X1–X5, purchased from the most capable sellers of the good, Z1–Z5. At the conclusion of the exchange, then, the possessors are X1–X5, and the excluded sellers Z6–Z8. It is these individuals who finish by possessing the eight horses, and these are the most capable possessors. At a price of 89 barrels of fish per horse, these were the ones who preferred the horse on their value scales to 89 barrels of fish, and they acted on the basis of this preference. For five of the individuals, this meant exchanging their fish for a horse; for three it meant refusing to part with their horses for the fish. The other nine individuals on the market were the less capable possessors, and they concluded by possessing the fish instead of the horse (even if they started by possessing horses). These were the ones who ranked 89 barrels of fish above one horse on their value scale. Five of these were original possessors of horses who exchanged them for fish; four simply retained the fish without purchasing a horse.

The total demand-stock analysis is a useful twin companion to the supply-demand analysis. Each has advantages for use in different spheres. One relative defect of the total demand-stock analysis is that it does not reveal the differences between the buyers and the sellers. In considering total demand, it abstracts from actual exchanges, and therefore does not, in contrast to the supply-demand curves, determine the quantity of exchanges. It reveals only the equilibrium price, without demonstrating the equilibrium quantity exchanged. However, it focuses more sharply on the fundamental truth that price is determined solely by *utility*. The supply curve is reducible to a *reservation demand curve* and to a *quantity of physical stock*. The demand-stock analysis therefore shows that the supply curve is not based on some sort of "cost" that is independent of utility on individual value scales. We see that the fundamental determinants of price are the value scales of all individuals (buyers and sellers) in the market and that the physical stock simply assumes its place on these scales.[28]

It is clear, in these cases of direct exchange of useful goods, that even if the utility of goods for buyers or sellers is at present determined by its subjective exchange-value for the individual, the sole *ultimate* source of utility of each good is its direct use-value. If the major utility of a horse to its possessor is the fish or the cow that he can procure in exchange, and the major value of the latter to their possessors is the horse obtainable in exchange, etc., the ultimate determinant of the utility of each good is its direct use-value to its individual consumer.

9. *Continuing Markets and Changes in Price*

How, then, may we sum up the analysis of our hypothetical horse-and-fish market? We began with a stock of eight horses in existence (and a certain stock of fish as well), and a situation where the relative positions of horses and fish on different people's value scales were such as to establish conditions for the exchange of the two goods. Of the original possessors, the "most capable sellers" sold their stock of horses, while among the original non-possessors, the "most capable buyers" purchased units of the stock with their fish. The final price of their sale was the equilibrium price determined ultimately by their various value scales, which also determined the quantity of exchanges that took place at that price. The net result was a shift of the stock of each good into the hands of its most capable possessors in accordance with the relative rank of the good on their value scales. The exchanges having been completed, the relatively most capable possesors own the stock, *and the market for this good has come to a close.*

With arrival at equilibrium, the exchanges have shifted the goods to the most capable possessors, and there is no further motive for exchange. The market has ended, and there is no longer an active "ruling market price" for either good because there is no longer any motive for exchange. Yet in our experience the markets for almost all goods are being continually renewed.

The market can be renewed again only if there is a change in the relative position of the two goods under consideration on the value scales of at least two individuals, one of them a possessor of one good and the other a possessor of the second good. Exchanges will then take place in a quantity and at a final price determined by the intersection of the *new* combination of supply and demand schedules. This may set a different quantity of exchanges at the old equilibrium price or at a new price, depending on their specific content. Or it may happen that the new combination of schedules—in the new period of time—will be identical with the old and therefore set the same quantity of exchanges and the same price as on the old market.

The market is always tending quickly toward its equilibrium position, and the wider the market is, and the better the communication among its participants, the more quickly will this position be established for any set of schedules. Furthermore, a growth of specialized speculation will tend to improve the forecasts of the equilibrium point and hasten the arrival at equilibrium. However, in those cases where the market does not arrive at equilibrium before the supply or demand schedules themselves change, the market does not reach the equilibrium point. It becomes *continuous,* moving toward a new equilibrium position before the old one has been reached.[29]

The types of change introduced by a shift in the supply and/ or the demand schedule may be depicted by the diagrams in Fig. 24.

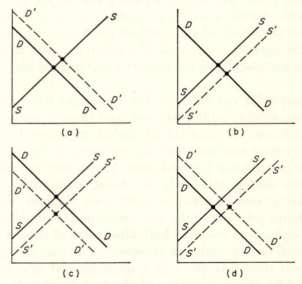

FIG. 24. CHANGES IN SUPPLY AND DEMAND SCHEDULES

These four diagrams depict eight types of situations that may develop from changes in the supply and demand schedules. It must be noted that these diagrams may apply *either* to a market that has already reached equilibrium and is then *renewed* at some later date *or* to one continuous market that experiences a change in supply and/or demand conditions before reaching the old equilibrium point. Solid lines depict the old schedules, while broken lines depict the new ones.

In all these diagrams straight lines are assumed purely for convenience, since the lines may be of any shape, provided the aforementioned restrictions on the slope of the schedules are met (rightward-sloping demand schedules, etc.).

In diagram *A*, the *demand schedule* of the individuals on the market *increases*. At each hypothetical price, people will wish to add more than before to their stock of the good—and it does not matter whether these individuals already possess some units of the good or not. The supply schedule remains the same. *As a result, the new equilibrium price is higher than the old, and the quantity of exchanges made at the new equilibrium position is greater than at the old position.*

In diagram *B*, the *supply schedule increases,* while the demand schedule remains the same. At each hypothetical price, people will wish to dispose of more of their stock. The result is that the new equilibrium price is *lower* than the old, and the equilibrium *quantity exchanged is greater.*

Diagrams *A* and *B* also depict what will occur when the demand curve decreases and the supply curve decreases, the other schedule remaining the same. All we need do is think of the broken lines as the old schedules, and the solid lines as the new ones. On diagram *A* we see that a *decrease in the demand schedule* leads to a fall in price and a fall in the quantity exchanged. On diagram *B*, we see that a *decrease in the supply schedule* leads to a rise in price and a fall in the quantity exchanged.

For diagrams *C* and *D*, the restriction that one schedule must remain the same while the other one changes is removed. In diagram *C*, the demand curve decreases and the supply curve increases. This will definitely lead to a *fall in equilibrium price,* although what will happen to the quantity exchanged depends on the relative proportion of change in the two schedules, and therefore this result cannot be predicted from the fact of an increase in the supply schedule and a decrease in the demand schedule. On the other hand, a decrease in the supply schedule plus an increase in the demand schedule will definitely lead to a *rise in the equilibrium price.*

Diagram *D* discloses that an *increase* in both demand and supply schedules will definitely lead to an *increase in the quantity exchanged,* although whether or not the price falls depends on the relative proportion of change. Also, a decrease in both supply and demand schedules will lead to a *decline in the quantity exchanged.* In diagram *C* what happens to the quantity, and in diagram *D* what happens to the price, depends on the specific shape and change of the curves in question.

The conclusions from these diagrams may be summarized in Table 5.

TABLE 5

If DEMAND and SUPPLY SCHEDULE	Then EQUILIBRIUM and QUANTITY PRICE EXCHANGED
Increases.....The Same	Increases........Increases
Decreases.....The Same	Decreases.......Decreases
The Same....Increases	Decreases.......Increases
The Same....Decreases	Increases........Decreases
Decreases.....Increases	Decreases..............
Increases.....Decreases	Increases..............
Increases.....Increases	..............Increases
Decreases.....Decreases	..............Decreases

If these are the effects of changes in the demand and supply schedules from one period of time to another, the next problem is to explain the causes of these changes themselves. A change in the demand schedule is due purely to a change in the relative utility-rankings of the two goods (the purchase-good and the sale-good) on the value scales of the individual buyers on the market. An increase in the demand schedule, for example, signifies a general rise in the purchase-good on the value scales of the buyers. This may be due to either (*a*) a rise in the direct use-value of the good; (*b*) poorer opportunities to exchange the sale-good for some other good—as a result, say, of a higher price of cows in terms of fish; or (*c*) a decline in speculative waiting for the price of the good to fall further. The last case has been discussed in detail and has been shown to be self-correcting, impelling the market more quickly towards the true equilibrium. We can therefore omit this case now and conclude that an increase in the demand schedule is due either to an increase in the direct use-value of the good or to a higher price of other potential purchase-goods in terms of the sale-good that buyers offer in exchange. A decrease in demand schedules is due precisely to the converse cases—a fall in the value in direct use or greater opportunities to buy other purchase-goods for this sales-good. The latter would mean a greater exchange-value—of fish, for example—in other fields of exchange. Changes in opportunities for other types of exchange may be a result of higher or lower prices for the other purchase-goods, or they may be the result of the fact that new types of goods are being offered for fish on the market. The sudden appearance of cows being offered for fish where none had been offered before is a widening of exchange opportunities for fish and will result in a general decline of the demand curve for *horses* in terms of fish.

A change in the market supply curve is, of course, also the result of a change in the relative rankings of utility on the sellers' value scales. This curve, however, may be broken down into the amount of physical stock and the reservation-demand schedule of the sellers. If we assume that the *amount of physical stock is constant* in the two periods under comparison, then a shift in supply curves is purely the result of a change in reservation-demand curves. A decrease in the supply curve caused by an increase in reservation demand for the stock may be due to either (*a*) an increase in the direct use-value of the good for the sellers; (*b*) greater opportunities for making exchanges for other purchase-goods; or (*c*) a greater speculative anticipation of a higher price in the future. We may here omit the last case for the same reason we omitted it from our discussion of the demand curve. Conversely, a fall in the reservation-demand schedule may be due to either (*a*) a decrease in the direct use-value of the good to the sellers or (*b*) a dwindling of exchange opportunities for other purchase-goods.

Thus, with the total stock constant, changes in both supply and demand curves are due solely to changes in the demand to hold the good by either sellers or buyers, which in turn are due to shifts in the relative utility of the two goods. Thus, in both diagrams *A* and *B* above, the *increase* in the demand schedule and a *decrease* in the supply schedule from *S'S'* to *SS* are a result of increased total demand to hold. In one case the increased total demand to hold is on the part of the buyers, in the other case of the sellers. The relevant diagram is shown in Fig. 25. In both cases of an increase in the total demand-to-hold schedule, say from *TD* to *T'D'*, the *equilibrium price increases*. On the contrary, when the demand schedule declines, and/or when the supply schedule increases, these signify a general decrease in the total demand-to-hold schedule and consequently a *fall in equilibrium price*.

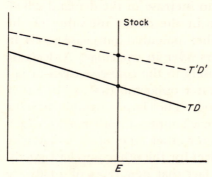

Fig. 25.   Increase in the Total Demand to Hold

A total demand-stock diagram can convey no information about the quantity exchanged, but only about the equilibrium price. Thus, in diagram *C*, the broken lines both represent a fall in demand to hold, and we could consequently be sure that the total demand to hold declined, and that therefore price declined. (The opposite would be the case for a shift from the broken to the solid lines.) In diagram *D*, however, since an increase in the supply schedule represented a fall in demand to hold, and an increase in demand was a rise in the demand to hold, we could not always be sure of the net effect on the total demand to hold and hence on the equilibrium price.

From the beginning of the supply-demand analysis up to this point we have been assuming the existence of a constant physical stock. Thus, we have been assuming the existence of eight horses and have been considering the principles on which this stock will go into the hands of different possessors. The analysis above applies to *all goods*—to all cases where an existing stock is being exchanged for the stock of another good. For some goods this point is as far as analysis can be pursued. This applies to those goods of which the stock is fixed and cannot be increased through production. They are either once produced by man or given by nature, but the stock cannot be increased by human action. Such a good, for example, is a Rembrandt painting after the death of Rembrandt. Such a painting would rank high enough on individual value scales to command a high price in exchange for other goods. The stock can never be increased, however, and its exchange and pricing is solely in terms of the previously analyzed exchange of existing stock, determined by the relative rankings of these and other goods on numerous value scales. Or assume that a certain quantity of diamonds have been produced, and no more diamonds are available anywhere. Again, the problem would be solely one of exchanging the existing stock. In these cases there is no further problem of *production*—of deciding how much of a stock should be produced in a certain period of time. For most goods, however, the problem of deciding how much to produce is a crucial one. Much of the remainder of this volume, in fact, is devoted to an analysis of the problem of production.

We shall now proceed to cases in which the existing stock of a good *changes* from one period to another. A stock may increase from one period to the next because an amount of the good has been *newly produced* in the meantime. This amount of new production constitutes an *addition to the stock*. Thus, three days after the beginning of the horse-market referred to above, two new horses might be produced and added to the existing stock. If the demand schedule of buyers and the reservation demand schedule of sellers remain the same, what will occur can be represented as in Fig. 26.

The increased stock will lower the price of the good. At the old equilibrium price, individuals find that their stock is in excess of the total demand to hold, and the consequence is an underbidding to sell that lowers the price to the new equilibrium.

In terms of supply and demand curves, an increase in stock, with demand and reservation-demand schedules remaining the same, is equivalent to a *uniform increase in the supply schedule*

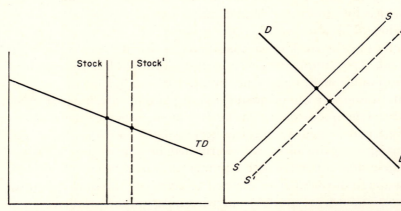

FIG. 26.   EFFECT OF AN INCREASE IN STOCK   FIG. 27.   EFFECT OF AN INCREASE IN THE
                                                              SUPPLY SCHEDULE

by the amount of the increased stock—in this case by two horses. The amount supplied would be the former total plus the added two. Possessors with an excess of stock at the old equilibrium price must underbid each other in order to sell the increased stock. If we refer back to Table 2, we find that an increase in the supply schedule by 2 lowers the equilibrium price to 88, where the demand is 6 and the new supply is 6.

Diagrammatically, the situation may be depicted as in Fig. 27.

The increased stock is reflected in a uniform increase in the supply curve, and a consequent fall in price and an increase in the quantity exchanged.

Of course, there is no reason to assume that, in reality, an increased stock will necessarily be accompanied by an unchanged reservation-demand curve. But in order to study the various causal factors that interact to form the actual historical result, it is necessary to isolate each one and consider what would be its effect if the others remained unchanged. Thus, if an increased stock were at the same time absorbed by an equivalent increase in the reservation-demand schedule, the supply curve would not increase at all, and the price and quantity exchanged would remain unchanged. (On the total demand-stock schedule, this situation would be reflected in an increase in stock, accompanied by an offsetting rise in the total-demand curve, leaving the price at the original level.)

A *decrease* in stock from one period to another may result from the *using up* of the stock. Thus, if we consider only consumers' goods, a part of the stock may be consumed. Since goods are generally used up in the process of consumption, if there is not sufficient production during the time considered, the total stock in existence may decline. Thus, one new horse may be produced, but two may die, from one point of time to the next, and the result may be a market with one less horse in existence. A *decline* in stock, with demand remaining the same, has the exactly reverse effect, as we may see on the diagrams by moving from the broken to the solid lines. At the old equilibrium price, there is an excess demand to hold compared to the stock available, and the result is an upbidding of prices to the new equilibrium. The supply schedule uniformly decreases by the decrease in stock, and the result is a higher price and a smaller quantity of goods exchanged.

We may summarize the relation between stock, production, and time, by stating that the stock at one period (assuming that a period of time is defined as one during which the stock remains unchanged) is related to the stock at a previous period as follows:

If S_t equals stock at a certain period (t)

S_{t-n} equals stock at an earlier period $(t - n)$ which is n units of time before period (t)

P_n equals production of the good over the period n

U_n equals amount of the good used up over the period n

Then: $$S_t = S_{t-n} + P_n - U_n$$

Thus, in the case just mentioned, if the original stock is 8 horses, and one new horse is produced while two die, the new stock of the good is $8 + 1 - 2 = 7$ horses.

It is important to be on one's guard here against a common confusion over such a term as "an increase in demand." Whenever this phrase is used by itself in this work, it always signifies an *increase in the demand schedule*, i.e., an increase in the

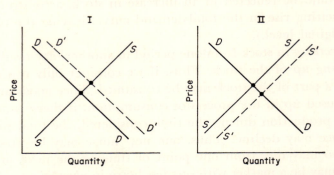

FIG. 28.   INCREASE IN THE DEMAND SCHEDULE AND IN THE QUANTITY DEMANDED

amounts that will be demanded at each hypothetical price. This "shift of the demand schedule to the right" always tends to cause an increase in price. It must never be confused with the "increase in quantity demanded" that takes place, for example, in response to an increased supply. An increased supply schedule, by lowering price, induces the market to demand the larger quantity offered. This, however, is *not* an increase in the demand schedule, but an *extension along the same demand schedule*. It is a larger quantity demanded in response to a more attractive price offer. This simple movement along the same schedule must not be confused with an increase in the demand schedule at *each* possible price. The diagrams in Fig. 28 highlight the difference:

Diagram I depicts an increase in the demand schedule, while diagram II depicts an extension of quantity demanded along the same schedule as a result of an increase in the supply offered. In both cases, the value scales of the various individuals determine the final result, but great confusion can ensue if the concepts are not clearly distinguished when such terms as "increase" or "decrease" in demand are being used.

10. *Specialization and Production of Stock*

We have analyzed the exchanges that take place in existing stock and the effect of *changes* in the stock of a good. The question still remains: On what principles is the size of the stock itself determined? Aside from the consumers' or producers' goods given directly by nature, *all goods must be produced by man.* (And even seemingly nature-given products must be searched for and then used by man, and hence are ultimately products of human effort.) The size of the stock of any good depends on the rate at which the good has been and is being *produced.* And since human wants for most goods are continuous, the goods that are worn out through use must constantly be replaced by new production. An analysis of the rate of production and its determinants is thus of central importance in an analysis of human action.

A complete answer to this problem cannot be given at this point, but certain general conclusions on production can be made. In the first place, while any one individual can at different times be both a buyer and a seller of existing stock, in the *production* of that stock there must be *specialization.* This omnipresence of specialization has been treated above, and the further an exchange economy develops, the further advanced will be the specialization process. The basis for specialization has been shown to be the varying abilities of men and the varying location of natural resources. The result is that a good comes first into existence by production, and then is sold by its producer in exchange for some other good, which has been produced in the same way. The initial sales of any new stock will all be made by original producers of the good. Purchases will be made by buyers who will use the good either for their direct use or for holding the good in speculative anticipation of later reselling it at a higher price. At any given time, therefore, new stock will be sold by its original producers. The old stock will be sold by: (*a*) original producers who through past reservation demand had accumulated old stock; (*b*) previous buyers who had bought in speculative anticipation of reselling at a higher price; and (*c*) previous buyers on whose value scales the relative utility of the good for their direct use has fallen.

At any time, then, the *market supply schedule* is formed by the addition of the supply schedules of the following groups of sellers:[30]

  a) The supply offered by *producers* of the good.
    1. The initial supply of new stock.
    2. The supply of old stock previously reserved by the producers.
  b) The supply of old stock offered by previous buyers.
    1. Sales by speculative buyers who had anticipated reselling at a higher price.
    2. Sales by buyers who had purchased for direct use, but on whose value scales the relative utility of the good has fallen.

The market demand schedule at any time consists of the sum of the demand schedules of:

  c) Buyers for direct use.
  d) Speculative buyers for resale at a higher price.

Since the good consists of equally serviceable units, the buyers are necessarily indifferent as to whether it is old or new stock that they are purchasing. If they are not, then the "stock" refers to two different goods, and not the same good.

The supply curve of the class (*b*) type of sellers has already been fully analyzed above, e.g., the relationship between stock and reservation demand for speculative resellers and for those whose utility position has changed. What more can be said, however, of the supply schedule of the class (*a*) sellers—the original producers of the good?

In the first place, the stock of newly produced goods in the hands of the producers is also *fixed* for any given point in time. Say that for the month of December the producers of copper decide to produce 5,000 tons of copper. At the end of that month their stock of newly produced copper is 5,000 tons. They might regret their decision and believe that if they could have made it again, they would have produced, say, 1,000 tons. But they have their stock, and they must use it as best they can. The distinguishing feature of the original producers is that, as a result of specialization, the direct use-value of their product to them is likely to be almost nonexistent. The further specialization proceeds, the less possible use-value can the product have for its producer. Picture, for example, how much copper a copper manufacturer could consume in his personal use, or the direct use-value of the huge number of produced automobiles to the Ford family. Therefore, in the supply schedule of the producers, the direct-use element in their reservation demand disappers. The only reason for a producer to reserve,

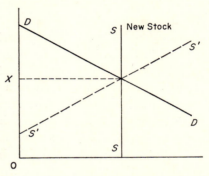

FIG. 29. EFFECT OF NEW STOCK OF CLASS (A) PRODUCERS

to hold on to, any of his stock is speculative—in anticipation of a higher price for the good in the future. (In direct exchange, there is also the possibility of exchange for a third good—say cows instead of fish, in our example.)

If, for the moment, we make the restrictive assumptions that there are no class (*b*) sellers on the market and that the producers have no present or accumulated past reservation demand, then the market supply-demand schedules can be represented as *SS, DD* in Fig. 29. Thus, with no reservation demand, the supply curve will be a vertical straight line (*SS*) at the level of the new stock. It seems more likely, however, that a price below equilibrium will tend to call forth a reservation demand to hold by the producers in anticipation of a higher price (called "building up inventory"), and that a price above equilibrium will result in the unloading of old stock that had been accumulated as a result of past reservation demand (called "drawing down inventory").

In that case, the supply curve assumes a more familiar shape (the broken line above—*S'S'*).

The removal of direct use-value from the calculation of the sellers signifies that all the stock must eventually be sold, so that *ultimately* none of the stock can be reserved from sale by the producers. The producers will make their sales at that point at which they expect the market price to be the greatest that they can attain—i.e., at the time when the market demand for the given stock is expected to be the greatest.[31] The length of time that producers can reserve supply is, of course, dependent on the durability of the good; a highly perishable good like strawberries, for example, could not be reserved for long, and its market supply curve is likely to be a vertical line.

Suppose that an equilibrium price for a good has been reached on the market. In this case, the speculative element of reservation demand drops out. However, in contrast to the market in re-exchange of *existing stock,* the market for *new production* does not end. Since wants are always being renewed in each successive period of time, new stock will also be produced in each period, and if the amount of stock is the same and the demand schedule given, the same amount will continue to be sold at the same equilibrium price. Thus, suppose that the copper producers produce 5,000 tons in a month; these are sold (no reservation demand) at the equilibrium price of *OX* on the foregoing diagram. The equilibrium quantity is *OS*. The following month, if 5,000 tons are produced, the equilibrium price will be the same. If more is produced, then, as we saw above, the equilibrium price is lower; if less, the equilibrium price will be higher.

If the speculative elements are also excluded from the demand schedule, it is clear that this schedule will be determined solely by the utility of the good in direct use (as compared with the utility of the sale-good). The only two elements in the value of a good are its direct use-value and its exchange-value, and the demand schedule consists of demand for direct use plus the speculative demand in anticipation of reselling at a higher price. If we exclude the latter element (e.g., at the equilibrium price), the only ultimate source of demand is the direct use-value of the good to the purchaser. If we abstract from the speculative elements in a market, therefore, the *sole* determinant of the market price of the stock of a good is its relative direct use-value to its purchasers.

It is clear, as has been shown in previous sections, that production must take place over a period of time. To obtain a certain amount of new stock at some future date, the producer must first put into effect a series of acts, using labor, nature, and capital goods, and the process must take time from the initial and intermediary acts until the final stock is produced. Therefore, the essence of specialized production is *anticipation of the future state of the market by the producers*. In deciding whether or not to produce a certain quantity of stock by a future date, the producer must use his judgment in estimating the market price at which he will be able to sell his stock. This market price is likely to be at some equilibrium, but an equilibrium is not likely to last for more than a short time. This is especially true when (as a result of ever-changing value scales) the demand curve for the good continually shifts. Each producer tries to use his resources—his labor and useful goods—in such a way as to obtain, in the production of stock, the maximum psychic revenue and hence a psychic profit. He is ever liable to error, and errors in anticipating the market will bring him a psychic loss. The essence of production for the market, therefore, is entrepreneurship. The key consideration is that the demand schedules, and consequently the future prices, are not and can never be definitely and automatically known to the producers. They must estimate the future state of demand as best they can.

Entrepreneurship is also the dominant characteristic of buyers and sellers who act speculatively, who specialize in anticipating higher or lower prices in the future. Their entire action consists in attempts to anticipate future market prices, and their success depends on how accurate or erroneous their forecasts are. Since, as was seen above, correct speculation quickens the movement toward equilibrium, and erroneous speculation tends to correct itself, the activity of these speculators tends to hasten the arrival of an equilibrium position.

The direct users of a good must *also anticipate their desires for a good* when they purchase it. At the time of purchase, their actual use of a good will be at some date in the future, even if in the very near future. The position of the good on their value scales is an estimate of its expected future value in these periods, discounted by time preferences. It is very possible for the buyer to make an erroneous forecast of the value of the good to him in the future, and the more durable the good, the greater the likelihood of error. Thus, it is more likely that the buyer of a house will be in error in forecasting his own future valuation than the buyer of strawberries. Hence, entrepreneurship is also a feature of the buyer's activity—even in direct use. However, in the case of specialized producers, entrepreneurship takes the form of estimating *other people's* future wants, and this is obviously a far more difficult and challenging task than forecasting one's *own* valuations.

Human action occurs in stages, and at each stage an actor must make the best possible use of his resources in the light of expected future developments. The past is forever bygone. The role of errors in different stages of human action may be considered in the comparatively simple case of the man who buys a good for direct use. Say that his estimate of his future uses is such that he purchases a good—e.g., 10 quarts of milk—in exchange for 100 barrels of fish, which also happens to be his maximum buying price for 10 quarts of milk. Suppose that after the purchase is completed he finds, for some reason, that his valuations have changed and that the milk is now far lower on his value scale. He is now confronted with the question of the best use to make of the 10 quarts of milk. The fact that he has made an error in using his resources of 100 barrels of fish does not remove the problem of making the best use of the 10 quarts of milk. If the price is still 100 barrels of fish, his best course at present would be to resell the milk and reobtain the 100 barrels of fish. If the price is now above 100, he has made a speculative gain, and he can resell the milk for more fish. And if the price of milk has fallen, but the fish is still higher on his value scale than the 10 quarts of milk, it would maximize his psychic revenue to sell the milk for less than 100 barrels of fish.

It is important to recognize that it is absurd to criticize such an action by saying that he suffered a clear loss of X barrels of fish from the two exchanges. To be sure, if he had correctly forecast later developments, the man would not have made the original exchange. His *original* exchange can therefore be termed erroneous in retrospect. But once the first exchange has been made, he must make the best possible present and future use of the milk, regardless of past errors, and therefore his second exchange was his best possible choice under the circumstances.

If, on the other hand, the price of milk has fallen below his new maximum buying price, then his best alternative is to use the milk in its most valuable direct use.

Similarly, a producer might decide to produce a certain amount of stock, and, after the stock has been made, the state of the market turns out to be such as to make him regret his decision. However, he must do the best he can with the stock, once it has been produced, and obtain the maximum psychic revenue from it. In other words, if we consider his action from the beginning— when he *invested* his resources in production—his act in retrospect was a psychic loss because it did not yield the best available alternative from these resources. But once the stock is produced, *this* is his available resource, and its sale at the best possible price now nets him a psychic gain.

At this point, we may summarize the expected (psychic) revenue and the expected (psychic) cost, factors that enter into the decision of buyers and sellers in any direct exchange of two goods.

Buyer Revenue	*Seller Revenue*
Either	Either
* A. Direct use of purchase-good	* A. Direct use of sale-good
or B. Anticipated later sale at higher price	or B. Anticipated later purchase at lower price
(whichever is the greater on his value scale)	(whichever is the greater on on his value scale)

Buyer Cost	*Seller Cost*
Either	Either
A. Direct use of sale-good	A. Direct use of purchase-good
or B. Anticipated later purchase at lower price	or * B. Exchange for a third good
or * C. Exchange for a third good	or C. Later sale at a higher price
(whichever is the greatest on his value scale)	(whichever is the greatest on his value scale)

If we eliminate the temporary speculative element, we are left with factors: revenue *A*, cost *A*, cost *C* for buyers; and revenue *A*, cost *A*, cost *B* for sellers. Similarly, if we consider the sellers as the specialized original producers—and this will be more true the greater the proportion of the rate of production to accumulated stock—cost *A* drops out for the sellers. If we also remember that, since the exchange involves two goods, the set of buyers for one good *is* the set of sellers for the other good, cost *A* is eliminated as a factor for buyers as well. Only the factors asterisked above ultimately remain. The revenue for both the buyers and the sellers is the expected direct use of the goods acquired; the costs are the exchange for a third good that is forgone because of this exchange.

The revenue and costs that are involved in making *the original decision regarding the production of stock* are, as we have indicated, of a different order, and these will be explored in subsequent chapters.

11. *Types of Exchangeable Goods*

For the sake of clarity, the examples of exchangeable goods in this chapter have mainly been taken from tangible *commodities,* such as horses, fish, eggs, etc. Such commodities are not the only type of goods subject to exchange, however. A may exchange his *personal services* for the commodity of B. Thus, for example, A may give his *labor* services to farmer B in exchange for farm produce. Furthermore, A may give personal services that function directly as *consumers' goods* in exchange for another good. An individual may thus exchange his medical advice or his musical performance for food or clothing. These services are as legitimately consumers' goods as those goods that are embodied in tangible, physical commodities. Similarly, individual labor services are as much producers' goods as are tangible capital goods. As a matter of fact, tangible goods are valued not so much for their physical content as for their *services* to the user, whether he is a consumer or a producer. The actor values the bread for its services in providing nourishment, the house for its services in providing shelter, the machine for its service in producing a lower-order good. In the last analysis, tangible commodities are also valued for their services, and are thus on the same plane as intangible personal "services."

Economics, therefore, is *not* a science that deals particularly with "material goods" or "material welfare." It deals in general with the action of men to satisfy their desires, and, specifically, with the process of exchange of goods as a means for each individual to "produce" satisfactions for his desires. These goods may be tangible commodities or they may be intangible personal services. The principles of supply and demand, of price determination, are exactly the same for any good, whether it is in one category or the other. The foregoing analysis is applicable to all goods.

Thus, the following types of possible exchanges have been covered by our analysis:

   a) A commodity for a commodity; such as horses for fish.
   b) A commodity for a personal service; such as medical advice for butter, or farm labor for food.
   c) A personal service for a personal service; such as mutual log-rolling by two settlers, or medical advice for gardening labor, or teaching for a musical performance.[32]

In cases where there are several competing homogeneous units, supply and demand schedules can be added; in cases where one or both parties are isolated or are the only ones exchanging, the zone of price determination will be established as indicated above. Thus, if one arithmetic teacher is bargaining with one violinist for an exchange of services, their respective utility rankings will set the zone of price determination. If several arithmetic teachers and several violinists who provide homogeneous services form a market for their two goods, the market price will be formed with the addition and intersection of supply and demand schedules. If the services of the different individuals are not considered as of equal quality by the demanders, they will be evaluated separately, and each service will be priced separately.[33] The supply curve will then be a supply of units of a commodity possessed by only *one* individual. This individual supply curve is, of course, sloped upward in a rightward direction. Where only one individual is the supplier of a good on the market, his supply curve is identical with the market supply curve.

One evident reason for the confusion of exchange with a mere trade of material objects is the fact that much intangible property *cannot,* by its very nature, be exchanged. A violinist may *own* his musicianly ability and exchange units of it, in the form of service, for the services of a physician. But other personal attributes, which cannot be exchanged, may be desired as goods. Thus, Brown might have a desired end: to gain the genuine approval of Smith. This is a particular consumers' good which he cannot purchase with any other good, for what he wants is the genuine approval rather than a show of approval that might be purchased. In this case, the consumers' good is a property of Smith's that cannot be exchanged; it might be acquired in some way, but not by exchange. In relation to exchange, this intangible good is an *inalienable* property of Smith's, i.e., it cannot be given up. Another example is that a man cannot permanently transfer his will, even though he may transfer much of his services and his property. As mentioned above, a man may not agree to permanent bondage by contracting to work for another man for the rest of his life. He might change his mind at a later date, and then he cannot, in a free market, be compelled to continue working thereafter. Because a man's self-ownership over his will is inalienable, he cannot, on the unhampered market, be compelled to continue an arrangement whereby he submits his will to the orders of another, even though he might have agreed to this arrangement previously.[34, 35] On the other hand, when property that *can* be alienated is transferred, it, of course, becomes the property—under the sole and exclusive jurisdiction—of the person who has received it in exchange, and no later regret by the original owner can establish any claim to the property.

Thus, exchange may occur with alienable goods; they may be consumers' goods, of varying degrees of durability; or they may be producers' goods. They may be tangible commodities or intangible personal services. There are other types of exchangeable items, which are based on these alienable goods. For example, suppose that Jones deposits a good—say 1,000 bushels of wheat— in a warehouse for safekeeping. He retains ownership of the good, but transfers its physical possession to the warehouse owner, Green, for safekeeping. Green gives Jones a *warehouse receipt* for the wheat, certifying that the wheat is there for safekeeping and giving the owner of the receipt a *claim* to receive the wheat whenever he presents the receipt to the warehouse. In exchange for this service as a guardian of the wheat, Jones pays him a certain agreed amount of some other good, say emeralds. Thus, the claim originates from an exchange of a commodity for a service—emeralds for storage—and the price of this exchange is determined according to the principles of the foregoing analysis. Now, however, the warehouse receipt has come into existence as a claim to the wheat. On an unhampered market, the claim would be regarded as absolutely secure and certain to be honored, and therefore Jones would be able to exchange the claim as a *substitute* for actual physical exchange of the wheat. He might find another party, Robinson, who wishes to purchase the wheat in exchange for horses. They agree on a price, and then Robinson accepts the *claim* on the warehouse as a perfectly good substitute for actual transfer of the wheat. He knows that when he wants to use the wheat, he will be able to *redeem* the claim at the warehouse; the claim therefore functions here as a *goods-substitute.* In this case, the claim is to a *present good,* since the good can be redeemed at any time that the owner desires.

Here, the nature and function of the claim is simple. The claim is a secure evidence of ownership of the good. Even simpler is a case where ownership of property, say a farm, is transferred from A to B by transferring written *title,* or evidence of ownership, which may be considered a claim. The situation becomes more complicated, however, when ownership is divided into pieces, and these pieces are transferred from person to person. Thus, suppose that Harrison is the owner of an iron mine. He decides to divide up the ownership, and sell the various divided pieces, or *shares,* of the good to other individuals. Assume that he creates a hundred tickets, with the total constituting the full ownership of the mine, and then sells all but ten tickets to numerous other individuals. The owner of two shares then becomes a $\frac{2}{100}$ owner of the mine. Since there is very little practical scope for such activity in a regime of *direct* exchange, analysis of this situation will be reserved for later chapters. It is clear, however, that the $\frac{2}{100}$ owner is entitled to his proportionate share of direction and control of, and revenue from, the jointly owned property. In other words, the *share* is evidence of part-ownership, or a claim to part-ownership, of a good. This property right in a proportionate share of the use of a good can also be sold or bought in exchange.

A third type of claim arises from a *credit exchange* (or *credit transaction*). Up to this point we have been discussing exchanges of one *present good* for another, i.e., the good can be used *at present*—or at any desired time—by each receiver in the exchange. In a credit transaction, a present good is exchanged for a *future good,* or rather, a *claim on a future good*. Suppose, for example, that Jackson desires to acquire 100 pounds of cotton at once. He makes the following exchange with Peters: Peters to give Jackson 100 pounds of cotton now (a present good); and, in return, Jackson gives Peters a *claim* on 110 pounds of cotton one year from now. This is a claim on a future good—110 pounds of cotton one year from now. The price of the present good in terms of the future good is 1.1 pounds of future cotton (one year from now) per pound of present cotton. Prices in such exchanges are determined by value scales and the meeting of supply and demand schedules, just as in the case of exchanges of present goods. Further analysis of the pricing of credit transactions must be left for later chapters; here it may be pointed out that, as explained in the previous chapter, every man will evaluate a homogeneous good more highly the earlier in time is his prospect of attaining it. A present good (a good consisting of units capable of rendering equivalent satisfaction) will always be valued more highly than the same good in the future, in accordance with the individual's rate of time preference. It is evident that the various rates of time preference—ultimately determined by relative positions on individual value scales—will act to set the price of credit exchanges. Moreover, the receiver of the present good—*the debtor*—will always have to repay *a greater amount* of the good in the future to the *creditor*—the man who receives the claim, since the same number of units is worth more as a present than as a future good. The creditor is rendering the debtor the service of using a good in the *present,* while the debtor pays for this service by repaying a greater amount of the good in the future.

At the date when the claim finally falls due, the creditor redeems the claim and acquires the good itself, thus ending the existence of the claim. In the meanwhile, however, the claim is in existence, and it can be bought and sold in exchange for other goods. Thus, Peters, the creditor, might decide to sell the claim—or promissory note—to Williams in exchange for a wagon. The price of this exchange will again be determined by supply and demand schedules. Demand for the note will be based on its security as a claim to the cotton. Thus, Williams' demand for the note (or Peter's demand to hold) in terms of wagons will be based (*a*) on the direct utility and exchange-value of the wagon, and (*b*) the marginal utility of the added units of cotton, *discounted* by him on two possible grounds: (1) the length of time the claim has left until the date of "maturity," and (2) the estimate of the security of the note. Thus, the less time there remains to elapse for a claim to any given good, the higher will it tend to be valued in the market. Also, if the eventual payment is considered less than absolutely secure, because of possible failure to redeem, the claim will be valued less highly in accordance with people's estimates of the likelihood of its failure. After a note has been transferred, it becomes the property of the new owner, who becomes the creditor and will be entitled to redeem the claim when due.

When a claim is thus transferred in exchange for some other good (or *claim*), this in itself is *not* a credit transaction. A credit exchange sets up an *unfinished payment* on the part of the debtor; in this case, Peters pays Williams the claim in return for the other good, and the transaction is finished. Jackson, on the other hand, remains the debtor as a result of the original transaction, which remains unfinished until he makes his agreed-upon payment to the creditor on the date of maturity.[36]

The several types of claims, therefore, are: on present goods, by such means as warehouse receipts or shares of joint ownership in a good; and on future goods, arising from credit transactions. These are evidences of ownership, or, as in the latter case, objects that *will become* evidence of ownership at a later date.

Thus, in addition to the three types of exchanges mentioned above, there are three other types whose terms and principles are included in the preceding analysis of this chapter:

  d) A commodity for a claim; examples of this are: (1) the deposit of a commodity for a warehouse receipt—the claim to a present good; (2) a credit transaction, with a commodity exchanged for a claim to a future commodity; (3) the purchase of shares of stock in a commodity by exchanging another type of commodity for them; (4) the purchase of promissory notes on a debtor by exchanging a commodity. All four of these cases have been described above.

  e) A claim for a service; an example is personal service being exchanged for a promissory note or warehouse receipt or stock.

  f) A claim for a claim; examples would be: exchange of a promissory note for another one; of stock shares for a note; of one type of stock share for another; of a warehouse receipt for any of the other types of claims.

With all goods analyzable into categories of tangible commodities, services, or claims to goods (goods-substitutes), all six possible types of exchanges are covered by the utility and supply-demand analysis of this chapter. In each case, different concrete considerations enter into the formation of the value scales—such as time preference in the case of credit exchanges; and this permits more to be said about the various specific types of exchanges. The level of analysis presented in this chapter, however, encompasses all possible exchanges of goods. In later chapters, when *indirect exchange* has been introduced, the present analysis will apply also, but further analysis will be made of production and exchange problems involved in credit exchanges (time preference); in exchanges for capital goods and consumer goods; and in exchanges for labor services (wages).

12. *Property: The Appropriation of Raw Land*

As we have stated above, the origin of all property is ultimately traceable to the appropriation of an unused nature-given factor by a man and his "mixing" his labor with this natural factor to produce a capital good or a consumers' good. For when we trace back through gifts and through exchanges, we must reach a man and an unowned natural resource. In a free society, any piece of nature that has never been used is *unowned* and is subject to a man's ownership through his first use or mixing of his labor with this resource.

How will an individual's title to the nature-given factor be determined? If Columbus lands on a new continent, is it legitimate for him to proclaim all the new continent his own, or even that sector "as far as his eye can see"? Clearly, this would not be the case in the free society that we are postulating. Columbus or Crusoe would have to *use* the land, to "cultivate" it in some way, before he could be asserted to own it. This "cultivation" does not have to involve tilling the soil, although that is one possible form of cultivation. If the natural resource is land, he may clear it for a house or a pasture, or care for some plots of timber, etc. If there is more land than can be used by a limited labor supply, then the unused land must simply remain unowned until a first user arrives on the scene. Any attempt to claim a new resource that someone does not use would have to be considered invasive of the property right of whoever the first user will turn out to be.

There is no requirement, however, that land *continue* to be used in order for it to continue to be a man's property. Suppose that Jones uses some new land, then finds it is unprofitable, and lets it fall into disuse. Or suppose that he clears new land and therefore obtains title to it, but then finds that it is no longer useful in production and allows it to remain idle. In a free society, would he lose title? No, for once his labor is mixed with the natural resource, it remains his owned land. His labor has been irretrievably mixed with the land, and the land is therefore his or his assigns' in perpetuity. We shall see in later chapters that the question whether or not labor has been mixed with land is irrelevant to its market price or capital value; in catallactics, the past is of no interest. In establishing the ownership of property, however, the question is important, for once the mixture takes place, the man and his heirs have appropriated the nature-given factor, and for anyone else to seize it would be an invasive act.

As Wolowski and Levasseur state:

Nature has been appropriated by him (man) for his use; she has become his *own;* she is his *property.* This property is legitimate; it constitutes a right as sacred for man as is the free exercise of his faculties. It is his because it has come entirely from himself, and is in no way anything but an emanation from his being. Before him, there was scarcely anything but matter; since him, and by him, there is interchangeable wealth. The producer has left a fragment of his own person in the thing which has thus become valuable, and may hence be regarded as a prolongation of the faculties of man acting upon external nature. As a free being he belongs to himself; now, the cause, that is to say, the productive force, is himself; the effect, that is to say, the wealth produced, is still himself. Who shall dare contest his title of ownership so clearly marked by the seal of his personality?[37]

Some critics, especially the Henry Georgists, assert that, while a man or his assigns may be entitled to the produce of his own labor or anything exchanged for it, he is not entitled to an original, nature-given factor, a "gift of nature." For one man to appropriate this gift is alleged to be an invasion of a common heritage that all men deserve to use equally. This is a self-contradictory position, however. A man cannot produce anything without the co-operation of original nature-given factors, if only as standing room. In order to produce and possess any capital good or consumers' good, therefore, he must appropriate and use an original nature-given factor. He cannot form products purely out of his labor alone; he *must* mix his labor with original nature-given factors. Therefore, if property in land or other nature-given factors is to be denied man, he cannot obtain property in the fruits of his labor.

Furthermore, in the question of land, it is difficult to see what better title there is than the first bringing of this land from a simple unvaluable thing into the sphere of production. For that is what the first user does. He takes a factor that was previously unowned and unused, and therefore worthless to anyone, and converts it into a tool for production of capital and consumers' goods. While such questions as communism of property will be discussed in later parts of this book, it is difficult indeed to see why the mere fact of being born should automatically confer upon one some aliquot part of the world's land. For the first user has mixed his labor with the land, while neither the newborn child nor his ancestors have done anything with the land at all.

The problem will be clearer if we consider the case of *animals*. Animals are "economic land," because they are equivalent to physical land in being original, nature-given factors of production. Yet will anyone deny title to a cow to the man that finds and domesticates her, putting her to use? For this is precisely what occurs in the case of land. Previously valueless "wild" land, like wild animals, is taken and transformed by a man into goods useful for man. The "mixing" of labor gives equivalent title in one case as in the other.

We must remember, also, what "production" entails. When man "produces," he does not create matter. He uses given materials and transforms and rearranges them into goods that he desires. In short, he moves matter further toward consumption. His finding of land or animals and putting them to use is also such a transformation.

Even if the value accruing to a piece of land at present is substantial, therefore, it is only "economic land" because of the innumerable past efforts of men at work on the land. When we are considering legitimacy of title, the fact that land always embodies past labor becomes extremely important.[38]

If animals are also "land" in the sense of given original na-

ture factors, so are water and air. We have seen that "air" is inappropriable, a condition of human welfare rather than a scarce
good that can be owned. However, this is true only of air for
breathing under usual conditions. For example, if some people
want their air to be changed, or "conditioned," then they will
have to pay for this service, and the "conditioned air" becomes
a scarce good that *is* owned by its producers.

Furthermore, if we understand by "air" the medium for the
transmission of such things as radio waves and television images,
there is only a limited quantity of wave lengths available for radio
and for television purposes. This scarce factor *is* appropriable and
ownable by man. In a free society, ownership of these channels
would accrue to individuals just like that of land or animals: the
first users obtain the property. The first user, Jones, of the wave
length of 1,000 kilocycles, would be the absolute owner of this
length for his wave area, and it will be his right to continue using it, to abandon it, to sell it, etc. Anyone else who set up a
transmitter on the owner's wave length would be as guilty of invasion of another's property right as a trespasser on someone else's
land or a thief of someone else's livestock.[39, 40]

The same is true of *water*. Water, at least in rivers and oceans,
has been considered by most people as also inappropriable and
unownable, although it is conceded to be ownable in the cases of
(small) lakes and wells. Now it is true that the high seas, in relation to shipping lanes, are probably inappropriable, because of
their abundance in relation to shipping routes.[41] This is *not* true,
however, of *fishing* rights in oceans. Fish are definitely not available in unlimited quantities relatively to human wants. Therefore, they are appropriable—their stock and source just as the
captured fish themselves. Indeed, nations are always quarreling
about "fishing rights." In a free society, fishing rights to the appropriate areas of oceans would be owned by the first users of
those areas and then usable or salable to other individuals. Ownership of areas of water that contain fish is directly analogous to
private ownership of areas of land or forests that contain animals
to be hunted. Some people raise the difficulty that water flows,
and has no fixed position, as land does. This is a completely in-

valid objection, however. Land "moves" too, as when soil is up-rooted in dust storms. Most important, water can definitely be marked off in terms of latitudes and longitudes. These bounda-ries, then, would circumscribe the area owned by individuals, in the full knowledge that fish and water can move from one per-son's property to another. The value of the property would be gauged according to this knowledge.[42]

Another argument is that appropriation of ownership by a first user would result in an uneconomic allocation of the nature-given factors. Thus, suppose that one man can fence, cultivate, or otherwise use, only five acres of a certain land, while the most economic allocation would be units of fifteen acres. However, the rule of *first ownership by the first user*, followed in a free society, would not mean that ownership must end with this allocation. On the contrary. In this case, either the owners would pool their assets in one corporate form, or the most efficient individual owners would buy out the others, and the final size of each unit of land in production would be fifteen acres.

It must be added that the theory of land ownership in a free society set forth here, i.e., first ownership by the first user, has nothing in common with another superficially similar theory of land ownership—that advanced by J. K. Ingalls and his disciples in the late nineteenth century. Ingalls advocated *continuing* own-ership only for actual occupiers and personal users of the land. This is in contrast to *original* ownership by the first user.

The Ingalls system would, in the first place, bring about a highly uneconomic allocation of land factors. Land sites where small "homestead" holdings are uneconomic would be forced into use in spite of this, and land would be prevented from entering other lines of use greatly demanded by consumers. Some land would be artificially and coercively withdrawn from use, since land that could not be used by owners *in person* would have to lie idle. Furthermore, this theory is self-contradictory, since it would not really permit ownership at all. One of the prime con-ditions of ownership is the right to buy, sell, and dispose of prop-erty as the owner or owners see fit. Since small holders would not have the right to sell to nonoccupying large holders, the small holders would not really be owners of the land at all. The result is that on the ownership question, the Ingalls thesis reverts, in the final analysis, to the Georgist view that Society (in the alleged person of the State) should own the land.[43]

13. *Enforcement against Invasion of Property*

This work is largely the analysis of a market society un-hampered by the use of violence or theft against any man's person or property. The question of the *means* by which this con-dition is best established is not at present under consideration. For the present purpose, it makes no difference whether this con-dition is established by every man's deciding to *refrain from in-vasive action* against others or whether some agency is established to enforce the abandonment of such action by every individual. (*Invasive action* may be defined as any action—violence, theft, or fraud—taking away another's personal freedom or property with-out his consent.) Whether the enforcement is undertaken by each person or by some sort of agency, we assume here that such a condition—the existence of an unhampered market—is maintained in some way.

One of the problems in maintaining the conditions of a free market is the role of the enforcing agency—whether individual or organizational—in exchange contracts. What type of contracts are to be enforced to maintain the conditions of an unhampered market? We have already seen that contracts assigning away the will of an individual cannot be enforced in such a market, be-cause the will of each person is by its nature inalienable. On the other hand, if the individual made such a contract and received another's property in exchange, he must forfeit part or all of the property when he decides to terminate the agreement. We shall see that fraud may be considered as theft, because one individual receives the other's property but does not fulfill his part of the exchange bargain, thereby taking the other's property without his consent. This case provides the clue to the role of contract and its enforcement in the free society. Contract must be considered as an agreed-upon exchange between two persons of two goods, present or future. Persons would be free to make any and all property contracts that they wished; and, for a free society to exist, all contracts, where the good is naturally alienable, must be enforced. Failure to fulfill contracts must be considered as theft of the other's property. Thus, when a debtor purchases a good in exchange for a promise of future payment, the good cannot be considered his property until the agreed contract has been fulfilled and payment made. Until then, it remains the creditor's property, and nonpayment would be equivalent to theft of the creditor's property.

An important consideration here is that contract *not* be enforced because a promise has been made that is not kept. It is not the business of the enforcing agency or agencies in the free market to enforce promises merely because they are promises; its business is to enforce against theft of property, and contracts are enforced because of the implicit theft involved.

Evidence of a *promise to pay property* is an enforceable claim, because the possessor of this claim is, in effect, the owner of the property involved, and failure to redeem the claim is equivalent to theft of the property. On the other hand, take the case of a promise to contribute personal services without an advance exchange of property. Thus, suppose that a movie actor agrees to act in three pictures for a certain studio for a year. Before receiving any goods in exchange (salary), he breaks the contract and decides not to perform the work. Since his personal will is inalienable, he cannot, on the free market, be forced to perform the work there. Further, since he has received none of the movie company property in exchange, he has committed no theft, and thus the contract cannot be enforced on the free market. Any suit for "damages" could not be entertained on an unhampered market. The fact that the movie company may have made considerable plans and investments on the expectation that the actor would keep the agreement may be unfortunate for the company, but it could not expect the actor to pay for its lack of foresight and poor entrepreneurship. It pays the penalty for placing too much confidence in the man. The movie actor has not received and kept any of the company's property and therefore cannot be

held accountable in the form of payment of goods as "damages." [44]
Any such enforced payment would be an invasion of his property rights on the free market rather than an attack upon invasion. It may be considered more moral to keep promises than to
break them, but the condition of a free market is that each individual's rights of person and property be maintained, and not
that some *further* standard of morals be coercively imposed on
all. Any coercive enforcement of such a moral code, going beyond the abolition of invasive acts, would in itself constitute an
invasion of individual rights of person and property and be an
interference in the free market. [45]

It certainly would be consonant with the free market, however, for the movie company to ask the actor to pay a certain
sum in consideration of his breaking the contract, and, if he refuses, to refuse to hire him again, and to notify other prospective contracting parties (such as movie companies) of the person's
action. It seems likely that his prospect of making exchanges in
the future will suffer because of his action. Thus, the "blacklist"
is permissible on the free market. Another legitimate action on
the free market is the *boycott,* by which A urges B not to make
an exchange with C, for whatever reason. Since A's and B's actions are purely voluntary and noninvasive, there is no reason for
a boycott not to be permitted on the unhampered market. On
the contrary, any coercive action against a boycott is an invasion
against the rights of free persons.

If default on contracted debts is to be considered as equivalent
to theft, then on the unhampered market its treatment by the
enforcing agency will be similar to that of theft. It is clear—for
example, in the case of burglary—that the recovery of the stolen
property to its owner would be the fundamental consideration for
the enforcing agency. Punishment of the wrongdoer would be a
consideration subsidiary to the former. Thus, suppose A has stolen
100 ounces of gold from B. By the time A has been apprehended
by the enforcing agency, he has dissipated the 100 ounces and
has no assets by which the 100 ounces can be obtained. The main
goal of the enforcement agency should be to force A to return
the 100 ounces. Thus, instead of simply idle imprisonment, the

agency could force the thief to labor and to attach his earnings to make up the amount of the theft, plus a compensation for the delay in time. Whether this forced labor is done in or out of prison is immaterial here. The main point is that the invader of another's rights on the free market gives up his rights to the same extent. The first consideration in the punishment of the aggressor against property in the free market is the forced return of the equivalent property.[46] On the other hand, suppose that B voluntarily decides to forgive A and grant the latter a gift of the property; he refuses to "press charges" against the thief. In that case, the enforcement agency would take no action against the robber, since he is now in the position of the receiver of a gift of property.

This analysis provides the clue to the treatment of defaulting debtors on the free market. If a creditor decides to forget about the debt and not press charges, he in effect grants a gift of his property to the debtor, and there is no further room for enforcement of contract. What if the creditor insists on keeping his property? It is clear that if the debtor can pay the required amount but refuses to do so, he is guilty of pure fraud, and the enforcing agency would treat his act as such. Its prime move would be to make sure that the debtor's assets are transferred to their rightful owner, the creditor. But suppose that the debtor has not got the property and would be willing to pay if he had it? Does this entitle him to special privilege or coerced elimination of the debt, as in the case of bankruptcy laws? Clearly not. The prime consideration in the treatment of the debtor would be his continuing and primary responsibility to redeem the property of the creditor. The only way by which this treatment could be eliminated would be for the debtor and the creditor to agree, as part of the original contract, that if the debtor makes certain investments and fails to have the property at the date due, the creditor will forgive the debt; in short, he grants the debtor the rights of a partial co-owner of the property.

There could be no room, in a free society such as we have outlined, for "negotiable instruments." Where the government designates a good as "negotiable," if A steals it from B and then sells it to C without the latter's knowledge of the theft, B cannot take the good back from C. Despite the fact that A was a thief and had no proper title to the good, C is decreed to be the legitimate owner, and B has no way of regaining his property. The law of negotiability is evidently a clear infringement of property right. Where property rights are fully defended, theft cannot be compounded in this manner. The buyer would have to purchase at his own risk and make sure that the good is not stolen; if he nonetheless does buy stolen goods, he must try to obtain restitution from the thief, and not at the expense of the rightful owner.

What of a cartel agreement? Would that be enforceable in a free society? If there has been no exchange of property, and A, B, C . . . firms agree among themselves to set quotas on their production of a good, this agreement would surely not be illegal, but neither would it be enforceable. It could be only a simple promise and not an enforceable case of implicit theft.[47]

One difficulty often raised against a free society of individual property rights is that it ignores the problem of "external diseconomies" or "external costs." But cases of "external diseconomy" all turn out to be instances of failure of *government*—the enforcing agency—adequately to enforce individual property rights. The "blame," therefore, rests not on the institution of private property, but on the failure of the government to enforce this property right against various subtle forms of invasion—the failure, e.g., to maintain a free society.

One instance of this failure is the case of smoke, as well as air pollution generally. In so far as the outpouring of smoke by factories pollutes the air and damages the persons and property of others, it is an invasive act. It is equivalent to an act of vandalism and in a truly free society would have been punished after court action brought by the victims. Air pollution, then, is not an example of a defect in a system of absolute property rights, but of failure on the part of the government to preserve property rights. Note that the remedy, in a free society, is not the creation of an administrative State bureau to prescribe regulations for smoke control. The remedy is *judicial* action to punish and proscribe pollution damage to the person and property of others.[48]

In a free society, as we have stated, every man is a self-owner. No man is allowed to own the body or mind of another, that being the essence of slavery. This condition completely overthrows the basis for a law of defamation, i.e., libel (written defamation) or slander (oral defamation). For the basis of outlawing defamation is that every man has a "property in his own reputation" and that therefore any malicious or untruthful attack on him or his character (or even more, a truthful attack!) injures his reputation and therefore should be punished. However, a man has no such objective property as "reputation." His reputation is simply what others think of him, i.e., it is purely a function of the *subjective* thoughts of others. But a man cannot own the minds or thoughts of others. Therefore, I cannot invade a man's property right by criticizing him publicly. Further, since I do not own others' minds either, I cannot force anyone else to think less of the man because of my criticism.[49]

The foregoing observations should firmly remind us that what the enforcing agency combats in a free society is invasion of the *physical* person and property, *not* injury to the *values* of property. For physical property is what the person owns; he does not have any ownership in monetary values, which are a function of what *others* will pay for his property. Thus, someone's vandalism against, or robbery of, a factory is an invasion of physical property and is outlawed. On the other hand, someone's shift from the purchase of this factory's product to the purchase of a competing factory's product may lower the monetary value of the former's property, but this is certainly not a punishable act. It is precisely the condition of a free society that a property owner have no unearned *claim* on the property of anyone else; therefore, he has no vested right in the value of his property, only in its physical existence. As for the value, this must take its chance on the free market. This is the answer, for example, to those who believe that "undesirable" businesses or people must be legally prevented from moving into a certain neighborhood because this may or will "lower the existing property value."

One method of acquiring property that we have so far not discussed, is *fraud*. Fraud involves cases where one party to an

agreed-upon exchange deliberately refuses to fulfill his part of
the contract. He thus acquires the property of the other person,
but he sacrifices either none of the agreed-upon goods or less
than he had agreed. We have seen that a debtor's deliberate failure to pay his creditor is equivalent to an outright theft of the
creditor's property.

Another example of fraudulent action is the following exchange: Smith agrees to give up fifteen ounces of gold to Jones
in exchange for a package of certain specified chinaware. When
he receives the package, after having given up the gold, Smith
finds that he has received an empty crate instead of the goods
that the two had agreed to exchange. Jones has falsely represented
the goods that he would exchange, and here again this is equivalent to outright theft of Smith's property. Since the exchange has
been made falsely, the actual form of which might not have
been contracted had the other party not been deceived, this is
not an example of voluntary exchange, but of one-sided theft.
We therefore exclude both explicit violence and the implicit
violence of fraud from our definition of the market—the pattern
of voluntary interpersonal exchanges. At this point we are dealing
only with an analysis of the market unhampered by fraud or violence.

We have not here been discussing what type of enforcing
agency will be set up or the means it will use, but what type
of actions the agency will combat and what type will be permissible. In a free market, all invasive acts by one person against
another's property, either against his person or his material goods,
will be combatted by the enforcing agency or agencies. We are
here assuming that there are no invasive acts in the society,
either because no individuals commit them or because they
are successfully combatted and prevented by some sort of enforcing agency. The problem then becomes one of defining invasive, as distinguished from noninvasive, acts, and this is what
has been done here in various typical examples. Each man would
be entitled to ownership over his own person and over any property that he has acquired by production, by appropriation of
unowned factors, by receiving gifts, or by voluntary exchange.

Never has the basis of the free, noninvasive, or "voluntaryist" society been described more clearly in a brief space than by the British political philosopher Auberon Herbert:

1) The great natural fact of each person being born in possession of a separate mind and separate body implies the ownership of such mind and body by each person, and rights of direction over such mind and body; it will be found on examination that no other deduction is reasonable.

2) Such self-ownership implies the restraint of violent or fraudulent aggressions made upon it.

3) Individuals, therefore, have the right to protect themselves by force against such aggressions made forcibly or fraudulently, and they may delegate such acts of self-defence to a special body called a government . . .

Condensed into a few words, our Voluntaryist formula would run: "The sovereignty of the individual must remain intact, except where the individual coerced has aggressed upon the sovereignty of another unaggressive individual."

Elaborating on the first point, Herbert continued:

If there is one thing on which we can safely build, it is the great natural fact that each human being forms with his or her body and mind a separate entity—from which we must conclude that the entities belong to themselves and not to each other. As I have said, no other deduction is possible. If the entities do not belong to themselves, then we are reduced to the most absurd conclusion. A or B cannot own himself; but he can own, or part own, C or D.[50]

3

The Pattern of Indirect Exchange

1. *The Limitations of Direct Exchange*

We have seen in the previous chapter how exchange benefits each participant and how the division of labor on a market increases productivity. The only exchange so far discussed, however, has been *direct exchange,* or *barter*—the exchange of one useful good for another, each for purposes of direct use by the party to the exchange. Although a treatment of direct exchange is important for economic analysis, the scope for direct exchange in society is extremely limited. In a very primitive society, for example, Crusoe could employ Jackson to labor on his farm in exchange for a part of the farm produce. There could, however, be no advanced system of production in a direct-exchange society and no accumulation of capital in higher stages of production—indeed no production at all beyond the most primitive level. Thus, suppose that A is a house-builder; he builds a house on contract and employs masons, carpenters, etc. In a regime of direct exchange, how would it be possible to pay these men? He could not give pieces of the house to each of the laborers. He would have to try to sell the house for precisely that combination of useful goods that each of the laborers and each of the sellers of raw material would accept. It is obvious that production could not be carried on and that the difficulties would be insuperable.

This problem of the lack of "coincidence of wants" holds even for the simple, direct exchange of consumers' goods, in addition to the insoluble problem of production. Thus, suppose that A, with a supply of eggs for sale, wants a pair of shoes in exchange. B has shoes but does not want eggs; there is no way for the two to get together. For anyone to sell the simplest commodity, he must find not only one who wants to purchase it, but one who has a commodity for sale that he must want to acquire. The market for anyone's commodities is therefore extremely limited, the extent of the market for any product is very small, and the scope for division of labor negligible. Furthermore, someone with a less divisible commodity, such as a plow, is in worse straits. Suppose that D, with a plow, would like to exchange it for eggs, butter, shoes, and various other commodities. Obviously, he cannot divide his plow into several pieces and then exchange the various pieces for eggs, butter, etc. The value of each piece to the others would be practically nil. Under a system of direct exchange, a plow would have almost no *marketability* in exchange, and few if any would be produced.

In addition to all these difficulties, which render a regime of direct exchange practically impossible, such a society could not solve the various problems of estimation, which (as was seen in chapter 1) even Crusoe had to face.[1] Since there would be no common denominator of units, there could be no way of estimating which line of production various factors should enter. Is it better to produce automobiles or tractors or houses or steel? Is it more productive to employ fewer men and more land on a certain product or less land and more men? Is the capital structure being maintained or consumed? None of these questions could be answered, since, in the stages beyond immediate consumption, there would be no way of comparing the usefulness or the productivity of the different factors or products.

The conclusion is evident that no sort of civilized society can be built on the basis of direct exchange, and that direct exchange, as well as Crusoe-like isolation, could yield only an economy of the most primitive type.[2]

2. *The Emergence of Indirect Exchange*

The tremendous difficulties of direct exchange can be overcome only by *indirect exchange,* where an individual buys a commodity in exchange, not as a consumers' good for the direct satisfaction of his wants or for the production of a consumers' good, but simply *to exchange again* for another commodity that he does desire for consumption or for production. Offhand, this might seem a clumsy and roundabout operation. Actually, it is indispensable for any economy above the barely primitive level.

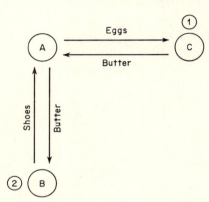

FIG. 30.   PATTERN OF INDIRECT EXCHANGE

Let us return, for example, to the case of A, with a supply of eggs, who wants a pair of shoes in exchange. B, the shoemaker, has shoes for sale but does not desire any more eggs than he has in stock. A cannot acquire shoes by means of direct exchange. If A wants to purchase a pair of shoes, he must find out what commodity B does want in exchange, and procure it. If A finds that B wants to acquire butter, A may exchange his eggs for the butter of C, and *then* exchange this butter for B's shoes. In this case, butter has been used as a *medium* of indirect exchange. The butter was worth more to A than the eggs (say the exchange was ten dozen eggs for ten pounds of butter, then for one pair of shoes), *not* because he wanted to consume the butter or to use the butter to produce some other good in a later stage of production, but because the butter greatly facilitated his obtaining the shoes in exchange. Thus, for A, the butter was more *marketable* than his eggs and was worth purchasing *because* of its superior marketability. The pattern of the exchange was as shown in Fig. 30.

Or consider the enormous benefit that D, the owner of a plow, acquires by using a medium of exchange. D, who would like to acquire many commodities but finds that his plow has a very limited marketability, can sell it in exchange for quantities of a more marketable commodity, e.g., butter. Butter, for one thing, is more marketable because, unlike the plow, its nature is such that it does not lose its complete value when divided into smaller pieces. D now uses the butter as a medium of indirect exchange to obtain the various commodities that he desires to consume.

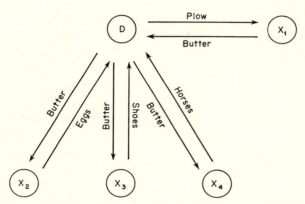

Fig. 31. Effect of Exchanging a Less Marketable for a More Marketable Commodity

Just as it is fundamental to human experience that there is great variety in resources, goods desired, and human skills, so is there great variety in the marketability of various commodities. Tending to increase the marketability of a commodity are its demand for use by more people, its divisibility into small units without loss of value, its durability, and its transportability over large distances. It is evident that people can vastly increase the extent of the market for their own products and goods by exchanging them for more marketable commodities and using the latter as media to exchange for goods that they desire. Thus, the pattern of D's, the plow-producer's, exchanges will be as shown in Fig. 31.

D first exchanges his plow for X_1's butter, and then uses the butter to exchange for the various goods that he desires to use, with X_2 for eggs, X_3 for shoes, X_4 for horses, etc.

As the more marketable commodities in any society begin to be picked by individuals as media of exchange, their choices will quickly focus on the few *most marketable* commodities available. If D saw, for example, that eggs were a more marketable commodity than butter, he would exchange his plow for eggs instead and use them as his medium in other exchanges. It is evident that, as the individuals center on a few selected commodities as the media of exchange, the demand for these commodities on the market greatly increases. For commodities, in so far as they are used as media, have an additional component in the demand for them—not only the demand for their direct use, but also a demand for their use as a medium of indirect exchange. This demand for their use as a medium is superimposed on the demand for their direct use, and this increase in the composite demand for the selected media *greatly increases their marketability*. Thus, if butter begins as one of the most marketable commodities and is therefore more and more chosen as a medium, this increase in the market demand for butter greatly increases the very marketability that makes it useful as a medium in the first place. The process is cumulative, with the most marketable commodities becoming enormously more marketable and with this increase spurring their use as media of exchange. The process continues, with an ever-widening gap between the marketability of the medium and the other commodities, until finally one or two commodities are far more marketable than any others and are in general use as media of exchange.[3]

Economic analysis is not concerned about *which* commodities are chosen as media of exchange. That is subject matter for economic *history*. The economic analysis of indirect exchange holds true regardless of the type of commodity used as a medium in any particular community. Historically, many different commodities have been in common use as media. The people in each community tended to choose the most marketable commodity available: tobacco in colonial Virginia, sugar in the West Indies, salt in Abyssinia, cattle in ancient Greece, nails in Scotland, copper in ancient Egypt, and many others, including beads, tea, cowrie shells, and fishhooks.[4] Through the centuries, gold and silver (specie) have gradually evolved as the commodities most widely used as media of exchange. Among the factors in their high marketability have been their great demand as ornaments, their scarcity in relation to other commodities, their ready divisibility, and their great durability. In the last few hundred years their marketable qualities have led to their general adoption as media throughout the world.

A commodity that comes into *general use* as a medium of exchange is defined as being a *money*. It is evident that, whereas the concept of a "medium of exchange" is a precise one, and indirect exchange can be distinctly separated from direct exchange, the concept of "money" is a less precise one. The point at which a medium of exchange comes into "common" or "general" use is not strictly definable, and whether or not a medium is a money can be decided only by historical inquiry and the judgment of the historian. However, for purposes of simplification, and since we have seen that there is a great impetus on the market for a medium of exchange to become money, we shall henceforth refer to all media of exchange as *moneys*.

3. Some Implications of the Emergence of Money

The establishment of a money on the market enormously increases the scope for specialization and division of labor, immensely widens the market for every product, and makes possible a society on a civilized productive level. Not only are the problems of coincidence of wants and indivisibility of goods eliminated, but individuals can now construct an ever-expanding edifice of remote stages of production to arrive at desired goods. Intricate and remote stages of production are now possible, and specialization can extend to every part of a production process as well as to the type of good produced. Thus, an automobile producer can sell an automobile in exchange for the money, e.g., butter or gold, and then exchange the gold partly for labor, partly for steel, partly for chrome, partly for rubber tires, etc. The steel producers can exchange the gold partly for labor, partly for iron, partly for machines, etc. Then the various laborers, landowners, etc., who receive the gold in the production process can use it as a medium to purchase eggs, automobiles, or clothing, as they desire.

The whole pattern of a modern society is thus built on the use of money, and the enormous importance of the use of money will become clearer as the analysis continues.[5] It is evident that it is a mistake on the part of many writers who wish to set forth the doctrines of modern economics to analyze direct exchange only and then to insert money somewhere at the end of the analysis, considering the task finished. On the contrary, the analysis of direct exchange is useful only as an introductory aid to the analysis of a society of indirect exchange; direct exchange would leave very little scope for the market or for production.

With the great variety in human skills and natural resources resulting in enormous advantages from the division of labor, the existence of money permits the splitting of production into minute branches, each man selling his product for money and using money to buy the products that he desires. In the field of consumers' goods, a doctor can sell his services, or a teacher his, for money, and then use the money to purchase goods that he demands. In production, a man can produce a capital good, sell it for money, and use the gold received to purchase the labor, land, and capital goods of a higher order needed for its production. He may use the surplus of money income over money outlay on factors to purchase consumers' goods for his own needs. Thus, at any stage in the production of any product, a man employs land and labor factors, exchanging money for their services as well as for the needed capital goods, and then sells the product for money to help in the next lower stage of production. This process continues until the final consumers' goods are sold to consumers. These consumers, on the other hand, obtain their money by *purchasing* it through the sale of their own goods— either durable consumers' goods or services in production. The latter may include the sale of labor services, the sale of services of their land, the sale of their capital goods, or inheritance from those who had previously contributed such services.[6]

Thus, nearly all exchanges are made against money, and money impresses its stamp upon the entire economic system. Producers of consumers' goods as well as owners of durable consumers' goods, owners of capital goods, and sellers of labor services, all sell their goods against money and purchase with money the factors that they need. They use their net money income to purchase consumers' goods produced by others in the society. Thus, all individuals, in their capacity as producers and owners, supply goods (commodities and services) and demand money in exchange. And, in their capacity as producers purchasing factors, as well as in their capacity as consumers, they supply money and demand an almost infinite variety of goods in exchange. The economy is therefore a "money economy," and almost all goods are compared with and exchanged against the money commodity. This fact is of crucial importance to the analysis of any society beyond the most primitive level. We may sum up the complex pattern of exchanges in a money economy in the following way:

Men in their capacity as:

Producers

Sell:	*Buy:*
Consumers' Goods,	Producers' Goods
Producers' Goods	Labor
Labor	Land
Land	Capital Goods
Capital Goods	
For Money	*With Money*

Consumers

Buy:
Consumers' Goods

With Money

4. *The Monetary Unit*

We have seen that every good is "in supply" if it can be divided into units, each of which is homogeneous with every other. Goods can be bought and sold only in terms of such units, and those goods which are indivisible and unique may be described as being in a supply of one unit only. Tangible commodities are generally traded in terms of *units of weight,* such as tons, pounds, ounces, grains, grams, etc. The money commodity is no exception to this rule. The most universally traded commodity in the community, it is bought and sold always in terms of units of its weight. It is characteristic of units of weight, as of other metrical scales, that each unit is convertible into every other. Thus, one pound equals 16 ounces; and one ounce equals 437.5 grains or 28.35 grams. Therefore, if Jones sells his tractor for 15 pounds of gold, he may also be described as having sold the tractor for 240 ounces of gold, or for 6,804 grams of gold, etc.

It is clear that the size of the unit of the money commodity chosen for any transaction is irrelevant for economic analysis and is purely a matter of convenience for the various parties. All the units will be units of weight, and they will be convertible into pounds, ounces, etc., by multiplying or dividing by some constant number, and therefore will all be convertible into one another in the same manner. Thus, one pound of gold will equal 16 ounces and will, of course, exchange for 16 ounces, should such an exchange be desired on the market. The economic irrelevance of the names or sizes of the units may be seen from the following example. Suppose that the residents of Texas use, in their exchanges, a unit known as the Houston, equalling 20 grains of gold, while the residents of Massachusetts use the Adams, equalling 10 grains. The citizens of the respective areas may make their exchanges and calculations in these terms, e.g., Jones sells his car for "2,000 Houstons of gold," or, more simply, "2,000 Houstons," or Jones might consider the money price of eggs as being "½ Houston per dozen." On the other hand, Smith might buy a house for "10,000 Adamses." It is obvious that the use of the different names will complicate matters but is economically *insignificant.* The "Houston" is still a unit of weight of gold, and is a shorthand name for "20 grains of gold." It is clear that, on the market, 1 Houston will exchange for 2 Adamses.[7]

To avoid unnecessary complications and to clarify the analysis, therefore, the names of the monetary units in this work will be in terms of universally acceptable units of weight (such as ounces, grams, etc.) rather than in terms of accidental names of only local significance (such as dollars or francs).

Obviously, the more valuable the units of a commodity are, the smaller the size of the units used in daily transactions; thus, platinum will be traded in terms of ounces, while iron is traded in terms of tons. Relatively valuable money commodities like gold and silver will tend to be traded in terms of smaller units of weight. Here again, this fact has no particular economic significance.

The *form* in which a unit weight of any commodity is traded depends on its usefulness for any specific, desired purpose. Thus, iron may be sold in the form of bars or chunks, cheese in rectangular or triangular shape, etc. Whereas other commodities will be traded in those forms suitable for production or consumption, money will be traded in forms suitable for exchange or storing until an exchange is made. Historically, the shapes of money have been innumerable.[8] In recent centuries large bars of gold or silver have been used for storage or for exchange in larger transactions, while smaller, circular pieces, known as *coins,* are used for smaller transactions.

5. *Money Income and Money Expenditures*

In a money economy, each individual sells goods and services that he owns for money and uses the money to buy desired goods. Each person may make a record of such monetary exchanges for any period of time. Such a record may be called his *balance of payments* for that period.

One record may be the transactions of goods sold for money in a certain period to other individuals. Suppose, for example, that Mr. Brown draws up the record of goods sold for money for the month of September, 1961. Suppose that he has sold his services as a carpenter to a Mr. Jones in building the latter's house and has sold his services also as a handyman to Messrs. Jones and Smith during the same period. Also, he has disposed of an old radio to Mr. Johnson. His account of money received, i.e., money *purchased* for goods and services *sold,* is as follows:

September, 1961—James Brown

Money Purchased	For Goods and Services Sold
20 ounces of gold	Labor as Carpenter to Jones
5 ounces of gold	Labor as Handyman to Jones & Smith
1 ounce of gold	Old Radio to Johnson
26 ounces of gold	

From the account, we know that by his sales of goods and services during this period, Brown has purchased 26 ounces of gold. This total of money purchased is his total of *money income* for that period.

It is clear that the more money income a man receives during any period, the more money he will be able to spend on desired goods. *Other things being equal* (an important qualification that will be examined in later sections), *he will strive to earn as much money income in any prospective period as he can.*

Mr. Brown acquired his income by selling his labor services and a durable consumers' good. There are other ways of acquiring money income on an unhampered market. The owner of land may sell it for agricultural, locational, or industrial, as well as other, purposes. The owner of capital goods may sell them to those interested in using them as factors of production. Tangible land and capital goods may be sold for money outright, or the owner may retain ownership of the good while selling ownership of its *services* over a certain period of time. Since any good is bought only for the services that it can bestow, there is no reason why a certain period of service of a good may not be purchased. This can be done, of course, only where it is technically possible. Thus, the owner of a plot of land or of a sewing machine or of a house may "rent it out" for a certain period of time in exchange for money. While such *hire* may leave legal ownership of the good in the hands of the "landlord," the actual owner of the good's service *for that period* is the renter, or "tenant." At the end of the hire period, the good is returned to the original owner, who may use or sell the remainder of the services.

In addition to the sale of goods and services, a man may receive money as a gift. A man does not *purchase* the money he receives in gifts. His money income for any period equals his money purchased, plus the money he receives in gifts. (One common form of receipt of gift is an inheritance, the result of a bequest at death.)

Thus, Mr. Green's account of money income for June to December, 1961, may be as follows:

	Money Income	*From Sale of Goods and Services*
	28 ounces of gold	Rent of Land to Mr. Jones
PURCHASED	300 ounces of gold	Sale of (other) Land to Mr. Forrest
	15 ounces of gold	Sale of a Threshing Machine to Mr. Woods
		From Gifts
GIVEN	400 ounces of gold	Inheritance from Uncle
	753 ounces of gold	

As was seen in the previous chapter, in order first to acquire the good or service that a man can sell for money, he must first either produce it himself or buy it from someone who has produced it (or who, in turn, has bought it from the original producer). If he has been given money, the original owner must have acquired it through producing a good, etc. Thus, in the last analysis, the first seller of a capital good or a durable consumers' good is the original producer, and later purchasers must have produced some service of their own in order to obtain the money to acquire it. The seller of labor service, of course, produces the service directly at the time. The seller of pure land must originally have appropriated unused land which he had found and transformed. On the unhampered market of a money economy, producers of commodities and services sell their goods for the money commodity, then use the money acquired to buy other desired goods.

Money is acquired in this way by all except the producers of the original gold on the market—those who mined and marketed it. However, the production of the money commodity, as with all other valuable commodities, itself requires the use of land, labor, and capital goods, and these must be paid for by the use of money. The gold miner, then, receives no money by gift, but must actively find and produce gold to acquire his money.

With the use of money acquired in these various ways, individuals purchase desired goods. They do so in two capacities: as consumers and as producers. As consumers, they purchase consumers' goods that they desire; in the case of durable goods, they may purchase the entire good, or they may hire the services of goods for some specified period of time. As producers, they use money to purchase the services of factors of production needed to produce consumers' goods or lower-order capital goods. Some factors they may purchase outright, to use *all* their anticipated future services; some they may hire for their services for a specified period of time. Thus, they may purchase capital goods that function as "raw material"; they may purchase some capital goods called "machines" and hire others; they may hire or purchase the land that they need to work on. In general, just as consumers cannot very well hire short-lived, nondurable goods, so producers cannot very well hire capital goods, dubbed "raw material" or "inventory," that are used up quickly in the process of production. On a free market, they cannot purchase labor services outright, as was explained in the preceding chapter. Since man's personal will is inalienable, he cannot, in a voluntary society, be compelled to work for another against his present will, and therefore no contracts can be made for purchase of his future will. Labor services, therefore, can only be bought for "hire," on a "pay-as-you-go" basis.

Any individual may draw up an account of his purchases of other goods with money for any period of time. The total amount of money given up in such exchanges is his *money expenditures* or *money outlays* for that period. Here it must be noted that his expenditure account, as well as his income account, can be itemized for each transaction or may be grouped into various classes.

Thus, in Brown's account above, he might have tabulated his income as 25 ounces from labor in general, and 1 ounce from his radio. How broad or narrow the classes are depends purely on the convenience of the person drawing up the account. The total, of course, is always unaffected by the type of classification chosen.

Just as money income equaled *money purchased* for goods and services sold *plus* money received as gifts, so money expenditure equals *money sold* for goods and services bought *plus* money given away as gifts. Thus, Mr. Brown's money expenditure account for September, 1961, might be the following:

September 1961—James Brown
Money Expended

Money Sold	For Goods and Services Bought
12 ounces of gold	Food
6 ounces of gold	Clothing
3 ounces of gold	Rent of House
2 ounces of gold	Entertainment
Money Given	
1 ounce of gold	Charity
24 ounces of gold	

In this account, Brown is spending money purely as a *consumer,* and his total money expenditures for the period are 24 ounces. If he had desired it, he could have subdivided the account further into such items as apples, ⅕ ounce; hat, 1 ounce, etc.

Here it may be noted that an individual's total money income for any period may be termed his *exports,* and the goods sold may be termed the "goods exported"; on the other hand, his total money expenditure may be termed his *imports,* and the goods and services bought are the "goods imported." These terms apply to goods purchased by producers or consumers.

Now, let us observe and compare Mr. Brown's income and expenditure accounts for September, 1961. Brown's total money income was 26 ounces of gold, his money expenditures 24 ounces. This must mean that 2 ounces of the 26 earned in this period *remained unspent*. These 2 ounces remain in the possession of Mr. Brown, and are therefore added to whatever previous stock of gold Brown might have possessed. If Brown's stock of money on September 1, 1961, was 6 ounces of gold, his stock of money on October 1, 1961, is 8 ounces of gold. The stock of money owned by any person at any point in time is called his *cash holding* or *cash balance* at that time. The 2 ounces of income remaining unspent on goods and services constituted a *net* addition to Brown's cash balance over the month of September. For any period, therefore, a person's money income is equal to his money outlay plus his addition to cash balance.

If we subdivide this income-expenditure account into smaller periods of time, the picture of what is happening to the cash balance within the larger period is likely to be far different from a simple addition of 2 ounces. Thus, suppose that all of Brown's money income came in two chunks on the first and the fifteenth of September, while his expenditures occurred every day in varying amounts. As a result, his cash balance rose drastically on September 1, say to 6 plus 13 or a total of 19 ounces. Then, the cash balance was gradually drawn down each day until it equaled 6 again on the 15th; then it rose sharply again to 19, finally being reduced to 8 at the month's end.

The pattern of Brown's supplies and demands on the market is clear. Brown *supplied* various goods and services on the market and *demanded* money in exchange. With this money income, he *demanded* various goods and services on the market and supplied money in exchange. The money *must go into the cash balance* before it can be spent on goods and services.[9]

Suppose, on the other hand, that Brown's expenditures for September had been 29 ounces instead of 24 ounces. This was accomplished by drawing down Brown's previous cash balance by 3 ounces and leaving him with 3 ounces in his cash holding. In this case, his money expenditures for the period equaled his money income *plus* the decrease in his cash balance. In sum, the following formula always holds true for any individual over any period of time:

Money Income = Money Expenditures + Net Additions to Cash Balance − Net Subtractions from Cash Balance

Alternatively, the term Exports can be substituted for Income, and Imports for Expenditures, in the above equation.

Let us assume for purposes of simplification that the total stock of the money commodity in the community has remained unchanged over the period. (This is not an unrealistic assumption, since newly mined gold is small compared to the existing stock.) Now it is obvious that, like all valuable property, all money must, at any point in time, be owned by *someone*. At any point in time, the sum of the cash holdings of all individuals is equal to the total *stock* of money in the community. Thus, if we consider Brown among a *group* of five persons living in a village, and their respective cash balances on September 1 were: 6, 8, 3, 12, and 5 ounces, then the total stock of money held in the village on that date was 34 ounces. If the data were available, the same sort of summation could be performed for the world as a whole, and the total stock of money discovered. *Now it is obvious that Brown's addition of 2 ounces to his cash balance for September must have been counterbalanced by a subtraction of 2 ounces from the cash balances of one or more other individuals.* Since the stock of money has not changed, Brown's addition to his cash balance must have been acquired by drawing down the cash balances of other individuals. Similarly, if Brown had drawn down his cash balance by 3 ounces, this must have been counterbalanced by the addition of 3 ounces to the cash balance of one or more individuals.

It is important to recognize that the additions to, or subtractions from, a cash balance are all voluntary acts on the part of the individuals concerned. In each period, some individuals decide to add to their cash balances, and others decide to reduce them, and each makes that decision which he believes will benefit him most.[10] For centuries, however, fallacious popular usage has asserted that one whose income is greater than expenditures (ex-

ports greater than imports) has a "favorable balance of trade,"
while one whose expenditures have been greater than income for
a period (imports greater than exports) has suffered an "unfavorable balance of trade." Such a view implies that the active,
important part of the balance of payments is the "trade" part,
the exports and imports, and that the changes in the individual's
cash balance are simply passive "balancing factors," serving to
keep the total payments always in balance. In other words, it assumes that the individual spends as much as he wants to on goods
and services and that the addition or subtraction from his cash
balance appears as an afterthought. On the contrary, changes in
cash balance are actively decided upon by each individual in the
course of his market actions. Thus, Brown decided to increase
his cash balance by 2 ounces and sold his labor services to obtain the money, forgoing purchases of consumers' goods to the
extent of 2 ounces. Conversely, in the later example, when he
spent 3 ounces more than he earned in the month, he decided
that his cash balance had been excessive and that he would rather
spend some of it on consumers' goods and services. *There is
therefore never a need for anyone to worry about anyone else's
balance of payments.* A person's "unfavorable" balance of trade
will continue so long as the individual wishes to reduce his cash
balance (and others are willing to purchase his money for goods).
His maximum limit is, of course, the point when his cash balance
is reduced to zero. Most likely, however, he will stop reducing
his cash balance long before this point.[11]

6. *Producers' Expenditures*

The previous section concentrated on the case of Mr. Brown,
whose entire money expenditures were on *consumers'* goods. His
money income, aside from the sale of old, previously produced
goods, came from the sale of current productive labor services.
His expenditures were purely on consumption; his income was
derived almost solely from his production of labor services. Every
man must be a consumer, and therefore this analysis of consumer
spending applies to all persons. Most people earn their income

from the sale of their labor services. However, if we except previously produced goods, because someone must have originally produced them, all other money incomes must derive from new production of capital goods or consumers' goods. (This is apart from the sellers of land or its services, whose ownership must have originally derived from the finding and reshaping of unappropriated land.)

Producers of capital goods and consumers' goods are in a different position from sellers of labor service only. Mr. Brown, for example, a seller solely of labor service, need not spend any money on purchasing capital goods. Purely from his expenditure on desired consumers' goods, he derives the energy to be able to produce and sell labor services on the market. But the producers of capital goods and consumers' goods—the nub of any civilized society, since labor services alone could produce very little—are not and cannot be in such a fortunate position. For a man to produce a consumers' good, he must obtain labor services and the services of land and capital goods, in order to use the technological "know-how" available in the production of the good. Pushing the problem back, we find that, in order to produce a capital good, the would-be producer must obtain the necessary land, labor, and capital goods. Each such individual producer (or group of individuals in partnership) obtains the required factors and then directs the combination of factors into producing a capital good. This process is repeated among numerous individuals, until the lowest stage of production is reached and a consumers' good is produced. The producer of the capital good must obtain the needed factors (land, labor, and capital) by purchasing them for money, and, when the (lower-order) capital good is completed, he sells it for money. This capital good is, in turn, used for the production of a still lower-order capital good, and the latter is sold for money. This process continues until the final producer of the consumers' good sells it for money to the ultimate consumer.

A simplified schematic representation of this process is shown in Fig. 32.

The solid arrows depict the movement of *goods* in exchange, as factors are bought by the producers at each stage, worked into a lower-order capital good, and then sold to lower-order producers. The broken arrows in the reverse direction depict the movement of *money* in the same exchanges. The producer of a capital good

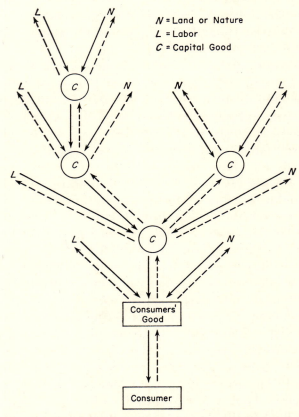

FIG. 32.   STAGES IN THE PROCESS OF PRODUCTION FOR THE ULTIMATE CONSUMER

employed money that he owned to purchase factors of production. He then used these owned factors, along with hired labor services, to produce a lower-order capital good that he owned until he could sell it for money to another producer. The producer of a consumers' good went through the same process, except that his final sale for money was to the ultimate consumer.

Now let us call those producers who use their money to *invest* in the purchase of factors (either outright or for hire) *capitalists*. The capitalists then produce and own the various stages of capital goods, exchanging them for money until their products reach the consumers. Those who participate in the productive process are therefore the capitalists and the sellers of land and labor services. The capitalists are the only ones who *spend money on producers' goods,* and they, therefore, may here be termed "the producers."

It is evident that a dominant characteristic of the production process is that each individual must produce *in anticipation* of the sale of his product. Any investment in production is made in anticipation of later sale to lower-order producers and, finally, to consumers.

Clearly, the consumer must have money in his cash balance in order to spend it on consumers' goods, and, likewise, the producer must have the original money to invest in factors. Where does the consumer get the money? As has been shown above, he may obtain it from gifts or from the sale of previously produced goods, but in the last analysis he must have obtained it from the sale of some productive service. The reader can inspect the final destinations of the broken arrows; these are the sellers of labor services and of the services of land. These laborers and landowners use the money thus obtained to buy the final products of the production system. The capitalist-producers also receive income at each stage of the production process. Evidently, the principles regulating these incomes require careful investigation, which will be undertaken below. Here it might be noted that the net incomes accruing to the owners of capital goods are not simply the result of the contribution to production by the capital goods, since these capital goods are in turn the products of other factors.

Where, then, do the *producers* acquire their money for investment? Clearly, from the same sources only. From the income acquired in production, individuals can, in addition to buying consumers' goods, purchase factors of production and engage in the productive process as producers of a good that is not simply their own labor service. In order to obtain the money for investment, then, an individual must *save money* by restricting his possible consumption expenditures. This saved money first goes into his cash balance and then is *invested* in the purchase of factors in the anticipation of a later sale of the produced good. It is obvious that investment can come only from funds that are saved by individuals from their possible consumption spending. The producers restrict their consumption expenditures, save their money, and "go into business" by investing their funds in factors that will yield them products in the future.[12]

Thus, while every man must spend part of his money income in consumption, some decide to become producers of capital or consumers' goods and to save money to invest in the required factors. Every person's income may be spent on consumption, on investment in the production of goods, or on an addition to his cash balance. For any period, an individual's *Money Income = his Consumption Expenditures + Investment Expenditures + Additions to Cash Balance − Subtractions from Cash Balance.* (Investment expenditures may be defined as the sum of the money expenditures made in investment in factors of production.)

Let us take the hypothetical case of Mr. Fred Jones and his "balance of payments" for November, 1961. Suppose his income from various sources during this month is 50 ounces. He decides to spend, during the month, 18 ounces on consumers' goods; to add 2 ounces to his cash balance; and to invest the other 30 ounces in a "business" for the production of some good. It must be emphasized that this business can involve the production of any good at all; it could be a steel factory, a farm, or a retail shoe store. It could be for the purchase of wheat in one season of the year in anticipation of sale in another season. All of this is productive enterprise, since, in each instance, a good is produced, i.e., goods are moved a step forward in their progress to the ultimate consumer. Since the investment is always in anticipation of later sale, the investors are also engaged in *entrepreneurship,* in enterprise.

Let us assume that Jones expends the saved funds on investment in a paper factory. His income-expenditure account for November may appear as follows:

November, 1961—Fred Jones

Income	Expenditures	
From sale of land........... 20 oz.	Food.........................	7 oz.
From sale of a building...... 30 oz.	Clothing.....................	4 oz.
	Shelter......................	4 oz.
	Entertainment................	3 oz.
50 oz.	Consumption Expenditures......	18 oz.
	On Paper Machinery...........	12 oz.
	On Wood Pulp................	10 oz.
	On Labor Services............	8 oz.
	Investment Expenditures........	30 oz.
	Addition to Cash Balance.......	2 oz.
	Total....................	50 oz.

Of course, these figures are purely illustrative of a possible situation; there are innumerable other illustrations; e.g., there could have been a subtraction from cash balance to enable greater investment.

Investment expenditures are always made in anticipation of future sale. Factors are purchased, they are transformed into the product, and the product is then sold by the enterpriser for money. The "businessman" makes his outlays with the expectation of being able to sell the product at a certain price on a certain future date. Suppose that Jones makes the investment of 30 ounces with the expectation of being able to transform his factors into the product (in this case, paper) and sell the product for 40 ounces at some date in November, 1962. If his expectation proves correct, he will succeed in selling the paper for 40 ounces at that date, and his income account, for any period that includes that date in November, 1962, will include "40 ounces from sale of paper."

It is obvious that, other things being equal, an investor will attempt to acquire the greatest possible net income from his investment, just as, with the same qualification, everyone attempts to acquire the greatest income from other types of sales. If Jones is confronted with investment opportunities for his 30 ounces in different possible lines or processes of production, and he expects that one will net him 40 ounces in a year, another 37 ounces, and another 34, etc., Jones will choose that investment promising the greatest return. A crucial difference, then, between man as an entrepreneur and man as a consumer is that in the latter case there is no drive to have exports greater than imports. A man's imports are his purchase of consumers' goods and are therefore the ends of his activity. The goods he imports are a source of satisfaction to him. On the other hand, the businessman is "importing" only producers' goods, which by definition are useless to him directly. He can gain from them only by selling them or their product, and therefore his imports are merely the necessary means to his later "exports." Therefore, he tries to attain the greatest net income, or, in other words, to attain the largest surplus of exports over imports. The larger his business income, the more the owner of the business will be able to spend (i.e., to import) on consumers' goods that he desires.

It is clear, however, that the man, *considered as a whole,* has no particular desire to export more than he imports or to have a "favorable balance of trade." He tries to export more than he imports *of producers' goods* in his business; then he uses this surplus to spend on *imports of consumers' goods* for his personal wants. On total balance, he may, like Mr. Brown above, choose to add to his cash balance or subtract from his cash balance, as he sees fit and considers most desirable.[13] Let us take as an example Mr. Jones, after he has been established in his business. Over a certain period, he may decide to subtract 5 ounces from his cash balance. Even though he tries his best to achieve the largest net income from business and thus add to his cash balance as much as possible from *this source,* in total he may well decide to reduce his cash balance. Thus:

Fred Jones

Income	Expenditures
From business... 150 oz.	In business, on factors of production (producers' goods).. 100 oz.
	For consumers' goods........ 55 oz.
	155 oz.
	Subtraction from cash balance. 5 oz.

7. Maximizing Income and Allocating Resources

We have seen that, in the money economy, *other things being equal,* men will attempt to attain the highest possible money income: if they are investors, they will try to obtain the largest net return; if they sell their labor service, they will sell it for the largest return. The higher their money income, the more money they will have available for expenditure on consumers' goods. Before we proceed to a deeper analysis of the money economy, it is important to examine the "other things being equal," or the *ceteris paribus,* qualification.

In chapter 1, we examined the truth that in every action, men try to obtain the greatest advantage, i.e., to attain the end located on the highest possible point on their value scale. This was also called attempting to "maximize psychic revenue" or "psychic income." This is a praxeological truth, a general law holding for all human action, with no qualification whatsoever. Now the establishment of indirect exchange, or a money economy, enables every person to obtain a vast number of consumers' goods that he could not obtain, or could barely obtain, in isolation or by way of barter. As we have demonstrated in this chapter, these consumers' goods are acquired by producing and selling a good for the money commodity and then using money to purchase them. Despite this development, however, by no means all goods can be bought and sold on the market. Some goods are attainable in this way; some cannot be. As was explained in chapter 2, some goods cannot be alienated from a person and therefore cannot be exchanged. They cannot come within the money nexus; they cannot be bought or sold for money. This fact does not mean that individuals disparage or revere them on that account. To some people, many of the unexchangeable consumers' goods are very precious and hold a high place on their value scale. To others, these goods mean little, as compared to those consumers' goods that can be bought in exchange. The ranking on his value scale depends entirely on the voluntary choice of each individual. It is nonsense to place the blame on "money" for the tendencies of some people to value exchangeable goods highly as compared to some nonexchangeable goods. There is no force in the existence of the money economy that compels men to make such choices; money simply enables men to expand enormously their acquisition of exchangeable goods. But the existence of the market leaves it to each individual to decide how he will value money and the goods that money will buy, as against other goods that are unexchangeable.

As a matter of fact, the existence of the money economy has the reverse effect. Since, as we know from the law of utility, the marginal utility of a unit of any good diminishes as its supply increases, and the establishment of money leads to an enormous increase in the supply of exchangeable goods, it is evident that this great supply enables men to enjoy unexchangeable goods to a far greater extent than would otherwise be the case. *The very fact that exchangeable consumers' goods are more abundant enables each individual to enjoy more of the nonexchangeable ones.*

There are many possible examples of grading exchangeable and nonexchangeable goods on one's value scale. Suppose that a man owns a piece of land containing an historic monument, which he prizes on aesthetic grounds. Suppose also that he has an offer for sale of the property for a certain sum of money, knowing that the purchaser intends to destroy the monument and use it for other purposes. To decide whether or not to sell the property, he must weigh the value to him of keeping the monument intact as against the value to him of the consumers' goods that he could eventually buy with the money. Which will take precedence depends on the constitution of the individual's value scale at that particular time. But it is evident that a greater abundance of consumers' goods already at his disposal will tend to raise the value of the (unexchangeable) aesthetic good to him as compared with the given sum of money. Contrary, therefore, to the common accusation that the establishment of a money economy tends to lead men to slight the importance of nonexchangeable goods, the effect is precisely the reverse. A destitute person is far less likely to prefer the nonexchangeable to the exchangeable than one whose "standard of living" in terms of the latter is high.[14]

Examples such as these are of great importance for human action, but of little importance for the rest of this volume, which is mainly concerned with analysis of the market under a system of indirect exchange. In this study of money exchanges—the subdivision of praxeology known as *catallactics*—there is not much more that could be said about this problem. Other examples of such choices, however, are more important for catallactics. Consider the case of a man who has three offers for the purchase of his labor services, one of a money income of 30 ounces per month, another of 24 ounces, and a third of 21 ounces. Now—and here we return to the original problem of this section—the man will clearly choose to accept the offer of 30 ounces, *provided* that the psychic, or more precisely, the nonexchangeable, factors are "equal" between the various alternatives. If the man is indifferent to any variations in conditions of work among the three offers, then no factors enter into his choice except money income and leisure, and, if he works at all, he will choose the income of 30 ounces. On the other hand, he may well have great differences in taste for the work itself and the varying conditions; thus, the job earning 30 ounces may be for a firm, or in a type of labor, which he dislikes. Or the job offering 24 ounces may have positive qualities that the man likes a great deal. We have seen in chapter 1 that labor is evaluated on the basis, not only of the monetary return, but also in terms of the individual's liking for or dislike of the work itself. The valuations that a man attaches to the work itself are nonexchangeable positive or negative goods, because they are, for the actor, inseparable attachments to the work itself. They may be weighed against monetary considerations, but they cannot be exchanged away or ignored. Thus, in the above case, along with the prospective money income, the man must weigh the nonexchangeable "consumers' goods" attached to the different jobs in his value scale. What he is weighing, in essence, is two "bundles" of utility: (*a*) the utility of 30 ounces per month plus work in what he considers an immoral trade or in unpleasant surroundings, vs. (*b*) the utility of 24 ounces per month plus work in a job which he likes. The choice will be made in accordance with the value scale of each individual; one man may choose the 30-ounce job, and another may choose the 24-ounce job. The important fact for catallactics is that a man always chooses a bundle of *money income plus other psychic factors* and that he will maximize his money income only if psychic factors are neutral with respect to his choices. If they are not, then these factors must always be kept in view by the economist.

Another similar example is the case of a prospective investor. Suppose that an investor faces the choice of investing his saved money in various alternative production projects. He can, say, invest 100 ounces, with the prospect of earning a net return of 10% in a year, in one project; 8% in a second; and 6% in a third. Other nonexchangeable psychic factors being equal, he will tend to invest in that line where he expects the greatest net money return—in this case, the 10% line. Suppose, however, that he has a great dislike for the product that would offer a 10% return, while he has a great fondness for the process and the product promising the 8% return. Here again, each prospect of investment carries with it a nondetachable positive or negative psychic factor. The pleasure in producing one product as against the distaste for producing another are *nonexchangeable consumers' goods,* positive and negative, which the actor has to weigh in deciding where to make his investment. He will weigh not simply 10% vs. 8%, but "10% plus a disliked production process and product" vs. "8% plus a delightful production process." Which alternative he chooses depends on his individual value scale. Thus, in the case of enterprise as well as in the case of labor, we must say that the entrepreneur will tend to choose the course that maximizes his prospective money income, *provided* that other nonexchangeable factors are neutral with respect to the various alternatives. In all cases whatsoever, of course, each man will move to maximize the *psychic* income on his value scale, on which scale all exchangeable and unexchangeable goods are entered.[15]

In deciding on the course that will maximize his psychic income, man therefore considers all the relevant factors, exchangeable and nonexchangeable. In considering whether to work and at what job, he must also consider the almost universally desired consumers' good, leisure. Suppose that, on the basis of the money return and the nonexchangeable values attached, the laborer in the example given above chooses to work at the 24-ounce job. As he continues to work at the job, the marginal utility of the money wage per unit of time that he earns (whether it be 24 ounces per month or $\frac{1}{4}$ ounce per hour, etc.), will decline. The marginal utility of money income will tend to decline as more money is acquired, since money is a good. In so far as money is desired for a nonmonetary use (such as ornaments) or for use as an addition to one's cash balance (see below for a discussion of the components in the demand for money), addition to its stock will lead to a decline in its marginal utility just as in the case of any other good. In so far as money is desired for the purchase of consumers' goods, an "ounce-worth" of consumers' goods will also decline in utility as new ounces are acquired. The first ounce of money spent on consumers' goods will fulfill the highest-ranking wants on the person's value scale, the next ounce spent the wants ranking second highest, etc. (Of course, this will not be true for a good costing more than one ounce, but this difficulty can be met by increasing the size of the monetary units so that each is homogeneous in what it can buy.) Consequently, the marginal utility of money income tends to decline as the income is increased.

On the other hand, as the input of labor increases, the stock of possible units of leisure declines, and the marginal utility of leisure forgone increases. As was seen in chapter 1, labor will tend to be supplied until the point at which the marginal utility reaped from labor no longer outweighs the marginal utility of leisure on the individual's value scale. In the money economy, labor will cease when the marginal utility of the additional money income per unit of time no longer exceeds the marginal utility of the leisure forgone by working for the additional time.[16]

Thus, man allocates his time between leisure and productive labor, between labor for money and labor on unexchangeable items, etc., in accordance with the principle of maximizing his psychic income. In deciding between labor and leisure, he weighs the marginal advantages of work with the marginal advantages of leisure.

Similarly, man as a prospective investor must weigh, not only the advantages and disadvantages, monetary and otherwise, from each prospective investment, but also whether or not to invest at all. *Every man must allocate his money resources in three and only three ways: in consumption spending, in investment expenditure, and in addition to his cash balance.* Assume that to the investor cited above, the 10% project is highest in utility in his value scale, all factors considered. But then he must decide: Shall he invest at all, or shall he buy consumers' goods now, or add to his cash balance? The marginal advantage of making the investment will be the prospective money return, weighted by the nonexchangeable utilities or disutilities involved. The advantage of a money return will be that he will have more money, in the future, that he could spend on consumers' goods. If he has 100 ounces of money now and invests it, in a year he might have 110 ounces which he could spend on consumers' goods. On the other hand, what chiefly militates against investment, as was explained in chapter 1, is the fact of time preference, the fact that he is giving up possible consumption *in the present*. If we assume that an ounce of money will buy the same quantity of goods as an ounce a year from now (an assumption that will be removed in later chapters), then one ounce of money now will always be worth *more* than one ounce a year from now, simply because enjoyment *of a given good* is always preferred as early as possible. Therefore, in deciding whether or not to invest, he must balance the *additional* return against his desire to consume in the present rather than the future. He must decide: if I value 100 ounces now more than 100 ounces a year from now, do I value 100 ounces now more or less than *110* ounces a year from now? He will decide in accordance with his value scale. Similarly, he must weigh each against the marginal utility of adding to his cash balance (in what this consists will be examined below).

Thus, every unit of the money commodity in a man's stock (his money resources owned) is always being allocated to the three categories of use in accordance with his value scale. The more money that he allocates to consumption, the lower will be the marginal utility of the goods consumed. Each further unit spent will be devoted to less urgently desired goods. And each further unit so spent will decrease his available stock of investment goods and his available cash balance, and therefore will, in accordance with the law of utility, raise the marginal utility forgone in each of these uses. The same will be true for each of the other uses; the more money he spends on each use, the less will be the marginal utility from that use, and the higher will be the marginal utility of other uses forgone. Every man will allocate his money resources on the same principles that the hypothetical actor allocated his stock of horses in chapter 1 above; each unit will be used for the most useful end not yet achieved. It is in accordance with these principles—the maximizing of his psychic income—that each man will allocate his money stock. In accordance with his value scale, each man will judge the respective marginal utilities to be obtained by each monetary unit in each use, and his allocation of money expenditures as revealed in his balance of payments will be determined by such judgments.

Just as, within the general category of investment expenditure, there are different projects with different expected returns, so there are an innumerable variety of consumers' goods within the general category of consumption. On what principles does a man allocate his expenditures among the numerous types of consumers' goods available? On precisely corresponding principles. His first unit of money spent on consumers' goods will be spent on that good satisfying the most highly valued end, the next unit on the next most highly valued end, etc. Each parcel of a con-

sumers' good bought decreases the marginal utility of this good
to the man and increases the marginal utility of all other goods
forgone. Again, a man will allocate his money resources within the
consumption category by apportioning each unit of money to that
good with the highest marginal utility on his value scale. A judgment of relative marginal utilities determines the allocation of
his money expenditures. It is evident that we may eliminate the
words "within the consumption category" in the sentence before
the preceding, to arrive at the rule which governs all a man's
money allocation within and between categories.

Our analysis may now be generalized still further. Each man,
at every point in time, has in his ownership a certain stock of
useful goods, a certain stock of *resources,* or *assets.* These resources
may include not only *money,* but also *consumers' goods, nonpersonal producers' goods* (land and capital goods), *personal energy,*
and *time.* He will allocate *each one* of these resources according
to the same principles by which he has allocated money—so that
each unit goes into the use with the highest prospective marginal utility on his value scale.

Here we must note that the sale of personal labor service is
not always made to an investing "employer" who purchases the
labor service for money and then tries to sell the resulting product. In many cases, the man who invests also works directly in
the production of the product. In some cases, the investor spends
saved funds on factors of production and hires the labor of someone to direct the actual production operation. In other cases, the
investor also spends his labor-time in the details of the production process. It is clear that this is just as much "labor" as the
labor of an employee who does not own and sell the product.

What principles will decide whether a prospective investor uses
his labor in his own investment in production (i.e., will be "self-
employed") or will invest only his money and sell his labor elsewhere as an employee? Clearly, the principle again will be the
best psychic advantage from the action. Thus, suppose that Jones
finds what he considers to be the best and most remunerative investment project, which he estimates will yield him a net money
income of 150 ounces for the forthcoming year, provided that

he does not labor on the project itself, but hires others for its direction and management. He also estimates that, if he were to perform the direction himself instead of hiring a manager to do it, he would be able to net a further income from the project of 50 ounces a year. With his own labor involved, then, the net income from the project will be 200 ounces for the year. This figure will be the higher, the more skilled his direction would be than the man he replaces, and the lower, the less comparatively skilled he is. In this case, the 200-ounce net income would include a 150-ounce investment income and 50 ounces for the labor income of direction. Whether or not he takes this course depends (setting leisure aside) on whether he can sell his labor service for a greater income elsewhere. This "greater income" will, of course, be in terms of psychic income, but, if nonexchangeable factors are assumed in this case to be neutral, then the "greater income" will be the greater money income. If, *ceteris paribus,* Jones can earn 60 ounces as an employee for some other investing producer, then he will take this job and hire someone else to use labor on his investment. His total money income will then be: 150 ounces from the project plus 60 ounces from the sale of his labor services to a producer, totaling 210 ounces. Of course, if nonexchangeable psychic factors countervail, such as a great preference for being self-employed in the use of his labor, then he may accept the 200-ounce income.

It is clear from this discussion that the common concept of the productive laborer, limited to the man who works in the fields or on an assembly line, is completely fallacious. Laborers are all those who expend their labor in the productive process. This labor is expended for a money income (which may be weighted by other psychic factors). If the labor service is sold to an investing employer who owns the final good produced by the co-operating factors, it might be rendered in any required task from that of a ditchdigger to that of a company president. On the other hand, labor income may be the result of the "self-employment" of the investing enterpriser. This type of laborer is also the owner of the final product, and his net monetary return from the sale of the product will include his labor income as well as his return from the money invested. The larger and more complex the enterprise and the production process, the greater will tend to be the development of specialized skill in management, and therefore the less will be the tendency for self-employment by the enterpriser. The smaller the enterprise, and the more direct the production methods, the more likely is self-employment to be the rule.

We have so far specifically treated the principles of allocating labor and money. The other exchangeable resources that a man may possess (and it is the *exchangeable* resources that catallactics is interested in) are consumers' goods and nonpersonal producers' goods (land and capital goods).

The consumers' goods in a man's stock are the *durable* ones. The nondurable goods and services will have disappeared in the process of consuming them. Now, as we have seen in chapter 2, any good may have either *direct use-value* to its owner or *exchange-value* or a mixture of both. At any time, each owner of a consumers' good must judge on his value scale whether its exchange-value or its highest direct use-value is the greater. In the money economy, the problem of exchange-value is simplified, since it will be exchange for *money* that will be especially important. The utility on his value scale of the highest direct use-value will be compared to the utility of the sum of money the good could procure in exchange. Suppose, for example, that Mr. Williams owns a house; he determines that he could sell the house for 200 ounces of gold. Now he judges the ranking of the direct use as against the exchange-value on his value scale. Thus, he might have three alternative direct uses for the house (a) living in it; (b) living in it part of the time and letting his brother live in it part of the time; (c) living in it part of the time, with no participation by his brother, and he may weigh each of these against the exchange-value as follows:

Williams' Value Scale

Ranking

1. Direct Use (a).
2. Exchanging good for 200 ounces of money.
3. Direct Use (b).
4. Direct Use (c).

In this case, Williams will decide to live in the house and not sell it. His decision will be determined solely by his value scale; someone else might rank the exchange above the direct use and therefore sell the house for money.

It is obvious that it is true, without qualification, for any *given good,* that the seller will try to obtain as high a money price for it as possible. The proof of this is analogous to the demonstration given in chapter 2 that the seller of a given good always tries to obtain the highest price, except that here the markets are simplified by being exchanges solely for *money,* and therefore it is the *money price* that is important. *The money income that a man will get from the sale of a good will always equal the money price of the sale times the quantity of units of the good.* Thus, if he sells one house at a money price of 200 ounces per house, his total money income from the good will be 200 ounces. His desire to sell at the highest price does not, of course, mean that he will *always* sell at that price. The highest money price for a good may still be lower than the psychic value of direct use to him, as was the case with Williams. It is possible, however, that if the money price for selling the house rose to 250 ounces, the exchange-value of the house would have ranked higher than Direct Use (*a*), and he would have sold the house.

It is clear that, if the owner of the consumers' good is also the original producer, the direct use-value to him will be almost nil. The specialized producer who produces and owns houses or television sets or washing machines finds that the direct use-value to him of this stock is practically nonexistent. For him, the exchange-value is the only important factor, and his interest lies *solely* in maximizing his money income from the stock and therefore in attaining the highest money prices in the sale of each good. The nonexchangeable factors that might loom large to the prospective investor or laborer in a certain line of production will be negligible to the producer who already has a stock of goods, since he had already taken the nonexchangeable factors into account when he made his original investment or his original choice of occupation. Thus, to the producer of a consumers' good, the way to maximize his psychic income from this revenue is to obtain the highest possible money price from its sale.

When will an owner sell the good, and when will he rent out its services? Clearly, he will take the course that he believes will yield him the highest money income, or, more precisely, the highest present value of money income.

What of the owner of a stock *of nonpersonal producers' goods?* How will he allocate these goods to attain the highest psychic income? In the first place, it is clear that, by definition, producers' goods can have no direct use-value to him as consumers' goods. But they may well have direct use-value *as producers' goods,* i.e., as factors of production in the making of a product further along in the process of being transformed into consumers' goods. For any given stock of a producers' good, or for any unit of that stock, there might be an exchange-value, a value in use for transformation into another product that would then have exchange-value, or both. It is also true for the owner of producers' goods that nonexchangeable factors will generally play a negligible role. The fact that he has already invested and perhaps worked in producing or purchasing these goods signifies that he has already accounted for the possible positive or negative psychic values in the work itself. Furthermore, in the economy of indirect exchange, it is only exchange of goods produced for money that is important, as there will be very little scope for barter. The owner of producers' goods is therefore interested in judging whether the goods will yield a higher money income from exchanging them directly for money or from transforming them via production into a product of "lower-order," and then selling the product for money.

As an example of the choices facing the owner of producers' goods, let us take Robertson. Robertson has invested in, and therefore owns, the following factors:

10 units of Producers' Good X
5 units of Producers' Good Y
6 units of Producers' Good Z

He knows, because of his technological knowledge, that he can transform these units of co-operating factors X, Y, and Z, into

10 units of a final product *P*. (The various "units," of course, are purely physical units of the various goods and are therefore completely incommensurable with one another.) He estimates that he will be able to sell these units of *P* for 15 ounces each, a total money income of *150 ounces.*

On the other hand, he sees that he could sell (or resell) the factors directly for money, without himself transforming them into *P*, as follows:

10 units of *X* @ 6 oz. of gold per unit (the money
    price of *X*) a money income from stock
    of *X* of   *60 ounces*
 5 units of *Y* @ 9 oz. per unit, a money income of *45 ounces*
 6 units of *Z* @ 4 oz. per unit, a money income of *24 ounces*

His total money income from the sale of the stock of each producers' good separately and directly is *129 ounces.* However, Robertson must also consider the money expenditures that he would have to make in buying labor services to help in this transformation. In a free economy, he cannot own a stock of laborers. If his expenditure on labor service is less than *21 ounces,* then it will pay him to transform the factors and sell the product *P* for 150 ounces; if the required expenditures on labor-service are more than 21 ounces, then it will pay him to sell the producers' goods directly for money.

In each one of these prospective sales, of course, it is to the owner's interest to be able to sell at the highest possible price, thus yielding the highest money income from each good.

Suppose, now, that Robertson had decided to go ahead with the production and that he now has in his stock 10 units of *P*. There is no prospect of his immediately going into the business that would make use of *P* as a factor in making another product. Therefore, there is only one alternative left to this owner—to sell the product for money, for the highest price that he can acquire. However, in those cases where *P* is durable, he still has the option of holding off the sale if he believes that its money price in the future will be higher, and provided that the higher price will cover the disadvantage to him of waiting (his time preference) and the expenses of storing *P* until the sale is made.

The owner of a producers' good, whether a product to him or a factor, may rent it out if he does not sell the entire good. In order for this to be feasible, of course, the good would have to be relatively durable. Here again, as in the case of a consumers' good, the owner will decide on outright sale of the good or hiring out of its services over a period of time in accordance with his judgment of which alternative will yield him the highest money income (precisely, the highest present value).

We have thus analyzed the actions of an owner of a stock of consumers' goods or of producers' goods in attempting to attain his most highly valued ends, i.e., to maximize his psychic income. Nonexchangeable factors for him will generally be negligible in importance, since they had already been discounted when the investment in them was made. If we set aside the value of the durable consumers' good in direct use for some owners, the aim of the owners will be to maximize their money income from the stock of the good. Since money income from sale of a good is the money price of the good multiplied by the quantity sold, this means that the sellers will try to attain the highest money price for their stock.

At this point we may, at least briefly, begin to answer the question which we did not have the information to answer in chapter 2: Granted the behavior of the owner of a given stock, what determines the *size* of that stock of goods? Now obviously, except in the case of personal energy, these goods must have been *previously produced by someone* (or previously found and transformed in the case of pure nature-given factors). This previous production was undertaken either by the present owner or by someone in the past, from whom he had acquired, by exchange or gift, this stock of goods. The past investment must have been made for the reason that we saw above: the expectation of a future money return from the investment, compensating for the sacrifice of waiting to consume in the future instead of the present. This previous investor expected that he would be able to sell the good for a money income greater than the money expenditures that he had to make on the factors of its production. As an example, let us take Robertson with a stock of ten units of *P*. How did he acquire this stock? By investing money in buying factors of its production, and then producing it, in the hope of making a certain net money income, i.e., in the expectation that the money income from the sale of *P* would be greater by a certain amount than the money expenditures invested in the various factors. Now how did the previously produced stock of the factors *X*, *Y*, and *Z* come into existence? By the same process. Various investors engaged in the production of these factors in the expectation of a net money income from the investment (total money income from the investment greater than total money expenditures). This investment decision accounts for the existence of all the stock of all producers' goods and durable consumers' goods for any community at any given point in time. In addition, the stock of pure nature-given factors was acquired through the owner's or some previous person's finding and using previously unused factors in a production process. The stock of the money commodity was, like that of the consumers' and producers' goods, the result of an investment decision by an investing producer, who expected his money income to be higher than his money expenditure. On the other hand, the stock of *personal energy* owned by any person is inherent in his nature as a human being.

We have thus analyzed each type of exchangeable resource that a person may have, what governs his use of them in order to maximize his psychic income, and to what extent such maximization involves attempted maximization of money income from the resource. In analyzing the determinants of the money income from any sale, we have seen that they are the quantity and the money price, and we have just seen how the quantities involved in the "given stock" of any good can be accounted for. What yet remains unaccounted for is the money prices. All we know about them so far is that the *seller* of any good—consumers' or producers' good or labor service—wishes to sell it for as *high a money price as possible*. Nonexchangeable goods on the owner's value scale may modify this rule, but generally these modifications will be important only for sellers of labor services.

We have so far been considering man as the allocator, or seller, of a given good. What of man as a *buyer* of a good? (And here we recall the discussion in the early parts of this chapter.) As a buyer, he uses money for investment expenditures and for consumption expenditures. In our discussion of an individual's consumption expenditures, we saw that he decided on them upon considering a "unit's worth" of goods. But what determines what his unit's worth shall be? What is an ounce of money's worth of eggs, or hats, or butter, etc.? This can be determined only by the *money price* that the buyer would have to pay for the good. If a man can buy eggs at $\frac{1}{10}$ of an ounce per dozen, then one ounce's worth of eggs is 10 dozen. Now it is obvious that man, in his capacity as a buyer of consumers' goods with money, will seek to buy each particular good at the *lowest money price possible*. For a man who owns money and seeks to buy consumers' goods, it is clear that the lower the money prices of the goods he seeks to buy, the *greater is his psychic income;* for the more goods he can buy, the more uses he can make with the same amount of his money. The buyer will therefore seek the lowest money prices for the goods he buys.

Thus, *ceteris paribus,* the psychic income of man as a seller for money is maximized by selling the good at the highest money price obtainable; the psychic income of man as a buyer with money is maximized by buying the good for the lowest money price obtainable.

Let us now sum up the results of the analysis of this chapter. We have seen how the common medium of exchange emerges in the market out of direct exchange; we have noted the pattern of exchanges with and for money in an economy of indirect exchange; we have described how each individual has a pattern of money income and money expenditures. Then, we investigated what is involved in the maximization of psychic income in a money economy, how this principle governs the actions of people in their various functions—as owners of different types of resources and as laborers or investors. We have seen to what extent such pursuit after the most highly valued ends involves the maximization of money income in the various cases, and to what extent it does not. We have just concluded that such maximization of psychic income always leads the seller of a good to seek the highest money price for it, and the buyer of a good to seek the lowest money price, with such exceptions as the laborer who spurns a higher money price for his labor because of the nonexchangeable conditions attached to the work, or the investor who spurns a greater prospective income for a line of production that he prefers for its own sake. These exceptions aside, pursuit of the rule: "Buy on the cheapest market and sell on the dearest" leads to satisfaction of the most highly valued ends for each individual, both as a consumer and as a producer.

Although we know that man tries to maximize his psychic income, and therefore his money income, *ceteris paribus,* we still do not know on what basis the money income that he does acquire is determined. We know that the nonexchangeable values are simply determined by the value scales of each individual. But though we know that, *ceteris paribus,* a man will sell a service or a good for a greater rather than a lesser money price and income, we do not yet know what makes the money prices what they are. What determines the money prices of consumers' goods, of labor services, of capital goods, of nature-given factors? What determines the money price of the entire durable good and the money price of the "hired-out" services? And, with the enormous importance of investment as the determinant of the given stock of every good, what determines the spread between gross money income from goods and the money expenditures on the factors needed to produce them? It is only the anticipation of this spread between money income from the sale of the product, and money expenditure on factors, that brings about investment and production. And what, if any, are the relations that tend to be established among the various prices?

To put it differently, all human action uses scarce resources to attempt to arrive at the most highly valued of not-yet-attained ends, i.e., to maximize psychic income. We have seen how this is done by individuals in isolation and by individuals in direct exchange—although these can exist only to a drastically limited extent. We have seen how it is done, on an immensely greater scale, in the money economy; and we have seen that the specific components of psychic maximization in the money economy are, ultimately, nonexchangeable values, quantities of goods in stock, and the money prices that these goods can exchange for on the market. We have explained the operations of the nonexchangeable values, and we have very briefly indicated how the quantity of the given stock of each good is determined. We have now to investigate the classic problem in the analysis of indirect exchange: *the determination of money prices*. The analysis of money prices, moreover, will enable investigation into the reasons for, and the determinants of, the "spread" between expected gross money income from sales and the expenditure on factors, which induces people to invest in the production of stock.

4

Prices and Consumption

1. *Money Prices*

We have seen the enormous importance of the money prices of goods in an economy of indirect exchange. The money income of the producer or laborer and the psychic income of the consumer depend on the configuration of these prices. How are they determined? In this investigation, we may draw extensively from almost all of the discussion in chapter 2 above. There we saw how the prices of one good in terms of others are determined under conditions of direct exchange. The reason for devoting so much consideration to a state of affairs that can have only a very limited existence was that a similar analysis can be applied to conditions of indirect exchange.

In a society of barter, the *markets* that established prices (assuming that the system could operate) were innumerable markets of one good for every other good. With the establishment of a money economy, the *number* of markets needed is immeasurably reduced. A large variety of goods exchange against the money commodity, and the money commodity exchanges for a large variety of goods. Every single market, then (with the exception of isolated instances of barter) includes the money commodity as one of the two elements.

Aside from loans and claims (which will be considered below), the following types of exchange are made against money:

Old Consumer Goods   against Money
New Consumer Goods
    and Services   against Money
Capital Goods   against Money
Labor Services   against Money
Land Factors   against Money

For durable goods, each unit may be sold *in toto,* or it may be hired out for its services over a certain period of time.

Now we remember from chapter 2 that the price of one good in terms of another is the amount of the other good divided by the amount of the first good in the exchange. If, in a certain exchange, 150 barrels of fish exchanged for 3 horses, then the price of horses in terms of fish, the "fish-price of horses," was 50 barrels of fish per horse in that exchange. Now suppose that, in a money economy, 3 horses exchange for 15 ounces of gold (money). The *money price* of horses in this exchange is *5 ounces per horse.* The money price of a good in an exchange, therefore, is the quantity of units of gold, divided by the quantity of units of the good, yielding a numerical ratio.

To illustrate how money prices may be computed for any exchange, suppose that the following exchanges are made:

15 ounces of gold for 3 horses
 5 ounces of gold for 100 barrels of fish
$\frac{1}{8}$ ounces of gold for 2 dozen eggs
24 ounces of gold for 3 hours of X's labor

The money prices of these various exchanges were:

$$\frac{15 \text{ oz.}}{3 \text{ horses}} = \frac{5 \text{ oz.}}{1 \text{ horse}}$$

$$\frac{5 \text{ oz.}}{100 \text{ bbls. of fish}} = \frac{1 \text{ oz.}}{20 \text{ bbls. of fish}} = \frac{\frac{1}{20} \text{ oz.}}{1 \text{ bbl. of fish}}$$

$$\frac{\frac{1}{8} \text{ oz.}}{2 \text{ doz. eggs}} = \frac{\frac{1}{16} \text{ oz.}}{1 \text{ doz. eggs}}$$

$$\frac{24 \text{ oz.}}{8 \text{ hrs. of } X\text{'s labor}} = \frac{3 \text{ oz.}}{1 \text{ hr. of } X\text{'s labor}}$$

The last ratios on each line are the money prices of the units of each good for each exchange.

It is evident that, with money being used for all exchanges, money prices serve as a *common denominator* of all exchange ratios. Thus, with the above money prices, anyone can calculate that if 1 horse exchanges for 5 ounces, and 1 barrel of fish exchanges for $\frac{1}{20}$ ounces, then 1 horse can, indirectly, exchange for 100 barrels of fish, or for 80 dozen eggs, or $\frac{5}{3}$ of an hour of X's labor, etc. Instead of a myriad of isolated markets for each good and every other good, each good exchanges for money, and the exchange ratios between every good and every other good can easily be estimated by observing their money prices. Here it must be emphasized that these exchange ratios are only hypothetical, and can be computed at all only because of the exchanges against money. It is only through the use of money that we can hypothetically estimate these "barter ratios," and it is only by intermediate exchanges against money that one good can finally be exchanged for the other at the hypothetical ratio.[1] Many writers have erred in believing that money can somehow be abstracted from the formation of money prices and that analysis can accurately describe affairs "as if" exchanges really took place by way of barter. With money and money prices pervading all exchanges, there can be no abstraction from money in analyzing the formation of prices in an economy of indirect exchange.

Just as in the case of direct exchange, there will always be a tendency on the market for *one money price to be established for each good.* We have seen that the basic rule is that each seller tries to sell his good for the highest attainable money price, and each buyer tries to buy the good for the lowest attainable money price. The actions of the buyers and sellers will always and rapidly tend to establish one price on the market at any given time. If the "ruling" market price for 100 barrels of fish, for example, is 5 ounces—i.e., if sellers and buyers believe that they can sell and buy the fish they desire for 5 ounces per 100 barrels—then no buyer will pay 6 ounces, and no seller will accept 4 ounces for the fish. Such action will obtain for all goods on the market, establishing the rule that, for the entire market society, every homogeneous good will tend to be bought and sold at one particular money price at any given time.

What, then, are the forces that determine at what point this uniform money price for each good tends to be set? We shall soon see that, as demonstrated in chapter 2, the determinants are the individual value scales, expressed through demand and supply schedules.

We must remember that, in the course of determining the "fish-price of horses" in the direct exchange of fish as against horses, at the same time there was also determined the "horse-price of fish." In the exchanges of a money economy, what is the "goods-price of money" and how is it determined?

Let us consider the foregoing list of typical exchanges against money. These exchanges established the money prices of four different goods on the market. Now let us reverse the process and divide the quantities of goods by the quantity of money in the exchange. This gives us:

$$\frac{\text{$\frac{1}{5}$ horse}}{\text{1 oz.}} \; ; \; \frac{\text{20 bbls. of fish}}{\text{1 oz.}} \; ; \; \frac{\text{16 doz. eggs}}{\text{1 oz.}} \; ; \; \frac{\text{$\frac{1}{3}$ hr. of X's labor}}{\text{1 oz.}}$$

This sort of list, or "array," goes on and on for each of the myriad exchanges of goods against money. *The inverse of the money price of any good gives us the "goods-price" of money in terms of that particular good.* Money, in a sense, is the only good that remains, as far as its prices are concerned, in the same state that every good was in a regime of barter. In barter, every good had only its ruling market price in terms of *every other good:* fish-price of eggs, horse-price of movies, etc. In a money economy, every good except money now has *one* market price in terms of money. Money, on the other hand, still has an almost infinite *array* of "goods-prices" that establish the "goods-price of money." The entire array, considered together, yields us the general "goods-price of money." For if we consider the whole array of goods-prices, we know what one ounce of money will buy in terms of any desired combination of goods, i.e., we know what that "ounce's worth" of money (which figures so largely in consumers' decisions) will be.

Alternatively, we may say that the money price of any good discloses what its "purchasing power" on the market will be. Suppose that a man possesses 200 barrels of fish. He estimates that the ruling market price for fish is 6 ounces per 100 barrels, and that therefore he can sell the 200 barrels for 12 ounces. The "purchasing power" of 100 barrels on the market is 6 ounces of money. Similarly, the purchasing power of a horse may be 5 ounces, etc. *The purchasing power of a stock of any good is equal to the amount of money it can "buy" on the market* and is therefore directly determined by the money price that it can obtain. As a matter of fact, *the purchasing power of a unit of any quantity of a good is equal to its money price.* If the market money price of a dozen eggs (the unit) is ⅛ of an ounce of gold, then the purchasing power of the dozen eggs is also ⅛ of an ounce. Similarly, the purchasing power of a horse, above, was 5 ounces; of an hour of *X*'s labor 3 ounces; etc.

For every good except money, then, the purchasing power of its unit is identical with the money price that it can obtain on the market. *What is the purchasing power of the monetary unit?* Obviously, the purchasing power of, e.g., an ounce of gold can be considered only in relation to *all* the goods that the ounce could purchase or help to purchase. *The purchasing power of the monetary unit consists of an array of all the particular goods-prices in the society in terms of the unit.*[2] It consists of a huge array of the type above: ⅕ horse per ounce; 20 barrels of fish per ounce; 16 dozen eggs per ounce; etc.

It is evident that the money commodity and the determinants of its purchasing power introduce a complication in the demand and supply schedules of chapter 2 that must be worked out; there cannot be a mere duplication of the demand and supply schedules of barter conditions, since the demand and supply situation for money is a unique one. Before investigating the "price" of money and its determinants, we must first take a long detour and investigate the determination of the money prices of all the other goods in the economy.

2. Determination of Money Prices

Let us first take a typical good and analyze the determinants of its money price on the market. (Here the reader is referred back to the more detailed analysis of price in chapter 2.) Let us take a homogeneous good, Grade A butter, in exchange against money.

The money price is determined by actions decided according to individual value scales. For example, a typical buyer's value scale may be ranked as follows:

> —7 grains of gold
> —(1st pound of butter)
> —6 grains of gold
> —5 grains of gold
> —(2nd pound of butter)
> —4 grains of gold
> —3 grains of gold
> —(3rd pound of butter)
> —2 grains of gold

The quantities in parentheses are those which the person does not possess but is considering adding to his ownership; the others are those which he has in his possession. In this case, the buyer's *maximum buying money price* for his first pound of butter is 6 grains of gold. At any market price of 6 grains or under, he will exchange these grains for the butter; at a market price of 7 grains or over, he will not make the purchase. His maximum buying price for a second pound of butter will be considerably lower. This result is always true, and stems from the law of utility; as he adds pounds of butter to his ownership, the marginal utility of each pound declines. On the other hand, as he dispenses with grains of gold, the marginal utility to him of each remaining grain increases. Both these forces impel the maximum buying price of an additional unit to decline with an increase in the quantity purchased.[3] From this value scale, we can compile this buyer's *demand schedule*, the amount of each good that he will consume at each hypothetical money price on the market. We may also draw his demand curve, if we wish to see the schedule in graphic form. The individual demand schedule of the buyer considered above is as shown in Table 6.

TABLE 6

MARKET PRICE	QUANTITY DEMANDED (PURCHASED)
Grains of gold per pound of butter	Pounds of butter
8	0
7	0
6	1
5	1
4	2
3	2
2	3
1	3

We note that, because of the law of utility, an individual demand curve must be either "vertical" as the hypothetical price declines, or else rightward-sloping (i.e., the quantity demanded, as the money price falls, must be either the same or greater), not leftward-sloping (not a lower quantity demanded).

If this is the necessary configuration of every buyer's demand schedule, it is clear that the existence of more than one buyer will tend greatly to *reinforce* this behavior. There are two and only two possible classifications of different people's value scales: either they are all identical, or else they differ. In the extremely unlikely case that everyone's relevant value scales are identical with everyone else's (extremely unlikely because of the immense variety of valuations by human beings), then, for example, buyers B, C, D, etc. will have the same value scale and therefore the same individual demand schedules as buyer A who has just been described. In that case, the shape of the aggregate market-demand curve (the sum of the demand curves of the individual buyers) will be identical with the curve of buyer A, although the aggregate quantities will, of course, be much greater. To be sure, the value scales of the buyers will almost always differ, which means that their maximum buying prices for any given pound of butter will differ. The result is that, as the market price is lowered, more and more buyers of different units are brought into the market. This effect greatly reinforces the rightward-sloping feature of the market-demand curve.

As an example of the formation of a market-demand schedule from individual value scales, let us take the buyer described above as buyer A and assume two other buyers on the market, B and C, with the following value scales:

Buyer B	*Buyer C*
┌─6 grains	┌─5 grains
├─(1st lb. of butter)	├─4 grains
├─5 grains	├─(1st lb. of butter)
├─(2nd lb. of butter)	├─3 grains
├─4 grains	├─(2nd lb. of butter)
├─3 grains	├─(3rd lb. of butter)
├─2 grains	├─2 grains
├─(3rd lb. of butter)	├─(4th lb. of butter)
├─(4th lb. of butter)	├─(5th lb. of butter)
└─1 grain	└─1 grain

From these value scales, we can construct their individual demand schedules (Table 7).

TABLE 7

Buyer B		Buyer C	
PRICE Grains/lb.	QUANTITY DEMANDED lbs. butter	PRICE Grains/lb.	QUANTITY DEMANDED lbs. butter
7	0	5	0
6	0	4	0
5	1	3	1
4	2	2	3
3	2	1	5
2	2		
1	4		

We notice that, in each of the varied patterns of individual demand schedules, none can ever be leftward-sloping as the hypothetical price declines.

Now we may summate the individual demand schedules, A, B, and C, into the *market-demand schedule*. The market-demand schedule yields the total quantity of the good that will be bought by all the buyers on the market at any given money price for the good. The market-demand schedule for buyers A, B, and C is as shown in Table 8.

TABLE 8

AGGREGATE MARKET-DEMAND SCHEDULE

PRICE	QUANTITY DEMANDED
8	0
7	0
6	1
5	2
4	4
3	5
2	8
1	12

Fig. 33 is a graphical representation of these schedules and their addition to form the market-demand schedule.

The principles of the formation of the market-supply schedule are similar, although the causal forces behind the value scales will differ.[4] Each supplier ranks each unit to be sold and the amount of money to be obtained in exchange on his value scale. Thus, one seller's value scale might be as follows:

Seller X

—(7 grains)
—(6 grains)
—6th lb. of butter
—(5 grains)
—5th lb. of butter
—4th lb. of butter
—(4 grains)
—3rd lb. of butter
—(3 grains)
—2nd lb. of butter
—1st lb. of butter
—(2 grains)
—(1 grain)

If the market price were 2 grains of gold, this seller would sell no butter, since even the first pound in his stock ranks above the acquisition of 2 grains on his value scale. At a price of 3 grains, he would sell 2 pounds, each of which ranks below 3 grains on his value scale. At a price of 4 grains, he would sell three

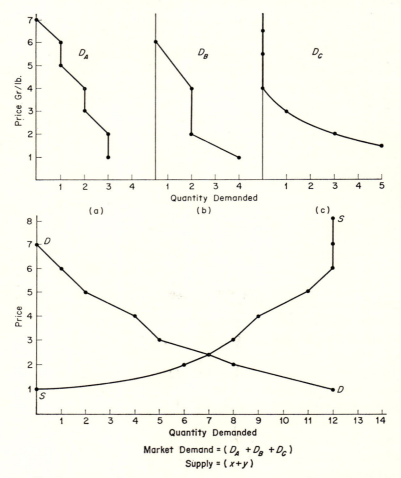

Fig. 33.   Effect of Adding Market-Demand and Market-Supply Schedules

pounds, etc. It is evident that, as the hypothetical price is lowered, the individual supply curve must be either vertical or leftward-sloping, i.e., a lower price must lead either to a lesser or to the same supply, never to more. This is, of course, equivalent to the statement that as the hypothetical price *increases,* the supply curve is either vertical or rightward-sloping. Again, the reason is the law of utility; as the seller disposes of his stock, its marginal utility to him tends to rise, while the marginal utility of the money acquired tends to fall. Of course, if the marginal utility of the stock to the supplier is nil, and if the marginal utility of money to him falls only slowly as he acquires it, the law may not change his quantity supplied during the range of action on the market, so that the supply curve may be vertical throughout almost all of its range. Thus, a supplier *Y* might have the following value scale:

Seller Y

—(6 grains)
—(5 grains)
—(4 grains)
—(3 grains)
—(2 grains)
—6th lb. of butter
—5th lb. of butter
—4th lb. of butter
—3rd lb. of butter
—2nd lb. of butter
—1st lb. of butter
—(1 grain)

This seller will be willing to sell, above the minimum price of 1 grain, every unit in his stock. His supply curve will be shaped as in Fig. 34.

In seller *X's* case, his minimum selling price was 3 grains for the first and second pounds of butter, 4 grains for the third pound, 5 grains for the fourth and fifth pounds, and 6 grains for the sixth pound. Seller *Y's* minimum selling price for the first pound and for every subsequent pound was 1 grain. In no case, however, can the supply

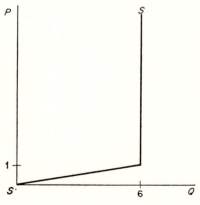

Fig. 34. Seller Y's Supply Curve

curve be rightward-sloping as the price declines; i.e., in no case can a lower price lead to more units supplied.

Let us assume, for purposes of exposition, that the suppliers of butter on the market consist of just these two, *X* and *Y*, with the foregoing value scales. Then their individual and aggregate market-supply schedules will be as shown in Table 9.

TABLE 9

	QUANTITY SUPPLIED		
Price	*X*	*Y*	Market
8.	6	6	12
7.	6	6	12
6.	6	6	12
5.	5	6	11
4.	3	6	9
3.	2	6	8
2.	0	6	6
1.	0	0	0

This market-supply curve is diagramed above in Fig. 33.

We notice that the *intersection* of the market-supply and market-demand curves, i.e., the price at which the quantity supplied and the quantity demanded are equal, here is located at a point *in between* two prices. This is necessarily due to the lack of *divisibility* of the units; if a unit grain, for example, is indivisible, there is no way of introducing an intermediate price, and the *market-equilibrium price* will be at *either* 2 or 3 grains. This will be the best approximation that can be made to a price at which the market will be *precisely* cleared, i.e., one at which the would-be suppliers and the demanders at that price are satisfied. Let us, however, assume that the monetary unit can be further divided, and therefore that the equilibrium price is, say, 2½ grains. Not only will this simplify the exposition of price formation; it is also a realistic assumption, since one of the important characteristics of the money commodity is precisely its *divisibility* into minute units, which can be exchanged on the market. It is this divisibility of the monetary unit that permits us to draw continuous lines between the points on the supply and demand schedules.

The money price on the market will tend to be set at the equilibrium price—in this case, at 2½ grains. At a higher price, the quantity offered in supply will be greater than the quantity demanded; as a result, part of the supply could not be sold, and the sellers will underbid the price in order to sell their stock. Since only one price can persist on the market, and the buyers always seek their best advantage, the result will be a general lowering of the price toward the equilibrium point. On the other hand, if the price is below 2½ grains, there are would-be buyers at this price whose demands remain unsatisfied. These demanders bid up the price, and with sellers looking for the highest attainable price, the market price is raised toward the equilibrium point. Thus, the fact that men seek their greatest utility sets forces into motion that establish the money price at a certain equilibrium point, at which further exchanges tend to be made. The money price will remain at the equilibrium point for further exchanges of the good, *until* demand or supply schedules change. Changes in demand or supply conditions establish a new equilibrium price, toward which the market price again tends to move.

What the equilibrium price will be depends upon the configuration of the supply and demand schedules, and the causes of these schedules will be subjected to further examination below.

The stock of any good is the total quantity of that good in existence. Some will be supplied in exchange, and the remainder will be *reserved*. At any hypothetical price, it will be recalled, adding the demand to buy and the *reserved* demand of the supplier gives the *total demand to hold* on the part of both groups.[5] The total demand to hold includes the demand in exchange by present nonowners and the reservation demand to hold by the present owners. Since the supply curve is either vertical or increasing with a rise in price, the sellers' reservation demand will fall with a rise in price or will be nonexistent. In either case, the total demand to hold rises as the price falls.

Where there is a rise in reservation demand, the increase in

the total demand to hold is greater—the curve far more elastic—
than the regular demand curve, because of the addition of the
reservation-demand component.[6] Thus, the higher the market
price of a stock, the less the willingness on the market to hold
and own it and the greater the eagerness to sell it. Conversely,
the lower the price of a good on the market, the greater the
willingness to own it and the less the willingness to sell it.

It is characteristic of the total demand curve that it *always*
intersects the physical stock available at the same equilibrium
price as the one at which the demand and supply schedules intersect. The Total Demand and Stock lines will therefore yield
the same market equilibrium price as the other, although the
quantity exchanged is not revealed by these curves. They do
disclose, however, that, since all units of an existing stock must
be possessed by someone, the market price of any good tends to
be such that the aggregate demand to keep the stock will equal
the stock itself. Then the stock will be in the hands of the most
eager, or most capable, possessors. These are the ones who are
willing to demand the most for the stock. That owner who would
just sell his stock if the price rose slightly is the *marginal possessor:*
that nonowner who would buy if the price fell slightly is the
marginal nonpossessor.[7]

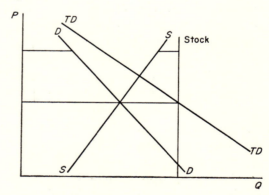

FIG. 35. SUPPLY, DEMAND, TOTAL DEMAND, AND STOCK CURVES

Fig. 35 is a diagram of the supply, demand, total demand,
and stock curves of a good.

The total demand curve is composed of demand plus reserved supply; both slope rightward as prices fall. The equilibrium price is the same both for the intersection of the S and D curves, and for TD and Stock.

If there is no reservation demand, then the supply curve will be vertical, and equal to the stock. In that case, the diagram becomes as in Fig. 36.

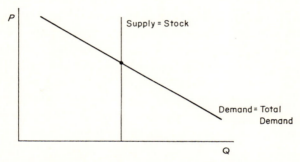

FIG. 36. EFFECT OF THE ABSENCE OF RESERVATION DEMAND

3. Determination of Supply and Demand Schedules

Every money price of a good on the market, therefore, is determined by the supply and demand schedules of the individual buyers and sellers, and their action tends to establish a uniform equilibrium price on the market at the point of intersection, which changes only when the schedules do.[8] Now the question arises: What are the determinants of the demand and supply schedules themselves? Can any conclusions be formed about the value scales and the resulting schedules?

In the first place, the analysis of speculation in chapter 2 can be applied directly to the case of the money price. There is no need to repeat that analysis here.[9] Suffice it to say, in summary, that, in so far as the equilibrium price is anticipated correctly by speculators, the demand and supply schedules will reflect the fact: above the equilibrium price, demanders will buy less than they otherwise would because of their anticipation of a later drop in the money price; below that price, they will buy more because of an anticipation of a rise in the money price. Similarly, sellers will sell more at a price that they anticipate will soon be lowered; they will sell less at a price that they anticipate will soon be raised. The general effect of speculation is to make both the supply and demand curves more elastic, viz., to shift them from *DD* to *D'D'* and from *SS* to *S'S'* in Fig. 37. The more people engage in such (correct) speculation, the more elastic will be the

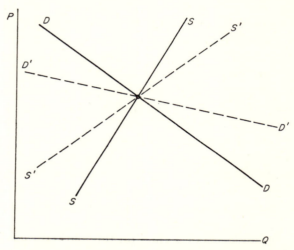

FIG. 37.   EFFECT OF SPECULATION ON SUPPLY AND DEMAND CURVES

curves, and, by implication, the more rapidly will the equilibrium price be reached.

We also saw that preponderant errors in speculation tend inexorably to be self-correcting. If the speculative demand and supply schedules (*D'D'—S'S'*) preponderantly do not estimate the correct equilibrium price and consequently intersect at another price, then it soon becomes evident that that price does not really clear the market. Unless the equilibrium point set by the speculative schedules is identical with the point set by the schedules minus the speculative elements, the market again tends to bring the price (and quantity sold) to the true equilibrium point. For if the speculative schedules set the price of eggs at 2 grains, and the schedules without speculation would set it at 3 grains, there is an excess of quantity demanded over quantity supplied at 2 grains, and the bidding of buyers finally brings the price to 3 grains.[10]

Setting speculation aside, then, let us return to the buyer's demand schedules. Suppose that he ranks the unit of a good above a certain number of ounces of gold on his value scale. What can be the possible *sources* of his *demand for the good?* In other words, what can be the sources of the utility of the good to him? There are three and only three sources of utility that any purchase good can have for any person.[11] One of these is (*a*) the *anticipated later sale* of the same good for a higher money price. This is the speculative demand, basically ephemeral—a useful path to uncovering the more fundamental demand factors. This demand has just been analyzed. The second source of demand is (*b*) direct use as a consumers' good; the third source of demand is (*c*) direct use as a producers' good. Source (*b*) can apply only to consumers' goods; (*c*) to producers' goods. The former are directly consumed; the latter are used in the production process and, along with other co-operating factors, are transformed into lower-order capital goods, which are then sold for money. Thus, the third source applies solely to the investing producers in their purchases of producers' goods; the second source stems from consumers. If we set aside the temporary speculative source, (*b*) is the source of the individual demand schedules for all consumers' goods, (*c*) the source of demands for all producers' goods.

What of the *seller* of the consumers' good or producers' good —why is he demanding money in exchange? The seller demands money because of the marginal utility of money to him, and for this reason he ranks the money acquired above possession of the goods that he sells. The components and determinants of the utility of money will be analyzed in a later section.

Thus, the buyer of a good demands it because of its direct use-value either in consumption or in production; the seller demands money because of its marginal utility in exchange. This, however, does not exhaust the description of the components of the market supply and demand curves, for we have still not explained the rankings of the good on the seller's value scale and the rankings of money on the buyer's. When a seller keeps his stock instead of selling it, what is the source of his *reservation demand* for the good? We have seen that the quantity of a good reserved at any point is the quantity of stock that the seller refuses to sell at the given price. The sources of a reservation demand by the seller are two: (*a*) anticipation of later sale at a higher price; this is the speculative factor analyzed above; and (*b*) direct use of the good by the seller. This second factor is not often applicable to producers' goods, since the seller produced the producers' good for sale and is usually not immediately prepared to use it directly in further production. In some cases, however, this alternative of direct use for further production does exist. For example, a producer of crude oil may sell it or, if the money price falls below a certain minimum, may use it in his own plant to produce gasoline. In the case of consumers' goods, which we are treating here, direct use may also be feasible, particularly in the case of a sale of an old consumers' good previously used directly by the seller—such as an old house, painting, etc. However, with the great development of specialization in the money economy, these cases become infrequent.

If we set aside (*a*) as being a temporary factor and realize that (*b*) is frequently not present in the case of either consumers' or producers' goods, it becomes evident that many market-supply curves will tend to assume an almost vertical shape. In such a case, *after* the investment in production has been made and the stock of goods is on hand, the producer is often willing to sell it at any money price that he can obtain, regardless of how low the market price may be. This, of course, is by no means the same as saying that *investment in further production* will be made if the seller *anticipates* a very low money price from the sale of the product. In the latter case, the problem is to determine how much to invest *at present* in the production of a good to be produced and sold at a point *in the future*. In the case of the market-supply curve, which helps set the day-to-day equilibrium price, we are dealing with already given stock and with the reservation demand for this stock. In the case of production, on the other hand, we are dealing with investment decisions concerning how much stock to produce for some later period. What we have been discussing has been the market-supply curve. Here the seller's problem is *what to do with given stock,* with already produced goods. The problem of production will be treated in chapter 5 and subsequent chapters.

Another condition that might obtain on the market is a previous buyer's re-entering the market and reselling a good. For him to be able to do so, it is obvious that the good must be *durable.* (A violin-playing service, for example, is so nondurable that it is not resalable by the purchasing listeners.) The total stock of the good in existence will then equal the producers' new supply *plus* the producers' reserved demand *plus* the supply offered by old possessors *plus* the reserved demand of the old possessors (i.e., the amount the old buyers retain). The market-supply curve of the old possessors will increase or be vertical as the price rises; and the reserved-demand curve of the old possessors will increase or be constant as the price falls. In other words, their schedules behave similarly to their counterpart schedules among the producers. The aggregate market-supply curve will be formed simply by adding the producers' and old possessors' supply curves. The total-demand-to-hold schedule will equal the demand by buyers plus the reservation demand (if any) of the producers and of the old possessors.

If the good is Chippendale chairs, which cannot be further produced, then the market-supply curves are *identical* with the supply curves of the old possessors. There is no new production, and there are no additions to stock.

It is clear that the greater the proportion of old stock to new production, other things being equal, the greater will tend to be the importance of the supply of old possessors compared to that of new producers. The tendency will be for old stock to be more important the greater the durability of the good.

There is one type of consumers' good the supply curve of which will have to be treated in a later section on labor and earnings. This is *personal service,* such as the services of a doctor, a lawyer, a concert violinist, a servant, etc. These services, as we have indicated above, are, of course, nondurable. In fact, they are con-

sumed by the seller immediately upon their production. Not being material objects like "commodities," they are the direct emanation of the effort of the supplier himself, who produces them
instantaneously upon his decision. The supply curve depends on
the decision whether or not to produce—supply—personal effort,
not on the sale of already produced stock. There is no "stock"
in this sphere, since the goods disappear into consumption immediately on being produced. It is evident that the concept of
"stock" is applicable only to tangible objects. The price of personal services, however, is determined by the intersection of supply and demand forces, as in the case of tangible goods.

For all goods, the establishment of the equilibrium price tends
to establish a *state of rest,* a cessation of exchanges. After the price
is established, sales will take place until the stock is in the hands
of the most capable possessors, in accordance with the value scales.
Where new production is continuing, the market will tend to
be *continuing,* however, because of the inflow of new stock from
producers coming into the market. This inflow alters the state
of rest and sets the stage for new exchanges, with producers eager
to sell their stock, and consumers to buy. When total stock is
fixed and there is no new production, on the other hand, the
state of rest is likely to become important. Any changes in price
or new exchanges will occur as a result of changes of valuations,
i.e., a change in the relative position of money and the good on
the value scales of at least two individuals on the market, which
will lead them to make further exchanges of the good against
money. Of course, where valuations are changing, as they almost
always are in a changing world, markets for old stock will again
be continuing.[12]

An example of that rare type of good for which the market
may be intermittent instead of continuous is Chippendale chairs,
where the stock is very limited and the money price relatively
high. The stock is always distributed into the hands of the most
eager possessors, and the trading may be infrequent. Whenever
one of the collectors comes to value his Chippendale below a
certain sum of money, and another collector values that sum in
his possession below the acquisition of the furniture, an exchange

is likely to occur. Most goods, however, even nonreproducible ones, have a lively, continuing market, because of continual changes in valuations and a large number of participants in the market.

In sum, buyers decide to buy consumers' goods at various ranges of price (setting aside previously analyzed speculative factors) because of their *demand for the good for direct use*. They decide to *abstain from buying* because of their *reservation demand for money*, which they prefer to retain rather than spend on that particular good. Sellers supply the goods, in all cases, because of their *demand for money*, and those cases where they reserve a stock for themselves are due (aside from speculation on price increases) to their demand for the good for direct use. Thus, the general factors that determine the supply and demand schedules of any and all consumers' goods, by *all persons on the market*, are the balancing on their value scales of their demand for the good for direct use and their demand for money, either for reservation or for exchange. Although we shall further discuss investment-production decisions below, it is evident that decisions to invest are due to the demand for an expected money return *in the future*. A decision *not* to invest, as we have seen above, is due to a competing demand to use a stock of money *in the present*.

4. *The Gains of Exchange*

As in the case considered in chapter 2, the sellers who are included in the sale at the equilibrium price are those whose value scales make them the most capable, the most eager, sellers. Similarly, it will be the most capable, or most eager, buyers who will purchase the good at the equilibrium price. With a price of 2½ grains of gold per pound of butter, the sellers will be those for whom 2½ grains of gold is worth more than one pound of butter; the buyers will be those for whom the reverse valuation holds. Those who are excluded from sale or purchase by their own value scales are the "less capable," or "less eager," buyers and sellers, who may be referred to as "submarginal." The "marginal" buyer and the "marginal" seller are the ones whose schedules just barely permit them to stay in the market. The marginal seller is the one whose minimum selling price is just 2½; a slightly lower selling price would drive him out of the market. The marginal buyer is the one whose maximum buying price is just 2½; a slightly higher selling price would drive him out of the market. Under the law of price uniformity, all the exchanges are made at the equilibrium price (once it is established), i.e., between the valuations of the marginal buyer and those of the marginal seller, with the demand and supply schedules and their intersection determining the point of the margin. It is clear from the nature of human action that all buyers will benefit (or decide they will benefit) from the exchange. Those who abstain from buying the good have decided that they would lose from the exchange. These propositions hold true for all goods.

Much importance has been attached by some writers to the "psychic surplus" gained through exchange by the most capable buyers and sellers, and attempts have been made to measure or compare these "surpluses." The buyer who would have bought the same amount for 4 grains is obviously attaining a subjective benefit because he can buy it for 2½ grains. The same holds for the seller who might have been willing to sell the same amount for 2 grains. However, the psychic surplus of the "supramarginal" cannot be contrasted to, or measured against, that of the marginal buyer or seller. For it must be remembered that the marginal buyer or seller also receives a psychic surplus: he gains from the exchange, or else he would not make it. Value scales of each individual are *purely ordinal,* and there is no way whatever of measuring the distance between the rankings; indeed, any concept of such distance is a fallacious one. Consequently, there is no way of making interpersonal comparisons and measurements, and no basis for saying that one person subjectively benefits more than another.[13]

We may illustrate the impossibility of measuring utility or benefit in the following way. Suppose that the equilibrium market price for eggs has been established at 3 grains per dozen. The following are the value scales of some selected buyers and would-be buyers:

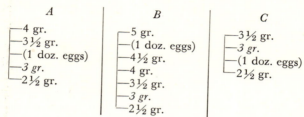

A	B	C
─4 gr.	─5 gr.	─3½ gr.
─3½ gr.	─(1 doz. eggs)	─*3 gr.*
─(1 doz. eggs)	─4½ gr.	─(1 doz. eggs)
─*3 gr.*	─4 gr.	─2½ gr.
─2½ gr.	─3½ gr.	
	─*3 gr.*	
	─2½ gr.	

The money prices are divided into units of ½ grain; for purposes of simplification, each buyer is assumed to be considering the purchase of *one unit*—one dozen eggs. C is obviously a submarginal buyer; he is just excluded from the purchase because 3 grains is higher on his value scale than the dozen eggs. A and B, however, will make the purchase. Now A is a marginal buyer; he is just able to make the purchase. At a price of 3½ grains, he would be excluded from the market, because of the rankings on his value scale. B, on the other hand, is a supramarginal buyer: he would buy the dozen eggs even if the price were raised to 4½ grains. But can we say that B benefits from his purchase *more than A? No, we cannot.* Each value scale, as has been explained above, is purely ordinal, a matter of rank. Even though B prefers the eggs to 4½ grains, and A prefers 3½ grains to the eggs, we still have no standard for comparing the two surpluses. All we can say is that *above* the price of 3 grains, B has a psychic surplus from exchange, while A becomes submarginal, with no surplus. But, even if we assume for a moment that the concept of "distance" between ranks makes sense, for all we know, A's surplus over 3 grains may give him a far greater subjective utility than B's surplus over 3 grains, even though the latter is also a surplus over 4½ grains. There can be no interpersonal comparison of utilities, and the relative rankings of money and goods on different value scales cannot be used for such comparisons.

Those writers who have vainly attempted to measure psychic gains from exchange have concentrated on "consumer surpluses." Most recent attempts try to base their measurements on the price a man would have paid for the good if confronted with the possibility of being deprived of it. These methods are completely fallacious. The fact that A would have bought a suit at 80 gold grains as well as at the 50 grains' market price, while B would not have bought the suit if the price had been as high as 52 grains, does not, as we have seen, permit any measurement of the psychic surpluses, nor does it permit us to say that A's gain was in any way "greater" than B's. The fact that even if we could identify the marginal and supramarginal purchasers, we could never assert that one's gain is greater than another's is a conclusive reason for the rejection of all attempts to measure consumers' or other psychic surpluses.

There are several other fundamental methodological errors in such a procedure. In the first place, individual value scales are here separated from concrete action. But economics deals with the universal aspects of real action, not with the actors' inner psychological workings. We deduce the existence of a specific value scale on the basis of the *real act;* we have no knowledge of that part of a value scale that is not revealed in real action. The question how much one would pay if threatened with deprivation of the whole stock of a good is strictly an academic question with no relation to human action. Like all other such constructions, it has no place in economics. Furthermore, this particular concept is a reversion to the classical economic fallacy of dealing with the whole supply of a good as if it were relevant to individual action. It must be understood that only *marginal* units are relevant to action and that there is no determinate relation at all between the marginal utility of a unit and the utility of the supply as a whole.

It is true that the total utility of a supply increases with the size of the supply. This is deducible from the very nature of a good. Ten units of a good will be ranked higher on an individual's value scale than four units will. But this ranking is completely unrelated to the utility ranking of *each unit* when the supply is 4, 9, 10 or any other amount. This is true regardless of the size of the unit. We can affirm only the trivial ordinal relationship, i.e., that five units will have a higher utility than one unit, and that the first unit will have a higher utility than the second unit, the third unit, etc. But there is no determinate way of lining up the single utility with the "package" utility.[14] Total utility, indeed, makes sense as a real and relevant rather than as a hypothetical concept only when actual decisions must be made concerning the whole supply. In that case, it is still *marginal* utility, although with the size of the margin or unit now being the whole supply.

The absurdity of the attempt to measure consumers' surplus would become clearer if we considered, as we logically may, *all* the consumers' goods at once and attempted to measure in any way the undoubted "consumers' surplus" arising from the fact that production for exchange exists at all. This has never been attempted.[15]

5. *The Marginal Utility of Money*

A. THE CONSUMER

We have not yet explained one very important problem: the ranking of money on the various individual value scales. We know that the ranking of units of goods on these scales is determined by the relative ranking of the marginal utilities of the units. In the case of barter, it was clear that the relative rankings were the result of people's evaluations of the marginal importance of the direct uses of the various goods. In the case of a monetary economy, however, the direct use-value of the money commodity is overshadowed by its exchange-value.

In chapter 1, section 5, on the law of marginal utility, we saw that the marginal utility of a unit of a good is determined in the following way: (1) if the unit is in the possession of the actor, the marginal utility of the unit is equal to the ranked value he places on the least important end, or use, which he would have to *give up* on losing the unit; or (2) if the unit is not yet in his possession, the marginal utility *of adding* the unit is equal to the value of the most important end that the unit could serve. On this basis, a man allocates his stock of various units of a good to his most important uses first, and his less important uses in succession, while he gives up his *least* important uses first. Now we saw in chapter 3 how every man allocates his stock of money among the various uses. The money commodity has numerous different uses, and the number of uses multiplies the more highly developed and advanced are the money economy, division of labor, and the capital structure. Decisions concerning numerous consumer goods, numerous investment projects, consumption at present versus expected increased returns in the future, and addition to cash balance, must all be made. We say that each individual allocates each unit of the money commodity to its most important use first, then to the next most important use, etc., thus determining the allocation of money in each possible use and line of spending. The least important use is given up first, as with any other commodity.

We are not interested here in exploring all aspects of the analysis of the marginal utility of money, particularly the cash-balance decision, which must be left for later treatment. We are interested here in the marginal utility of money as relevant to consumption decisions. Every man is a consumer, and therefore the analysis applies to everyone taking part in the nexus of monetary exchange.

Each succeeding unit that the consumer allocates among different lines of spending, he wishes to allocate to the most highly valued use that it can serve. His *psychic revenue* is the marginal utility—the value of the most important use that will be served. His *psychic cost* is the next most important use which must be forgone—the use which must be sacrificed in order to attain the most important end. The highest ranked utility *forgone,* therefore, is defined as the *cost* of any action.

The utility a person derives or expects to derive from an act of exchange is the marginal utility of adding the good purchased, i.e., the most important use for the units to be acquired. The utility that he forgoes is the highest utility that he could have derived from the units of the good that he gives up in the exchange. When he is a consumer purchasing a good, his marginal utility of addition is the most highly valued use to which he could put the units of the good; this is the psychic revenue that he expects from the exchange. On the other hand, what he forgoes is the use of the units of money that he "sells" or gives up. His *cost*, then, is the value of the most important use to which he could have put the money.[16] Every man strives in action to achieve a psychic revenue greater than his psychic cost, and thereby a psychic profit; this is true of the consumer's purchases as well. Error is revealed when his choice proves to be mistaken, and he realizes that he would have done better to have pursued the other, forgone course of action.

Now, as the consumer adds to his purchases of a good, the marginal utility which the added good has for him must *diminish*, in accordance with the law of marginal utility. On the other hand, as he gives up units of a good in sale, the marginal utility that this good has for him becomes greater, in accordance with the same law. Eventually, he must cease purchasing the good, because the marginal utility of the good forgone becomes greater than the marginal utility of the good purchased. This is clearly true of direct goods, but what of money?

It is obvious that money is not only a useful good, but one of the most useful in a money economy. It is used as a medium in practically every exchange. We have seen that one of a man's most important activities is the allocation of his money stock to various desired uses. It is obvious, therefore, *that money obeys the law of marginal utility, just as any other commodity does.* Money is a commodity divisible into homogeneous units. Indeed, one of the reasons the commodity is picked as money is its ready divisibility into relatively small homogeneous units. The first unit of money will be allocated to its most important and valued use to an individual; the second unit will be allocated to its second most valued use, etc. Any unit of money that must be given up will be surrendered at the sacrifice of the least highly valued use previously being served or which would have been served. Therefore, it is true of money as of any other commodity, that *as its stock increases, its marginal utility declines; and that as its stock declines, its marginal utility to the person increases.*[17] Its marginal utility of addition is equal to the rank of the most highly valued end the monetary unit can attain; and its marginal utility is equal in value to the most highly valued end *that would have to be sacrificed* if the unit were surrendered.

What are the various ends that money can serve? They are: (*a*) the nonmonetary uses of the money commodity (such as the use of gold for ornament); (*b*) expenditure on the many different kinds of consumers' goods; (*c*) investment in various alternative combinations of factors of production; and (*d*) additions to the cash balance. Each of these broad categories of uses encompasses a large number of types and quantities of goods, and each particular alternative is ranked on the individual's value scale. It is clear what the uses of consumption goods are: they provide immediate satisfaction for the individual's desires and are thus immediately ranked on his value scale. It is also clear that when money is used for nonmonetary purposes, it becomes a direct consumers' good itself instead of a medium of exchange. Investment, which will be further discussed below, aims at a greater level of future consumption through investing in capital goods at present.

What is the usefulness of keeping or adding to a cash balance? This question will be explored in later chapters, but here we may state that the desire to keep a cash balance stems from fundamental *uncertainty* as to the right time for making purchases, whether of capital or of consumers' goods. Also important are a basic *uncertainty* about the individual's own future value scale and the desire to keep cash on hand to satisfy any changes that might occur. Uncertainty, indeed, is a fundamental feature of all human action, and uncertainty about changing prices and changing value scales are aspects of this basic uncertainty. If an individual, for example, anticipates a rise in the purchasing power of the monetary unit in the near future, he will tend to postpone his purchases toward that day and add now to his cash balance. On the other hand, if he anticipates a fall in purchasing power, he will tend to buy more at present and draw down his cash balance. An example of general uncertainty is an individual's typical desire to keep a certain amount of cash on hand "in case of a rainy day" or an emergency that will require an unanticipated expenditure of funds in some direction. His "feeling safer" in such a case demonstrates that money's only value is not simply when it makes exchanges; because of its very marketability, its mere *possession* in the hands of an individual performs a service for that person.

That money in one's cash balance is performing a service demonstrates the fallacy in the distinction that some writers make between "circulating" money and money in "idle hoards." In the first place, all money is *always* in someone's cash balance. It is never "moving" in some mysterious "circulation." It is in A's cash balance, and then when A buys eggs from B, it is shifted to B's cash balance. Secondly, regardless of the length of time any given unit of money is in one person's cash balance, it is performing a service to him, and is therefore never in an "idle hoard."

What is the marginal utility and the cost involved in any act of consumption exchange? When a consumer spends five grains of gold on a dozen eggs, this means that he anticipates that the most valuable use for the five grains of gold is to acquire the dozen eggs. This is his marginal utility of addition of the five grains. This utility is his anticipated psychic revenue from the exchange. What, then, is the "opportunity cost" or, simply, the "cost," of the exchange, i.e., the next best alternative forgone? This is the most valuable use that he could have made with the five grains of gold. This could be any one of the following alternatives, whichever is the highest on his value scale: (*a*) expenditure on some other consumers' good; (*b*) use of the money commodity for purposes of direct consumption; (*c*) expenditure on some line of investment in factors of production to increase future monetary income and consumption; (*d*) addition to his cash balance. It should be noted that since this cost refers to a decision on a marginal unit, of whatever size, this is also the "marginal cost" of the decision. This cost is subjective and is ranked on the individual's value scale.

The nature of the cost, or utility forgone, of a decision to spend money on a particular consumers' good, is clear in the case where the cost is the value that could have been derived from another act of consumption. When the cost is forgone investment, then what is forgone is expected future increases in consumption, expressed in terms of the individual's rate of time preference, which will be further explored below. At any rate, when an individual buys a particular good, such as eggs, the more he continues to buy, the lower will be the marginal utility of addition that each successive unit has for him. This, of course, is in accordance with the law of marginal utility. On the other hand, the more money he spends on eggs, the greater will be the marginal utility forgone in whatever is the next best good—e.g., butter. Thus, the more he spends on eggs, the less will be his marginal utility derived from eggs, and the greater will be his marginal cost of buying eggs, i.e., the value that he must forgo. Eventually, the latter becomes greater than the former. When this happens and the marginal cost of purchasing eggs becomes greater than the marginal utility of addition of the commodity, he switches his purchases to butter, and the same process continues. With any stock of money, a man's consumption expenditures come first, and expenditures on each good follow the same law. In some cases, the marginal cost of consumption on a consumers' good becomes investment in some line, and the man may invest some money in factors of production. This investment continues until the marginal cost of such investment, in terms of forgone consumption or cash balance, is greater than the present value of the expected return. Sometimes, the most highly valued use is an addition to one's cash balance, and this continues until the marginal utility derived from this use is less than the marginal cost in some other line. In this way, a man's monetary stock is allocated among all the most highly valued uses.

And in this way, individual demand schedules are constructed for every consumers' good, and market-demand schedules are determined as the summation of the individual demand schedules on the market. Given the stocks of all the consumers' goods (this *given* will be analyzed in succeeding chapters), their market prices are thereby determined.

It might be thought, and many writers have assumed, that money has here performed the function of measuring and rendering comparable the utilities of the different individuals. It has, however, done nothing of the sort. The marginal utility of money differs from person to person, just as does the marginal utility of any other good. The fact that an ounce of money can buy various goods on the market and that such opportunities may be open to all does not give us any information about the ways in which various people will rank these different combinations of goods. *There is no measuring or comparability in the field of values or ranks.* Money permits only *prices* to be comparable, by establishing money prices for every good.

It might seem that the process of ranking and comparing on value scales by each individual has established and determined the prices of consumers' goods without any need for further analysis. The problem, however, is not nearly so simple. Neglect or evasion of the difficulties involved has plagued economics for many years. Under a system of barter, there would be no analytic difficulty. All the possible consumers' goods would be ranked and compared by each individual, the demand schedules of each in terms of the other would be established, etc. Relative utilities would establish individual demand schedules, and these would be summed up to yield market-demand schedules. But, in the monetary economy, a grave analytic difficulty arises.

To determine the price of a good, we analyze the market-demand schedule for the good; this in turn depends on the individual demand schedules; these in their turn are determined by the individuals' value rankings of units of the good and units of money as given by the various alternative uses of money; *yet the latter alternatives depend in turn on given prices of the other goods.* A hypothetical demand for eggs must assume as given some money price for butter, clothes, etc. *But how, then, can value scales and utilities be used to explain the formation of money prices, when these value scales and utilities themselves depend upon the existence of money prices?*

B. THE MONEY REGRESSION

It is obvious that this vitally important problem of *circularity* (X depends on Y, while Y depends on X) exists not only in regard to decisions by consumers but also in regard to any exchange decision in the money economy. Thus, let us consider the *seller* of the stock of a consumers' good. At a given offered money price, he must decide whether to sell the units of his stock or whether to hold on to them. His eagerness to sell in exchange for acquiring money is due to the use that the money would have for him. The money would be employed in its most important uses for him, and this will determine his evaluation of the money—or its marginal utility of addition. But the *marginal utility of addition of money to the seller of the stock* is based *on its already being money* and its ready command of other goods that the seller will buy—consumers' goods and factors of production alike. The seller's marginal utility therefore also depends on the previous existence of money prices for the various goods in the economy.

Similarly, for the laborer, landowner, investor, or owner of a capital good: in selling his services or goods, money has a marginal utility of addition, which is a necessary prior condition to his decision to sell the goods and therefore a determinant in his supply curve of the good for money. And yet this marginal utility always depends on there being a previous array of money prices in existence. The seller of any good or service for money, therefore, ranks the marginal utility of the money that he will obtain against the marginal utility of holding on to the good or service. Whoever spends money to buy any good or service ranks the marginal utility which keeping the money has for him against the marginal utility of acquiring the good. These value scales of the various buyers and sellers determine the individual supply-demand schedules and hence all money prices; yet, in order to rank money and goods on his value scale, money must *already* have a marginal utility for each person, and this marginal utility *must* be based on the fact of pre-existing money prices of the various goods.[18]

The solution of this crucial problem of circularity has been provided by Professor Ludwig von Mises, in his notable theory of the money regression.[19] The theory of money regression may be explained by examining the period of time that is being considered in each part of our analysis. Let us define a "day" as the period of time just sufficient to determine the market prices of every good in the society. On day X, then, the money price of each good is determined by the interactions of the supply and demand schedules of money and the good by the buyers and sellers on that day. Each buyer and seller ranks money and the given good in accordance with the relative marginal utility of the two to him. Therefore, a money price at the *end* of day X is determined by the marginal utilities of money and the good as they existed at the *beginning* of day X. But the marginal utility of money is based, as we have seen above, on a *previously* existing array of money prices. Money is demanded and considered useful because of its *already existing* money prices. Therefore, the price of a good on day X is determined by the marginal utility of the good on day X and the marginal utility of money on day X, which last in turn depends on the prices of goods on day $X - 1$.

The economic analysis of money prices is therefore *not* circular. If prices today depend on the marginal utility of money today, the latter is dependent on money prices *yesterday*. Thus, in every money price in any day, there is contained a *time component,* so that this price is partially determined by the money prices of yesterday. This does *not* mean specifically that the price of eggs today is partially determined by the price of eggs yesterday, the price of butter today by that of yesterday, etc. On the contrary, the time component essential to each specific price today is the *general array* of yesterday's money prices for all goods, and, of course, the subsequent evaluation of the monetary unit by the individuals in the society. If we consider the *general array* of today's prices, however, an essential time component in their determination is the general array of yesterday's prices.

This time component is purely on the money side of the determining factors. *In a society of barter, there is no time component* in the prices of any given day. When horses are being exchanged against fish, the individuals in the market decide on the relative marginal utilities solely on the basis of the direct uses of the commodities. These direct uses are immediate and do not require any previously existing prices on the market. Therefore, the marginal utilities of direct goods, such as horses and fish, have no previous time components. And, therefore, there is no problem of circularity in a system of barter. In such a society, if all previous markets and knowledge of previous prices were somehow wiped out, there would, of course, be an initial period of confusion while each individual consulted his value scales and tried to estimate those of others, but there would be no great difficulty in speedily re-establishing the exchange markets. The case is different in a monetary economy. Since the marginal utility of the money commodity depends on previously existing money prices, a wiping out of existing markets and knowledge of money prices would render impossible the direct re-establishment of a money economy. The economy would be wrecked and thrown back into a highly primitive state of barter, after which a money economy could only slowly be re-established as it had been before.

Now the question may be raised: Granted that there is no circularity in the determination of money prices, does not the fact that the causes partially *regress* backward in time simply push the unexplained components back further without end? If today's prices are partly determined by yesterday's prices, and yesterday's by those of the day before yesterday, etc., is not the regression simply pushed back infinitely, and part of the determination of prices thus left unexplained?

The answer is that the regression is not infinite, and the clue to its stopping point is the distinction just made between conditions in a money economy and conditions in a state of barter. We remember that the utility of money consists of *two* major elements: the utility of the money as a medium of exchange, and the utility of the money commodity in its direct, commodity use (such as the use of gold for ornaments). In the modern economy, after the money commodity has fully developed as a medium of exchange, its use as a medium tends greatly to overshadow its direct use in consumption. The demand for gold as money far exceeds its demand as jewelry. However, the latter use and demand continue to exist and to exert some influence on the total demand for the money commodity.

In any day in the money economy, the marginal utility of gold and therefore the demand for it enter into the determination of every money price. The marginal utility of gold and the demand for it today depend on the array of money prices existing yesterday, which in turn depended on the marginal utility of gold and the demand for it yesterday, etc. Now, as we regress backwards in time, we must eventually arrive at the original point when people first began to use gold as a medium of exchange. Let us consider the *first* day on which people passed from the system of pure barter and began to use gold as a medium of exchange. On that day, the money price, or rather, the gold price, of every other good depended partially on the marginal utility of gold. This marginal utility had a *time component,* namely, the previous array of gold prices, which had been determined in barter. In other words, when gold first began to be used as a medium of exchange, its marginal utility for use in that capacity depended on the existing previous array of gold prices established through *barter.* But if we regress one day further *to the last day of barter,* the gold prices of various goods on that day, like all other prices, had *no* time components. They were determined, as were all other barter prices, solely by the marginal utility of gold and of the other goods on that day, and the marginal utility of gold, since it was used *only* for direct consumption, had *no* temporal component.

The determination of money prices (gold prices) is therefore completely explained, with no circularity and no infinite regression. The demand for gold enters into every gold price, and today's demand for gold, in so far as it is for use as a *medium of exchange,* has a time component, being based on yesterday's array of gold prices. This time component regresses until the last day of barter, the day before gold began to be used as a medium of exchange. On that day, gold had no utility in that use; the demand for gold was solely for direct use, and consequently, the determination of the gold prices, for that day and for all previous days, had no temporal component whatever.[20, 21]

The causal-temporal pattern of the regression may be portrayed as in the diagram in Fig. 38. Consecutive days are numbered 1, 2, 3, etc., and, for each period, arrows depict the underlying causal factors determining the gold prices of goods on the market. For each period of time, the gold prices of goods are fundamentally determined by the relative marginal utilities of gold and other goods on individual value scales, and the marginal utilities of gold are based on the gold prices during the preceding period. This temporal component, depicted by an arrow, continues back-

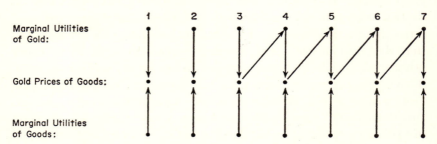

FIG. 38.   CAUSAL-TEMPORAL PATTERN OF THE MONEY REGRESSION

ward until the period of barter, when gold is used only for direct consumption or production purposes and not as a medium of exchange. At that point there is no temporal dependence on preceding gold prices, and the temporal arrow disappears. In this diagram, a system of barter prevails on days 1, 2, and 3, and gold is used as a medium of exchange on day 4 and thereafter.

One of the important achievements of the regression theory is its establishment of the fact that money *must* arise in the manner described in chapter 3, i.e., it must develop out of a commodity already in demand for direct use, the commodity then being used as a more and more general medium of exchange. Demand for a good as a medium of exchange *must* be predicated on a previously existing array of prices in terms of other goods. A medium of exchange can therefore *originate only* according to our previous description and the forgoing diagram; it can arise only out of a commodity previously *used directly in a barter situation,* and therefore having had an array of prices in terms of other goods. *Money must develop out of a commodity with a previously existing purchasing power, such as gold and silver had.* It cannot be created out of thin air by any sudden "social compact" or edict of government.

On the other hand, it does *not* follow from this analysis that if an extant money were to lose its direct uses, it could no longer be used as money. Thus, if gold, after being established as money, were suddenly to lose its value in ornaments or industrial uses, it would not necessarily lose its character as a money. Once a medium of exchange has been established as a money, money prices continue to be set. If on day X gold loses its direct uses, there will still be previously existing money prices that had been established on day $X - 1$, and these prices form the basis for the marginal utility of gold on day X. Similarly, the money prices thereby determined on day X form the basis for the marginal utility of money on day $X + 1$. From X on, gold could be demanded for its exchange value alone, and not at all for its direct use. Therefore, while it is absolutely necessary that a money *originate* as a commodity with direct uses, it is not absolutely necessary that the direct uses continue after the money has been established.

The money prices of consumers' goods have now been completely explained in terms of individual value scales, and these value scales have been explained up to the point of the content of the subjective use-valuations of each good. Economics is not concerned with the specific content of these ends, but with the explanation of various phenomena of action based on *any* given ends, and therefore its task in this sphere is fully accomplished by tracing these phenomena back to subjective valuations of useful goods.[22]

C. UTILITY AND COSTS

We may sum up the utility and cost considerations in decisions of buyers and sellers of consumers' goods—or, rather, of potential buyers and sellers (cf. chapter 2, pp. 139 f.)—as follows:

Seller:

Revenue: Marginal Utility of Addition of the Units of Money = value rank in most valuable prospective use

Cost:

Either
1) Marginal Utility of good in direct use
   —highest-ranked use that would have to be sacrificed
                              Or
2) Marginal Utility of holding for anticipated future sale at higher price
   —whichever is the higher on his value scale

In cases where neither cost item is present, the sale is costless.

Buyer:

Revenue: Marginal Utility of Addition of the Units of the Good = highest-ranked direct use of units

Cost: Marginal Utility of Units of Money—value rank in highest-ranked use that will have to be sacrificed in making the exchange

The aim of the actor is always to achieve a psychic profit from an action by having his marginal revenue exceed his marginal cost. Only after the decision has been made, the action taken, and the consequences assessed, can the actor know if his decision was correct, i.e., if his psychic revenue really did exceed his cost. It is possible that his cost may prove to have been greater than his revenue and that therefore he lost on the exchange.

It is convenient to distinguish the two vantage points by which an actor judges his action as *ex ante* and *ex post*. *Ex ante* is his position when he must decide on a course of action; it is the relevant and dominant consideration for human action. It is the actor considering his alternative courses and the consequences of each. *Ex post* is his recorded observation of the results of his past action. It is the judging of his past actions and their results. *Ex ante,* then, he will always take the most advantageous course of action, and will always have a psychic profit, with revenue exceeding cost. *Ex post,* he may have profited or lost from a course of action. Revenue may or may not have exceeded cost, depending on how good an entrepreneur he has been in making his original action. It is clear that his *ex post* judgments are mainly useful to him in the weighing of his *ex ante* considerations for future action.

Suppose that an ultimate consumer buys a product and then finds that he was mistaken in this purchase and that the good has little or no value to him. Thus, a man might buy a cake and find that he does not like it at all. *Ex ante* the (expected) utility of the cake was greater than the marginal utility of the money forgone in purchasing it; *ex post* he finds that he was in error and that if he had it to do over again, he would not have bought the cake. The purchase was the consumer's responsibility, and he must bear the loss as well as the gain from his voluntary transaction. Of course, no one can relive the past, but he can use this knowledge, for example, to avoid purchasing such a cake again. It should be obvious that the cake, once purchased, may have little or no value even though the man originally paid several grains of gold for it. The *cost* of the cake was the forgone marginal utility of the three grains of gold paid for it. But this cost incurred *in the past* cannot confer any value on the cake *now*. This would seem obvious, and yet economics has always suffered from neglect of this truth, particularly during the nineteenth century, in the form of various "cost" theories of value. These cost theories asserted that the value of goods is conferred by the costs or sacrifices incurred in their acquisition in the past. On the contrary, it is clear that value can be conferred on a good only by individuals' desires to use it directly in the *present* or in the present expectation of selling to such individuals in the *future*.[23]

We may modify the buyer summary above by considering the case in which the buyer is not an ultimate consumer, but rather a speculative buyer anticipating a future price rise. In that case, a higher revenue for him will be the marginal utility of holding for anticipated future sale at a higher price, which he considers net of the cost of storage.

D. PLANNING AND THE RANGE OF CHOICE

It should be evident that the the establishment of money tremendously broadens the range of choice open to everybody. The range of alternative uses that can be satisfied by units of money is far wider than the number of uses to which individual goods can be put. Horses or houses can be allocated to several uses, raw materials to many areas of production, but money can be allocated in expenditure on *every* single type of exchangeable good in the society, whether a tangible commodity or an intangible service, a consumers' or a capital or a natural good or claims to these goods. Money serves greatly to expand the range of choice; and it itself becomes a key *means* to be allocated to the most highly valued of alternative ends.[24]

It might be worth while to consider at this point what each person does in action. He is always engaged in allocating means to the most highly valued of his alternative ends, as ranked on his value scale. His actions in general, and his actions *in exchange* in particular, are always the result of certain expectations on his part, expectations of the most satisfactory course that he could follow. He always follows the route that he *expects* will yield him the most highly ranked available end at a certain future time (which might in some cases be so near as to be almost immediate) and therefore a psychic profit from the action. If he proves to have acted erroneously, so that another course of action would have yielded him a greater psychic revenue, then he has incurred a loss. *Ex ante* he appraises his situation, present and prospective future, chooses among his valuations, tries to achieve the highest ones according to his "know-how," and then chooses courses of action on the basis of these *plans*. Plans are his decisions concerning future action, based on his ranking of ends and on his assumed knowledge of how to attain the ends. Every individual, therefore, is constantly engaged in *planning*. This planning may range from an impressive investment in a new steel plant to a small boy's decision to spend two cents on candy, but it is planning nevertheless.[25] It is erroneous, therefore, to assert that a free market society is "unplanned"; on the contrary, each individual plans for himself.

But does not "chaos" result from the fact that individual plans do not seem to be co-ordinated? On the contrary, the exchange system, in the first place, co-ordinates individual plans by benefiting *both* parties to every exchange. In the second place, the bulk of the present volume is devoted to an explanation and analysis of the principles and order that determine the various exchange phenomena in a monetary economy: prices, output, expenditures, etc. Far from being chaotic, the structure of the monetary economy presents an intricate, systematic picture and is deducible from the basic existence of human action and indirect exchange.[26]

6. *Interrelations among the Prices of Consumers' Goods*

Thus, at any given point in time, the consumer is confronted with the previously existing money prices of the various consumers' goods on the market. On the basis of his utility scale, he determines his rankings of various units of the several goods and of money, and these rankings determine how much money he will spend on each of the various goods. Specifically, *he will spend money on each particular good until the marginal utility of adding a unit of the good ceases to be greater than the marginal utility that its money price on the market has for him.* This is the law of consumer action in a market economy. As he spends money on a good, the marginal utility of the new units declines, while the marginal utility of the money forgone rises, until he ceases spending on that good. In those cases where the marginal utility of even one unit of a good is lower than the marginal utility of its money price, the individual will not buy any of that good.

In this way are determined the individual demand schedules for each good and, consequently, the aggregate market-demand schedules for all buyers. The position of the market-demand schedule determines what the market price will be in the immediate future. Thus, if we consider action as divided into periods consisting of "days," then the individual buyers set their rankings and demand schedules on the basis of the prices existing at the end of day 1, and these demand schedules determine what the prices will be by the end of day 2.

The reader is now referred back to the discussion in chapter 2 above, sections 9 and 10. The analysis, there applied to barter conditions, applies to money prices as well. At the end of each day, the demand schedules (or rather, the total demand schedules) and the stock in existence on that day set the market equilibrium price for that day. In the money economy, these factors determine the money prices of the various goods during that day. The analysis of changes in the prices of a good, set forth in chapter 2, is directly applicable here. In the money economy, the most important markets are naturally continuous, as goods continue to be produced in each day. Changes in supply and demand schedules or changes in total demand schedules and quantity of stock have exactly the same directional effect as in barter. An increase in the market's total demand schedule over the previous day tends to increase the money price for the day; an increase in stock available tends to lower the price, etc. As in barter, the stock of each good, at the end of each day, has been transferred into the hands of the most eager possessors.

Up to this point we have concentrated on the determination of the money price of each consumers' good, without devoting much attention to the relations among these prices. The interrelationships should be clear, however. The available goods are ranked, along with the possibility of holding the money commodity in one's cash balance, on each individual's value scale. Then, in accordance with the rankings and the law of utility, the individual allocates his units of money to the most highly valued uses: the various consumers' goods, investment in various factors, and addition to his cash balance. Let us here set aside the question of the distribution chosen between consumption and investment, and the question of addition to the cash balance, until later chapters, and consider the interrelations among the prices of consumers' goods alone.

The law of the interrelation of consumers' goods is: *The more substitutes are available for any given good, the more elastic will tend to be the demand schedules (individual and market) for that good.* By the definition of "good," two goods cannot be "perfect substitutes" for each other, since if consumers regarded two goods as completely identical, they would, by definition, be one good. *All* consumers' goods are, on the other hand, *partial* substitutes for one another. When a man ranks in his value scale the myriad of goods available and balances the diminishing utilities of each, he is treating them all as partial substitutes for one another. A change in ranking for one good by necessity changes the rankings of all the other goods, since all the rankings are ordinal and relative. A higher price for one good (owing, say, to a decrease in stock produced) will tend to shift the demand of consumers from that to other consumers' goods, and therefore their demand schedules will tend to increase. Conversely, an increased supply and a consequent lowering of price for a good will tend to shift consumer demand from other goods to this one and lower the demand schedules for the other goods (for some, of course, more than for others).

It is a mistake to suppose that only technologically similar goods are substitutes for one another. The more money consumers spend on pork, the less they have to spend on beef, or the more money they spend on travel, the less they have to spend on TV sets. Suppose that a reduction in its supply raises the price of pork on the market; it is clear that the quantity demanded, and the price, of beef will be affected by this change. *If the demand schedule for pork is more than unitarily elastic in this range,* then the higher price will cause less money to be spent on pork, and more money will tend to be shifted to such a substitute as beef. The demand schedules for beef will increase, and the price of beef will tend to rise. On the other hand, if the demand schedule for pork is *inelastic,* more consumers' money will be spent on pork, and the result will be a fall in the demand schedule for beef and consequently in its price. Such interrelations of substitute goods, however, hold true in some degree for all goods, since all goods are substitutes for one another; for every good is engaged in competing for the consumers' stock of money. Of course, some goods are "closer" substitutes than others, and the interrelations among them will be stronger than among the others. The closeness of the substitution depends, however, on the particular circumstances of the consumer and his preferences rather than on technological similarity.

Thus, consumers' goods, in so far as they are substitutes for one another, are related as follows: When the stock of *A* rises and the price of *A* therefore *falls,* (1) *if* the demand schedule for *A* is elastic, there will be a tendency for a decline in the demand schedules for *B, C, D,* etc., and consequent declines in their prices; (2) if the demand schedule for *A* is inelastic, there will be a rise in the demand schedules for *B, C, D,* etc., and a consequent *rise* in their prices; (3) if the demand schedule has exactly neutral (or unitary) elasticity, so that there is no change in the amount of money expended on *A,* there will be no effect on the demands for and the prices of the other goods.

As the money economy develops and civilization flowers, there is a great expansion in the types of goods available and therefore in the number of goods that can be substituted for one another. Consequently, there is a tendency for the demands for the various consumers' goods to become more elastic, although they will continue to vary from highly elastic to highly inelastic. In so far as the multiplication of substitutes tends to render demand curves for individual goods elastic, the first type of interaction will tend to predominate. Furthermore, when *new* types of goods are established on the market, these will clearly draw monetary demand away from other, substitute products, and hence bring about the first type of reaction.

The substitutive interrelations of consumers' goods were cogently set forth in this passage by Philip Wicksteed:

It is sufficiently obvious that when a woman goes into the market uncertain whether she will or will not buy new potatoes, or chickens, the price at which she finds that she can get them may determine her either way . . . For the price is the first and most obvious indication of the nature of the alternatives that she is foregoing, if she makes a contemplated purchase. But it is almost equally obvious that not only the price of these particular things, but the price of a number of other things also will affect the problem. If good, sound, old potatoes are to be had at a low price, the marketer will be less likely to pay a high price for new ones, because there is a good alternative to be had on good terms . . . If the housewife is thinking of doing honour to a small party of neighbours by providing a couple of chickens for their entertainment at supper, it is possible that she could treat them with adequate respect, though not with distinction, by substituting a few pounds of cod. And in that case not only the price of chickens but the price of cod will tend to affect her choice. . . .

But on what does the significance . . . [of the price difference between chicken and cod] depend? Probably upon the price of things that have no obvious connection with either chicken or cod. A father and mother may have ambitions with respect to the education or accomplishments of their children, and may be willing considerably to curtail their expenditure on other things in order to gratify them. Such parents may be willing to incur . . . entertaining their guests less sumptuously than custom demands, and at the same time getting French or violin lessons for their children. In such cases the question whether to buy new or old potatoes, or whether to entertain friends with chicken or cod, or neither, may be affected by the terms on which French or music lessons of a satisfactory quality can be secured.[27]

While all consumers' goods compete with one another for consumer purchases, some goods are also *complementary* to one another. These are goods whose uses are closely linked together by consumers, so that movements in demand for them are likely to be closely tied together. An example of complementary consumers' goods is *golf clubs* and *golf balls,* two goods the demands for which tend to rise and fall together. In this case, for example, an increase in the supply of golf balls will tend to cause a *fall* in their prices, which will tend to raise the demand schedule for golf *clubs* as well as to increase the quantity of golf balls demanded. This will tend to *increase* the price of golf clubs. In so far, then, as two goods are *complementary* to each other, when the stock of A rises, and the price of A therefore *falls,* the demand schedule for B increases and its price will tend to *rise.* Since a fall in the price of a good will always increase the quantity of the good demanded (by the law of demand), this will always stimulate the demand schedule for a complementary good and thus tend to raise its price.[28] For this effect the elasticity of demand for the original good has no relevance.

Summing up these interrelations among consumers' goods:

Substitutable goods:

If stock of A rises, and price of A *falls,* and
  Demand curve for A is:

Inelastic:	Demand for, Price of, B, C, D, . . . *rise*
Elastic:	Demand for, Price of, B, C, D, . . . *fall*
Neutral:	No effect on B, C, D . . .

Complementary goods:

If stock of *A* rises, price of *A falls,* and: Demand for, and Price
of, *B, C, D,* . . . *rise.*

(Unless Demand Curve for *A* is vertical, then there is no effect.)

All goods are substitutable for one another, while fewer are
complementary. When they are also complementary, then the
complementary effect will be mixed with the substitutive effect,
and the nature of each particular case will determine which effect
will be the stronger.

This discussion of the interrelation of consumers' goods has
treated the effect only of changes from the *stock,* or supply, side.
The effects are different when the change occurs in *the demand
schedule* instead of in the quantity of stock. Suppose that the
market-demand schedule for good *A increases*—shifts to the right.
This means that, for every hypothetical price, the quantity of
A bought, and therefore the amount of money spent on *A, increases.* But, given the supply (stock) of money in the society,
this means that there will be decreases in the demand schedules
for one or more other goods.[29] More money spent on good *A,*
given the stock of money, signifies that less money is spent on
goods *B, C, D* . . . The demand curves for the latter goods "shift
to the left," and the prices of these goods *fall.* Therefore, the
effect of the substitutability of all goods for one another is that
an increased demand for *A,* resulting in a *rise* in the price of *A,*
will lead to decreased demand schedules and *falling* prices for
goods *B, C, D* . . . We can see this relation more fully when we
realize that the demand schedules are determined by individual
value scales and that a rise in the marginal utility of a unit of
A necessarily means a relative fall in the utility of the other consumers' goods.

In so far as two goods are complementary, another effect tends
to occur. If there is an increase in the demand schedule for golf
clubs, it is likely to be accompanied by an increase in the demand schedule for golf balls, since both are determined by in-

creased relative desires to play golf. When changes come from the demand side, the prices of complementary goods tend to rise and fall together. In this case, we should not say that the rise in demand for *A led* to a rise in demand for its complement *B,* since both increases were due to an increased demand for the consumption "package" in which the two goods are intimately related.

We may now sum up both sets of interrelations of consumers' goods, for changes in stock and in demand (suppliers' reservation demand can be omitted here, since this speculative element tends toward correct estimates of the basic determinant, consumer demand).

Table 10 indicates the reactions of other goods, *B, C, D,* to changes in the determinants for good *A,* in so far as these goods are substitutable for it or complementary to it. A + sign signifies that the prices of the other goods react in the *same* direction as the price of good *A;* a — sign signifies that the prices of the other goods react in the *opposite* direction:

TABLE 10

CHANGE IN PRICES OF *B, C, D,* ...

If *A* and the Good are:	If Change in Stock of *A*		If Change in Demand for *A*
Substitutable for each other	+	if Demand for *A* is *elastic*	
	—	if Demand for *A* is *inelastic*	—
	None 0	if Demand for *A* is *unitary*	
Complementary to each other	—		+

In some cases, an *old* stock of a good may be evaluated differently from the *new* and therefore may become a separate good. Thus, while well-stored old nails might be considered the same good as newly produced nails, an old Ford will not be considered the same as a new one. There will, however, definitely be a close relation between the two goods. If the supply schedule for the new Fords decreases and the price rises, consumers will tend to shift to the purchase of old Fords, tending to raise the price of the latter. Thus, old and new commodities, technologically similar, tend to be very close substitutes for each other, and their demands and prices tend to be closely related.

Much has been written in the economic literature of consumption theory on the "assumption" that each consumers' good is desired quite independently of other goods. Actually, as we have seen, the desires for various goods are of necessity interdependent, since all are ranged on the consumers' value scales. Utilities of each of the goods are relative to one another. These ranked values for goods and money permit the formation of individual, and then aggregate, demand schedules in money for each particular good.

7. *The Prices of Durable Goods and Their Services*

Why does a man purchase a consumers' good? As we saw back in chapter 1, a consumers' good is desired and sought because the actor believes that it will serve to satisfy his urgently valued desires, that it will enable him to attain his valued ends. In other words, the good is valuable because of the expected *services* that it will provide. Tangible commodities, then, such as food, clothing, houses, etc., and intangible personal services, such as medical attention and concert performances, are similar in the life of the consumer. Both are evaluated by the consumer in terms of their services in providing him with satisfactions.

Every type of consumers' good will yield a certain amount of *services per unit of time*. These may be called *unit services*. When they are exchangeable, these services may be sold individually. On the other hand, when a good is a physical commodity and is durable, it may be sold to the consumer in one piece, thereby embodying an expected future accrual of many unit services.

What are the interrelations among the markets for, and prices of, the unit services and the durable good as a whole?

Other things being equal, it is obvious that a *more* durable good is more valuable than a *less* durable good, since it embodies more future unit services. Thus, suppose that there are two television sets, each identical in service to the viewer, but that A has an expected life of five years, and B of ten. Though the service is identical, B has twice as many services as A to offer the consumer. On the market, then, the price of B will tend to be twice the price of A.[30]

For nondurable goods, the problem of the separate sale of the service of the good and of the good itself does not arise. Since they embody services over a relatively short span of time, they are almost always sold as a whole. Butter, eggs, Wheaties, etc., are sold as a whole, embodying all their services. Few would think of "renting" eggs. Personal services, on the other hand, are never sold as a whole, since, on the free market, slave contracts are not enforceable. Thus, no one can purchase a doctor or a lawyer or a pianist for life, to perform services at will with no further payment. Personal services, then, are always sold in their individual units.

The problem whether services should be sold separately or with the good as a whole arises in the case of durable commodities, such as houses, pianos, tuxedos, television sets, etc. We have seen that goods are sold, not as a total class, e.g., "bread" or "eggs," but in separate homogeneous units of their supply, such as "loaves of bread," or "dozens of eggs." In the present discussion, a good can be sold either as a complete physical unit—a house, a television set, etc.—or in service units over a period of time. This sale of service units of a durable good is called *renting* or *renting out* or *hiring out* the good. The price of the service unit is called the *rent*.

Since the good itself is only a bundle of expected service units, it is proper to base our analysis on the *service unit*. It is clear that the demand for, and the price of, a service unit of a consumers' good will be determined on exactly the same principles as those set forth in the preceding analysis of this chapter.

A durable consumers' good embodies service units as they will accrue over a period of time. Thus, suppose that a house is expected to have a life of 20 years. Assume that a year's rental of the house has a market price, as determined by the market supply and demand schedules, of 10 ounces of gold. Now, what will be the market price of the house itself should it be sold? Since the annual rental price is 10 ounces (and if this rental is expected to continue), the buyer of the house will obtain what amounts to 20×10, or 200 ounces, of prospective rental income. The price of the house as a whole will tend inexorably to equal the present value of the 200 ounces. Let us assume for convenience at this point that there is no phenomenon of time preference and that the present value of 200 ounces is therefore equal to 200 ounces. In that case, the price of the house as a whole will tend to equal 200 ounces.

Suppose that the market price of the house as a whole is 180 ounces. In that case, there will be a rush to buy the house, since there is an expected monetary profit to be gained by purchasing for 180 ounces and then renting out for a total income of 200 ounces. This action is similar to speculative purchasers' buying a good and expecting to resell at a higher price. On the other hand, there will be a great reluctance by the present owners of such houses (or of *the* house, if there is no other house adjudged by the market as the same good), to sell at that price, since it is far more profitable to rent it out than to sell it. Thus, under these conditions, there will be a considerable excess of demand over supply of this type of house for sale, at a price of 180 ounces. The upbidding of the excess demand tends to raise the price toward 200. On the other hand, suppose that the market price is above 200. In that case, there will be a paucity of demand to purchase, since it would be cheaper to pay rental for it instead of paying the sum to purchase it. On the contrary, possessors will be eager to sell the house rather than rent it out, since the price for sale is better. The excess supply over demand at a price over 200 will drive the price down to the equilibrium point.

Thus, while every type of market price is determined as in the foregoing sections of this chapter, the market also determines price *relations*. We see that there is a definite relationship between the price of the unit services of a durable consumers' good and the price of the good as a whole. If that relationship is disturbed or does not apply at any particular time, the actions of individuals on the market will tend to establish it, because prospects of monetary gain arise until it is established, and action to obtain such gain inevitably tends to eliminate the opportunity. This is a case of "arbitrage" in the same sense as the establishment of *one price* for a good on the market. If two prices for one good exist, people will tend to rush to purchase in the cheaper market and sell more of the good in the more expensive market, until the play of supply and demand on each market establishes an "equilibrium" price and eliminates the arbitrage opportunity. In the case of the durable good and its services, there is an *equilibrium-price relation,* which the market tends to establish. *The market price of the good as a whole is equal to the present value of the sum of its expected (future) rental incomes or rental prices.*

The expected future rental incomes are, of course, not necessarily a simple extrapolation of present rental prices. Indeed, since prices are always changing, it will almost always be the case that rental prices will change in the future. When a person buys a durable good, he is buying its services for a length of time extending into the future; hence, he is more concerned with *future* than with *present* rates; he merely takes the latter as a possible guide to the future.[31] Now, suppose that the individuals on the market generally estimate that rents for this house over the next decade or so will be much lower than at present. The price of the house will then not be 20×10 ounces, but some correspondingly smaller amount.

At this point we shall define the "price of the good as whole" as its *capital value* on the market, even though there is risk of confusion with the concept of "capital good." The *capital value* of any good (be it consumers' or capital good or nature-given factor) is the money price which, as a durable good, it presently sells for on the market. The concept applies to durable goods, embodying future services.[32] The capital value of a consumers' good will tend to equal the present value of the sum of expected unit rentals.

The capital value at any time is based on expectations of future rental prices. What happens when these expectations are erroneous? Suppose, for example, that the market expects the rental prices of this house to increase in the next few years and therefore sets the capital value higher than 200 ounces. Suppose, further, that the rental prices actually decline instead. This means that the original capital value on the market had overestimated the rental income from the house. Those who had sold the house at, say, 250, have gained, while those who bought the house in order to rent it out have lost, on the transaction. Thus, those who have forecast better than their fellows gain, while the poorer forecasters lose, as a result of their speculative transactions.

It is obvious that such monetary profits come *not* simply from correct forecasting, *but from forecasting more correctly than other individuals.* If all the individuals had forecast correctly, then the original capital value would have been below 200, say, 150, to account for the eventually lower rental prices. In that case no such monetary profit would have appeared.[33] It should be clear that the gains or losses are the consequences of the freely undertaken action of the gainers and losers themselves. The man who has bought a good to rent out at what proves to be an excessive capital value has only himself to blame for being overoptimistic about the monetary return on his investment. The man who sells at a capital value higher than the eventual rental income is rewarded for his sagacity through decisions voluntarily taken by all parties. And since successful forecasters are, in effect, rewarded, and poor ones penalized, and in proportion to good and poor judgment respectively, the market tends to establish and maintain as high a quality of forecasting as is humanly possible to achieve.

The equilibrium relation between the capital value on the market and the sum of *expected* future rents is a day-to-day equilibrium that tends always to be set by the market. It is similar to the day-to-day *market equilibrium* price for a good set by supply and demand. On the other hand, the equilibrium relation between present capital value and *actual* future rents is only a long-range tendency fostered by the market's encouragement of successful forecasters. This relation is a *final* equilibrium, similar to the *final equilibrium* prices that set the goal toward which the day-to-day prices tend.

Study of capital value and rental prices requires additional supply-demand analysis. The determination of the unit rental price presents no problem. Price determination of the capital value, however, needs to be modified to account for this dependence on, and relationship to, the rental price. The *demand* for the durable good will now be, not only for direct use, but *also,* on the part of others, *demand for investment in future renting out.* If a man feels that the market price of the capital value of a good is lower than the income he can obtain from future rentals, he will purchase the good and enter the renting-out market as a supplier. Similarly, the *reserved demand* for the good as a whole will be not only for direct use or for speculative price increases, but *also* for future renting out of the good. If the possessor of a durable good believes that the selling price (capital value) is lower than what he can get in rents, he will reserve the supply and rent out the good. The capital value of the good will be such as to clear the total stock, and the total of all these demands for the good will be in equilibrium. The reserved demand of the buyers will, as before, be due to their reserved demand for money, while the sellers of both the good as a whole and of its unit services will be demanding money in exchange.

In other words, for any consumers' good, the possessors have the choice of either consuming it directly or selling it for money. In the case of durable consumers' goods, the possessors can do any one of the following with the good: use it directly, sell it whole, or *hire it out*—selling its unit services over a period of time. We have already seen that if using it directly is highest on his value scale, then the man uses the good and reserves his stock from the market. If selling it whole is highest on his value scale, he enters the "capital" market for the good as a supplier. If renting it out is highest on his value scale, then he enters the "renting" market for the good as a supplier. Which of these latter alternatives will be higher on his value scale depends on his estimate of which course will yield him the higher money income. The shape of the supply curves in both the capital and rental markets will be either rightward- and upward-sloping or vertical, since the greater the expected income, the less will be the amount reserved for direct use. It is clear that the supply schedules on the two markets are interconnected. They will tend to come into equilibrium when the equilibrium-price relation is established between them.

Similarly, the nonpossessors of a good at any given time will choose between (*a*) not buying it and reserving their money, (*b*) buying it outright, and (*c*) renting it. They will choose the course highest on their value scales, which depends partially on their demand for money and on their estimate of which type of purchase will be cheaper. If they decide to buy, they will buy on what they estimate is the cheaper market; then they can either use the good directly or resell it on the more expensive market. Thus, if the capital value of the house is 200 and a buyer estimates that total rental prices will be 220, he buys outright at 200, after which he may either use it directly or enter the rental market as a supplier in order to earn the expected 220 ounces. The latter choice again depends on his value scale. This is another example of the arbitrage action already explained, and the effect is to link the demand curves for the two types of markets for durable goods.

Here it must be pointed out that in some cases the renting contract itself takes on the characteristics of a capital contract and the estimating of future return. Such is the case of a *long-term* renting contract. Suppose that A is planning to rent a house to B for thirty years, at a set annual price. Then, instead of continual changes in the rental price, the latter is *fixed* by the original contract. Here again, the demand and supply schedules are set according to the various individual estimates of the changing course of other varying rents for the same type of good. Thus, if there are two identical houses, and it is expected that the sum of the varying rents on house *A* for the next thirty years will be

300 ounces, then the long-term renting price for house *B* will tend to be set at 10 ounces per year. Here again, there is a similar connection between markets. *The price of presently established long-term rents will tend to be equal to the present value of the sum of the expected fluctuating rents for identical goods.* If the general expectation is that the sum of rents will be 360 ounces, then there will be a heavy demand for long-term rent purchases at 300 ounces and a diminished supply for rent at that price, until the long-term rental price is driven to 12 ounces per year, when the sum will be the same. And here again, the ever-present uncertainty of the future causes the more able forecasters to gain and the less able ones to lose.[34]

In actuality, time preference exists, and the present value of the future rentals is always less by a certain discount than the sum of these rentals. If this were not so, the capital value of very durable goods, goods which wear out only imperceptibly, would be almost infinite. An estate expected to last and be in demand for hundreds of years would have an almost infinitely high selling price. The reason this does not happen is that *time preference* discounts future goods in accordance with the length of time being considered. How the rate of time preference is arrived at will be treated in later chapters. However, the following is an illustration of the effect of time preference on the capital-value of a good. Assume a durable good, expected to last for 10 years, with an expected rental value of 10 ounces each year. If the rate of time preference is 10% per annum, then the future rents and their *present* value are as follows:

Years:	1	2	3	4	5	6	7	8	9	10
Expected Rents:	10	10	10	10	10	10	10	10	10	10
Present Value:	9	8.1	7.3	6.7	6.0	5.4	4.9	4.4	4.0	3.6

(assuming first year payment at one year from present date)

Sum of these present values = 59.4 ounces = Capital value, as compared to a sum of 100 ounces of future rent.

As the date of time recedes into the future, the compounded discount becomes greater, finally reducing the present value to a negligible amount.

It is important to recognize that the time-preference factor does *not,* as does relatively correct forecasting of an uncertain situation, confer monetary profits or losses. If the time-preference rate is 10%, purchasing the aforementioned good for 59.4 ounces, holding it, and renting it out for 10 years to acquire 100 ounces does *not* constitute a monetary profit. Present money was at this premium over future money, and what this man earned was simply the amount of future income that the market had evaluated as equal to 59.4 ounces of present money.

In general, we may sum up the action of entrepreneurs in the field of durable consumers' goods by saying that they will tend to *invest* in the outright purchase of (already existing) durable consumers' goods when they believe that the present capital value of the good on the market is less than the sum of future rentals (discounted by time preference) that they will receive. They will sell such goods outright when they believe that the present capital value is higher than the discounted sum of future rentals. Better forecasters will earn profits, and poorer ones will suffer losses. In so far as the forecasting is correct, these "arbitrage" opportunities will tend to disappear.

Although we have analyzed the arbitrage profits and losses of entrepreneurship in the case of selling outright as against renting, we have yet to unravel fully the laws that govern entrepreneurial incomes—the incomes that the producers strive to obtain in the process of production. This problem will be analyzed in later chapters.[35]

8. *Welfare Comparisons and the Ultimate Satisfactions of the Consumer*

In our preoccupation with analysis of the action of man in the monetary economy, it must not be thought that the general truths presented in chapter 1 remain no longer valid. On the contrary, in chapter 1 they were applied to isolated Crusoe-type situations because we logically begin with such situations in order to be able to analyze the more complex interrelations of the monetary economy. However, the truths formulated in the first chapter are applicable still, not only through logical inferences applied to the monetary nexus, but also directly to all situations in the monetary economy in which money is not involved.

There is another sense in which the analysis of the first chapter is directly applicable in a money economy. We may be primarily concerned in the analysis of exchange with the consumer's allocation of money to the most highly valued of its uses—based on the individual's value scales. We must not forget, however, the *ultimate* goal of the consumers' expenditures of money. This goal is the actual use of the purchased goods in attaining his most highly valued ends. Thus, for the purposes of analysis of the *market,* once Jones has purchased three pounds of butter, we have lost interest in the butter (assuming there is no chance of Jones' re-entering the market to sell the butter). We call the retail sale of the butter the sale of the *consumers' good,* since this is its *last sale for money* along the path of the butter's production. Now the good is in the hands of the ultimate consumer. The consumer has weighed the purchase on his value scale and has decided upon it.

Strictly, we must never lose sight of the fact that this purchase by the consumer is *not* the last stopping point of the butter, when we consider human action in its entirety. The butter must be carried to the man's home. Then, Jones allocates the units of butter to their most highly valued uses: buttered toast, butter in a cake, butter on a bun, etc. To use the butter in a cake or sandwich, for example, Mrs. Jones bakes the cake and prepares the sandwich and then brings it to the table where Jones eats it. We can see that the analysis of chapter 1 holds true, in that useful goods—horses, butter, or anything else—in the hands of the consumer are allocated, in accordance with their utility, to the most highly valued uses. Also, we can see that actually the *butter when last sold for money* was not a consumers' good, but a *cap-*

ital good—albeit one of lower order than at any other previous stage of its production. Capital goods are produced goods that must be combined still further with other factors in order to provide the consumers' good—the good that finally yields the ultimate satisfaction to the consumer. From the full praxeological point of view, the butter becomes a consumers' good only when it is actually being eaten or otherwise "consumed" by the ultimate consumer.

From the standpoint of praxeology proper—the complete formal analysis of human action in all its aspects—it is inadmissible to call the good at its last retail sale to the consumer a "consumers' good." From the point of view of that subdivision of praxeology that covers traditional economics—that of *catallactics,* the science of monetary exchanges—however, it becomes convenient to call the good at the last retail stage a "consumers' good." This is the last stage of the good in the monetary nexus—the last point, in most cases, at which it is open to producers to invest money in factors. To call the good at this final monetary stage a "consumers' good" is permissible, provided we are always aware of the foregoing qualifications. We must always remember that without the final stages and the final allocation by consumers, there would be no *raison d'être* for the whole monetary exchange process. Economics cannot afford to dismiss the ultimate consumption stage simply because it has passed beyond the monetary nexus; it is the final goal and end of the monetary transactions by individuals in society.

Attention to this point will clear up many confusions. Thus, there is the question of consumers' income. In chapter 3, we analyzed consumers' money income and the universal goal of maximizing psychic income, and we indicated to some extent the relation between the two. Everyone attempts to maximize the latter, which includes on its value scale a vast range of all consumers' goods, both exchangeable and nonexchangeable. Exchangeable goods are generally in the monetary nexus, and therefore can be purchased for money, whereas nonexchangeable goods are not. We have indicated some of the consequences of the fact that it is *psychic* and not *monetary* income that is being maximized, and how this introduces qualifications into the expenditure of effort or labor and in the investment in producers' goods. It is also true that psychic income, being purely subjective, cannot be measured. Further, from the standpoint of praxeology, we cannot even ordinally compare the psychic income or utility of one person with that of another. We cannot say that A's income or "utility" is greater than B's.

We can, at least theoretically, measure monetary incomes by adding the amount of money income each person obtains, but this is by no means a measure of psychic income. Furthermore, it does not, as we perhaps might think, give any exact indication of the amount of services that each individual obtains purely from *exchangeable* consumers' goods. An income of 50 ounces of gold in one year may not, and most likely will not, mean the same to him in terms of services from exchangeable goods as an income of 50 ounces in some other year. The purchasing power of money in terms of all other commodities is continually changing, and there is no way to measure such changes.

Of course, as historians rather than economists, we can make imprecise judgments comparing the "real" income rather than the monetary income between periods. Thus, if Jones received 1,000 ounces of income in one year and 1,200 in the next, and prices generally rose during the year, Jones' "real income" in terms of goods purchasable by the money has risen considerably less than the nominal monetary increase or has perhaps fallen. However, as we shall see further below, there is no precise method of measuring or even identifying the purchasing power of money and its changes.

Even if we confine ourselves to the same period, monetary incomes are not an infallible guide. There are, for example, many consumers' goods that are obtainable *both* through monetary exchange and outside the money nexus. Thus, Jones may be spending 18 ounces a month on food, rent, and household maintenance, while Smith spends only 9 ounces a month. This does not necessarily mean that Jones obtains twice as much of these services as Smith. Jones may live in a hotel, which provides him with these services in exchange for money. Smith, on the other hand, may be married and may obtain household and cooking services outside the monetary nexus. Smith's psychic income from these services may be equal to, or greater than, Jones', despite the lower monetary expenditures.

Neither can we measure psychic incomes if we confine ourselves to goods in the monetary nexus. A and B might live in the same sort of house, but how can the economist-observer deduce from this that the two are deriving the same amount of enjoyment from the house? Obviously, the degree of enjoyment will most likely differ, but the mere fact of the income or property will provide no clue to the direction or extent of the difference.

It follows that the law of the diminishing marginal utility of money applies only to the valuations of *each individual* person. There can be no comparison of such utility between persons. Thus, we cannot, as some writers have done, assert that an extra dollar is enjoyed less by a Rockefeller than by a poor man. If Rockefeller were suddenly to become poor, each dollar would be worth more to him than it is now; similarly, if the poor man were to become rich, his value scales remaining the same, each dollar would be worth less than it is now. But this is a far cry from attempting to compare different individuals' enjoyments or subjective valuations. It is certainly possible that a Rockefeller enjoys the services of each dollar more than a poor, but highly ascetic, individual does.

9. *Some Fallacies Relating to Utility*

A doctrine commonly held by writers on utility is that the consumer acts so as to bring the marginal utility that any good has for him into *equality* with the price of that good. To understand this thesis, let us examine the preference scale of Mr. Jones in contemplating the purchase of one or more suits (and we shall assume that each suit is of the same quality—the same "good"). Suppose his value scale is as follows:

```
 ─3.4 grains of gold
 ─3.3    "     "    "
 ─(1st suit)
 ─3.2    "     "    "
 ─3.1    "     "    "
 ─(2nd suit)
 ─3.0    "     "    "
 ─2.9    "     "    "
 ─2.8    "     "    "
 ─(3rd suit)
 ─2.7    "     "    "
```

And suppose also that the market price is 2.9 grains per suit. Jones will buy not one or three, but two, suits. *He will buy up to the last unit at which the diminishing marginal utility that the suit has for him exceeds the increasing marginal utility of money.*[36] This is obvious. Now, if a writer couches the exposition in terms of highly divisible goods, such as butter, and in terms of small units of money, such as pennies, it is easy to leap unthinkingly to the conclusion that the consumer for each good will act in such a way as to equalize, at the market price, the marginal utility of the sum of money and the marginal utility of the good. It should be clear, however, that there is never any such "equalization." In the case of the suit, the rank of the second suit is still considerably above the rank of the 2.9 grains. So there is no equalization. Even in the case of the most divisible of goods, there will still be a *difference in rank,* not an equalization, between the two utilities. A man may buy 11 ounces of butter at 10 cents an ounce, until there is nothing ranking between the 11th ounce and the 10 cents on his utility scale; yet there is still no *equality,* but a difference in rank, with the last ounce bought ranking higher than the last sum of money spent. Of course, the consumer tries to spend his money so as to bring the two as close as possible, but they can never be equal.

Furthermore, the marginal utility of each particular good, after the purchases are made, differs in rank from that of every other. Thus, let us take one grain of gold as the monetary unit under consideration. Let us say that the given market-prices of various goods are as follows:

eggs—1 dozen per grain;
butter—1 pound per grain;
bread—1 loaf per grain;
candy—1 bar per grain.

Now each individual will purchase each commodity until the last point at which the marginal utility of the unit exceeds the marginal utility of a grain of gold. For one man this might mean the purchase of 5 pounds of butter, 3 loaves of bread, 2 bars of candy, etc. This would mean that either a sixth pound of butter or a third loaf of bread would have a lower marginal utility than a grain of gold forgone. However, the marginal utility of each good will still differ in rank from that of every other and will not be equal to that of any other.

Another, even more curious doctrine holds that in equilibrium the ratio of the marginal utilities of the various goods equals the ratio of their prices. Without entering in detail into the manner by which these writers arrive at this conclusion, we can see its absurdity clearly, since utilities are not quantities and therefore cannot be divided.

These fallacies stem from a related one: the idea that an individual will act so as to *equalize* the marginal utility that any good will have in each of its uses. Applied to money, this would imply that the marginal utility of a unit of money is equal for each field of expenditure for each person. This is incorrect, as we have just seen that the marginal utilities of the various goods are not equalized. Successive units of a good are allocated to the most desired end, then to the next most desired satisfaction, etc. If there are several uses for the good, each one involving many possible units, the marginal utility of a unit in each use continues to decline as the supply increases. As goods are purchased, the marginal utility of each good purchased diminishes, and a man may allocate his money first to one use, then to another, and then to the first use again. However, in no case is there any equalization of marginal utilities.

The dogma of the equalization of marginal utilities may best be illustrated in the following passage from perhaps the originator of this line of argument:

Let s be the whole stock of some commodity, and let it be capable of two distinct uses. Then we may represent the two quantities appropriated to these uses by x_1 and y_1, it being a condition that x_1 plus y_1 equal s. The person may be conceived as successively expending small quantities of the commodity; now it is the inevitable tendency of human nature to choose that course which appears to offer the greatest advantage at the moment. Hence, when the person remains satisfied with the distribution he has made, it follows that no alteration would yield him more pleasure; which amounts to saying that an increment of commodity would yield exactly as much utility in one use as in another. Let Δu_1, Δu_2, be the increments of utility, which might arise respectively from consuming an increment of commodity in the two different ways. When the distribution is completed, we ought to have $\Delta u_1 = \Delta u_2$ . . . The same reasoning . . . will evidently apply to any two uses, and hence to all uses simultaneously, so that we obtain a series of equations less numerous by a unit than the number of ways of using the commodity. The general result is that the commodity, if consumed by a perfectly wise being, must be consumed with a maximum production of utility.[37]

The chief errors here consist in conceiving utility as a certain quantity, a definite function of an increment in the commodity, and in treating the problem in terms of infinitely small steps. Both procedures are fallacious. Utilities are not quantities, but ranks, and the successive amounts of a commodity that are used are always discrete units, not infinitely small ones. If the units are discrete, then the rank of each unit differs from that of every other, and there can be no equalization.

Many errors in discussions of utility stem from an assumption that it is some sort of quantity, measurable at least in principle. When we refer to a consumer's "maximization" of utility, for example, we are *not* referring to a definite stock or quantity of something to be maximized. We refer to the *highest-ranking position* on the individual's value scale. Similarly, it is the assumption of the infinitely small, added to the belief in utility as a quantity, that leads to the error of treating marginal utility as the mathematical derivative of the integral "total utility" of several units of a good. Actually, there is no such relation, and there is no such thing as "total utility," only the marginal utility of a *larger-*

sized unit. The size of the unit depends on its relevance to the particular action.[38]

This illustrates one of the grave dangers of the mathematical method in economics, since this method carries with it the bias of the assumption of continuity, or the infinitely small step. Most writers on economics consider this assumption a harmless, but potentially very useful, fiction, and point to its great success in the field of physics. They overlook the enormous differences between the world of physics and the world of human action. The problem is not simply one of acquiring the microscopic measuring tools that physics has developed. The crucial difference is that physics deals with inanimate objects that *move* but do not *act*. The movements of these objects can be investigated as being governed by precise, quantitatively determinate laws, well expressed in terms of mathematical functions. Since these laws precisely describe definite paths of movement, there is no harm at all in introducing simplified assumptions of continuity and infinitely small steps.

Human beings, however, do not move in such fashion, but act purposefully, applying means to the attainment of ends. Investigating causes of human action, then, is radically different from investigating the laws of motion of physical objects. In particular, human beings act on the basis of things that are *relevant* to their action. The human being cannot see the infinitely small step; it therefore has no meaning to him and no relevance to his action. Thus, if one ounce of a good is the smallest unit that human beings will bother distinguishing, then the ounce is the basic unit, and we cannot simply assume infinite continuity in terms of small fractions of an ounce.

The key problem in utility theory, neglected by the mathematical writers, has been *the size of the unit*. Under the assumption of mathematical continuity, this is not a problem at all; it could hardly be when the mathematically conceived unit is infinitely small and therefore literally *sizeless*. In a praxeological analysis of human action, however, this becomes a basic question. The relevant size of the unit varies according to the particular situation, and in each of these situations this relevant unit be-

comes the *marginal* unit. There is none but a simple ordinal relation among the utilities of the variously sized units.

The tendency to treat problems of human action in terms of
equality of utility and of infinitely small steps is also apparent
in recent writings on "indifference maps." Almost the entire edifice of contemporary mathematical economics in consumption
theory has been built on the "indifference" assumption. Its basis
is the treatment of large-sized classes of combinations of two
goods, between which the individual is indifferent in his valuations. Furthermore, the differences between them are infinitely
small, so that smooth lines and tangents can be drawn. The crucial fallacy is *that "indifference" cannot be a basis for action.* If
a man were really indifferent between two alternatives, he could
not make any choice between them, and therefore the choice
could not be revealed in action. We are interested in analyzing
human action. Any action demonstrates choice based on preference: preference for one alternative over others. There is therefore no role for the concept of indifference in economics or in
any other praxeological science. If it is a matter of indifference
for a man whether he uses 5.1 or 5.2 ounces of butter, for example, because the unit is too small for him to take into consideration, then there will be no occasion for him to act on this
alternative. He will use butter in ounce units, instead of tenths
of an ounce. For the same reason, there are no infinitely small
steps in human action. Steps are only those that are significant
to human beings; hence, they will always be finite and discrete.

The error in reasoning on the basis of "indifference" is the
failure to appreciate the fact that a problem important in the
field of *psychology* may have no significance in the realm of
praxeology, to which economics belongs. Psychology deals with
the problem of *how* or why the individual forms value scales, and
for this question it is relevant to consider whether the individual
is decisive or inclined to be "indifferent" between various alternatives. Praxeology, however, is a logical science based on the
existence of action *per se;* it is interested in explaining and inter-
preting real action in its universal sense rather than in its concrete content. Its discussion of value scales is therefore a deduc-

tion from the nature of human action and not a speculative essay on the internal workings of the mind. It is consequently irrelevant for praxeology whether a man, in having to decide between alternatives *A* and *B*, makes a choice firmly and decisively, or whether he decides by tossing a coin. This is a problem for psychology; praxeology is concerned only with the fact that he chooses, for example, *A* rather than *B*, and that therefore *A* ranked higher in his preference scale than *B*. Utility theory is not concerned with psychology or the internal operations of the mind, but is part of a separate science based on the logical consequences of the simple existence of action.

Neither is praxeology based on behaviorist psychology. In fact, in so far as praxeology touches on psychology, its principles are the reverse of those of behaviorism. As we have seen, far from simply observing action in the same way as we observe and record the movements of stones, praxeology is based on a fundamental distinction between human action and the motion of inorganic matter, namely, that human action is *motivated* toward the achievement of certain ends. Means and resources are used for the achievement of these ends. Far from leaving mind out of the picture, praxeology rests fundamentally on the basic axiom of action, action caused and put into effect by human minds. However, praxeology is not concerned with the content of these ends, the manner of arriving at them, or their order; it is concerned with analysis of the logical implications of the existence of these ends.

Some writers, in their artificial separation of value scales from real action, have actually gone to the length of attempting to discover people's indifference maps by means of questionnaires. These attempts, besides being open to the stricture that indifference is not praxeologically valid, fail to realize that value scales may and do change continually and that therefore such questionnaires have no relevance to the business of economics. Economics is interested not in value scales professed in response to questionnaires, but in the values implied by real action. As Ludwig von Mises states, with regard to all attempts to separate value scales from action:

. . . the scale of value is nothing but a constructed tool of thought. The scale of value manifests itself only in real acting; it can be discerned only from the observation of real acting. It is therefore impermissible to contrast it with real acting and to use it as a yardstick for the appraisal of real actions.[39]

Since indifference is not relevant to human action, it follows that two alternatives for choice cannot be ranked equally on an individual's value scale. If they are really ranked equally, then they cannot be alternatives for choice, and are therefore not relevant to action. Hence, not only are alternatives ranked ordinally on every man's value scale, but they are ranked *without ties;* i.e., every alternative has a different rank.

The famous illustration used by the indifference theorists to demonstrate the relevance of indifference to human action is the case of Buridan's ass. This is the fable of the ass who stands, hungry, equidistant from two equally attractive bales of hay, or, thirsty, equidistant from two water holes. Since the two bales or water holes are equally attractive in every way, the ass can choose neither one and must therefore starve. This example is supposed to prove the great relevance of indifference to action and to be an indication of the way that indifference is *revealed* in action. Compounding confusion, Schumpeter refers to this ass as "perfectly rational." [40]

In the first place, it is of course difficult to conceive of an ass or a person that could be *less* rational. He is confronted not with *two* choices, but with *three,* the third being to starve where he is. Even on the indifferentists' own grounds, this third choice will be ranked lower than the other two on the actor's value scale. He will *not* choose starvation.

If both left and right water holes are equally attractive, and he can find no reason for preferring one or the other, the ass or the man will allow pure chance, such as a flip of a coin, to decide on either one. But on one he must and will decide. Again, we are interested in preference *as revealed through choice* and not in the *psychology* of preferences. If the flipped coin indicated the left water hole, then the left water hole was finally placed higher on the actor's value scale, as was revealed when he went toward it. Far from being a proof of the importance of indifference, the case of Buridan's ass is an excellent demonstration of the fact that indifference can play no part whatever in an analysis of human action.

Another way of attempting a justification of the indifference analysis is to suppose that a man, Jones, chooses each of two alternatives *A* and *B* about fifty per cent of the time, upon repeated opportunities. This shifting is alleged to be a demonstration that Jones is really indifferent as between the two alternatives. Yet what is the reasonable inference? Clearly, that in some cases, *A* was *preferred* to *B* on Jones' value scale, and that in the others, the positions were shifted so that *B* was *preferred* to *A*. *In no case* was there indifference between the two alternatives. The shift of choice indicates a shift in the preference scale, and not indifference on a constant value scale. Of course, if we were dealing with psychology, we could enter into a discussion of intensities of preferences and opine that the man, with respect to his underlying personality, was relatively indifferent rather than intensely biassed, as between the two alternatives. But in praxeology we are not interested in the concrete content of his value scales nor in his underlying personality. We are interested in value scales as revealed through choice.

APPENDIX A: THE DIMINISHING MARGINAL UTILITY OF MONEY

Some writers, while admitting the validity of the law of diminishing marginal utility for all other goods, deny its application to money. Thus, for example, a man may allocate each ounce of money to his most preferred uses. However, suppose that it takes 60 ounces of gold to buy an automobile. Then the acquisition of the 60th ounce, which will enable him to buy an automobile, will have considerably more value than the acquisition of the 58th or of the 59th ounce, which will not enable him to do so.

This argument involves a misconception identical with that of the argument about the "increasing marginal utility of eggs" discussed in chapter 1, above.[41] There we saw that it is erroneous to argue that because a fourth egg might enable a man to bake a cake, which he could not do with the first three, the marginal utility of the eggs has increased. We saw that a "good" and, consequently, the "unit" of a good are defined in terms of whatever quantity of which the units give an *equally serviceable supply*. This last phrase is the key concept. The fourth egg was not equally serviceable as, and therefore not interchangeable with, the first egg, and therefore a *single egg* could not be taken as the *unit*. The units of a good must be homogeneous in their serviceability, and it is only to such units that the law of utility applies.

The situation is similar in the case of money. The serviceability of the money commodity lies in its use in exchange rather than in its direct use. Here, therefore, a "unit" of money, in its relevance to individual value scales, must be such as to be homogeneous with every other unit in exchange-value. If another ounce permits a purchase of an automobile, and the issue is relevant to the case in question, then the "unit" of the money commodity must be taken not as one ounce, but as sixty ounces.

All that needs to be done, then, to account for and explain "discontinuities" because of possible large purchases is to *vary the size of the monetary unit* to which the law of utility and the preferences and choices apply.[42] This is what each man actually does in practice. Thus, suppose that a man is considering what to do with 60 ounces of gold. Let us assume, for the sake of simplicity, that he has a choice of parceling out the 60 ounces into 5-ounce units. This, we will say, is alternative *A*. In that case, he decides that he will parcel out each 5 ounces in accordance with the highest rankings on his utility scale. The first 5 ounces will be allocated to, or spent on, the most highly valued use *that can be served by 5 ounces;* the next 5 ounces to the next most highly valued use, and so on. Finally, his twelfth 5 ounces he will allocate to his twelfth most highly valued use. Now, however, he is also confronted with alternative *B*. This alternative is to spend the entire 60 ounces on whatever single use will be most valuable on his value scale. This will be the single highest-ranked use for a *unit* of 60 ounces of money. Now, to decide which alternative course he will take, the man compares the utility of the highest-ranked single use of a lump sum of 60 ounces (say, the purchase of a car) with the utility of the "package"—the expenditure of 5 ounces on *a*, 5 ounces on *b*, etc. Since the man knows his own preference scale—otherwise he could never choose any action—it is no more difficult to assume that he can rank the utility of the whole package with the utility of purchasing a car than to assume that he can rank the uses of each 5 ounces. In other words, he posits a unit of 60 ounces and determines which alternative ranks higher on his value scale: purchase of the car or a certain package distribution by 5-ounce (or other-sized) units. At any rate, the 60 ounces are distributed to what each man believes will be its highest-ranking use, and the same can be said for each of his monetary exchange decisions.

Here we must stress the fact that there is no numerical relation— aside from pure ordinal rank—between the marginal utilities of the various 5-ounce units and the utilities of the 60-ounce units, and this is true even of the package combination of distribution that we have considered. All that we can say is that the utility of 60 ounces will clearly be higher than any *one* of the utilities of 5 ounces. But there is no way of determining the numerical difference. Whether or not the rank of the utility of this *package* is higher or lower than the utility of the car purchase, moreover, can be determined only by the individual himself.

We have reiterated several times that utility is only ranked, and never measurable. There is no numerical relationship whatever between the utility of large-sized and smaller-sized units of a good. Also, there is no numerical relationship between the utilities of one unit and several units of the same size. Therefore, there is no possible way of adding or combining marginal utilities to form some sort of "total utility"; the latter can only be a *marginal* utility of a large-sized unit, and there is no numerical relationship between that and the utilities of small units.

As Ludwig von Mises states:

Value can rightly be spoken of only with regard to specific acts of appraisal. . . . Total value can be spoken of only with reference to a particular instance of an individual . . . having to choose between the total available quantities of certain economic goods. Like every other act of valuation, this is complete in itself . . . When a stock is valued as a whole, its marginal utility, that is to say, the utility of the last available unit of it, coincides with its total utility, since the total supply is one indivisible quantity.[43]

There are, then, two laws of utility, both following from the apodictic conditions of human action: first, that *given the size of a unit of a good, the (marginal) utility of each unit decreases as the supply of units increases;* second, that *the (marginal) utility of a larger-sized unit is greater than the (marginal) utility of a smaller-sized unit.* The first is the law of diminishing marginal utility. The second has been called the law of increasing total utility. The relationship between the two laws and between the items considered in both is purely one of rank, i.e., ordinal. Thus, 4 eggs (or pounds of butter, or ounces of gold) are worth more on a value scale than 3 eggs, which in turn are worth more than 2 eggs, 2 eggs more than 1 egg, etc. This illustrates the second law. One egg will be worth more than a second egg, which will be worth more than a third egg, etc. This illustrates the first law. But there is no arithmetical relationship between the items apart from these rankings.[44]

The fact that the units of a good must be homogeneous in serviceability means, in the case of money, that the given array of money prices remains constant. The serviceability of a unit of money consists in its direct use-value and especially in its exchange-value, which rests on its power to purchase a myriad of different goods. We have seen in our study of the money regression and the marginal utility of money that the evaluation and the marginal utility of the money commodity rests on an already given structure of money prices for the various goods. It is clear that, in any given application of the foregoing law, the money prices cannot change in the meantime. If they do, and for example, the fifth unit of money is valued more highly than the fourth unit because of an intervening change in money prices, then the "units" are no longer equally serviceable and therefore cannot be considered as homogeneous.

As we have seen above, this power of the monetary unit to purchase quantities of various goods is called the *purchasing power of the monetary unit*. This purchasing power of money consists of the *array* of all the given money prices on the market at any particular time, considered in terms of the prices of goods per unit of money. As we saw in the regression theorem above, today's purchasing power of the monetary unit is determined by today's marginal utilities of money and of goods, expressed in demand schedules, while today's marginal utility of money is directly dependent on yesterday's purchasing power of money.[45]

APPENDIX B: ON VALUE

Economics has made such extensive use of the term "value" that it would be inexpedient to abandon it now. However, there is undoubtedly confusion because the term is used in a variety of different ways. It is more important to keep distinct the subjective use of the term in the sense of *valuation* and preference, as against the "objective" use in the sense of *purchasing power* or price on the market. Up to this chapter, "value" in this book has meant the subjective individual "valuing" process of ranking goods on individual "value scales."

In this chapter, the term "value of capital" signifies the purchasing power of a durable good in terms of money on the market. If a house can be sold on the market for 250 ounces of gold, then its "capital value" is 250 ounces. The difference between this and the subjective type of value is apparent. When a good is being subjectively valued, it is ranked by someone in relation to other goods on his value scale. When a good is being "evaluated" in the sense of finding out its capital value, the evaluator *estimates* how much the good could be sold for in terms of money. This sort of activity is known as *appraisement* and is to be distinguished from subjective evaluation. If Jones says: "I shall be able to sell this house next week for 250 ounces," he is "appraising" its purchasing power, or "objective exchange-value," at 250 ounces of gold. He is not thereby ranking the house and gold on his own value scale, but is estimating the money price of the house at some point in the future. We shall see below that appraisement is fundamental to the entire economic system in an economy of indirect exchange. Not only do the renting and selling of consumers' goods rest on appraisement and on hope of monetary profits, but so does the activity of all the investing producers, the keystone of the entire productive system. We shall see that the term "capital value" applies, not only to durable consumers' goods, but to all nonhuman factors of production as well—i.e., land and capital goods, singly and in various aggregates. The use and purchase of these factors rest on appraisement by entrepreneurs of their eventual yield in terms of monetary income on the market, and it will be seen that their capital value on the market will also tend to be equal to the discounted sum of their future yields of money income.[46]

5

Production: The Structure

1. *Some Fundamental Principles of Action*

The analysis of production activities—the actions that eventually result in the attainment of consumers' goods—is a highly intricate one for a complex, monetary market economy. It is best, therefore, to summarize now some of the most applicable of the fundamental principles formulated in chapter 1. In that chapter we applied those principles to a Crusoe economy only. Actually, however, they are applicable to any type of economy and are the indispensable keys to the analysis of the complex modern economy. Some of these fundamental principles are:

1) Each individual acts so that the expected psychic revenue, or achievement of utility, from his action will exceed its psychic cost. The latter is the forgone utility of the next best alternative that he could adopt with the available means. Both the psychic revenue and the psychic cost are purely subjective to the individual. Since all action deals with units of supply of a good, we may refer to these subjective estimates as marginal utility and marginal cost, the *marginal* signifying action in steps.

2) Each person acts in the *present* instant, on the basis of present value scales, to obtain *anticipated* end results *in the future*. Each person acts, therefore, to arrive at a certain satisfactory state in the future. Each has a temporal horizon of future dates toward which his actions are directed. He uses present given *means*, according to his technological ideas, to attain his ends in the future.

3) Every person prefers and will attempt to achieve the satis-

faction of a given end in the present to the satisfaction of that
end in the future. This is the law of time preference.

4) All goods are distributed by each individual in accordance
with their utility to him. A stock of the units of a good is allocated
first to its most highly valued uses, then to its next most highly
valued use, etc. The definition of a *good* is that it consists of an
interchangeable supply of one or more units. Therefore, every
unit will always be valued equally with every other. If a unit of
a stock is given up or disposed of, the *least highly valued use* for
one unit will be the one given up. Therefore, the value of each
unit of the supply of a good is equal to the utility of the least
highly valued of its present uses. This marginal utility diminishes
as the stock of each good increases. The marginal utility of *addition* of a unit to the stock equals the utility of a unit in its next
most highly valued use, i.e., *the most highly valued of the not
yet satisfied ends.* This provides us with the law of marginal utility
and the law of allocation of goods.

5) In the technical combination of factors of production to
yield a product, as one factor varies and the others remain constant, there is an optimum point—a point of maximum average
product produced by the factor. This is the law of returns. It
is based on the very fact of the existence of human action.

6) And we know from chapter 2 that the price of any good
on the market will tend to be *uniform* throughout the market.
The price is determined by supply and demand schedules, which
are themselves determined by the value scales of the individuals
in the market.

2. *The Evenly Rotating Economy*

Analysis of the activities of production in a monetary market
economy is a highly complex matter. An explanation of these
activities, in particular the determination of prices and therefore
the return to factors, the allocation of factors, and the formation
of capital, can be developed only if we use the mental construction
of the *evenly rotating economy.*

This construction is developed as follows: We realize that the real world of action is one of continual change. Individual value scales, technological ideas, and the quantities of means available are always changing. These changes continually impel the economy in various directions. Value scales change, and consumer demand shifts from one good to another. Technological ideas change, and factors are used in a different way. Both types of change have differing effects on prices. Time preferences change, with certain effects on interest and capital formation. The crucial point is this: before the effects of any one change are completely worked out, other changes intervene. What we must consider, however, by the use of reasoning, is what would happen if no changes intervened. In other words, what would occur if value scales, technological ideas, and the given resources remained constant? What would then happen to prices and production and their relations? Given values, technology, and resources, whatever their concrete form, remain constant. In that case, the economy tends toward a state of affairs in which it is *evenly rotating*, i.e., in which the same activities tend to be repeated in the same pattern over and over again. Rates of production of each good remain constant, all prices remain constant, total population remains constant, etc. Thus, if values, technology, and resources remain constant, we have two successive states of affairs: (*a*) the period of transition to an unchanging, evenly rotating economy, and (*b*) the unchanging round of the evenly rotating economy itself. This latter stage is the state of *final equilibrium*. It is to be distinguished from the market equilibrium prices that are set each day by the interaction of supply and demand. *The final equilibrium state is one which the economy is always tending to approach.* If our *data*—values, technology, and resources—remained constant, the economy would move toward the final equilibrium position and remain there. In actual life, however, the data are always changing, and therefore, before arriving at a final equilibrium point, the economy must shift direction, towards some other final equilibrium position.

Hence, the final equilibrium position is always changing, and consequently no one such position is ever reached in practice. But even though it is never reached in practice, it has a very real importance. In the first place, it is like the mechanical rabbit being chased by the dog. It is never reached in practice and it is always changing, but it explains the direction in which the dog is moving. Secondly, the complexity of the market system is such that we cannot analyze factor prices and incomes in a world of continual change unless we first analyze their determination in an evenly rotating world where there is no change and where given conditions are allowed to work themselves out to the full.

Certainly at this stage of inquiry we are not interested in ethical evaluations of our knowledge. We are attaching no ethical merit to the equilibrium position. It is a concept for scientific explanation of human activity.

The reader might ask why such an "unrealistic" concept as final equilibrium is permissible, when we have already presented and will present grave strictures against the use of various unrealistic and antirealistic premises in economics. For example, as we shall see, the theory of "pure competition," so prevalent among writers today, is based on impossible premises. The theory is then worked out along these lines and not only applied uncritically to the real world, but actually used as an ethical base from which to criticize the real "deviations" from this theory. The concepts of "indifference classes" and of infinitely small steps are other examples of false premises that are used as the basis of highly elaborate theoretical structures. The concept of the evenly rotating economy, however, when used with care, is not open to these criticisms. For this is an ever-present force, since it is the goal toward which the actual system is always moving, the *final position of rest,* at which, on the basis of the given, actually existing value scales, all individuals would have attained the highest positions on their value scales, given the technology and resources. This concept, then, is of legitimate and realistic importance.

We must always remember, however, that while a final equilibrium is the goal toward which the economy is moving at any particular time, changes in the data alter this position and therefore shift the direction of movement. Therefore, *there is nothing in a dynamic world that is ethically better about a final equilib-*

rium position. As a matter of fact, since wants are unsatisfied (otherwise there would be no action), such a position of no change would be most unfortunate, since it would imply that no further want-satisfaction would be possible. Furthermore, we must remember that a final equilibrium situation tends to be, though it can never actually be, the *result* of market activity, and not the *condition* of such activity. Far too many writers, for example, discerning that in the evenly rotating economy entrepreneurial profits and losses would all be zero, have somehow concluded that this must be the *condition* for any legitimate activity on the market. There could hardly be a greater misconception of the market or a greater abuse of the equilibrium concept.

Another danger in the use of this concept is that its purely static, essentially timeless, conditions are all too well suited for the use of mathematics. Mathematics rests on *equations*, which portray mutual relationships between two or more "functions." Of themselves, of course, such mathematical procedures are unimportant, since they do not establish causal relationships. They are of the greatest importance in physics, for example, because that science deals with certain observed regularities of motion by particles of matter that we must regard as unmotivated. These particles move according to certain precisely observable, exact, quantitative laws. Mathematics is indispensable in formulating the laws among these variables and in formulating theoretical explanations for the observed phenomena. In human action, the situation is entirely different, if not diametrically opposite. Whereas in physics, causal relations can only be assumed hypothetically and later approximately verified by referring to precise observable regularities, in praxeology we *know* the causal force at work. This causal force is human action, *motivated,* purposeful behavior, directed at certain ends. The universal aspects of this behavior can be logically analyzed. We are not dealing with "functional," quantitative relations among variables, but with human reason and will causing certain action, which is not "determinable" or reducible to outside forces. Furthermore, since the data of human action are always changing, there are no precise, quantitative relationships in human history. In physics, the quantitative relationships, or laws, are constant; they are considered to be valid for any point in human history, past, present, or future. In the field of human action, there are no such quantitative constants. There are no constant relationships valid for different periods in human history. The only "natural laws" (if we may use such an old-fashioned but perfectly legitimate label for such constant regularities) in human action are *qualitative* rather than *quantitative*. They are, for example, precisely the laws educed in praxeology and economics—the fact of action, the use of means to achieve ends, time preference, diminishing marginal utility, etc.[1]

Mathematical equations, then, are appropriate and useful where there are constant quantitative relations among unmotivated variables. They are singularly inappropriate in praxeology and economics. In the latter fields, verbal, logical analysis of action and its processes through time is the appropriate method. It is not surprising that the main efforts of the "mathematical economists" have been directed toward describing the final equilibrium state by means of equations. For in this state, since activities merely repeat themselves, there seems to be more scope for describing conditions by means of functional equations. These equations, at best, however, can do no more than describe this equilibrium state.

Aside from doing no more than verbal logic can do, and therefore violating the scientific principle of *Occam's razor*—that science should be as simple and clear as possible—such a use of mathematics contains grave errors and defects within itself. In the first place, it cannot describe the *path* by which the economy approaches the final equilibrium position. This task can be performed only by verbal, logical analysis of the causal action of human beings. It is evident that this task is the important one, since it is this analysis that is significant for human action. Action moves along a path and is not describable in an unchanging, evenly rotating world. The world is an uncertain one, and we shall see shortly that we cannot even pursue to its logical conclusion the analysis of a static, evenly rotating economy. The assumption of an evenly rotating economy is only an auxiliary tool in aiding us in the analysis of real action. Since mathematics is least badly accommodated to a static state, mathematical writers have tended to be preoccupied with this state, thus providing a particularly misleading picture of the world of action. Finally, the mathematical equations of the evenly rotating economy describe only a static situation, outside of time.[2] They differ drastically from the mathematical equations of physics, which describe a *process through time;* it is precisely through this description of constant, quantitative relations in the *motion* of elements that mathematics renders its great service in natural science. How different is economics, where mathematics, at best, can only inadequately describe a timeless end result![3]

The use of the mathematical concept of "function" is particularly inappropriate in a science of human action. On the one hand, action itself is *not* a function of anything, since "function" implies definite, unique, mechanical regularity and determination. On the other hand, the mathematics of simultaneous equations, dealing in physics with unmotivated motion, stresses mutual determination. In human action, however, the known causal force of action unilinearly determines the results. This gross misconception by mathematically inclined writers on the study of human action was exemplified during a running attack on Eugen Böhm-Bawerk, one of the greatest of all economists, by Professor George Stigler:

. . . yet the postulate of continuity of utility and demand functions (which is unrealistic only to a minor degree, and essential to analytic treatment) is never granted. A more important weakness is Böhm-Bawerk's failure to understand some of the most essential elements of modern economic theory, the concepts of mutual determination and equilibrium (developed by the use of the theory of simultaneous equations). Mutual determination is spurned for the older concept of cause and effect.[4]

The "weakness" displayed here is not that of Böhm-Bawerk, but of those, like Professor Stigler, who attempt vainly and fallaciously to construct economics on the model of mathematical physics, specifically, of classical mechanics.[5]

To return to the concept of the evenly rotating economy, the error of the mathematical economists is to treat it as a real and even ideal state of affairs, whereas it is simply a mental concept enabling us to analyze the market and human activities on the market. It is indispensable because it is the goal, though ever-shifting, of action and exchange; on the other hand, the data can never remain unchanged long enough for it to be brought into being. We cannot conceive in all consistency of a state of affairs without change or uncertainty, and therefore without action. The evenly rotating state, for example, would be incompatible with the existence of money, the very medium at the center of the entire exchange structure. For the money commodity is demanded and held only because it is more marketable than other commodities, i.e., because the holder is more sure of being able to exchange it. In a world where prices and demands remain perpetually the same, such demand for money would be unnecessary. Money is demanded and held only because it gives greater assurance of finding a market and because of the uncertainties of the person's demands in the near future. If everyone, for example, knew his spending precisely over his entire future—and this would be known under the evenly rotating system—there would be no point in his keeping a cash balance of money. It would be invested so that money would be returned in precisely the needed amounts on the day of expenditure. But if no one wishes to hold money, there will be no money and no system of money prices. The entire monetary market would break down. Thus, the evenly rotating economy is unrealistic, for it cannot actually be established and we cannot even conceive consistently of its establishment. But the idea of the evenly rotating economy is indispensable in analyzing the real economy; through hypothesizing a world where all change has worked itself out, we can analyze the directions of actual change.

3. *The Structure of Production: A World of Specific Factors*

Crucial to understanding the process of production is the question of the *specificity* of factors, a problem we touched on in chapter 1. A *specific* factor is one suitable to the production of only one product. A *purely nonspecific* factor would be one equally suited to the production of *all* possible products. It is clear that not all factors could be purely nonspecific, for in that case all factors would be purely interchangeable, i.e., there would be need for only one factor. But we have seen that human action implies more than one existing factor. Even the existence of *one* purely nonspecific factor is inconceivable if we properly consider "suitability in production" in *value* terms rather than in *technological* terms.[6] In fact, if we analyze the concept, we find that there is no sense in saying that a factor is "equally suitable" in purely technological terms, since there is no way of comparing the physical quantities of one product with those of another. If X can help to produce three units of A or two units of B, there is no way by which we can compare these units. Only the *valuation* of consumers establishes a hierarchy of valued goods, their interaction setting the prices of the consumers' goods. (Relatively) nonspecific factors, then, are allocated to those products that the consumers have valued most highly. It is difficult to conceive of any good that would be purely nonspecific and equally valuable in all processes of production. Our major distinction, then, is between the *specific* factor, which can be used in only one line of production, and the *nonspecific* factor (of varying degrees of convertibility), which can be used in more than one production process.

Now let us for a time consider a world where every good is produced *only* by several *specific* factors. In this world, a world that is conceivable, though highly unlikely, every person, every piece of land, every capital good, would necessarily be irrevocably committed to the production of one particular product. There would be no alternative uses of any good from one line of production to another. In the entire world of production, then, there would be little or no "economic problem," i.e., no problem of allocating scarce means to alternative ends. Certainly, the *consumers* would still have to allocate their scarce monetary resources to the most preferred consumers' goods. In the nonmarket sphere, everyone—again as a consumer—would have to allocate his time and energies to the enjoyment of various consumers' goods.

There would still, in the sphere of production of exchangeable goods, be *one* allocation that every man would make: how much time to devote to labor and how much to leisure. But there would be no problem of *which* field to labor in, no problem of what to do with any piece of land, no problem of how to allocate capital goods. The employment of the factors would all depend on the consumers' demand for the final product.

The structure of production in such a world of purely specific

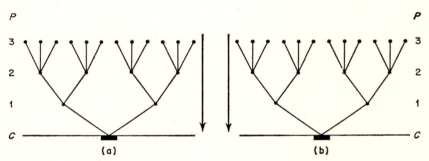

FIG. 39.   STRUCTURE OF PRODUCTION IN A WORLD OF PURELY SPECIFIC FACTORS

factors would be somewhat as in Fig. 39. In this diagram, we see two typical consumers' goods, *A* and *B*. Each, depicted as a solid rectangle at the bottom of the diagram, is produced by co-operating factors of the next higher rank, designated *P* 1, or the first order of producers' goods. The *capital goods* of the first rank are, in turn, produced with the help of co-operating factors, these being of the second-rank, and so on upward. The process logically continues upward until capital goods are produced completely by land and labor factors, although this stage is not depicted on the diagram. Lines connect the dots to designate the causal pattern of the factors. In the diagram, all factors are purely *specific,* since no good is used at different stages of the process or for different goods. The center arrows indicate the causal direction of *effort* downward, from the highest ranked producers' goods through the intermediate ranks, finally concluding in consumers' goods. At each stage, labor uses nature-given factors to produce capital goods, and the capital goods are again combined with labor and nature-given factors, transformed into lower and lower orders of capital goods, until consumers' goods are reached.

Now that we have traced the direction of productive effort, we must trace the direction of monetary income. This is a reverse one, from the consumers back to the producers. The consumers purchase the stock of a consumers' good at a price determined on the market, yielding the producers a certain income. Two of the crucial problems of production theory are the method by which the monetary income is allocated and the corollary problem of the pricing of the factors of production. First, let us consider only the "lowest" stage of production, the stage that brings about the *final* product. In that stage, numerous factors, all now assumed to be specific, co-operate in producing the consumers' good. There are three types of such factors: labor, original nature and produced capital goods.[7] Let us assume that on a certain day, consumers purchase a certain quantity of a good *X* for, say, 100 ounces of gold. Given the quantity of the good sold, the *price* of the total quantity is equal to the (gross) income obtained from the sale of the good. How will these 100 ounces be allocated to the producing factors?

In the first place, we must make an assumption about the *ownership* of the consumers' good just before it is sold. It is obvious that this owner or these owners will be the *immediate* recipients of the 100 ounces of gold income. Let us say that, in the final stage, there have been seven factors participating in the production: two types of labor, two types of land, and three types of capital goods. There are two alternatives in regard to the final ownership of the product (*before* it is sold to the consumer): (*a*) all the owners of these factors *jointly* own the final product; or (*b*) the owner of each of the factors sells the services of his factor to someone else, and the latter (who may himself contribute a factor) sells the good at a later date to the consumer. Although the latter is the nearly universal condition, it will be convenient to begin by analyzing the first alternative.

Those who own the final product, whatever the alternative adopted, are "capitalists," since they are the owners of capital goods. It is better, however, to confine the term "capitalists" to those who have saved money capital with which to buy factors. This, by definition, does not occur under the first alternative, where owners of factors are joint owners of the products. The term "product-owner" suffices for designating the owner of the capital assets, whatever the alternative adopted. Product-owners are also "entrepreneurs," since they assume the major entrepreneurial burden of adjusting to uncertain future conditions. To call them "entrepreneurs" alone, however, is to run the danger of forgetting that they are also capitalists or product-owners and that they would continue to perform that function in an evenly rotating economy.

4. *Joint Ownership of the Product by the Owners of the Factors*

Let us first consider the case of joint ownership by the owners of all the final co-operating factors.[8] It is clear that the 100 ounces of gold accrue to the owners jointly. Let us now be purely arbitrary and state that a total of 80 ounces accrues to the owners of capital goods and a total of 20 ounces to the owners of labor and nature-given factors. It is obvious that, whatever the allocation, it will be, on the unhampered market, in accordance with the voluntary contractual agreement of each and every factor-owner concerned. Now it is clear that there is an important difference between what happens to the monetary income of the *laborer* and the *landowner,* on the one hand, and of the owner of *capital goods,* on the other. For the capital goods must in turn be produced by labor, nature, and other capital goods. Therefore, while the contributor of personal "labor" energy (and this, of course, includes the energy of direction as well as what are called "laborers" in popular parlance) has earned a pure return, the owner of capital goods has previously spent some money for the production or the purchase of *his* owned factors.

Now it is clear that, since only factors of production may obtain income from the consumer, *the price of the consumers' good, i.e., the income from the consumers' good, equals the sum of the prices accruing to the producing factors, i.e., the income accruing to the factors.* In the case of joint ownership, this is a truism, since *only a factor* can receive income from the sale of a good. It is the same as saying that 100 ounces equals 100 ounces.

But what of the 80 ounces that we have arbitrarily allocated to the owners of capital goods? To whom do they finally accrue? Since we are assuming in this example of joint ownership that all products are owned by their factor-owners, it also follows that capital goods, which are *also* products, are *themselves* jointly owned by the factors on the second rank of production. Let us say that each of the three first-order capital goods was produced by five co-operating factors: two types of labor, one type of land, two types of capital goods. All these factor-owners jointly own the 80 ounces. Let us say that each of the first-order capital goods had obtained the following:

> Capital good *A*: 30 ounces
> Capital good *B*: 30 ounces
> Capital good *C*: 20 ounces

The income to each capital good will then be owned by five factor-owners on the second rank of production.

It is clear that, conceptually, *no one, in the last analysis, receives a return as the owner of a capital good.* Since every capital good analytically resolves itself into original nature-given and labor factors, it is evident that no money could accrue to the owner of a capital good. All 100 ounces must eventually be allocated to labor and owners of nature-given factors exclusively. Thus, the 30 ounces accruing to the owners of capital good *A* will be allocated to the five factor-owners, while the, say, four ounces accruing to one of the capital goods of third rank helping to produce good *A* will, in turn, be allocated to land, labor, and capital-goods factors of the fourth rank, etc. Eventually, all the money is allocated to labor and nature-given factors only. The diagram in Fig. 40 illustrates this process.

At the bottom of the diagram, we see that 100 ounces of gold are transferred from the consumers to the producers. Some of this money goes to owners of capital goods, some to landowners, some to owners of labor. (The proportion going to one group and the other is arbitrarily assumed in the example and is of no importance for this analysis.) The amount accruing to the capital-goods owners is included in the *shaded* portion of the diagram and the amount accruing *both* to labor and nature-owners is included in the clear portion of the diagram. In the lowest, the

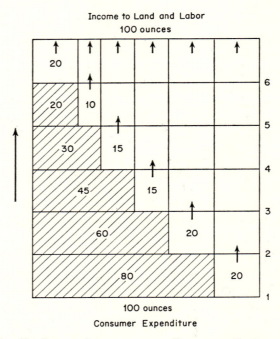

Income to Land and Labor
100 ounces

Fig. 40.   Income Accruing to the Factors of Production

first, block, the 20 ounces received by owners of land and of labor factors is marked with an upward arrow, followed by a similar upward arrow at the top of the diagram, the top line designating the money ultimately received by the owners of the various factors. The width of the top line (100 ounces) must be equal to the width of the bottom line (100 ounces), since the money ultimately received by the owners of the factors must equal the money spent by the consumers.

Moving up to line 2, we follow the fortunes of the 80 ounces which had accrued to the owners of capital goods of the first order. We assume that 60 ounces accrue to the owners of second-order capital goods and 20 ounces to second-order labor and nature-given factors. Once again, the 20 ounces' clear area is marked with an upward arrow designating the ultimate receipt of money by the owners of the factors and is equally marked off on the top line of the diagram. The same process is repeated as we go further and further upward in the order of capital goods. At each point, of course, the amount obtained by owners of capital goods becomes smaller, because more and more has accrued to labor and nature owners. Finally, at the highest conceivable stage, all the remaining 20 ounces earned by the owners of capital goods accrue to land and labor factors only, since eventually we must come to the stage where no capital good has yet been produced and only labor and nature remain. The result is that the 100 ounces are all eventually allocated to the clear spaces, to the land and labor factors. The large upward arrow on the left signifies the general upward course of the monetary income.

To the truism that the income from sale of the consumers' good equals the consumers' expenditure on the good, we may add a corresponding truism for each stage of production, namely, that *the income from sale of a capital good equals the income accruing to the factors of its production.*

In the world that we have been examining, where all products, at whatever stage, are owned jointly by the owners of their factors, it is clear that *first* work is done on the highest stage. Owners of land and of labor *invest* their land and labor to produce the highest-order (in this case the fifth) capital good; then these owners turn the good over to the owners of labor and land at the next lower stage; these produce the fourth-order capital good, which in turn co-operates with labor and land factors on that stage to produce the lower-order good, etc. Finally, the lowest stage is reached, and the final factors co-operate to produce the consumers' good. The consumers' good is then sold to consumers.[9]

In the case of joint ownership, then, there does not arise any separate class of owners of capital goods. All the capital goods produced are jointly owned by the owners of the producing land and labor factors; the capital goods of the next lower order are owned by the owners of the land and labor factors at the next lower stage along with the previously co-operating owners, etc. In sum, the entire capital-goods structure engaged in any line of production is jointly owned by the owners of land and labor. And the income gained from the final sale of the product to the consumers accrues only to the owners of land and labor; there is no separate group of owners of capital goods to whom income accrues.[10]

It is obvious that the production process takes *time,* and the more complex the production process the more time must be taken. During this time, all the factors have had to work without earning any remuneration; they have had to work only in *expectation* of *future* income. Their income is received only at a much later date.

The income that would be earned by the factors, in a world of purely specific factors, depends entirely on consumer demand for the particular final product. If consumers spend 100 ounces on the good, then the factors will jointly earn 100 ounces. If they spend 500 ounces, the factors will earn that amount. If they spend nothing on the product, and the producers have made the enormous entrepreneurial error of working on a product that the consumers do not buy, the factors earn precisely zero. The joint monetary income earned by the owners of the factors fluctuates *pari passu* with consumer demand for the product.

At this point, a question naturally arises: What happens to owners of factors who earn a zero return? Must they "starve"? Fundamentally, we cannot answer this question for concrete individual persons, since economics demonstrates truths about "functional" earnings in production, and not about the entire earnings of a given person. A particular person, in other words, may experience a zero return on this good, while at the same time earning a substantial return on ownership of another piece of land. In cases where there is no such ownership in another area, the individual may pursue isolated production that does not yield a monetary return, or, if he has an accumulated monetary cash balance, he may purchase goods by reducing the balance. Furthermore, if he has such a balance, he may invest in land or capital goods or in a production organization owning them, in some other line of production. His labor, on our assumptions, may be a specific factor, but his *money* is usable in every line of production.

Suppose we assume the worst possible case—a man with no cash balance, with no assets of capital, and whose labor is a *specific* factor the product of which has little or no consumer demand.[11] Is he not truly an example of an individual led astray by the existence of the market and of the specialization prevalent on it? By subjecting himself to the consumer has he not placed his happiness and existence in jeopardy? Even granting that people chose a market, could not the choice turn out to be tragic for many people?

The answer is that there is no basis whatever for such strictures on the market process. For even in this impossible case, the individual is no worse off than he would have been in isolation or barter. He can always revert to isolation if he finds he cannot attain his ends via the market process. The very fact that we consider such a possibility ludicrous is evidence of the enormous advantages that the market confers upon everyone. Indeed, empirically, we can certainly state that without the modern, developed market, and thrown back into isolation, the overwhelming majority of individuals could not obtain enough exchangeable goods to exist at all. Yet this choice always remains open to anyone who, for any reason, voluntarily prefers isolation to the vast benefits obtainable from the market system. Certainly, therefore, complaints against the market system by disgruntled persons are misplaced and erroneous. Any person or group, on the unhampered market, is free to abandon the social market at any time and to withdraw into any other desired form of co-operative arrangement. People may withdraw into individual isolation or establish some sort of group isolation or start from the beginning to re-create their own market. In any case, on the free market, their choice is entirely their own, and they decide according to their preferences unhampered by the use or threat of violence.[12]

Our example of the "worst possible case" enables us to analyze one of the most popular objections to the free society: that "it leaves people free to starve." First, from the fact that this objection is so widespread, we can easily conclude that there will be enough charitable people in the society to present these unfortunates with gifts. There is, however, a more fundamental refutation. It is that the "freedom-to-starve" argument rests on a basic confusion of "freedom" with "abundance of exchangeable goods." The two must be kept conceptually distinct. Freedom is meaningfully definable only as absence of interpersonal restrictions. Robinson Crusoe on the desert island is absolutely free, since there is no other person to hinder him. But he is not necessarily living an abundant life; indeed, he is likely to be constantly on the verge of starvation. Whether or not man lives at the level of poverty or abundance depends upon the success that he and his ancestors have had in grappling with nature and in transforming naturally given resources into capital goods and consumers' goods. The two problems, therefore, are logically separate. Crusoe is absolutely free, yet starving, while it is certainly possible, though not likely, for a given person at a given instant to be a slave while being kept in riches by his master. Yet there is an important connection between the two, for we have seen that a free market tends to lead to abundance for all of its participants, and we shall see below that violent intervention in the market and a hegemonic society tend to lead to general poverty. That a person is "free to starve" is therefore *not* a condemnation of the free market, but a simple fact of nature: every child comes into the world without capital or resources of his own. On the contrary, as we shall see further below, it is the free market in a free society that furnishes the only instrument to reduce or eliminate poverty and provide abundance.

5. Cost

At this point, let us reintroduce the concept of "cost" into the analysis. We have seen above that the cost, or "marginal" cost, of any decision is the next highest utility that must be forgone because of the decision. When a means M must be distributed among ends E_1, E_2, and E_3, with E_1 ranked highest on the individual's value scale, the individual attempts to allocate the means so as to attain his most highly valued ends and to forgo those ranked lower, although he will attain as many of his ends as he can with the means available. If he allocates his means to E_1 and E_2, and must forgo E_3, E_3 is the marginal cost of his decision. If he errs in his decision, and arrives at E_3 instead of E_2, then *ex post*—in retrospect—he is seen to have suffered a loss compared to the course he could have taken.

What are the costs involved in the decisions made by the owners of the factors? In the first place, it must be stressed that these costs are subjective and cannot be precisely determined by outside observers or be gauged *ex post* by observing accountants.[13] Secondly, it is clear that, *since* such factors as land and the produced capital goods have only one use, namely, the production of this product (by virtue of being purely specific), they involve *no cost* to their owner in being used in production. By the very terms of our problem, the only alternative for their owner would be to let the land lie unused, earning no return. The use of labor, however, does have a cost, in accordance with the value of the leisure forgone by the laborers. This value is, of course, unmeasurable in money terms, and necessarily differs for each individual, since there can be no comparison between the value scales of two or more persons.

Once the final product has been produced, the analysis of the previous chapter follows, and it becomes clear that, in most cases, the sale of the good at the market price, whatever the price may be, is *costless,* except for rare cases of direct consumption by the producer or in cases of anticipation of a price increase in the near future. This sale is *costless* from the proper point of view— the point of view of acting man at the relevant instant of action. The fact that he would not have engaged in the labor at all if he had known in advance of the present price might indicate a deplorable instance of poor judgment, but it does not affect the present situation. At present, with all the labor already exerted and the product finished, the original—subjective—cost has already been incurred and vanished with the original making of the decision. At present, there is no alternative to the sale of the good at the market price, and therefore the sale is costless.[14]

It is evident, therefore, that once the product has been made, "cost" has *no influence* on the price of the product. Past costs, being ephemeral, are irrelevant to present determination of prices. The agitation that often takes place over sales "below cost" is now placed in its proper perspective. It is obvious that, in the relevant sense of "cost," no such sales can take place. The sale of an already produced good is likely to be costless, and if it is not, and price is below its costs, then the seller will hold on to the good rather than make the sale.

That costs do have an influence in production is not denied by anyone. However, the influence is not directly on the price, but on the amount that will be produced or, more specifically, on the degree to which factors will be used. We have seen in our example that land and capital goods will be used to the fullest extent practicable, since there is no return or benefit in allowing them to remain idle.[15] But man laboring bears the cost of leisure forgone. What he expects will be the monetary return from his labor is the deciding factor in his decision concerning how much or whether or not to employ his labor on the product. The monetary return is ranked on his subjective value scale along with the costs of forgoing leisure, and his decision is made on the quantity of labor he will put forth in production. The height of costs on individual value scales, then, is *one* of the determinants of the quantity, the *stock,* that will be produced. This stock, of course, *later* plays a role in the determination of market price, since stock is evaluated by consumers according to the law of diminishing marginal utility. This, however, is a far cry from stating that cost either determines, or is co-ordinate with utility in determining, price. We may briefly summarize the law of price (which can be stated at this point only in regard to specific factors and joint ownership, but which will be later seen as true for any arrangement of production): Individuals, on their value scales, evaluate a given stock of goods according to their utilities, setting the prices of consumers' goods; the stock is produced according to previous decisions by producers, who had weighed on their value scales the expected monetary revenue from consumers against the subjective costs (themselves simply *utilities forgone*) of engaging in the production. In the former case, the utility valuations are generally (though by no means always) the ones made by *consumers;* in the latter case, they are made by *producers.* But it is clear that the determinants of price are *only the subjective utilities of individuals* in valuing given conditions and alternatives. There are no "objective" or "real" costs that determine, or are co-ordinate in determining, price.[16]

If we investigate the costs of laborers in production more closely, we see that what is involved is not simply a question of leisure forgone. There is another, though in this case intertwined, element: *present goods* are being forgone in exchange for an expectation of return *in the future.* Thus, added to the leisure-labor element, the workers, in this case, must wait for some time before earning the return, while they must give up their leisure in the present or in various periods earlier than the return is obtained. Time, therefore, is a critical element in production, and its analysis must pervade any theory of production.

When the owners of the factors embark on a process of production the yield of which will be necessarily realized in the future, they are giving up leisure and other consumers' goods that they either could have enjoyed without working or could have earned earlier from shorter processes of production. In order to *invest* their labor and land in a process of production, then, they must restrict their *present* consumption to less than its possible maximum. This involves forgoing either immediate consumption or the consumption made possible from shorter processes of production. *Present* consumption is given up in anticipation of *future* consumption. Since we have seen that the universal law of time preference holds that any given satisfaction will be preferred earlier than later, an equivalent satisfaction will be preferred as early as possible. Present consumption of a good will be given up only in anticipation of a *greater future* consumption, the degree of the premium being dependent on time preferences. This restriction of present consumption is *saving.* (See the discussion in chapter 1, above.)

In a world where products are all jointly owned by owners of factors, the original owners of land and labor must do their own saving; there is no monetary expression to represent total saving, even in a monetary economy. The owners of land and labor forgo a certain amount of present or earlier consumption and save in various amounts in order to invest their time and labor to produce the final product. Their income is finally earned, say after one year, when the good is sold to the consumers and the 100 ounces is received by the joint owners. It is impossible, however, for us to say what this saving or investment was in monetary terms.

6. *Ownership of the Product by Capitalists: Amalgamated Stages*

Up to this point we have discussed the case in which the owners of land and labor, i.e., of the original factors, restrict their possible consumption and invest their factors in a production process, which, after a certain time, produces a consumers' good to be sold to consumers for money. Now let us consider a situation in which the owners of the factors do *not* own the final product. How could this come about? Let us first forget about the various stages of the production process and assume for the moment that all the stages can be lumped together as one. An individual or a group of individuals acting jointly can then, *at present,* offer to pay money to the owners of land and labor, thus buying the services of their factors. The factors then work and produce the product, which, under the terms of their agreement, belongs to the new class of product-owners. These product-owners have purchased the services of the land and labor factors as the latter have been contributing to production; they then sell the final product to the consumers.

What has been the contribution of these product-owners, or "capitalists," to the production process? It is this: the saving and restriction of consumption, instead of being done by the owners of land and labor, has been done by the *capitalists.* The capitalists originally saved, say, 95 ounces of gold which they could have then spent on consumers' goods. They refrained from doing so, however, and, instead, *advanced* the money to the original owners of the factors. They *paid* the latter for their services while they were working, thus advancing them money before the product was actually produced and sold to the consumers. The capitalists, therefore, made an essential contribution to production. They relieved the owners of the original factors from the necessity of sacrificing present goods and waiting for future goods. *Instead,* the capitalists have supplied present goods *from their own savings* (i.e., money with which to buy present goods) to the owners of the original factors. In return for this supply of present goods, the latter contribute their productive services to the capitalists, who become the owners of the product. More precisely, the capitalists become the owners of the capital structure, of the whole structure of capital goods as they are produced. Keeping to our assumption that one capitalist or group of capitalists owns all the stages of any good's production, the capitalists continue to advance present goods to owners of factors as the "year" goes on. As the period of time continues, highest-order capital goods are first produced, are then transformed into lower-order capital goods, etc., and ultimately into the final product. At any given time this whole structure is owned by the capitalists. When one capitalist owns the whole structure, these capital goods, it must be stressed, *do him no good whatever.* Thus, suppose that a capitalist has already advanced 80 ounces over a period of many months to owners of labor and land in a line of production. He has in his ownership, as a result, a mass of fifth-, fourth-, and third-order capital goods. None of these capital goods is of any use to him, however, until the goods can be further worked on and the final product obtained and sold to the consumer.

Popular literature attributes enormous "power" to the capitalist and considers his owning a mass of capital goods as of enormous significance, giving him a great advantage over other people in the economy. We see, however, that this is far from the case; indeed, the opposite may well be true. For the capitalist has already saved from possible consumption and hired the services of factors to produce his capital goods. The owners of these factors have the money already for which they otherwise would have had to save and wait (and bear uncertainty), while the capitalist has only a mass of capital goods, a mass that will prove worthless to him unless it can be further worked on and the product sold to the consumers.

When the capitalist purchases factor services, what is the precise exchange that takes place? The capitalist gives money (a present good) in exchange for receiving factor services (labor and land), which work to supply him with capital goods. They supply him, in other words, with *future goods*. The capital goods for which he pays are way stations on the route to the final product—the consumers' good. At the time when land and labor are hired to produce capital goods, therefore, these capital goods, and therefore the services of the land and labor, are *future* goods; they represent the embodiment of the expected yield of a good in the future—a good that can then be consumed. The capitalist who buys the services of land and labor in year 1 to work on a product that will eventually become a consumers' good ready for sale in year 2 is advancing money (a present good) in exchange for a future good—for the present anticipation of a yield of money in the future from the sale of the final product. A present good is being exchanged for an expected future good.

Under the conditions of our example, we are assuming that the capitalists own *no* original factors, in contrast to the first case, in which the products were jointly owned by the owners of these factors. In our case, the capitalists originally owned money, with which they purchased the services of land and labor in order to produce capital goods, which are finally transformed by land and labor into consumers' goods. In this example we have assumed that the capitalists do not at any time own any of the co-operating labor or land factors. In actual life, of course, there may be and are capitalists who both work in some managerial capacity in the production process and also own the land on which they operate. Analytically, however, it is necessary to isolate these various functions. We may call those capitalists who own only the capital goods and the final product before sale "pure capitalists."

Let us now add another temporary restriction to our analysis —namely, that all producers' goods and services are only *hired*, never bought outright. This is a convenient assumption that will be maintained long after the assumption of specific factors is dropped. We here assume that the pure capitalists never purchase as a whole a factor that in itself could yield several units of service. They can only *hire* the services of factors per unit of time. This situation is directly analogous to the conditions described in chapter 4, section 7 above, in which consumers bought or "rented" the unit services of goods rather than the goods as a whole. In a free economy, of course, this hiring or renting must always occur in the case of labor services. The laborer, being a free man, *cannot be bought;* i.e., he cannot be paid a cash value for his total future anticipated services, after which he is at the permanent command of his buyer. This would be a condition of slavery, and even "voluntary slavery," as we have seen, cannot be enforced on the free market because of the inalienability of personal will. A laborer cannot be bought, then, but his *services* can be bought over a period of time; i.e., he can be rented or hired.

7. *Present and Future Goods: The Pure Rate of Interest*

We are deferring until later the major part of the analysis of the pricing of productive services and factors. At this point we can see, however, that the purchasing of labor and land services are directly analogous. The classical discussion of productive income treats labor as earning wages whereas land earns rents, and the two are supposed to be subject to completely different laws. Actually, however, the earnings of labor and land services are analogous. Both are original and productive factors; and in the case in which land is hired rather than bought, both are rented per unit of time rather than sold outright. Generally, writers on economics have termed those capitalists "entrepreneurs" who buy labor and land factors in expectation of a future monetary return from the final product. They are entrepreneurs, however, only in the actual economy of uncertainty. *In an evenly rotating economy,* where all the market actions are repeated in an endless round and there is therefore no uncertainty, *entrepreneurship* disappears. There is no uncertain future to be anticipated and about which forecasts are made. To call these capitalists simply entrepreneurs, then, is tacitly to imply that in the evenly rotating economy there will be no capitalists, i.e., no group that saves money and hires the services of factors, thereby acquiring capital and consumers' goods to be sold to the consumers. Actually, however, there is no reason why pure capitalists should not continue in the ERE (the evenly rotating economy). Even if final returns and consumer demand are certain, *the capitalists are still providing present goods to the owners of labor and land* and thus relieving them of the burden of waiting until the future goods are produced and finally transformed into consumers' goods. Their function, therefore, remains in the ERE to provide present goods and to assume the burden of waiting for future returns over the period of the production process. Let us assume simply that the sum the capitalists paid out was 95 ounces and that the final sale was for 100 ounces. The 5 ounces accruing to the capitalists is payment for their function of supplying present goods and waiting for a future return. In short, the capitalists, in year 1, bought future goods for 95 ounces and then sold the transformed product in year 2 for 100 ounces when it had become a *present* good. In other words, in year 1 the market price of an anticipated (certain) income of 100 ounces was only 95 ounces. It is clear that this arises out of the universal fact of time preference and of the resulting premium of a given good at present over the present *prospect* of its *future* acquisition.

In the monetary economy, since money enters into all transactions, the discount of a future good against a present good can, in all cases, be expressed in terms of one good: money. This is so because the money commodity is a present good and because claims to future goods are almost always expressed in terms of future money income.

The factors of production in our discussion have all been assumed to be purely *specific* to a particular line of production. When the capitalists have saved money ("money capital"), however, they are at liberty to purchase factor services in any line of production. *Money, the general medium of exchange, is precisely nonspecific.* If, for example, the saver sees that he can invest 95 ounces in the aforementioned production process and earn 100 ounces in a year, whereas he can invest 95 ounces in some other process and earn 110 ounces in a year, he will invest his money in the process earning the greater return. Clearly, the line in which he will feel impelled to invest will be the line that earns him the greatest *rate* of return on his investment.

The concept of *rate* of return is necessary in order for him to compare different potential investments for different periods of time and involving different sums of money. For any amount of money that he saves, he would like to earn the greatest amount of net return, i.e., the greatest rate of net return. The absolute amount of return has to be reduced to units of time, and this is done by determining the rate per unit of time. Thus, a return of 20 ounces on an investment of 500 ounces after 2 years is 2% per annum, while a return of 15 ounces on the same investment after 1 year is a return of 3% per annum.

After data work themselves out and continue without change, the rate of net return on the investment of money capital will, in the ERE, be the *same* in every line of production. If capitalists can earn 3% per annum in one production process and 5% per annum in another, they will cease investing in the former and invest more in the latter until the rates of return are uniform. In the ERE, there is no entrepreneurial uncertainty, and the rate of net return is the pure exchange ratio between present and future goods. This rate of return is *the rate of interest.* This *pure rate of interest* will be uniform for all periods of time and for all lines of production and will remain constant in the ERE.[17]

Suppose that at some time the rates of interest earned are not uniform as between several lines of production. If capitalists are generally earning 5% interest, and a capitalist is obtaining 7% in a particular line, other capitalists will enter this line and bid away the factors of production from him by raising factor prices. Thus, if a capitalist is paying factors 93 ounces out of 100 income, a competing capitalist can offer 95 ounces and outbid the first for the use of the factors. The first, then, forced to meet the competition of other capitalists, will have to raise his bid eventually to 95 (disregarding for simplicity the variation in percentages based on the investment figure rather than on 100). The same equalization process will occur, of course, between capitalists and firms within the same line of production—the same "industry." There is always competitive pressure, then, driving toward a uniform rate of interest in the economy. This competition, it must be pointed out, does not take place simply between firms in the same industry or producing "similar" products. Since money is the general medium of exchange and can be invested in all products, this close competition extends throughout the length and breadth of the production structure.

A fuller discussion of the determination of the rate of interest will take place in chapter 6 below. But one thing should here be evident. The classical writers erred grievously in their discussion of the income-earning process in production. They believed that wages were the "reward" of labor, rents the "reward" of land, and interest the "reward" of capital goods, the three supposedly co-ordinate and independent factors of production. But such a discussion of interest was completely fallacious. As we have seen and shall see further below, capital goods are *not* independently productive. They are the imputable creatures of land and labor (and time). Therefore, capital goods generate no interest income. We have seen above, in keeping with this analysis, that *no* income accrues to the owners of capital goods *as such*.[18]

If the owners of land and labor factors receive all the income (e.g., 100 ounces) when they own the product jointly, why do their owners consent to sell their services for a total of 5 ounces less than their "full worth"? Is this not some form of "exploitation" by the capitalists? The answer again is that the capitalists do *not* earn income from their possession of capital goods or because capital goods generate any sort of monetary income. The capitalists earn income in their capacity as *purchasers of future goods in exchange for supplying present goods to owners of factors.* It is this *time element,* the result of the various individuals' time preferences, and *not* the alleged independent productivity of capital goods, from which the interest rate and interest income arise.

The capitalists earn their interest income, therefore, by supplying the services of present goods to owners of factors in advance of the fruits of their production, acquiring their products by this purchase, and selling the products *at the later date when they become present goods*. Thus, capitalists supply present goods in exchange for future goods (the capital goods), hold the future goods, and have work done on them until they become present goods. They have given up money in the present for a greater sum of money in the future, and the interest rate that they have earned is the agio, or discount on future goods as compared with present goods, i.e., the premium commanded by present goods over future goods. We shall see below that this exchange rate between present and future goods is not only uniform in the production process, but throughout the entire market system. It is the "social rate of time preference." It is the "price of time" on the market as the resultant of all the individual valuations of that good.

How the agio, or pure interest rate, is determined, in the particular time-exchange markets, will be discussed below. Here we shall simply conclude by observing that there is some agio which will be established uniformly throughout the economy and which will be the pure interest rate on the certain expectation of future goods as against present goods.

8. *Money Costs, Prices, and Alfred Marshall*

In the ERE, therefore, every good sold to consumers will sell at a certain "final equilibrium" price and at certain total sales. These receipts will accrue in part to capitalists in the form of interest income, and the remainder to owners of land and labor. The payments of income to the producers have also been popularly termed "costs." These are clearly *money* costs, or money expenses, and are obviously not the same thing as "costs" in the psychic sense of subjective opportunity forgone. Money costs may be *ex post* as well as *ex ante*. (In the ERE, of course, *ex ante* and *ex post* calculations are always the same.) However, the two concepts become linked when psychic costs are appraised as much as possible in monetary terms. Thus, payment to factors may be

95 ounces and recorded as a cost, while the capitalist who earns an interest of five ounces considers 100 as an opportunity cost, since he could have invested elsewhere and earned five (actually, a bit higher) per cent interest.

If, *for the moment,* we include as *money costs* factor payments and interest,[19] then in the ERE, money costs equal total money sales for every firm in every line of production. A firm earns entrepreneurial *profits* when its return is more than interest, suffers entrepreneurial *losses* when its return is less. In our production process, consumers will pay 100 ounces (money sales) and money costs are 100 ounces (factor plus interest income) and there will be similar equality for all other goods and processes. What this means, in essence, is that there are no entrepreneurial profits or losses in the ERE, because there is no change of data or uncertainty about possible change. If total money sales equal total money costs, then it evidently follows that total money sales *per unit sold* will equal total money costs per unit sold. This follows from elementary rules of arithmetic. But the money sales per unit are equal to the *money price* of the good, by definition; while we shall call the total money costs per unit the *average money cost* of the good. It likewise follows, therefore, that *price will equal average money cost for every good in the ERE.*

Strange as it may seem, a great many writers on economics have deduced from this a curious conclusion indeed. They have deduced that "in the long run" (i.e., in the ERE), the fact that costs equal sales or that "cost equals price" implies that *costs determine price.* The price of the good discussed above is 100 ounces per unit, allegedly *because* the cost (average money cost) is 100 ounces per unit. This is supposed to be the law of price determination "in the long run." It would seem to be crystal clear, however, that the truth is precisely the reverse. The price of the final product is determined by the valuations and demands of the consumers, and this price *determines what the cost will be.* If the consumers value the product mentioned above so that its price is 50 ounces instead of 100 ounces, as a result, say, of a change in their valuations, then it is precisely in the "long run," when the effects of uncertainty are removed, that "costs of production" (here, factor payment plus interest payment) will equal the final price. We have seen above how factor incomes are at the mercy of consumer demand and fluctuate according to that demand. Factor payments are the *result* of sales to consumers and *do not determine the latter in advance.* Costs of production, then, are at the mercy of final price, and not the other way around. It is ironic that it is precisely in the ERE that this causative phenomenon should be the clearest. For in the ERE we see quite evidently that consumers pay and determine the final price of the product; that it is through these payments and these payments alone that factors and interest are paid; that therefore the amount of the payments and the total "costs of production" are determined by price and not vice versa. Money costs are the opposite of a basic, determining factor; they are dependent on the price of the product and on consumer demands.

In the real world of uncertainty it is more difficult to see this, because factors are paid in *advance* of the sale of the product, since the capitalist-entrepreneurs speculatively advance money to the factors in the *expectation* of being able to recoup their money with a surplus for interest and profit after sale to the consumers.[20] Whether they do so or not depends on their foresight regarding the state of consumer demand and the future prices of consumers' goods. In the real world of immediate market prices, of course, the existence of entrepreneurial profit and loss will always prevent costs and receipts, cost and price, from being identical, and it is obvious to all that price is solely determined by valuations of stock—by "utilities"—and not at all by money cost. But although most economists recognize that in the real world (the so-called "short-run") costs cannot determine price, they are seduced by the habit of the individual entrepreneur of dealing in terms of "cost" as the determining factor, and they apply this procedure to the case of the ERE and therefore to the inherent long-run tendencies of the economy. Their grave error, as will be discussed further below, comes from viewing the economy from the standpoint of an individual entrepreneur rather than from that of an economist. To the individual entrepreneur, the "cost" of factors is largely determined by forces outside himself and his own sales; the economist, however, must see how money costs are determined and, taking account of all the interrelations in the economy, must recognize that they are determined by final prices reflecting consumer demands and valuations.

The source of the error will become clearer below when we consider a world of nonspecific as well as specific factors. However, the essentials of our analysis and its conclusion remain the same in that more complex and realistic case.

The classical economists were under the delusion that the price of the final product is determined by "costs of production," or rather they fluctuated between this doctrine and the "labor theory of value," which isolated the money costs of labor and picked that segment of the cost of production as the determinant of price. They slurred over the determination of the prices of such goods as old paintings that already existed and needed no further production. The correct relation between prices and costs, as outlined above, was developed, along with other outstanding contributions to economics, by the "Austrian" economists, including the Austrians Carl Menger, Eugen von Böhm-Bawerk, and Friedrich von Wieser, and the Englishman W. Stanley Jevons. It was with the writings of the Austrian school in the 1870's and 1880's that economics was truly established as a science.[21]

Unfortunately, in the science of economics *retrogression* in knowledge has taken place almost as often as progression. The enormous advance provided by the Austrian school, on this point as on others, was blocked and reversed by the influence of Alfred Marshall, who attempted to rehabilitate the classicists and integrate them with the Austrians, while disparaging the contributions of the latter. It was unfortunately the Marshallian and not the Austrian approach that exerted the most influence over later writers. This influence is partly responsible for the current myth among economists that the Austrian school is effectively dead and has no more to contribute and that everything of lasting worth that it had to offer was effectively stated and integrated in Alfred Marshall's *Principles*.

Marshall tried to rehabilitate the cost-of-production theory of the classicists by conceding that, in the "short run," in the immediate market place, consumers' demand rules price. But in the long run, among the important reproducible goods, cost of production is determining. According to Marshall, both utility and money costs determine price, like blades of a scissors, but one blade is more important in the short run, and another in the long run. He concludes that

as a general rule, the shorter the period we are considering, the greater must be the share of our attention which is given to the influence of demand on value; and the longer the period, the more important will be the influence of cost of production on value. . . . The actual value at any time, the market value as it is often called, is often more influenced by passing events and by causes whose action is fitful and short-lived, than by those which work persistently. But in long periods these fitful and irregular causes in large measure efface one another's influence; so that in the long run persistent causes dominate value completely.[22]

The implication is quite clear: if one deals with "short-run" market values, one is being quite superficial and dwelling only on fitful and transient causes—so much for the Austrians. But if one wants to deal with the "really basic" matters, the really lasting and permanent causes of prices, he must concentrate on costs of production—*pace* the classicists. This impression of the Austrians—their alleged neglect of the "long period," and "one-sided neglect of costs"—has been stamped on economics ever since.

Marshall's analysis suffers from a grave methodological defect —indeed, from an almost hopeless methodological confusion as regards the "short run" and the "long run." He considers the "long run" as actually existing, as being the permanent, persistent, observable element beneath the fitful, basically unimportant flux of market value. He admits (p. 350) that "even the most persistent causes are, however, liable to change," but he clearly indicates that they are *far less* likely to change than the fitful market values; herein, indeed, lies their long-run nature. He regards the long-run data, then, as underlying the transient market values in a way similar to that in which the basic sea level underlies the changing waves and tides.[23] For Marshall, then, the long-run data are something that can be spotted and marked by an observer;

indeed, since they change far more slowly than the market values, they can be observed more accurately.

Marshall's conception of the long run is completely fallacious, and this eliminates the whole groundwork of his theoretical structure. The long run, by its very nature, *never does and never can exist*. This does not mean that "long-run," or ERE, analysis is not important. On the contrary, only through the concept of the ERE can we subject to catallactic analysis such critical problems as entrepreneurial profit, the structure of production, the interest rate, and the pricing of productive factors. The ERE is the goal (albeit shifting in the concrete sense) toward which the market moves. But the point at issue is that it *is not observable,* or real, as are actual market prices.

We have seen above the characteristics of the evenly rotating economy. The ERE is the condition that comes into being and continues to obtain when the present, existing market data (valuations, technology, resources) remain constant. It is a theoretical construct of the economist that enables him to point out in what directions the economy tends to be moving at any given time; it also enables the economist to isolate various elements in his analysis of the economy of the real world. To analyze the determining forces in a world of change, he must construct hypothetically a world of nonchange. This is far different from, indeed it is the reverse of, saying that the long run exists or that it is somehow *more permanently* or more persistently existent than the actual market data. The actual market prices, on the contrary, are the only ones that *ever* exist, and they are the resultants of actual market data (consumer demands, resources, etc.) that themselves change continually. The "long run" is *not* more stable; its data necessarily change along with the data on the market. The fact that costs equal prices in the "long run" does not mean that costs will actually equal prices, but that the tendency exists, a tendency that is continually being *disrupted* in reality by the very fitful changes in market data that Marshall points out.[24]

In sum, rather than being in some sense more persistent and more real than the actual market, the "long run" of the ERE is not real at all, but a very useful theoretical construct that enables the economist to point out the direction in which the market is moving at any given time—specifically, toward the elimination of profits and losses if existing market data remain the same. Thus, the ERE concept is especially helpful in the analysis of profits and losses as compared to interest. But the market data are the only actual reality.

This is not to deny, and the Austrians never did deny, that subjective costs, in the sense of opportunity costs and utilities forgone, are important in the analysis of production. In particular, the disutilities of labor and of waiting—as expressed in the time-preference ratios—determine how much of people's energies and how much of their savings will go into the production process. This, in the broadest sense, will determine or help to determine the total supply of all goods that will be produced. But these costs are themselves subjective utilities, so that both "blades of the scissors" are governed by the subjective utility of individuals. This is a *monistic* and not a dualistic causal explanation. The costs, furthermore, have no direct influence on the relative amount of the stock of *each good* to be produced. Consumers will evaluate the various stocks of goods available. *How much* productive energy and savings will go into producing stock of one particular good and how much into producing another, in other words the relative stocks of each product, will depend in turn on entrepreneurial expectations of where the greatest monetary profit will be found. These expectations are based on the anticipated direction of consumer demand.

As a result of such anticipations, the *nonspecific* factors will move to the production of those goods where, *ceteris paribus,* their owners will earn the highest incomes. An exposition of this process will be presented below.

Marshall's treatment of subjective costs was also highly fallacious. Instead of the idea of opportunity costs, he had the notion that they were "real costs" that could be added in terms of measurable units. Money costs of production, then, became the "necessary supply prices" which entrepreneurs had to pay in order "to call forth an adequate supply of the efforts and waitings" to produce a supply of the product. These real costs were then supposed to be the fundamental, persisting element that backstops money costs of production, and allowed Marshall to talk of the more persisting, long-run, normal situation.[25]

Marshall's great error here, and it has permeated the works of his followers and of present-day writers, is to regard costs and production exclusively from the point of view of an isolated individual entrepreneur or an isolated individual industry, rather than viewing the whole economy in all of its interrelations.[26] Marshall is dealing, of necessity, with particular prices of different goods, and he is attempting to show that alleged "costs of production" determine these prices in the long run. But it is completely erroneous to tie up particular goods with labor vs. leisure and with consuming vs. waiting costs, for the latter are only *general* phenomena, applying and diffusing throughout the entire economic system. The price necessary to call forth a non-specific factor is the highest price this factor can earn elsewhere— an opportunity cost. What it can attain elsewhere is basically determined by the state of consumer demand elsewhere. The forgone leisure-and-consumption costs, in general, only help to determine the size—the general stock—of labor and savings that will be applied to production. All this will be treated further below.

9. *Pricing and the Theory of Bargaining*

We have seen that, for all goods, total receipts to sellers will tend to equal total payments to factors, and this equality will be established in the evenly rotating economy. In the ERE, interest income will be earned at the same uniform rate by capitalists throughout the economy. The remainder of income from production and sale to consumers will be earned by the owners of the original factors: land and labor.

Our next task will be to analyze the determination of the prices of factor services and the determination of the interest rate, as they tend to be approached in the economy and would be reached in the ERE. Until now, discussion has centered on the capital-goods structure, treated *as if* it were in one composite stage of production. Clearly, there are numerous stages, but we have seen above that earnings in production ultimately resolve themselves, and certainly do so in the ERE, into the earnings of the original factors: land and labor. Later on, we shall expand the analysis to include the case of *many* stages in the production process, and we shall defend this type of temporal analysis of production against the very fashionable current view that production is "timeless" under modern conditions and that the original-factor analysis might have been useful for the primitive era but not for a modern economy. As a corollary to this, we shall develop further an analysis of the nature of capital and time in the production process.

What will be the process of pricing productive factors in a world of purely specific factors? We have been assuming that only *services* and not whole goods can be acquired. In the case of labor this is true because of the nature of the free society; in the case of land and capital goods, we are assuming that the capitalist product-owners hire or rent rather than own any of the productive factors outright. In our example above, the 95 ounces went to all the factor-owners jointly. By what *principles* can we determine how the joint income is allocated to the various *individual* factor services? If all the factors are purely specific, we can resort to what is usually called the *theory of bargaining*. We are in a very analogous situation to the *two-person* barter of chapter 2. For what we have is not relatively determinate prices, or proportions, but exchange ratios with wide zones between the "marginal pairs" of prices. The maximum price of one is widely separated from the minimum price of the other.

In the present case, we have, say, twelve labor and land factors, each of which is indispensable to the production of the good. None of the factors, furthermore, can be used anywhere else, in any other line of production. The question for these factor-owners to solve is the proportionate share of each in the total joint income. Each factor-owner's maximum goal is something slightly less than 100% of the income from the consumers. What the final decision will be cannot be indicated by praxeology. There is, for all practical purposes, no theory of bargaining; all that can be said is that since the owner of each factor wants to participate and earn some income, all will most likely arrive at some sort of voluntary contractual arrangement. This will be a formal type of partnership agreement if the factors jointly own the product; or it will be the *implicit* result if a pure capitalist purchases the services of the factors.

Economists have always been very unhappy about bargaining situations of this kind, since economic analysis is estopped from saying anything more of note. We must not pursue the temptation, however, to condemn such situations as in some way "exploitative" or bad, and thereby convert barrenness for economic analysis into tragedy for the economy. Whatever agreement is arrived at by the various individuals will be beneficial to every one of them; otherwise he would not have so agreed.[27]

It is generally assumed that, in the jockeying for proportionate shares, labor factors have less "bargaining power" than land factors. The only meaning that can be seen in the term "bargaining power" here is that some factor-owners might have minimum reservation prices for their factors, below which they would not be entered in production. In that case, these factors would *at least* have to receive the minimum, while factors with no minimum, with no reservation price, would work even at an income of only slightly more than zero. Now it should be evident that the owner of every labor factor has *some* minimum selling price, a price below which he will not work. In our case, where we are assuming (as we shall see, quite unrealistically) that *every* factor is specific, it is true that no laborer would be able to earn a return in any other type of work. But he could always enjoy leisure, and this sets a minimum supply price for labor service. On the other hand, the use of land sacrifices no leisure. Except in rare cases where the owner enjoys a valuable esthetic pleasure from contemplating a stretch of his own land not in use, there is no revenue that the land can bring him except a monetary return in production. Therefore, land has no reservation price, and the landowner would have to accept a return of almost zero rather than allow his land to be idle. The bargaining power of the owner of labor, therefore, is almost always superior to that of the owner of land.

In the real world, labor, as will be seen below, is uniquely the *nonspecific* factor, so that the theory of bargaining could never apply to labor incomes.[28]

Thus, when two or more factors are specific to a given line of production, there is nothing that economic analysis can say further about the allocation of the joint income from their product; it is a matter of voluntary bargaining between them. Bargaining and indeterminate pricing also take place even between two or more nonspecific factors in the rare case where the proportions in which these factors *must* be used are *identical* in each employment. In such cases, also, there is no determinate pricing for any of the factors separately, and the result must be settled by mutual bargaining.

Suppose, for example, that a certain machine, containing two necessary parts, can be used in several fields of production. The two parts, however, must always be combined in use in a certain fixed proportion. Suppose that two (or more) individuals owned these two parts, i.e., two different individuals produced the different parts by their labor and land. The combined machine will be sold to, or used in, that line of production where it will yield the highest monetary income. But the price that will be established for that machine will necessarily be a *cumulative* price so far as the two factors—the two parts—are concerned. The price of each part and the allocation of the income to the two owners must be decided by a process of bargaining. Economics cannot here determine separate prices. This is true because the proportions between the two are always the same, even though the combined product can be used in several different ways.[29]

Not only is bargaining theory rarely applicable in the real world, but zones of indeterminacy between valuations, and therefore zones of indeterminacy in pricing, tend to dwindle radically in importance as the economy evolves from barter to an advanced monetary economy. The greater the number and variety of goods available, and the greater the number of people with differing valuations, the more negligible will zones of indeterminacy become.[30]

At this point, we may introduce another rare, explicitly empirical, element into our discussion: that on this earth, labor has been a far scarcer factor than land. As in the case of Crusoe, so in the case of a modern economy, men have been able to choose which land to use in various occupations, and which to leave idle, and have found themselves with idle "no-rent" land, i.e., land yielding no income. Of course, as an economy advances, and population and utilization of resources grow, there is a tendency for this superfluity of land to diminish (barring discoveries of new, fertile lands).

6

Production: The Rate of
Interest and Its Determination

1. *Many Stages: the Pure Rate of Interest* [1]

Up to this point we have been treating the structure of production as amalgamated into one stage. One or several firms have all been *vertically integrating* all the stages of production of a product (with all factors specific), until finally the product is sold to the consumer. This is certainly an unrealistic assumption. We shall now consider the production situation in the real world, where (*a*) factors are nonspecific as well as specific, and (*b*) production is divided into numerous stages, as the factors continue to work and advance from the higher to the lower stages of the production process.[2] Instead of assuming that one firm—one set of capitalists—purchases factors and retains ownership of the product up through the sale to consumers, let us suppose that there are different firms and different sets of capitalists at definite intervals, and at each interval the product, in the stage it has reached up to that point, is sold for money to another capitalist or group of capitalists. It is not necessary to make any restrictive assumptions about how many separate stages occur or what the time intervals between individual stages might be. For purposes of convenience, let us return to our example and the diagram in Fig. 40. We shall assume that exchanges of product and service take place at each line marked on the diagram. We shall further assume, for convenience only, that each stage takes the same length of time.

Now, instead of collecting interest income for services in one lump sum at the final stage, the capitalist or capitalists acquire interest income *at each stage*.[3] If each stage takes one year, then

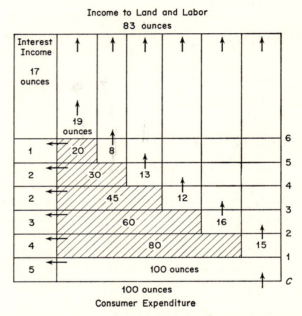

Fig. 41.   Income Accruing to Factors at Various Stages of Production

the entire production process for the good takes six years. When the stages are all lumped together, or vertically integrated, then one capitalist (or set of capitalists) advances the owners of original factors their money six years ahead of time and then waits for this period to acquire his revenue. (Strictly, since the work and pay of labor and land would be continual as the product advanced to its final form, the earliest hired labor and land would be paid, say, in year 1, and the latest toward the end of year 6.) With separate stages, however, each capitalist advances the money for only one year.

Let us see the picture on a diagram (Fig. 41). We must modify the previous diagram somewhat. A lower bar of 100 ounces is added, and the *interest* income that accrues to the capitalist at this lowest stage is indicated by an arrow going off to the left side. The upward arrow then represents the amount going to owners of original factors, land and labor, at this stage, and the shaded area the amount going to owners of capital-goods factors of a higher rank, i.e., intermediate products. The previous diagram did not depict interest income, but simply presented all income as going to the owners of original factors; the time element had not yet been introduced into our discussion.

The structure of production and payment depicted in this basic diagram is as follows: Consumers spend 100 ounces on the good in question. Of the 100 ounces, 5 ounces go as interest income to the sellers of the consumers' good, and 95 are paid out to the owners of factors. In our example, 15 ounces go for the use of land and labor (original) factors, and 80 go into the purchase of factor services of capital goods of a higher order. At the second stage, capitalists receive 80 ounces in revenue from the sale of their product.

Of the 80 ounces, 16 go into the purchase of land and labor factors, and 4 accrue as interest income to the second-level capitalists. The remaining 60 are used for the purchase of higher-order capital goods. The same process is repeated until, on the highest stage, the highest-order capitalists receive 20 ounces of revenue, retain 1 for themselves, and pay out 19 to land and labor factors. The sum total of income to land and labor factors is 83 ounces; total interest income is 17 ounces.

In the foregoing section on interest we showed that money is always nonspecific, and the result is that in the ERE the interest return on monetary investment (the pure rate of interest) is the same everywhere in the economy, regardless of the type of product or the specific conditions of its production. Here we see an amplification of this principle. *Not only must the interest rate be uniform for each good; it must be uniform for every stage of every good.* In our diagram, the interest rate return received by product-owners, i.e., by capitalists, is equal at each stage. At the lowest stage, producers have invested 95 ounces in factors (both capital goods and original factors) and receive 100 ounces from consumers—a net income of 5 ounces. This represents a return on the investment of $\frac{5}{95}$, or approximately 5.2%. In the ERE, which we are considering, there are no profits or losses due to uncertainty, so that this return represents the rate of pure interest.[4] The capitalist at the next higher stage invests 60 plus 16 or 76 ounces in factors and receives a net return of 4 ounces, again approximately 5.2%. And so on for each stage of investment, where, except for the vagaries of the arithmetic in our example, the interest rate is uniform for each stage. At the highest stage, the capitalist has invested 19 ounces in land and labor, and receives a net return of 1, again about 5.2%.

The interest rate must be equal for each stage of the production process. For suppose that the interest rate were higher in the higher stages than in the lower stages. Then capitalists would abandon producing in the lower stage, and shift to the higher stage, where the interest return is greater. What is the effect of such a shift? We can answer by stressing the *implications* of differences in the interest rate. A higher interest rate in stage *A* than in stage *B* means that the *price* spread between the sum of factors entering into stage *A* and the selling price of its product, *is greater,* in percentage terms, than the price spread in stage *B*. Thus, if we compare stage 4 and stage 1 in the diagram in Fig. 41, we find a price spread of 43 to 45 in the former case, and 95 to 100 in the latter, for a net interest return of approximately 5.2% in each. Let us suppose, however, that the sum of the factor prices for stage 4 is 35 instead of 43, while the sum of factor prices in stage 1 is 98. (The sum of factor prices here *excludes* interest income, of course.) Capitalists investing in stage 4 would earn a net return of 8, or 23%, while investors in stage 1 earned about 2%. Capitalists would begin to stop investing in stage 1 and shift to stage 4. As a consequence of this shifting, the aggregate demand in stage 1 for its factors diminishes, and the prices of the factors used in stage 1 therefore decline. In the meanwhile, greater investment in stage 4 raises factor prices there, so that the cumulative price rises from 35. Products of stage 4 increase, and the increased supply lowers the selling price, which falls from 43. These arbitrage actions continue until the percentage spread in each of the two stages is equal.

It is important to realize that the *interest rate is equal to the rate of price spread in the various stages.* Too many writers consider the rate of interest as only the price of loans on the loan market. In reality, as we shall see further below, the rate of interest pervades all time markets, and the productive loan market is a strictly subsidiary time market of only derivative importance.[5]

Not only will the rate of interest be equal in each stage of any given product, but the *same* rate of interest will prevail in *all* stages of *all* products in the ERE. In the real world of uncertainty, the *tendency* of entrepreneurial actions is always in the direction of establishing a uniform rate of interest throughout all time markets in the economy. The reason for the uniformity is clear. If stage 3 of good X earns 8% and stage 1 of good Y earns 2%, capitalists will tend to cease investing in the latter and shift to greater investments in the former. The price spreads change accordingly, in response to the changing demands and supplies, and the interest rates become uniform.

We may now remove our restrictive assumption about the equality of duration of the various stages. Any stage of any product may be as long or as short as the techniques of production, and the organizational structure of industry require. Thus, a technique of production might require a year's harvest for any particular stage. On the other hand, a firm might "vertically integrate" two stages and advance the money to owners of factors for the period covering *both* stages before selling the product for money. The net return on the investment in any stage will adjust itself in accordance with the length of the stage. Thus, suppose that the uniform interest rate in the economy is 5%. This is 5% for a certain unit period of time, say a year. A production process or investment covering a period of two years will, in equilibrium, then earn 10%, the equivalent of 5% *per year.* The same will obtain for a stage of production of any length of time. Thus, *irregularity or integration of stages does not hamper the equilibrating process in the slightest.*

It is already clear that the old classical trinity of "land, labor, and capital" earning "wages, rents, and interest" must be drastically modified. It is *not* true that capital is an independent productive factor or that it earns interest for its owner, in the same way that land and labor earn income for their owners. As we have seen above and will discuss further below, capital is not an independently productive factor. Capital goods are vital and of crucial importance in production, but their production is, in the long run, imputable to land, labor, and time factors. Futhermore, land and labor are not homogeneous factors within themselves, but simply categories of *types* of uniquely varying factors. Each land and each labor factor, then, has its own physical features, its own power to serve in production; each, therefore, receives its own income from production, as will be detailed below. Capital goods too have infinite variety; but, in the ERE, they earn no incomes. What does earn an income is the conversion of future goods into present goods; because of the universal fact of time preference, future satisfactions are always at a discount compared to present satisfactions. The *owning* and holding of capital goods from date 1, when factor services are purchased, until the product is sold at date 2 is what capitalist investors accomplish. This is equivalent to the purchase of future goods (the factor services producing capital goods) with money, followed by the sale at a later date of the present goods for money. The latter occurs when consumers' goods are being sold, for consumers' goods *are* present goods. When intermediate, lower-order capital goods are sold for money, then it is not present goods, but *less distantly future* goods, that are sold. In other words, capital goods have been advanced from an earlier, *more distantly future* stage toward the consumption stage, to a later or *less distantly future* stage. The time for this transformation will be covered by a rate of time preference. Thus, if the market time preference rate, i.e., interest rate, is 5% per year, then a present good worth 100 ounces on the market will be worth about 95 ounces for a claim on it one year from now. The *present value* for a claim on 100 ounces one year from now will be 95 ounces. On this basis, the estimated worth of the good could be worked out for various points in time; thus, the claim for ½ year in the future will be worth roughly 97.5 ounces. The result will be a uniformity of rates over a period of time.

Thus, capitalists advance present goods to owners of factors in return for future goods; then, later, they sell the goods which have matured to become present or less distantly future goods in exchange for present goods (money). They have advanced present goods to owners of factors and, in return, wait while these factors, which are future goods, are transformed into goods that are *more nearly present* than before. The capitalists' function is thus a *time* function, and their income is precisely an income representing the agio of present as compared to future goods. This interest income, then, is *not* derived from the concrete, heterogeneous capital *goods,* but from the generalized investment of time.[6] It comes from a willingness to sacrifice present goods for the purchase of future goods (the factor services). As a result of the purchases, the owners of factors obtain their money in the present for a product that matures only in the future.

Thus, capitalists restrict their present consumption and use these *savings* of money to supply money (present goods) to factor owners who are producing only future goods. This is the service—an advance of time—that the capitalists supply to the owners of factors, and for which the latter voluntarily pay in the form of the interest rate.

2. *The Determination of the Pure Rate of Interest: The Time Market* [7]

It is clear that the rate of interest plays a crucial role in the system of production in the complex, monetary economy. How is the rate of interest determined? The *pure* rate of interest, with which we are now concerned, we have seen will tend to be equal throughout all stages of all production processes in the economy and thus will be uniform in the ERE.

The level of the pure rate of interest is determined by the market for the exchange of present goods against future goods, a market which we shall see permeates many parts of the economic system. The establishment of money as a general medium of exchange has greatly simplified the present-future market as compared to the laborious conditions under barter, where there were separate present-future markets for every commodity. In the monetary economy, the present-future market, or what we may call the "time market," is expressed completely in terms of money. *Money* is clearly the present good *par excellence*. For, aside from the consumption value of the monetary metal itself, the money commodity is the one completely marketable good in the entire society. It is the open sesame to exchange for consumption goods at any time that its owner desires. It is therefore a present good. Since consumers' goods, once sold, do not ordinarily re-enter the exchange nexus, money is the dominant present good in the market. Furthermore, since money is the medium for *all* exchanges, it is also the medium for exchanges on the time market.

What are the future goods that exchange for money? *Future goods are goods that are now expected to become present goods at some future date*. They therefore have a present value. Because of the universal fact of time preference, a particular good is worth more at present than is the present *prospect* of its becoming available as a present good at some time in the future. In other words, a good at present is worth more now than its present value as a future good. Because money is the general medium of exchange, for the time market as well as for other markets, money is the present good, and the future goods *are present expectations of the future acquisition of money*. It follows from the law of time preference that *present money is worth more than present expectations of the same amount of future money*. In other words, future money (as we may call present expectations of money in the future) will always exchange at a discount compared to present money.

This discount on future goods as compared with present goods (or, conversely, the premium commanded by present goods over future goods) is the rate of interest. Thus, if, on the time market, 100 ounces of gold exchange for the prospect of obtaining 105 ounces of gold one year from now, then the rate of interest is approximately 5% per annum. This is the time-discount rate of future to present money.

What do we mean specifically by "prospects for obtaining money in the future"? These prospects must be carefully analyzed in order to explain all the causal factors in the determination of the rate of interest. In the first place, in the real world, these prospects, like any prospects over a period of time, are always more or less *uncertain*. In the real world this ever-present uncertainty necessarily causes interest and profit-and-loss elements to be intertwined and creates complexities that will be analyzed further below. In order to separate the time market from the entrepreneurial elements, we must consider the certain world of the evenly rotating economy, where anticipations are all fulfilled and the pure rate of interest is equal throughout the economy. The *pure* rate of interest will then be the going rate of time discount, the ratio of the price of present goods to that of future goods.

What, then, are the specific types of future goods that enter the time market? There are two such types. One is a *written claim to a certain amount of money at a future date.* The exchange on the time market in this case is as follows: A gives money to B in exchange for a claim to future money. The term generally used to refer to A, the purchaser of the future money, is "lender," or "creditor," while B, the seller of the future money, is termed the "borrower" or "debtor." The reason is that this *credit transaction,* as contrasted to a *cash* transaction, remains *unfinished* in the present. When a man buys a suit for cash, he transfers money in exchange for the suit. The transaction is finished. In a credit transaction he receives simply a written I. O. U., or note, entitling him to claim a certain amount of money at a future date. The transaction remains to be completed in the future, when B, the borrower, "repays the loan" by transferring the agreed money to the creditor.

Although the loan market is a very conspicuous type of time transaction, it is by no means the only or even the dominant one. There is a much more subtle, but more important, type of transaction which permeates the entire production system, but which is not often recognized as a time transaction. This is the purchase of producers' goods and services, which are transformed over a period of time, finally to emerge as consumers' goods. When capitalists purchase the services of factors of production (or, as we shall later see, the factors themselves), they are purchasing a certain amount and value of net produce, discounted to the *present* value of that produce. For the land, labor, and capital services purchased are *future goods,* to be transformed into *final form as present goods.*

Suppose, for example, that a capitalist-entrepreneur hires labor services, and suppose that it can be determined that this amount of labor service will result in a net revenue of 20 gold ounces to the product-owner. We shall see below that the service will tend to be paid the net value of its product; but it will earn its product *discounted* by the time interval until sale. For if the labor service will reap 20 ounces five years from now, it is obvious that the owner of the labor cannot expect to receive from the capitalist the full 20 ounces *now,* in advance. He will receive his net earnings discounted by the going agio, the rate of interest. And the interest income will be earned by the capitalist who has assumed the task of advancing present money. The capitalist then waits for five years until the product matures before recouping his money.

The pure capitalist, therefore, in performing a capital-advancing function in the productive system, plays a sort of intermediary role. He sells money (a present good) to factor-owners in exchange for the services of their factors (prospective future goods). He holds these goods and continues to hire work on them until they have been transformed into consumers' goods (present goods), which are then sold to the public for money (a present good). The premium that he earns from the sale of present goods, compared to what he paid for future goods, is the *rate of interest* earned on the exchange.

The time market is therefore not restricted to the loan market. It permeates the entire production structure of the complex economy. All productive factors are future goods: they provide for their owner the expectation of being advanced toward the final goal of consumption, a goal which provides the *raison d'être* for the whole productive enterprise. It is a time market where the future goods sold do not constitute a credit transaction, as in the case of the loan market. The transaction is complete in itself and needs no further payment by either party. In this case, the buyer of the future goods—the capitalist—earns his income through transforming these goods into present goods, rather than through the presentation of an I. O. U. claim on the original seller of a future good.

The time market, the market where present goods exchange for future goods, is, then, an aggregate with several component parts. In one part of the market, capitalists exchange their money savings (present goods) for the services of numerous factors (future goods). This is one part, and the most important part, of the time market. Another is the consumers' loan market, where savers lend their money in a credit transaction, in exchange for an I. O. U. of future money. The savers are the suppliers of present money, the borrowers the suppliers of future money, in the form of I. O. U.'s. Here we are dealing only with those who borrow to spend on consumption goods, and *not* with producers who borrow savings in order to invest in production. For the borrowers of savings for production loans are not independent forces on the time market, but are rather completely dependent on the interest agio between present and future goods as determined in the production system, equaling the ratio between the prices of consumers' and producers' goods, and between the various stages of producers' goods. This dependence will be seen below.

3. *Time Preference and Individual Value Scales*

Before considering the component parts of the time market further, let us go to the very root of the matter: the value scale of the individual. As we have seen in the problem of pricing and demand, the individual's value scale provides the key to the determination of all events on the market. This is no less true in regard to the interest rate. Here the key is the schedule of time-preference valuations of the individual.

Let us consider a hypothetical individual, abstracting from any particular role that he may play in the economic system. This individual has, of necessity, a diminishing marginal utility of money, so that each additional unit of money acquired ranks lower on his value scale. This is necessarily true. Conversely, and this also follows from the diminishing marginal utility of money, each successive unit of money given up will rank higher on his value scale. The same law of utility applies to future money, i.e., to prospects of future money. To both present money and future money there applies the general rule that *more* of a good will have greater utility than *less* of it. We may illustrate these general laws by means of the following hypothetical value scale of an individual:

John Smith

....(19 oz. future) (10 yrs. from now)	
....................4th unit of 10 oz.	
....(18 oz. future)	
....(17 oz. future)	
....(16 oz. future)	
...................3rd unit of 10 oz.	
....(15 oz. future)	
....(14 oz. future)	
....(13 oz. future)	
..................2nd unit of 10 oz.	
....(12 oz. future)	
..................1st unit of 10 oz.	
....(11 oz. future)	
..................(1st added unit of 10 oz.)	
....(10 oz. future)	
..................(2nd added unit of 10 oz.)	

We see in this value scale an example of the fact that all possible alternatives for choice are ranged in one scale, and the truths of the law of utility are exemplified. The "1st unit of 10 oz." refers to the rank accorded to the first unit of 10 ounces (the unit arbitrarily chosen here) to be given up. The "2nd unit of 10 ounces" of money to be given up is accorded higher rank, etc. The "1st added unit of 10 oz." refers to the rank accorded to the next unit of 10 ounces which the man is considering acquiring, with parentheses to indicate that he does not now have the good in his possession. Above we have a schedule of John Smith's value scale with respect to time, i.e., his scale of time preferences. Suppose that the market rate of interest, then, is 3%; i.e., he can obtain 13 ounces of future money (considered here as 10 years from now), by selling 10 ounces of present money. To see what he will do, we are privileged to be able to consult his time-preference scale. We find that 13 ounces of future money is preferred to his first unit of 10 ounces and also to the second unit of 10 ounces, but that the 3rd unit of 10 ounces stands higher in his valuation. Therefore, with a market rate of 3% per year, the individual will save 20 ounces of gold and sell them for future money on the time market. He is a supplier of present goods on the time market to the extent of 20 ounces.[8]

If the market rate of interest is 2%, so that 12 future ounces would be the price of 10 present ounces, then John Smith would be a *supplier of 10 ounces of present money.* He is never a *supplier of future money* because, in his particular case, there are no quantities of future money above 10 ounces that are ranked below "1st added unit of 10 oz."

Suppose, for example, that James Robinson has the following time-value scale:

James Robinson

```
............................................(19 oz. future) (10 yrs. from now)
..................2nd unit of 10 oz.
.........................................(18 oz. future)
.........................................(17 oz. future)
..................1st unit of 10 oz.
.........................................(16 oz. future)
.........................................(15 oz. future)
.........................................(14 oz. future)
..................(1st added unit of 10 oz.)
.........................................(13 oz. future)
.........................................(12 oz. future)
..................(2nd added unit of 10 oz.)
.........................................(11 oz. future)
..................(3rd added unit of 10 oz.)
.........................................(10 oz. future)
```

If the market rate of interest is 3%, then Robinson's valuations are such that no savings will be supplied to the time market. On the contrary, 13 ounces future *is lower than* "1st added unit of 10 oz.," which means that Robinson would be willing to exchange 13 ounces of future money for 10 ounces of present money. Thereby he becomes, in contrast to Smith, a supplier of future money. If the rate of interest were 1%, then he would supply 22 ounces of future money in exchange for 20 ounces of present money, thus increasing his demand for present money at the lower price.

It will be noticed that there is no listing for less than 10 ounces of future goods, to be compared with 10 ounces of present goods. The reason is that every man's time preference is positive, i.e., 1 ounce of present money will always be preferred to 1 ounce or less of future money. Therefore, there will never be any question of a zero or negative pure interest rate. Many economists have made the great mistake of believing that the interest rate determines the time-preference schedule and rate of savings, rather than *vice versa*. This is completely invalid. The interest rates discussed here are simply hypothetical schedules, and they *indicate* and reveal the time-preference schedules of each individual. In the aggregate, as we shall see presently, the interaction of the time preferences and hence the supply-demand schedules of individuals on the time market determine the pure rate of interest on the market. They do so in the same way that individual valuations determine aggregate supply and demand schedules for goods, which in turn determine market prices. And once again, it is utilities and utilities alone, here in the form of time preferences, that determine the market result; the explanation does not lie in some sort of "mutually determining process" of preferences and market consequences.

Continuing with our analysis, let us tabulate the schedules of John Smith and James Robinson, from their time-value scales above, in relation to their position on the time market. John Smith's schedule is given in Table 11. James Robinson's schedule is given in Table 12.

The Robinson time schedule is of particular interest. Referring to his time-value scale, we find that at an interest rate of 9%, 19 ounces of future money is above the 2nd unit of 10 ounces of

TABLE 11

INTEREST RATE %	SUPPLY OF PRESENT MONEY = DEMAND FOR FUTURE MONEY = SAVINGS OZ. OF GOLD	SUPPLY OF FUTURE MONEY = DEMAND FOR PRESENT MONEY OZ. OF GOLD
9..........	40	0
8..........	30	0
7..........	30	0
6..........	30	0
5..........	20	0
4..........	20	0
3..........	20	0
2..........	10	0
1..........	0	0

TABLE 12

INTEREST RATE %	SUPPLY OF PRESENT MONEY = DEMAND FOR FUTURE MONEY = SAVINGS OZ. OF GOLD	SUPPLY OF FUTURE MONEY = DEMAND FOR PRESENT MONEY OZ. OF GOLD
9..........	20	0
8..........	10	0
7..........	10	0
6..........	0	0
5..........	0	0
4..........	0	0
3..........	0	10
2..........	0	10
1..........	0	20

present money and therefore also above the first unit. At this
interest rate, his supply of present money on the time market,
i.e., his savings, equals 20 ounces. Because his valuation of the
first unit (of 10 ounces—an arbitrary size of unit that we have

picked for this discussion) is between 16 and 17 ounces of future money, when the market interest rate is 6%, his return of 16 ounces is less valuable to him than his first unit. Therefore, he will not be a saver and supplier of present money at this rate. On the other hand, he will not be a supplier of future goods (i.e., a demander of present goods on the time market) either. In order to be a supplier of future goods, his valuation of the future money that he would have to give up at the ruling rate of interest has to be lower than the present money that he would get. In other words, what he gives up in prospective future money will have to be worth less to him than the utility of the "1st additional unit of 10 oz." on his scale. While the market rate is in the 4% to 6% range, this will not be true, for the 14 to 16 ounces of future money that he would have to supply would be worth more to him than the additional 10 ounces of present money that he would gain from the exchange. In Robinson's case, the critical point takes place when the hypothetical interest rate drops to 3%, for 13 future ounces are worth less than an additional 10 ounces of present money, and he will supply the future ounces on the market. If the interest rate were 1%, he would supply 20 ounces of future goods.[9]

It should be evident that an individual, at any one time, will either be a net saver (i.e., a net demander of future goods), a net supplier of future goods, or not be on the time market at all. The three categories are mutually exclusive.

The diagram in Fig. 42 sketches the schedules of Smith and Robinson in graphic form. Interest rate is on the vertical axis, and money on the horizontal. The supplies of present goods are also demands for future goods, and the demand for present goods is also the supply of future goods.

We cannot compare utilities or values between persons, but we certainly may say that Robinson's time-preference schedule is *higher* than Smith's. In other words, it cannot make sense to compare the rankings or utilities that the two men accord to any particular unit of a good, but we can (if we know them) compare their *schedules* based purely on their demonstrated time preferences. Robinson's time-preference schedule is *higher* than

Smith's, i.e., at each hypothetical rate of interest Robinson's values are such that he will part with less of his present goods in exchange for future goods.[10]

Let us explore the typical individual time-preference schedule, or time-supply-and-demand schedule, more closely. In the first place, there is no necessity for the unit chosen to be 10 ounces.

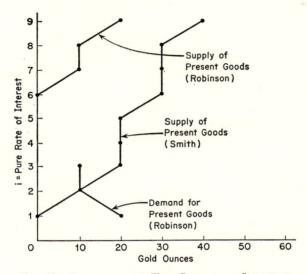

FIG. 42.   COMPARISON OF TIME-PREFERENCE SCHEDULES

Since money is perhaps the most *divisible* of goods, it is possible to break down the units into far smaller sizes. Furthermore, because of the arbitrage of the market, the rate of interest return on investments of present in future goods will be equal for all the various sizes of units. We may therefore visualize a comparatively smooth curve, even for each individual.

One inevitable characteristic of an individual's time-preference schedule is that eventually, after a certain amount of present money has been supplied on the market, no conceivable interest rate could persuade him to purchase more future goods. The reason is that as present money dwindles and future money increases in a man's possession, the marginal utility of the former increases on the man's value scale, and the marginal utility of the latter decreases. In particular, every man must consume in the present, and this drastically limits his savings regardless of the interest rate. As a result, after a certain point, a man's time preference for the present becomes infinite, and the line representing his supply of present goods becomes vertical upward. At the other end of the scale, the fact of time preference will imply that at some minimum rate of interest the man will not save at all. At what point the supply curve hits the vertical axis depends on the valuations of the individual; but it must do so, as a result of the operation of the law of time preference. A man could not prefer 10 ounces or even less of future money to 10 ounces of present money.[11]

What happens after the individual supply curve hits the vertical axis depends entirely on the time preferences of the individual. In some cases, as in that of John Smith above, the person's marginal utility of money falls too fast, as compared with that of future money, for him to participate as a net demander of present goods at low rates of interest. In other words, Smith's time-preference ratio is too low in this area for him to become a demander of present goods and a supplier of future goods. On the other hand, Robinson's higher schedule of time preferences is such that, at low rates of interest, he becomes a supplier of future goods for present goods. (See Fig. 42.)

We may of course, diagram a typical individual's supply and demand curve conventionally, as we have done in Fig. 42. On the other hand, we may also modify this diagram, so as to make one continuous curve of the individual's activity on the time market. We may call this curve the "individual's time-market curve." At higher interest rates, down to where it hits the vertical axis, this curve is simply the individual's supply curve of present goods. But below this, we are *reversing* his demand curve and continuing it on to the left on the horizontal axis. (See Fig. 43.)

Every individual on the market has a similar type of time-market schedule, reflecting his particular value scale. The schedule of each will be such that at higher rates of interest there will be a greater tendency toward net saving, and at lower rates of interest, less saving, until the individual becomes a net demander.

At each *hypothetical* rate of interest there is a possible net saving, net demanding, or abstaining from the market, for each individual. For some changes in the rate of interest, there will be no change (vertical curve), but there will never be a situation where the supply will be greater, or demand less, with lower rates of interest.

The time-market schedules of all individuals are aggregated on

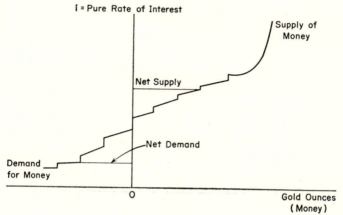

FIG. 43.   INDIVIDUAL TIME-MARKET CURVE

the market to form market-supply and market-demand schedules for present goods in terms of future goods. The supply schedule will increase with an increase in the rate of interest, and the demand schedule will fall with the higher rates of interest.

A typical aggregate market diagram may be seen in Fig. 44. Aggregating the supply and demand schedules on the time market for all individuals in the market, we obtain curves such as *SS* and *DD*. *DD* is the demand curve for present goods in terms of the supply of future goods; it slopes rightward as the rate of interest falls. *SS* is the supply curve of present goods in terms of the demand for future goods; it slopes rightward as the rate of interest increases. The intersection of the two curves determines the *equilibrium rate of interest*—the rate of interest as it would tend to be in the evenly rotating economy. This pure rate of interest, then, is determined *solely by the time preferences of the individuals in the society, and by no other factor.*

The intersection of the two curves determines an equilibrium rate of interest, *BA, and* an equilibrium amount saved, *OB. OB* is the total amount of money that will be saved and invested in future money. At a higher interest rate than *BA,* present goods supplied would exceed future goods supplied in exchange, and

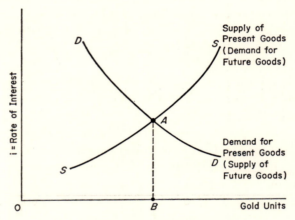

FIG. 44.   AGGREGATE TIME-MARKET CURVES

the excess savings would compete with one another until the price of present goods in terms of future goods would decline toward equilibrium. If the rate of interest were below *BA,* the demand for present goods by suppliers of future goods would exceed the supply of savings, and the competition of this demand would push interest rates up toward equilibrium.

Perhaps more fallacies have been committed in discussions concerning the interest rate than in the treatment of any other aspect of economics. It took a long while for the crucial importance of time preference in the determination of the pure rate of interest to be realized in economics; it took even longer for economists to realize that time preference is the *only* determining factor. Reluctance to accept a monistic causal interpretation has plagued economics to this day.[12]

4. *The Time Market and the Production Structure*

The time market, like other markets, consists of component individuals whose schedules are aggregated to form the market supply and demand schedules. The intricacy of the time market (and of the money market as well) consists in the fact that it is also divided and subdivided into various distinguishable submarkets. These are aggregable into a total market, but the subsidiary components are interesting and highly significant in their own right and deserve further analysis. They themselves, of course, are composed of individual supply and demand schedules.

As we have indicated above, we may divide the present-future market into two main subdivisions: *the production structure* and the *consumer loan market*. Let us turn first to the production structure. This may be done most clearly by considering once again a typical production-structure diagram. This diagram is the one in Fig. 41, with one critical difference. Previously the diagram represented a typical production structure for any particular consumers' good. *Now the same diagram represents the aggregate production structure for all goods.* Money moves from consumers' goods back through the various stages of production, while goods flow from the higher through the lower stages of production, finally to be sold as consumers' goods. The pattern of production is not changed by the fact that both specific and nonspecific factors exist. Since the production structure is aggregated, the degree of specificity for a *particular product* is irrelevant in a discussion of the time market.

There is no problem in the fact that different production processes for different goods take unequal lengths of time. This is not a difficulty because the flow from one stage to another can be aggregated for any number of processes.

There are, however, two more serious problems that seem to be involved in aggregating the production structure for the entire economy. One is the fact that in various processes there will not necessarily be an exchange of capital goods for money at each stage. One firm may "vertically integrate" within itself one or more stages and thereby advance present goods for a greater period of time. We shall see below, however, that this presents no difficulty at all, just as it presented no difficulty in the case of particular processes.

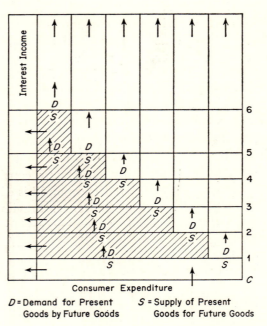

FIG. 45. AGGREGATE PRODUCTION STRUCTURE FOR ALL GOODS

A second difficulty is the purchase and use of *durable* capital goods. We have been assuming, and are continuing to assume, that no capital goods or land are *bought*—that they are only *hired,* i.e., "rented" from their owners. The purchase of durable goods presents complications, but again, as we shall see, this will lead to no essential change whatever in our analysis.

The production-structure diagram in Fig. 45 omits the numbers that indicated the size of payments between the various sectors and substitutes instead *D*'s and *S*'s to indicate the points where present-future transactions ("time transactions") take place and what groups are engaging in these various transactions. D's indicate demanders of present goods, and S's are suppliers of present goods, for future goods.

Let us begin at the bottom—the expenditure of consumers on consumers' goods. The movement of money is indicated by arrows, and money moves from consumers to the sellers of consumers' goods. This is *not* a time transaction, because it is an exchange of *present goods* (money) *for present goods* (consumers' goods).[13]

These producers of consumers' goods are necessarily capitalists who have invested in the services of factors to produce these goods and who then sell their products. Their investment in factors consisted of purchases of the services of land factors and labor factors (the original factors) and first-order capital goods (the produced factors). In both these two large categories of transactions (exchanges that are made a stage earlier than the final sale of consumers' goods), present goods are exchanging for future goods. In both cases, the capitalists are supplying *present money* in exchange for factor services whose yield will materialize in the future, and which therefore are *future goods*.

So the capitalists who are producing consumers' goods, whom we might call "first-stage capitalists," engage in time transactions in making their investments. The components of this particular subdivision of the time market, then, are:

Supply of Present Goods: Capitalists$_1$
Supply of Future Goods: Landowners, Laborers, Capitalists$_2$
   (Demand for Present Goods)

Capitalists$_1$ are the first-stage capitalists who produce consumers' goods. They purchase capital goods from the producer-owners—the second-stage capitalists, or Capitalists$_2$. The appropriate S's and D's indicate these transactions, and the arrows pointing upward indicate the direction of money payment.

At the next stage, the Capitalists$_2$ have to purchase services of factors of production. They supply present goods and purchase future goods, goods which are even more distantly in the future than the product that they will produce.[14] These future goods are supplied by landowners, laborers, and Capitalists$_3$. To sum up, at the second stage:

Supply of Present Goods: Capitalists$_2$
Supply of Future Goods: Landowners, Laborers, Capitalists$_3$

These transactions are marked with the appropriate S's and D's, and the arrows pointing upward indicate the direction of money payment in these transactions.

This pattern is continued until the very last stage. At this final stage, which is here the sixth, the sixth-stage capitalists supply future goods to the fifth-stage capitalists, but also supply present goods to laborers and landowners in exchange for the extremely distant future services of the latter. The transactions for the two highest stages are, then, as follows (with the last stage designated as N instead of 6):

5th Stage:

Supply of Present Goods: Capitalists$_5$
Supply of Future Goods: Landowners, Laborers, Capitalists$_N$

Nth Stage:

Supply of Present Goods: Capitalists$_N$
Supply of Future Goods: Landowners, Laborers.

We may now sum up our time market for any production structure of N stages:

Suppliers of Present Goods	Suppliers of Future Goods (Demanders of Present Goods)
Capitalists$_1$	All Landowners
Capitalists$_2$	All Laborers
Capitalists$_3$	Capitalists$_2$
. . . .	Capitalists$_3$
. . . .	. . . .
. . . .	. . . .
Capitalists$_N$	Capitalists$_N$

To illustrate clearly the workings of the production structure, let us hark back to the numerical example given in Fig. 41 and summarize the quantities of present goods supplied and received by the various components of the time market. We may use the same figures here to apply to the *aggregate* production structure, although the reader may wish to consider the units as multiples of gold ounces in this case. The fact that different durations of production processes and different degrees of vertical integration make no difficulties for aggregation permits us to use the diagram almost interchangeably for a single production process and for the economy as a whole. Furthermore, the fact that the ERE interest rate will be the same for all stages and all goods in the economy especially permits us to aggregate the comparable stages of all goods. For if the rate is 5%, then we may say that for a certain stage of one good, payments by capitalists to owners of factors are 50 ounces, and receipts from sales of products are 52.5 ounces, while we can also assume that the aggregate payments for the whole economy in the same period are 5,000 ounces, and receipts 5,250 ounces. The same interest rate connotes the same rate of return on investments, whether considered separately or for all goods lumped together.

The following, then, are the supplies and demands for present goods from Fig. 41, the diagram now being treated as an aggregate for the whole economy:

(Savers) Suppliers of Present Goods		Demanders of Present Goods Suppliers of Future Goods	
Capitalists$_1$..	95 oz. →	15 oz. Land and Labor Owners; Capitalists$_2$.....	80 oz.
Capitalists$_2$..	76 oz. →	16 oz. Land and Labor Owners; Capitalists$_3$.....	60 oz.
Capitalists$_3$..	57 oz. →	12 oz. Land and Labor Owners; Capitalists$_4$.....	45 oz.
Capitalists$_4$..	43 oz. →	13 oz. Land and Labor Owners; Capitalists$_5$.....	30 oz.
Capitalists$_5$..	28 oz. →	8 oz. Land and Labor Owners; Capitalists$_N$.....	20 oz.
Capitalists$_N$..	19 oz. →	19 oz. Land and Labor Owners................	
	318 oz. 83 oz.		235 oz.

The horizontal arrows at each stage of this table depict the movement of money as supplied from the savers to the recipient demanders at that stage.

From this tabulation it is easy to derive the *net* money income of the various participants: their *gross* money income minus their money payments, if we include the entire period of time for all of their transactions on the time market. The case of the owners of land and labor is simple: they receive their money in exchange for the future goods to be yielded by their factors; this money is their gross *and* their net money income from the productive system. The total of net money income to the owners of land and labor is 83 ounces. This is the sum of the money incomes to the various owners of land and labor at each stage of production.

The case of the capitalists is far more complicated. They pay out present goods in exchange for future goods and then sell the maturing less distantly future products for money to lower-stage capitalists. Their *net* money income is derived by subtracting their money outgo from their gross income over the period of the production stage. In our example, the various net incomes of the capitalists are as follows:

Net Incomes of Capitalists Producing Capital Goods

Capitalists$_2$...............	$80 - 76 = 4$ oz.
Capitalists$_3$...............	$60 - 57 = 3$ oz.
Capitalists$_4$...............	$45 - 43 = 2$ oz.
Capitalists$_5$...............	$30 - 28 = 2$ oz.
Capitalists$_N$...............	$20 - 19 = 1$ oz.

$$12 \text{ oz.}$$

The total net income of the capitalists producing capital goods (orders 2 through N) is *12 ounces*. What, then, of Capitalists$_1$, who apparently have not only no net income, but a deficit of 95 ounces? They are recouped, as we see from the diagram (in Fig. 41), *not* from the savings of capitalists, but from the expenditure of consumers, which totals 100 ounces, yielding a net income to Capitalists$_1$ of 5 ounces.

It should be emphasized at this point that the general pattern of the structure of production and of the time market will be the same in the real world of uncertainty as in the ERE. The difference will be in the amounts that go to each sector and in the relations among the various prices. We shall see later what the discrepancies will be; for example, the rate of return by the capitalists in each sector will not be uniform in the real market.

But the *pattern* of payments, the composition of suppliers and demanders, will be the same.

In analyzing the income-expenditure balance sheets of the production structure, writers on economic problems have seen that we may consolidate the various incomes and consider only the net incomes. The temptation has been simply to write off the various intercapitalist transactions as "duplications." If that is done here, then the total net income in the market is: capitalists, 17 ounces (12 ounces for capital-good capitalists and 5 ounces for consumers'-good capitalists); land and labor factors, 83 ounces. The grand total net income is then 100 ounces. This is exactly equal to the total of consumer spending for the period.

Total net income is 100 ounces, and consumption is 100 ounces. There is, therefore, no new *net* saving. We shall deal with savings and their change in detail below. Here the point is that, in the endless round of the ERE, zero *net* savings, as thus defined, would mean that there is just enough *gross* saving to keep the structure of productive capital intact, to keep the production processes rolling, and to keep a constant amount of consumers' goods produced per given period.

It is certainly legitimate and often useful to consider net incomes and net savings, but it is not always illuminating, and its use has been extremely misleading in present-day economics.[15] Use of the net "national" income figures (it is better to deal with "social income" extending throughout the market community using the money rather than to limit the scope to national boundaries) leads one to believe that the really important element maintaining the production structure is consumers' spending. In our ERE example, the various factors and capitalists receive their net income and plow it back into consumption, thus maintaining the productive structure and future standards of living, i.e., the output of consumers' goods. The inference from such concepts is clear: capitalists' savings are necessary to increase and deepen the capital structure, but even without any savings, consumption expenditure is alone sufficient to maintain the productive capital structure intact.

This conclusion seems deceptively clear-cut: after all, is not consumer spending the bulwark and end product of activity? This thesis, however, is tragically erroneous. There is no simple automatism in capitalists' spending, especially when we leave the certain world of the ERE, and it is in this real world that the conceptual error plays havoc. For with production divided into stages, it is not true that consumption spending is sufficient to provide for the maintenance of the capital structure. When we consider the maintenance of the capital structure, we must consider *all the decisions* to supply present goods on the present-future market. These decisions are *aggregated;* they do not cancel one another out. Total savings in the economy, then, are not zero, but the aggregation of all the present goods supplied to owners of future goods during the production process. This is the sum of the supplies of Capitalists$_1$ through Capitalists$_N$, which totals *318 ounces.* This is the total *gross* savings—the supply of present goods for future goods in production—and also equals total *gross* investment. Investment is the amount of money spent on future-good factors and necessarily equals savings. Total expenditures on production are: 100 (Consumption) plus 318 (Investment = Savings), equals *418 ounces.* Total gross income from production equals the gross income of Capitalists$_1$ (100 ounces) plus the gross income of other capitalists (235 ounces) plus the gross income of owners of land and labor (83 ounces), which also equals *418 ounces.*

The system depicted in our diagram of the production structure, then, is of an economy in which *418 gold ounces* are earned in gross income, and *100 ounces* are spent on consumption, while *318 ounces* are saved and invested in a certain order in the production structure. In this evenly rotating economy, 418 ounces are earned and then spent, with no net "hoarding" or "dishoarding," i.e., no net additions or subtractions from the cash balance over the period as a whole.[16]

Thus, instead of no savings being needed to maintain capital and the production structure intact, we see that a very heavy proportion of savings and investment—in our example three times the amount spent on consumption—is necessary simply to keep the production structure intact. The contrast is clear when we consider *who* obtains income and who is empowered to decide whether to consume or to invest. The net-income theorists implicitly assume that the only important decisions in regard to consuming vs. saving-investing are made by the factor-owners out of their net income. Since the net income of capitalists is admittedly relatively small, this approach attributes little importance to their role in maintaining capital. We see, however, that what maintains capital is *gross* expenditures and *gross* investment and not net investment. The capitalists at each stage of production, therefore, have a vital role in maintaining capital through their savings and investment, through heavy savings from gross income.

Concretely, let us take the case of the Capitalists$_1$. According to the net-income theorists, their role is relatively small, since their net income is only 5 ounces. But actually their gross income is 100 ounces, and *it is their decision how much of this to save and how much to consume that is decisive.* In the ERE, of course, we simply state that they save and invest 95 ounces. But when we leave the province of the ERE, we must realize that there is nothing automatic about this investment. There is no natural law that they must reinvest this amount. Suppose, for example, that the Capitalists$_1$ decide to break up the smooth flow of the ERE by spending all of the 100 ounces for their own consumption rather than investing the 95 ounces. It is evident that the entire market-born production structure would be destroyed. No income at all would accrue to the owners of all the higher-order capital goods, and all the higher-order capital processes, all the production processes longer than the very shortest, would have to be abandoned. We have seen above, and shall see in more detail below, that civilization advances by virtue of additional capital, which lengthens production processes. Greater quantities of goods are made possible only through the employment of more capital in longer processes. Should capitalists shift from saving-investment to consumption, all these processes would be necessarily abandoned, and the economy would revert to barbarism, with the employment of only the shortest and most primitive production processes. The standard of living, the quantity and variety of goods produced, would fall catastrophically to the primitive level.[17]

What could be the reason for such a precipitate withdrawal of savings and investment in favor of consumption? The only reason —on the free market—would be a sudden and massive increase in the time-preference schedules of the capitalists, so that present satisfactions become worth very much more in terms of future satisfactions. Their higher time preferences mean that the existing rate of interest is not enough to induce them to save and invest in their previous proportions. They therefore consume a greater proportion of their gross income and invest less.

Each individual, on the basis of his time-preference schedule, decides between the amount of his money income to be devoted to saving and the amount to be devoted to consumption. *The aggregate time-market schedules (determined by time preferences) determine the aggregate social proportions between (gross) savings and consumption.* It is clear that the higher the time-preference schedules are, the greater will be the proportion of consumption to savings, while lower time-preference schedules will lower this proportion. At the same time, as we have seen, higher time-preference schedules in the economy lead to higher rates of interest, and lower schedules lead to lower rates of interest.

From this it becomes clear that *the time preferences of the individuals on the market determine simultaneously and by themselves both the market equilibrium interest rate and the proportions between consumption and savings (individual and aggregate).*[18] Both the latter are the obverse side of the same coin. In our example, the increase in time-preference schedules has caused a decline in savings, absolute and proportionate, and a rise in the interest rate.

The fallacies of the net product figures have led economists to include some "grossness" in their product and income figures. At present the favorite concept is that of the "gross national product" and its counterpart, gross national expenditures. These concepts were adopted because of the obvious errors encountered with the net income concepts.[19] Current "gross" figures, however, are the height of illogicality, because they are not gross at all, but only partly gross. They include only gross purchases by capitalists of *durable* capital goods and the consumption of their self-owned durable capital, approximated by depreciation allowances set by the owners. We shall consider the problems of durable capital more fully below, but suffice it to say that there is no great difference between durable and less durable capital. Both are consumed in the course of the production process, and both must be paid for out of the gross income and gross savings of lower-order capitalists. In evaluating the payment pattern of the production structure, then, it is inadmissible to leave the consumption of nondurable capital goods out of the investment picture. It is completely illogical to single out durable goods, which are themselves only discounted embodiments of their nondurable services and are therefore no different from nondurable goods.

The idea that the capital structure is maintained intact without savings, as it were automatically, is fostered by the use of the "net" approach. If even zero savings will suffice to maintain capital, then it seems as if the aggregate value of capital is a permanent entity that cannot be reduced. This notion of the permanence of capital has permeated economic theory, particularly through the writings of J. B. Clark and Frank H. Knight, and through the influence of the latter has molded current "neoclassical" economic theory in America. To maintain this doctrine it is necessary to deny the stage analysis of production and, indeed, to deny the very influence of *time* in production.[20] The all-pervading influence of time is stressed in the period-of-production concept and in the determination of the interest rate and of the investment-consumption ratio by individual time-preference schedules. The Knight doctrine denies any role to time in production, asserting that production "now" (in a modern, complex economy) is timeless and that time preference has *no* influence on the interest rate. This doctrine has been aptly called a "mythology of capital." Among other errors, it leads to the belief that there is no economic problem connected with the replacement and maintenance of capital.[21, 22]

A common fallacy, fostered directly by the net-income approach, holds that the important category of expenditures in the production system is consumers' spending. Many writers have gone so far as to relate business prosperity directly to consumers' spending, and depressions of business to declines in consumers' spending. "Business cycle" considerations will be deferred to later chapters, but it is clear that there is little or no relationship between prosperity and consumers' spending; indeed almost the reverse is true. For business prosperity, the important consideration is the price spreads between the various stages—i.e., the rate of interest return earned. It is this rate of interest that induces capitalists to save and invest present goods in productive factors. The rate of interest, as we have been demonstrating, is set by the configurations of the time preferences of individuals in the society. It is not the total quantity of money spent on consumption that is relevant to capitalists' returns, but the *margins*, the spreads, between the product prices and the sum of factor prices at the various stages—spreads which tend to be proportionately equal throughout the economy.

There is, in fact, *never any need to worry about the maintenance of consumer spending*. There must always be consumption; as we have seen, after a certain amount of monetary saving, there is always an irreducible minimum of his monetary assets that every man will spend on current consumption. The fact of human action insures such an irreducible minimum. And as long as there is a monetary economy and money is in use, it will be spent on the purchase of consumers' goods. The proportion spent on capital in its various stages and *in toto* gives a clue to the *important* consideration—the real output of consumers' goods in the economy. The total amount of money spent, however, gives no clue at all. Money and its value will be systematically studied in a later chapter. It is obvious, however, that the number of units spent could vary enormously, depending on the quantity of the money commodity in circulation. 100 or 1,000 or 10,000 or 100,000 ounces of gold might be spent on consumption, without signifying anything except that the quantity of money units available was less or greater. The total amount of money spent on consumption gives no clue to the quantity of goods the economy may purchase.

The important consideration, therefore, is time preferences and the resultant proportion between expenditure on consumers' and producers' goods (investment). The lower the proportion of the former, the heavier will be the investment in capital structure, and, after a while, the more abundant the supply of consumers' goods and the more productive the economy. The obverse of the coin is the determining effect of time preferences on the price spreads that set the rate of interest, and the income of the capitalist savers-investors in the economy. We have already seen the effect of a lowering of investment on the first rank, and below we shall analyze fully the effect on production and interest of a lowering of time preferences and the effects of various changes in the quantity of money on time preferences and the production structure.

Before continuing with an analysis of time preference and the production structure, however, let us complete our examination of the components of the time market.[23]

The pure demanders of present goods on the time market are the various groups of laborers and landowners—the sellers of the services of original productive factors. Their price on the market, as will be seen below, will be set equal to the *marginal value product* of their units, *discounted* by the prevailing rate of interest. The greater the rate of interest, the less will the price of their service be, or rather, the greater will be the *discount* from their marginal value product considered as the matured present good. Thus, if the marginal value product of a certain labor or land factor is 10 ounces per unit period, and the rate of interest is 10%, its earning price will be approximately 9 ounces per year if the final product is one year away. A higher rate of interest would lead to a lower price, and a lower rate to a higher price, although the maximum price is one slightly below the full MVP (marginal value product), since the interest rate can never disappear.

It seems likely that the demand schedule for present goods by the original productive factors will be highly inelastic in response to changes in the interest rate. With the large base amount, the discounting by various rates of interest will very likely make little difference to the factor-owner.[24] Large changes in the interest rate, which would make an enormous difference to capitalists and determine huge differences in interest income and the profitableness of various lengthy productive processes, would have a negligible effect on the earnings of the owners of the original productive factors.

On the time market, we are considering all factors in the aggregate; the interest rate of the time market permeates all particular aspects of the present-future market, including all purchases of land and labor services. Therefore, when we are considering the supply of a certain factor on the market, we are considering it *in general,* and not its supply schedule for a specific use. A group of homogeneous pieces of land may have three alternative uses: say, for growing wheat, raising sheep, or serving as the site of a steel factory. Its supply schedule for each of the three uses will be elastic (relatively flat curve) and will be determined by the amount it can obtain in the next best use—i.e., the use in which its discounted MVP is next highest. In the present analysis, we are not considering the factor's supply curve for a *particular* industry or use; we are considering its supply curve for all users *in the aggregate,* i.e., its supply curve on the time market in exchange for present goods. We are therefore considering the behavior of all owners of a homogeneous factor of land (or of one owner if the land factor is unique, as it often is). Land is very likely to have *no* reservation price, i.e., it will have little subjective use-value to the owner. A few landlords may place a valuation on the possibility of contemplating the virgin beauty of the unused land; in practice, however, the importance of such reservation-demand for land is likely to be negligible. It will, of course, be greater where the owner can use the land to grow food for himself.

Labor services are also likely to be inelastic with respect to the interest discount, but probably less so than land, since labor has a reservation demand, a subjective use-value, even in the aggregate labor market. This special reservation demand stems from the value of leisure as a consumers' good. Higher prices for labor services will induce more units of labor to enter the market, while lower prices will increase the relative advantages of leisure. Here again, however, the difference that will be made by relatively large changes in the interest rate will not be at all great, so that the aggregate supply-of-labor curve (or rather curves, one for each homogeneous labor factor) will tend to be inelastic with regard to the interest rate.

The two categories of independent demanders of present goods for future goods, then, are the *landowners* and the *laborers.* The suppliers of present goods on the time market are clearly the *capitalists,* who save from their possible consumption and invest their savings in future goods. But the question may be raised: Do not the capitalists also *demand* present goods as well as supply them?

It is true that capitalists, after investing in a stage of production, demand present goods in exchange for their product. This particular demand is inelastic in relation to interest changes since these capital goods also can have no subjective use-value for their producers. This demand, however, is strictly derivative and dependent. In the first place, the product for which the owner demands present goods is, of course, a future good, but it is also one stage *less distantly future* than the goods that the owner purchased in order to produce it. In other words, Capitalists$_3$ will sell their future goods to Capitalists$_2$, but they had bought future goods from Capitalists$_4$, as well as from landowners and laborers. Every capitalist at every stage, then, *demands* goods that are *more* distantly future than the product that he supplies, and he supplies present goods for the duration of the production stage until this product is formed. He is therefore a *net supplier of present goods,* and a *net demander of future goods.* Hence, his activities are guided by his role as a supplier. The higher the rate of interest that he will be able to earn, i.e., the higher the price spread, the more he will tend to invest in production. If he were not essentially a supplier of present goods, this would not be true.

The relation between his role as a supplier and as a demander of present goods may be illustrated by the diagram in Fig. 46.

This diagram is another way of conveniently representing the structure of production. On the horizontal axis are represented the various stages of production, the dots furthest to the left being the highest stages, and those further to the right being the lower stages. From left to right, then, the stages of production are

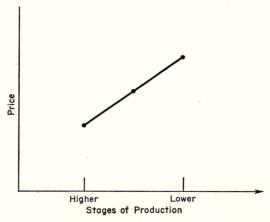

FIG. 46.   RELATION OF CUMULATIVE FACTOR PRICES TO STAGES OF PRODUCTION

lower and eventually reach the consumers'-good stage. The vertical axis represents prices, and it could interchangeably be either the production structure of one particular good or of all the goods in general. The prices that are represented at each stage are the *cumulative* prices of the factors at each stage, *excluding* the interest return of the capitalists. At each stage rightward, then, the level of the dots is higher, the difference representing the interest return to the capitalists at that stage. In this diagram, the interest return to capitalists at two adjacent stages is indicated, and the constant slope indicates that this return is equal.

Let us now reproduce the above diagram in Fig. 47.[25] The original production structure diagram is marked at points *A, B,* and *C.* Capitalists *X* purchase factors at *A* price and sell their product at point *B;* while capitalists *Y* buy at *B* and sell their product at *C*. Let us first consider the highest stage here portrayed—that of capitalists *X*. They purchase the factors at point *A*. Here they *supply* present goods to owners of factors. Capitalists *X*, of course, would prefer that the prices of the factors be lower; thus, they would prefer paying *A'* rather than *A*. Their interest spread cannot be determined until their selling prices are determined. Their activities as suppliers of present goods in exchange for

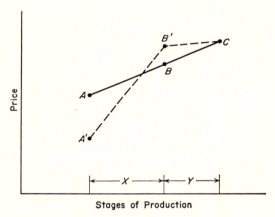

FIG. 47. EFFECT OF THE TENDENCY TOWARD A UNIFORM RATE OF INTEREST

interest return, therefore, are not really completed with their purchase of factors. Obviously, they could not be. The capitalists must transform the factors into products and sell their products for money before they obtain their interest return from their supply of present goods. The suppliers of future goods (landowners and laborers) *complete* their transactions immediately, as soon as they obtain present money. But the capitalists' transactions are incomplete until they obtain present money once again. Their demand for present goods is therefore strictly dependent on their previous supply.

Capitalists *X*, as we have stated, sell their products at *B* to the next lower rank of capitalists. Naturally, they would prefer a higher selling price for their product, and the point *B'* would be preferred to *B*. If we looked only at this sale, we might be tempted to state that, as demanders of present goods, capitalists *X* prefer a higher price, and therefore a lower discount for their product, i.e., a lower interest rate. This, however, would be a superficial point of view, for we must look at both of their exchanges, which are necessarily considered together if we consider their *complete* transaction. They prefer a lower buying point and a higher selling point, i.e., a more steeply sloped line, or a *higher rate of discount*. In other words, the capitalists prefer a higher rate of interest and therefore always act as *suppliers* of present goods. Of course, the result of this particular change (to a price spread of $A'B'$) is that the next lower rung of capitalists, capitalists Y, suffer a narrowing of their price spread, along the line $B'C$. It is, of course, perfectly agreeable to capitalists X if capitalists Y suffer a lowering of their interest return, so long as the return of the former improves. Each capitalist is interested in improving his own interest return and not necessarily the rate of interest in general. However, as we have seen, *there cannot for long be any differences in interest return between one stage and another or between one production process and another*. If the $A'B'C$ situation were established, capitalists would pour out of the Y stage and into the X stage, the increased demand would bid up the price above A', the sales at B' would be increased and the demand lowered, and the supply at C lowered, until finally the interest returns were equalized. There is always a tendency for such equalization, and this equalization is actually completed in the ERE.

5. *Time Preference, Capitalists, and Individual Money Stock*

When we state that the time-preference schedules of all individuals in the society determine the interest rate and the proportion of savings to consumption, we mean *all* individuals, and not some sort of separate class called "capitalists." There is a temptation, since the production structure is analyzed in terms of different classes—landowners, laborers, and capitalists—to conclude that there are three definite stratified groups of *people* in society corresponding to these classifications. Actually, in economic analysis of the market we are concerned with *functions* rather than *whole persons per se.* In reality, there is no special class of capitalists set off from laborers and landowners. This is not simply due to the trite fact that even capitalists must also be consumers. It is also due to the more important fact that *all* consumers *can be capitalists* if they wish. They will be capitalists if their time-preference schedules so dictate. Time-market diagrams such as shown above apply to every man, and not simply to some select group known as capitalists. The interchange of the various aggregate supply and demand diagrams throughout the entire time market sets the equilibrium rate of interest on the market. At this rate of interest, some individuals will be suppliers of present goods, some will be demanders, the curves representing the supply and demand schedules of others will be coinciding with their line of origin and they will not be in the time market at all. Those whose time-preference schedules at this rate permit them to be suppliers will be the *savers*—i.e., they will be the capitalists.

The role of the capitalists will be clarified if we ask the question: Where did they get the money that they save and invest? First, they may have obtained it in what we might call "current" production; i.e., they could have received the money in their current capacities as laborers, landowners, and capitalists. After they receive the money, they must then decide how to allocate it among various lines of goods, and between consumption and investment. Secondly, the source of funds could have been money earned in *past* rounds of production and previously "hoarded," now being "dishoarded." We are, however, leaving out hoarding and dishoarding at this stage in the analysis. The only other source, the third source, is *new* money, and this too will be discussed below.

For the moment, therefore, we shall consider that the money from which savings derive could only have come from recent earnings from production. Some earnings were obtained as capitalists, and some as owners of original factors.

The reader might here have detected an apparent paradox: How can a laborer or a landowner be a demander of present goods, and then turn around and be a supplier of present goods for investment? This seems to be particularly puzzling since we have stated above that one cannot be a demander and a supplier of present goods at the same time, that one's time-preference schedule may put one in one camp or the other, but not in both. The solution to this puzzle is that the two acts are *not performed at the same time,* even though both are performed to the same extent in their turn in the endless round of the evenly rotating economy.

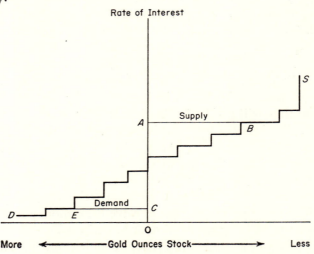

Fig. 48.   Relation of Individual Time-Preference Schedule to Money Stock

Let us reproduce the typical individual time-preference schedule (see Fig. 48). At a market interest rate of *OA,* the individual would supply savings of *AB;* at a market interest rate of *OC,* he would demand money of amount *CE.* Here, however, we are analyzing more carefully the horizontal axis. The point *O* is the point of origin. It is the point at which the person deliberates on his course of action, i.e., the position he is in when he is consulting, so to speak, his time-preference scales. Specifically, this is his position with respect to the *size of his money stock* at the time of origin. At point *O,* he has a certain money stock, and he is considering how much of his stock he is willing to give up in exchange for future goods or how much new stock he would like to acquire while giving up future goods. Suppose that he is a saver.

As the curve moves to the right, he is giving up more and more of his present money stock in exchange for future goods; therefore, his minimum interest return becomes greater. The further the curve goes to the right, then, the lower will his final money stock be. On the other hand, consider the same individual when he is a demander of present goods. As the curve proceeds to the left, he increases his stock of present goods and gives up future goods. Considering both sides of the point of origin, then, we see that the further right the curve goes, the less stock he has; the further left, the greater his stock.

Given his time-preference schedule, therefore, he is bound to be in a greater supply position the more money he has, and in more of a demand position the less money he has. Before the laborer or landowner sells his services, he has a certain money stock—a cash balance that he apparently does not reduce below a certain minimum. After he sells his services, he acquires his money income from production, thereby adding to his money stock. He then allocates this income between consumption and savings-investment, and we are assuming no hoarding or dishoarding. At this point, then, when he is allocating, he is in a far different position and at a different point in time. For now he has had a considerable addition to his money stock.

Let us consider (Fig. 49) the individual's time-market graph with two different points of origin, i.e., two different sizes of money stock, one before he earns his income (I), and one immediately after (II).

Here we see how a laborer or a landowner can be a demander at one time, in one position of his money stock, and a supplier at another time. With very little money stock, as represented in the first diagram, he is a demander. Then, he acquires money in the productive arena, greatly increases his money stock, and therefore the point of origin of his decision to allocate his money income shifts to the left, so that he might well become a supplier out of his income. Of course, in many cases, he is still a demander or is not on the time market at all. To coin a phrase to distinguish these two positions, we may call his original condition a "pre-in-

come position" (before he has sold his services for money), and
the latter a "post-income position"—his situation when he is allocating his money income. Both points of origin are relevant to his
real actions.

We have seen above that a landowner's pre-income demand

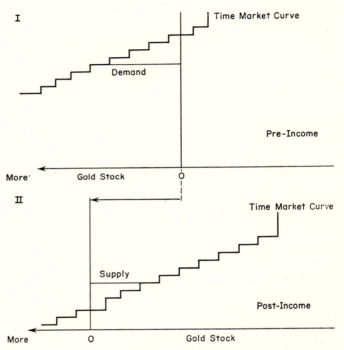

Fig. 49. Effect of Change in Individual's Money Stock on His Allocation of
Money to Savings and Consumption

for money is likely to be practically inelastic, or vertical, while
a laborer's will probably be more elastic. Some individuals in a
post-income position will be suppliers at the market rate of interest; some will be demanders; some will be neutral. The four
diagrams in Fig. 50 depict various pre-income and post-income
time-preference situations, establishing individual time-market
curves, with the same market rate of interest applied to each
one.

The line *AB,* across the page, is our assumed market rate of interest, equilibrated as a result of the individual time-preference scales. At this rate of interest, the landowner and the laborer (I and II) are shown with demands for present money (pre-income), and diagrams III and IV depict a demander at this rate and a neutral at this rate, one who is moved neither to supply nor to demand money in the time market. Both the latter are in post-income situations.

We conclude that any man can be a capitalist if only he wants to be. He can derive his funds solely from the fruits of previous

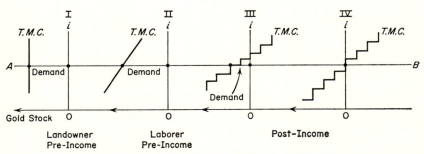

Fig. 50. Different Individuals' Time-Market Curves at a Given Rate of Interest

capitalist investment or from past "hoarded" cash balances or solely from his income as a laborer or a landowner. He can, of course, derive his funds from several of these sources. *The only thing that stops a man from being a capitalist is his own high time-preference scale,* in other words, his stronger desire to consume goods in the present. Marxists and others who postulate a rigid stratification—a virtual *caste* structure in society—are in grave error. The same person can be at once a laborer, a landowner, and a capitalist, in the same period of time.[26]

It might be argued that only the "rich" can afford to be capitalists, i.e., those who have a greater amount of money stock. This argument has superficial plausibility, since from our diagrams above we saw that, for *any given individual* and a given time-preference schedule, a greater money stock will lead to a greater supply of savings, and a lesser money stock to a lesser supply of savings. *Ceteris paribus,* the same applies to changes in money income, which constitute additions to stock. We *cannot,* how-

ever, assume that a man with (post-income) assets of 10,000 ounces
of gold will necessarily save more than a man with 100 ounces
of gold. We *cannot compare time preferences interpersonally,*
any more than we can formulate interpersonal laws for any other
type of utilities. What we can assert as an economic law for one
person we cannot assert in comparing two or more persons. Each
person has his own time-preference schedule, apart from the specific size of his monetary stock. Each person's time-preference
schedule, as with any other element in his value scale, is entirely
of his own making. All of us have heard of the proverbially
thrifty French peasant, compared with the rich playboy who is
always running into debt. The common-sense observation that it
is generally the rich who save more may be an interesting historical judgment, but it furnishes us with no scientific economic
law whatever, and the purpose of economic science is to furnish
us with such laws. As long as a person has any money at all, and
he must have some money if he participates in the market society
to any extent, he can be a capitalist.

6. *The Post-Income Demanders*

Up to this point we have analyzed the time-market demand
for present goods by landowners and laborers, as well as the
derived demand by capitalists. This aggregate demand we may
call the *producers' demand* for present goods on the time market.
This is the demand by those who are selling their services or
the services of their owned property in the advancing of production. This demand is all *pre-income demand* as we have defined
it; i.e., it takes place prior to the acquisition of money income
from the productive system. It is all in the form of selling factor
services (future goods) in exchange for present money. But there
is another component of net demand for present goods on the
time market. This is the *post-income* component; it is a demand
that takes place even after productive income is acquired. Clearly,
this demand cannot be a productive demand, since owners of
future goods used in production exercise that demand *prior* to
their sale. It is, on the contrary, a *consumers' demand.*

This subdivision of the time market operates as follows: Jones sells 100 ounces of future money (say, one year from now) to Smith in exchange for 95 ounces of present money. This future money is not in the form of an expectation created by a factor of production; instead, it is an I. O. U. by Jones promising to pay 100 ounces of money at a point one year in the future. He exchanges this *claim* on future money for present money—95 ounces. The discount on future money as compared with present money is precisely equivalent to that in the other parts of the time market that we have studied heretofore, except that the present case is more obvious. The rate of interest finally set on the market is determined by the aggregate net supply and net demand schedules throughout the entire time market, and these, as we have seen, are determined by the time preferences of all the individuals on the market. Thus, in the case of Fig. 50 above, in diagram III we have a case of a net (post-income) demander at the market rate of interest. The form that his demand takes is the sale of an I. O. U. of future money—usually termed the "borrowing" of present money. On the other hand, the person whose time-market curve is shown in diagram IV has such a time-preference configuration that he is neither a net supplier nor a net demander at the going rate of interest—he is not on the time market at all—in his post-income position.

The net borrowers, then, are people who have relatively higher time-preference rates than others at the going rate of interest, in fact so high that they will borrow certain amounts at this rate. It must be emphasized here that we are dealing *only* with consumption borrowing—borrowing to add to the present use of Jones' money stock for consumption. Jones' sale of future money differs from the sales of the landowners and laborers in another respect; their transactions are completed, while Jones has not yet completed his. His I. O. U. establishes a claim to future money on the part of the buyer (or "lender") Smith, and Smith, to complete his transaction and earn his interest payment, must present his note at the later date and claim the money due.

In sum, the *time market's components are as follows:*

I. *Supply of Present Goods for Future Goods:*
　　Savings (of all)
II. *Demand for Present Goods by Suppliers of Future Goods:*
　　a. *Producers' Demand*
　　　　Landowners　　Laborers
　　b. *Consumers' Demand*
　　　　Borrowing Consumers

These demands are aggregated without regard to whether they are

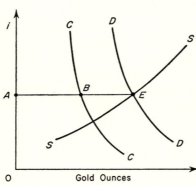

FIG. 51. DETERMINATION OF THE EQUI-
LIBRIUM RATE OF INTEREST ON THE TIME
MARKET

post- or pre-income; they both occur within a relatively brief time period, and they recur continually in the ERE.

Although the consumption and the productive demands are aggregated to set the market rate of interest, a point of great importance for the productive system is revealed if we separate these demands analytically. The diagram in Fig. 51 depicts the establishment of the rate of interest on the time market.

The vertical axis is the rate of interest; the horizontal axis is gold ounces. The *SS* curve is the supply-of-savings schedule, determined by individual time preferences. The *CC* curve is the schedule of consumers' loan demands for present goods, consisting of the aggregate net demand (post-income) at the various hypothetical rates of interest. The *DD* curve is the total demand for present goods by suppliers of future goods, and it consists of the *CC* curve *plus* a curve that is not shown—the demand for present goods by the owners of original productive factors, i.e., land and labor. Both the *CC* and the *DD* curves are determined by individual time preferences. The equilibrium rate of interest will be set by the market at the point of intersection of the *SS* and *DD* curves—point *E*.

The point of intersection at *E* determines two important resultants: the rate of interest, which is established at *OA*, and the total supply of savings *AE*. A vital matter for the productive system, however, is the position of the *CC* curve: the larger *CC* is at any given rate of interest, the larger the amount of total savings that will be competed for and drawn away from production into consumers' loans. In our diagram, the total savings going into investment in production is *BE*.

The relative strength of productive and consumption demand for present goods in the society depends on the configurations of the time-preference schedules of the various individuals on the market. We have seen that the productive demand for present goods tends to be inelastic with respect to interest rates; on the other hand, the consumers' loan curve will probably display greater elasticity. It follows that, on the demand side, changes in time preferences will display themselves mostly in the consumption demand schedule. On the supply side, of course, a rise in time preferences will lead to a shift of the *SS* curve to the left, with less being saved and invested at each rate of interest. The effects of time-preference changes on the rate of interest and the structure of production will be discussed further below.

It is clear that the gross savings that maintain the production structure are the "productive" savings, i.e., those that go into productive investment, and that these exclude the "consumption" savings that go into consumer lending. From the point of view of the production system, we may regard borrowing by a consumer as dissaving, for this is the amount by which a *person's consumption expenditures exceed his income,* as contrasted to savings, the amount by which a person's income exceeds his consumption. In that case, the savings loaned are canceled out, so to speak, by the dissavings of the consumption borrowers.

The consumers' and producers' subdivisions of the time market are a good illustration of how the rate of interest is equalized over the market. The connection between the returns on investment and money loans to consumers is not an obvious one. But it is clear from our discussion that both are parts of one time market. It should also be clear that there can be no long-run deviation of the rate of interest on the consumption loan market from the rate of interest return on productive investment. Both are aspects of one time market. If the rate of interest on consumers' loans, for example, were higher than the rate of interest return from investment, savings would shift from buying future goods in the form of factors to the more remunerative purchase of I. O. U.'s. This shift would cause the price of future factors to fall, i.e., the interest rate in investment to rise; and the rate of interest on consumers' loans to fall, as a result of the competition of more savings in the consumer loan arena. The everyday arbitrage of the market, then, will tend to equalize the rate of interest in both parts of the market. Thus, the rate of interest will tend to be equalized for all areas of the economy, as it were in three dimensions—"horizontally" in every process of production, "vertically" at every stage of production, and "in depth," in the consumer loan market as well as in the production structure.

7. *The Myth of the Importance of the Producers' Loan Market*

We have completed our analysis of the determination of the pure rate of interest as it would be in the evenly rotating economy—a rate that the market tends to approach in the real world. We have shown how it is determined by time preferences on the time market and have seen the various components of that time market. This statement will undoubtedly be extremely puzzling to many readers. Where is the producers' loan market? This market is always the one that is stressed by writers, often to the exclusion of anything else. In fact, "rate of interest" generally refers to money loans, including loans to consumers and producers, but particularly stressing the latter, which is usually quantitatively greater and more significant for production. The rate of interest of money loans to the would-be producer is supposed to be the significant rate of interest. In fact, the fashionable neoclassical doctrine holds that the producers' loan market *determines* the rate of interest and that this determination takes place as in Fig. 52, where *SS* is the supply of savings *entering the loan market,* and *DD* is the *demand for these loans* by producers or entrepreneurs. Their intersection allegedly determines the rate of interest.

It will be noticed that this sort of approach completely overlooks the *gross savings of the producers* and, even more, the *demand for present goods by owners of the original factors.* Instead of being fundamentally suppliers of present goods, capitalists are portrayed as demanders of present goods. What determines the *SS* and *DD* schedules, according to this neoclassical doctrine? The *SS* curve is admittedly determined by time preferences; the *DD* curve, on the other hand, is supposed to be determined by the "marginal efficiency of capital," i.e., by the expected rate of return on the investment.

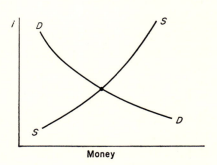

Fig. 52.   Neoclassical Conception of the Determination of the Rate of Interest

This approach misses the point very badly because it looks at the economy with the superficial eye of an average businessman. The businessman borrows on a producers' loan market from individual savers, and he judges how much to borrow on the basis of his expected rate of "profit," or rate of return. The writers assume that he has available a shelf of investment projects some of which would pay him, say 8%, some 7%, some 3%, etc., and that at each hypothetical interest rate he will borrow in order to invest in those projects where his return will be as high or higher. In other words, if the interest rate is 8%, he will borrow to invest in those projects that will yield him over 8%; if the rate is 4%, he will invest in many more projects—those that will yield him over 4%, etc. In that way, the demand curve for savings, for each individual, and still more for the aggregate on the market, will slope rightward as demand curves usually do, as the rate of interest falls. The intersection sets the market rate of interest.

Superficially, this approach might seem plausible. It usually happens that a businessman foresees such varying rates of return on different investments, that he borrows on the market from different individual savers, *and* that he is popularly considered the "capitalist" or entrepreneur, while the lenders are simply savers. This lends plausibility to terming the *DD* curve in Fig. 52, the demand by capitalists or entrepreneurs for money (present goods). And it seems to avoid mysterious complexities and to focus neatly and simply on the rate of interest for producers' loans—the loans from savers to businessmen—in which they and most writers on economics are interested. It is this rate of interest that is generally discussed at great length by economists.

Although popular, this approach is wrong through and through, as will be revealed in the course of this analysis. In the first place, let us consider the construction of this *DD* curve a little more closely. What is the basis for the alleged shelf of available projects, each with different rates of return? *Why does a particular investment yield any net monetary return at all?* The usual answer is that each dose of new investment has a "marginal value productivity," such as 10%, 9%, 4%, etc., that naturally the most productive investments will be made first and that therefore, as savings increase, further investments will be less and less value-productive. This provides the basis for the alleged "businessman's demand curve," which slopes to the right as savings increase and the interest rate falls. The cardinal error here is an old one in economics—the attribution of *value*-productivity to monetary investment. There is no question that investment increases the *physical* productivity of the productive process, as well as the productivity per man hour. Indeed, that is precisely why investment and the consequent lengthening of the periods of production take place at all. But what has this to do with value-productivity or with the monetary return on investment, especially in the long run of the ERE?

Suppose, for example, that a certain quantity of physical factors (and we shall set aside the question of how this quantity can be measured) produces 10 units of a certain product per period at a selling price of 2 gold ounces per unit. Now let us postulate that investment is made in higher-order capital goods to such an extent that productivity multiplies fivefold and that the same original factors can now produce 50 units per period. The selling price of the larger supply of product will be less; let us assume that it will be cut in half to 1 ounce per unit. The gross revenue per period is increased from 20 to 50 ounces. Does this mean that value-productivity has increased two and a half times, just as physical productivity increased fivefold? Certainly not! For, as we have seen, producers benefit, not from the gross revenue received, but from the *price spread* between their selling price and their aggregate factor prices. The increase in physical productivity will certainly increase revenue in the short run, but this refers to the profit-and-loss situations of the real world of uncertainty. The *long-run* tendency will be nothing of the sort. The long-run tendency, eventuating in the ERE, is toward an equalization of price spreads. How can there be any permanent benefit when the cumulative factor prices paid by this producer increase from, say, 18 ounces to 47 ounces? This is precisely what will happen on the market, as competitors vie to invest in these profitable situations. The price spread, i.e., the *interest rate,* will again be 5%.

Thus the productivity of production processes has no basic relation to the rate of return on business investment. This rate of return depends on the price spreads between stages, and these price spreads will tend to be equal. The size of the price spread, i.e., the size of the interest rate, is determined, as we have seen at length, by the time-preference schedules of all the individuals in the economy.

In sum, the neoclassical doctrine maintains that the interest rate, by which is largely meant the producers' loan market, is co-determined by time preference (which determines the supply of individual savings) and by marginal (value) productivity of investment (which determines the demand for savings by business men), which in turn is determined by the rates of return that can be achieved in investments. But we have seen that *these very rates of return are, in fact, the rate of interest* and that their size is determined by time preferences. The neoclassicists are partly right in only one respect—that the rate of interest in the producers' loan market is dependent on the rates of return on investment. They hardly realize the extent of this dependence, however. It is clear that these *rates of return,* which will be equalized into one uniform rate, *constitute the significant rate of interest in the production structure.*[27, 28]

Discarding the neoclassical analysis, we may ask: What, then, is the role of the productive loan market and of the rate of interest set therein? This role is one of complete and utter dependence on the rate of interest as determined above, and manifesting itself, as we have seen, in the rate of investment return, on the one hand, and in the consumers' loan market, on the other. These latter two markets are the independent and important subdivisions of the general time market, with the former being the important market for the production system.

In this picture, the producers' loan market has a purely subsidiary and dependent role. In fact, from the point of view of fundamental analysis, there need not be any producers' loan market at all. To examine this conclusion, let us consider a state of business affairs without a producers' loan market. What is needed to bring this about? Individuals save, consuming less than their income. They then *directly invest* these savings in the production structure, the incentive for investment being the rate of interest return—the price spread—on the investment. This rate is determined, along with the rate on the consumers' loan market, by the various components of the time market that we have portrayed above. There is, in that case, no producers' loan market. There are no loans from a saving group to another group of investors. And it is clear that the rate of interest in the production structure still exists; it is determined by factors that have nothing to do with the usual discussion by economists of the producers' loan market.

8. *The Joint-Stock Company*

It is clear that, far from being the centrally important element, the producers' loan market is of minor importance, and it is easy to postulate a going productive system with no such market at all. But, some may reply, this may be all very well for a primitive economy where every firm is owned by just one capitalist-investor, who invests his own savings. What happens in our modern complex economy, where savings and investment are *separated,* are processes engaged in by different groups of people— the former by scattered individuals, the latter by relatively few directors of firms? Let us, therefore, now consider a second possible situation. Up to this point we have not treated in detail the question whether each factor or business was owned by one person or jointly by many persons. Now let us consider an economy in which factors are *jointly owned* by many people, as largely happens in the modern world, and we shall see what difference this makes in our analyses.

Before studying the effect of such jointly owned companies on the producers' loan market, we must digress to analyze the nature of these companies themselves. In a *jointly* owned firm, instead of each individual capitalist's making his own investments and making all his own investment and production decisions, various individuals pool their money capital in one organization, or *business firm,* and jointly make decisions on the investment of their joint savings. The firm then purchases the land, labor, and capital-goods factors, and later sells the product to consumers or to lower-order capitalists. Thus, the firm is the joint owner of the factor services and particularly of the *product* as it is produced and becomes ready for sale. The firm is the product-owner until the product is sold for money. The individuals who contributed their saved capital to the firm are the joint owners, successively, of: (*a*) the initial money capital—the pooled savings, (*b*) the services of the factors, (*c*) the product of the factors, and (*d*) the money obtained from the sale of the product. In the evenly rotating economy, their ownership of assets follows this same step-by-step pattern, period after period, without change. In a jointly owned firm, in actual practice, the variety of productive assets owned by the firm is large. Any one firm is usually engaged in various production processes, each one involving a different period of time, and is likely to be engaged in different stages of each process at any one particular time. A firm is likely to be producing so that its output is continuous and so that it makes sales of new units of the product every day.

It is obvious, then, that if the firm keeps continually in business, its operations at any one time will be a mixture of investment and sale of product. Its assets at any one time will be a mixture of cash about to be invested, factors just bought, hardly begun products, and money just received from the sale of products. The result is that, to the superficial, it looks as if the firm is an automatically continuing thing and as if the production is somehow timeless and instantaneous, ensuing immediately after the factor input.

Actually, of course, this idea is completely unfounded. There is no automatic continuity of investment and production. Production is continued because the owners are continually making decisions to proceed; if they did not think it profitable to do so, they could and do at any point alter, curtail, or totally cease operations and investments. And production takes *time* from initial investment to final product.

In the light of our discussion, we may classify the types of assets owned by any firm (whether jointly or individually owned) as follows:

A. *Money*
B. *Productive Assets*
   Melange of factors, such as land and capital goods, embodying future services (this will be analyzed below); various stages of product; the completed product

On this entire package of assets, a monetary evaluation is placed by the market. How this is done will be examined in detail later.

At this point, let us revert to the simple case of a one-shot investment, an investment in factors on one date, and the sale of the resulting product a year later. This is the assumption involved in our original analysis of the production structure; and it will be seen below that the same analysis can be applied to the more complex case of a melange of assets at different stages of production and even to cases where one firm engages in several different production processes and produces different goods. Let us consider a group of individuals pooling their saved money capital to the extent of 100 ounces, purchasing factors with the 100 gold ounces, obtaining a product, and selling the product for 105 ounces a year later. The rate of interest in this society is 5% per annum, and the rate of interest return on this investment conforms with this condition. The question now arises: *On what principle do the individual owners mutually apportion their shares of the assets?* It will almost always be the case that every individual is vitally interested in knowing his share of the joint assets, and consequently firms are established in such a way that the principle of apportionment is known to all the owners.

At first one might be inclined to say that this is simply a case of bargaining, as in the case of the product jointly owned by all the owners of the factors. But the former situation does not apply here. For in the case discussed above, there was no principle whereby any man's share of ownership could be distinguished from that of anyone else. A whole group of people worked, contributed their land, etc., to the production process, and there was no way except simple bargaining by which the income from the sale of the product could be apportioned among them. Here, each individual is contributing a certain amount of money capital to begin with. Therefore, the proportions are naturally established from the outset. Let us say that the 100 ounces of capital are contributed by five men as follows:

$$
\begin{array}{ll}
A & 40 \text{ oz.} \\
B & 20 \text{ oz.} \\
C & 20 \text{ oz.} \\
D & 15 \text{ oz.} \\
E & 5 \text{ oz.}
\end{array}
$$

In other words, A contributes 40% of the capital, B 20%, C 20%, D 15%, E 5%. Each individual owner of the firm then owns the same percentage of all the assets that he contributed in the beginning. This holds true at each step of the way, and finally for the money obtained from the sale of the product. The 105 ounces earned from the sale will be either reinvested in or "disinvested" from the process. At any rate, the ownership of these 105 ounces will be distributed in the same percentages as the capital invested.

This natural structure of a firm is essentially the structure of a *joint-stock company*. In the joint-stock company, each investor-owner receives a *share*—a certification of ownership in proportion to the amount he has invested in the total capital of the company. Thus, if A, B, . . . E above form a company, they may issue 100 shares, each share representing a value, or an asset, of 1 ounce. A will receive 40 shares; B, 20 shares; C, 20 shares, etc. After the sale of the product, each share will be worth five percent more than its original, or *par,* value.

Suppose that after the sale, or indeed at any time before the sale, another person, F, wishes to invest in this company. Suppose that he wishes to invest 30 ounces of gold. In that case, the investment of money savings in the company increases from 100 (if before the sale) or 105 (if after the sale) by 30 ounces. Thirty new shares will be issued and turned over to F, and the capital value of the firm increases by 30 ounces. In the vast majority of cases where reinvestment of monetary revenue is going on continuously, at any point in time the capital value of a firm's assets will be the appraised value of all the productive assets, including cash, land, capital goods, and finished products. The capital value of the firm is increased at any given time by new investment and is maintained by the reinvestments of the owners after the finished product is sold.

The shares of capital are generally known as *stock;* the total *par* value of capital stock is the amount originally paid in on the formation of the company. From that point on, the total capital value of assets changes as income is earned, or, in the world of uncertainty, as losses are suffered, and as capital is reinvested or withdrawn from the company. The total value of capital stock changes accordingly, and the value of each share will differ from the original value accordingly.

How will the group of owners decide on the affairs of the company? Those decisions that must be made jointly will be made by some sort of voting arrangement. The natural voting arrangement, which one would expect to be used, is to have one vote per share of voting stock, with a majority of the votes deciding. This is precisely the arrangement used in the joint-stock company and its modern form, the *corporation*.

Of course, some joint-stock company arrangements differ from this, according to the desires of the owners. *Partnerships* can be worked out between two or more people on various principles. Usually, however, if one partner receives more than his proportionate share of invested capital, it is because he is contributing more of his labor or his land to the enterprise and gets paid accordingly. As we shall see, the rate paid to the labor of the "working partner" will be approximately equal to what he could earn in labor elsewhere, and the same is true for payment to the land or any other originally owned factor contributed by a partner. Since partnerships are almost always limited to a few, the relationships are more or less informal and need not have the formal patterns of the joint-stock company. However, partnerships will tend to work quite similarly. They provide more room for idiosyncratic arrangements. Thus, one partner may receive more than his share of capital because he is loved and revered by the others; this is really in the nature of a gift to him from the rest of the partners. Joint-stock companies hew more closely to a formal principle.

The great advantage of the joint-stock company is that it provides a more ready channel for new investments of saved capital. We have seen how easy it is for new capital to be attracted through the issuance of new shares. It is also easier for any owner to withdraw his capital from the firm. This greater ease of withdrawal vastly increases the temptation to invest in the company. Later on we shall explore the pricing of stock shares in the real world of uncertainty. In this real world, there is room for great differences of opinion concerning the appraised value of a firm's assets, and therefore concerning the monetary appraised value of each share of the firm's stock. In the evenly rotating economy, however, all appraisals of monetary value will agree—the principles of such appraisal will be examined below—and therefore the appraised value of the shares of stock will be agreed upon by all and will remain constant.

While the share market of joint-stock companies provides a ready channel for accumulating savings, *the share market is strictly dependent on the price spreads.* The savings or dissavings of capitalists are determined by time preferences, and the latter establish the price spread in the economy. The value of capital invested in the enterprise, i.e., its productive assets, will be the sum of future earnings from the capital discounted by the rate of interest. If the price spreads are five per cent, the rate of interest return yielded on the share market (the ratio of earnings per share to the market price of the share) will tend to equal the rate of interest as determined elsewhere on the time market—in this case, five per cent.

We still have a situation in which capitalists supply their own saved capital, which is used to purchase factors in expectation of a net monetary return. The only complications that develop from joint-stock companies or corporations are that many capitalists contribute and own the firm's assets jointly and that the price of a certain quantum of ownership will be regulated by the market so that the rate of interest yield will be the same for each individual share of stock as it is for the enterprise as a whole. If the whole firm buys factors for a total price of 100 and sells the product a year later for 105, for a five per cent return, then, say, $\frac{1}{5}$ of the shares of ownership of this firm will sell for an aggregate price of twenty, and earn an annual net return of one ounce. Thus, the rates of interest for the partial shares of capital will all tend to be equal to the rate of interest earned on the entire capital.[29]

Majority rule in the joint-stock companies, with respect to total shares owned, does not mean that the minority rights of owners are overridden. In the first place, the entire pooling of resources and the basis on which it is worked out are voluntary for all parties concerned. Secondly, all the stockholders, or owners, have one single interest in common—an increase in their monetary return and assets, although they may, of course, differ concerning the means to achieve this goal. Thirdly, the members of the minority may sell their stock and withdraw from the company if they so desire.

Actually, the partners may arrange their voting rights and ownership rights in any way they please, and there have been many variations of such arrangements. One such form of group ownership, in which each owner has one vote regardless of the number of shares he owns, has absurdly but effectively arrogated to itself the name of "co-operative." It is obvious that partnerships, joint-stock companies and corporations are *all* eminently *co-operative* institutions.[30]

Many people believe that economic analysis, while applicable to individually owned firms, does not hold true for the modern economy of joint-stock companies. Nothing could be further from the truth. The introduction of corporations has not fundamentally changed our analysis of the interest rate or the savings-investment process. What of the separation of "management" from ownership in a corporation? It is certainly true that, in a joint-stock firm, the owners hire managerial labor to supervise their workers, whereas individual owners generally perform their own managerial labor. A manager is just as much a hired laborer as any other worker. The president of a company, just like the ditchdigger, is hired by the owners; and, like the ditchdigger, he expends labor in the production process. The price of managerial labor is determined in the same way as that of other labor, as will be seen below. On the market, the income to an independent owner will *also* include the going wage for that type of managerial labor, which joint-stock owners, of course, will not receive. Thus, we see that, far from rendering economic analysis obsolete, the modern world of the corporation aids analysis by separating and simplifying functions in production—specifically, the managerial function.

In addition to the capital-supplying function, the corporate capitalists also assume the *entrepreneurial* function: the crucial directing element in guiding the processes of production to-

ward meeting the desires of the consumers. In the real world
of uncertainty, it takes sound judgment to decide how the market is operating, so that present investment will lead to future
profits, and not future losses. We shall deal further with the
nature of profit and loss, but suffice it to say here that the active entrepreneurial element in the real world is due to the
presence of uncertainty. We have been discussing the determination of the pure rate of interest, the rate of interest as it always tends to be and as it will be in the certain world of the
ERE. In the ERE, where all techniques, market demands and
supplies, etc., for the future are known, the investment function becomes purely passive and waiting. There might still be
a supervisory or managerial labor function, but this can be
analyzed under prices of labor factors. But there will no longer
be an entrepreneurial function because future events are known.

Some have maintained, finally, that joint-stock companies
make for a separation of savings and investment. Stockholders
save, and the managers do the investing. This is completely
fallacious. The managers are *hired agents* of the stockholders
and subject to the latters' dictation. Any individual stockholder
not satisfied with the decisions of the majority of owners can
dispose of his ownership share. As a result, it is effectively the
stockholders who save and the *stockholders* who invest the
funds.[31]

Some people maintain that since most stockholders are not
"interested" in the affairs of their company, they do not effectively
control the firm, but permit control to pass into the hands of
the hired managers. Yet surely a stockholder's interest is a
matter of his own preference and is under his own control. Preferring his lack of interest, he permits the managers to continue
their present course; the fundamental control, however, is still
his, and he has absolute control over his agents.[32] A typical view
asserts: "The maximizing of dividend income for stockholders
as a group is not an objective that is necessarily unique or
paramount. Instead, management officials will seek to improve
the long-run earnings and competitive position of the firm and
their own prestige as managers." [33] But to "improve the long-

run earnings" is identical with maximizing stockholders' income, and what else can develop the "prestige" of managers? Other theorists lapse into the sheer mysticism of considering the "corporation"—a conceptual name which we give to an institution owned by real individuals—as "really" existing and acting by itself.[34]

9. Joint-Stock Companies and the Producers' Loan Market

We are now ready to embark on an analysis of the effect of joint-stock companies on the producers' loan market.

Let us take the aforementioned firm with a total capital stock and capital value of 130 ounces and owned by six stockholders. The firm earns a net income of 5% per year for its owners, and this is the interest rate earned by all the firms in the economy.

We have already seen how the firm expanded its capital by 30 ounces through the sale of new capital stock to F. Let us see what happens when a productive loan is made. Suppose that the firm borrows 20 ounces from the producers' loan market for a five-year period. What has happened? The firm has exchanged a future good—a promise to pay money in the future—for present money. The present money has been supplied by a saver, G. It is clear that G has done the saving and is the capitalist in this transaction, while the joint stockholders A–F are here supplying future goods; and further, it is the stockholders who invest the new capital in the production system. On the surface, this seems to be a positive case of the separation of savings and investment.

However, let us look at the transaction further. G has supplied new capital, worth 20 ounces, to the firm, for a five-year period. The owners A–F take this new capital and invest it in future goods, i.e., factors of production. In other words, to the extent of 20 ounces, A–F are intermediary investors of the savings of the creditors. What will the rate of interest on this loan be? It is obvious that this rate of interest in the ERE, will be equal to 5%, i.e., it will be purely dependent on the rate of interest return that prevails in the price spreads of the production structure. The reason for this should be clear. We have already seen how the interest rate is determined in the production structure; we have assumed it to be 5% everywhere. Now, suppose that the firm offers to pay G 3% on the loan. Clearly, G will not lend the firm 20 ounces for a 3% return when he could get 5% as a stockholder either in the same firm or in any other firm. On the other hand, the firm is in no position to pay G any more than 5%, since its net return on the investment will be only 5%. If the maximum that the firm can pay in interest is 5%, and the minimum that the creditor can accept is 5%, it is obvious that the transaction will take place at 5%.

It is clear that, in essence, G, the creditor on the prospective loan market, is no different from F, the man who has invested in stock. Both have saved money instead of spending it on consumption, and both wish to sell their saved capital in exchange for future goods and to earn interest. The time-preference schedules of both F and G, as well as of everyone else, are aggregated on the time market to arrive at the rate of interest; both F and G are net savers at the market rate. The interest rate, then, is determined by the various time-preference schedules, and the final rate is set by the saving schedules, on the one hand, and by the demand-for-present-goods schedules, on the other. The demand schedules consist (and consist only) of the productive demand by laborers and landowners and the consumption demand by borrowing consumers. F and G are both net savers, interested in investing their capital for the highest return. There is no essential difference between F's method of investing his capital and G's method of investing his; *the difference between investing in stock and lending money to firms is mainly a technical one.* The separation between saving and investment that occurs in the latter case is completely unimportant. The interest return on investment, as set by total savings and total demands by owners of factors, *completely determines the rate of interest on the producers' loan market* as well as the rate of earning on stock. The producers' loan market is totally unimportant from the point of view of fundamental analysis; it is even useless to try to construct demand and supply schedules for this market, since its price is determined elsewhere.[35] Whether saved capital is channeled into investments *via* stocks or *via* loans is unimportant. The only difference is in the legal technicalities. Indeed, even the legal difference between the creditor and the owner is a negligible one. G's loan has increased the capital value of the assets in the firm from 130 to 150. The invested 150 pays 5%, or 7.5 ounces per year. Let us examine the situation and see who the actual owners of this capital are (see Fig. 53).

In this diagram, the left-hand rectangle represents assets at any one point in time. We see in the right-hand rectangle that 130 ounces of these assets is represented by owners' capital, and 20 by liabilities—i.e., by I. O. U.'s due to creditors. But what does this "representation" mean? It means that if, for example, the firm were to liquidate and go out of business, 20 ounces of its assets would be used to pay off the creditors, and 130

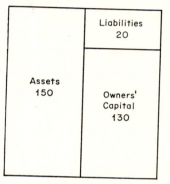

FIG. 53. DISTRIBUTION OF OWN-ERSHIP OF JOINT-STOCK COM-PANY'S ASSETS

would go to the legal owners. It means, further, that of the 7.5 ounces paid out as net earnings per year, 6.5 ounces go to the legal owners and 1 ounce to the creditors, each being 5% of their saving. In fact, each group gets 5% on its *investment,* for are not the creditors just as much investors as the stockholders? In fact, are not the creditors the *owners* of 20 ounces' worth of the firm's assets, and do they not own the prorata earnings of those 20 ounces? What functions of ownership do the creditors *not* have as compared to the stockholders? Even from the legal point of view, the creditors *get first claim* on the assets of a corporation, and they get paid before the stockholders. They are therefore definitely owners of these assets. It might be stated that since they are not shareholders, they do not vote on the decisions of the corporation, but there are many situations in which joint-stock companies issue *nonvoting* shares, the holders of which do not vote on company affairs, even though they receive their prorata value of the earnings.

We must conclude that economically and even in basic law, there is no difference between shareholders and productive creditors; both are equally suppliers of capital, both receive interest return as determined on the general time market, both own their proportionate share of the company's assets. The differences between the two are only technical and semantic. It is true that our discussion has so far applied only to the evenly rotating economy, but we shall see that the real world of uncertainty and entrepreneurship, while complicating matters, does not change the essentials of our analysis.[36]

In recent writings there has been a growing acknowledgment of the essential identity between shareholders and creditors, in contrast to the old tradition that postulated a sharp cleavage between them. But it is curious that the new literature interprets the identity in precisely the wrong way: instead of treating the creditors like shareholder-owners, it treats the shareholders like creditors. In other words, the correct approach is to consider creditors as actually part owners of the firm; but the new literature treats stockholders as merely creditors of the firm, in keeping with the new tradition of picturing the hired managers as its real controllers and owners. Managers are depicted as somehow owning the firm and paying out interest to creditors, as well as dividends to stockholders, just as any factor payment is made—as a grudging cost of production. In reality, the managers are only the hired agents of the stockholders, and it is the latter who decide how much of their earnings to reinvest in the firm and how much to "take out of the firm" in the form of "dividends."

The commonly made distinction between "dividends" and "retained earnings" is not a useful one for the purposes of economic analysis. Retained earnings are not necessarily reinvested; they may be held out of investment in a cash balance and later paid out as dividends. Dividends, on the other hand, are not necessarily spent on consumption; they may be invested in some other firm. Therefore, this distinction is a misleading one. Earnings are either reinvested or they are not; and all corporate earnings constitute earnings of the individual owners.

Savings may be channeled through intermediaries before entering the actual producers' loan (or the consumers' loan) market. *Finding* a productive investment is one of the tasks of entrepreneurs, and it is often far more convenient for all concerned when the individual, instead of making up his mind himself on the proper channels of investment, lends or invests his money in other institutions specially set up to be experts in investment. These institutions may serve as channels, gathering in the small savings of isolated individuals, whose investments by themselves are too small to be worth the cost of finding a market for them. The institutions then invest the funds knowledgeably in larger lump sums. A typical example is the *investment trust,* which sells its own stock to individuals and then uses this capital to buy stock of other companies. In the ERE, the interest that will be earned from individuals' savings via intermediaries will equal the interest earned from direct investments minus the cost of the intermediary's service, this price to be determined on the market just like other prices. Thus, if the interest rate throughout the market is 5%, and the cost of intermediary service is 1%, then, in the ERE, those who channel their savings via the convenient intermediary method will receive a 4% interest return on the investment of their savings.

We have thus seen the unimportance of the producers' loan market as an independent determining factor in the establishment of the market rate of interest or in the productive system.

In many cases it is convenient to designate by different terms the rate of interest on contractual loan markets and the rate of interest in the form of earnings on investments as a result of price spreads. The former we may call the *contractual rate of interest* (where the interest is fixed at the time of making the contract), and the latter the *natural rate of interest* (i.e., the interest comes "naturally" via investments in production processes, rather than being officially included in an exchange contract). The two interest rates will, of course, coincide in the ERE.

Throughout our analysis we have been making one underlying

assumption that might be modified: that individuals will always try to obtain the highest interest return. It is on this basis that we have traced the arbitrage actions and eventual uniformities of the ERE. We have assumed that each investor will try to earn as much as he can from his investment. This might not always be true, and critics of economics have never tired of reproaching economists for neglecting other than monetary ends. Economics does not neglect such ends, however. In fact, praxeological analysis explicitly includes them. As we have repeatedly pointed out, each individual attempts to maximize his *psychic* income, and this will translate itself into maximizing his *monetary* income only if other psychic ends are neutral. The ease with which economics can accommodate nonmonetary ends may readily be seen. Suppose that the interest rate in the society is 5%. Suppose, however, that there is a line of production that is distasteful to a large number of people, including investors. In a society, for example, where the making of arms is held in disfavor, simple arbitrage would not work to equate returns in the armament industry with those in other industries. We are not here referring to the displeasure of consumers of arms, which would, of course, reflect itself in a lowered demand for the product. We are referring to the particular displeasure of producers, specifically investors. Because of this psychic dislike, investors will require a higher return in the armament industry than in other industries. It is possible, for example, that they might require an interest return of 10% in the armament industry, even though the general rate of interest is 5%. What factors, then, will have to pay for this increased discount? We are not overly anticipating the results of our subsequent analysis if we state that the owners of *nonspecific* factors, i.e., those factors which can be employed elsewhere (or, strictly, the *services* of which can be thus employed) will certainly not accept a lower monetary return in the armament industry than in the other industries. In the ERE, their prices as determined in this industry will, then, be the same as in the other industries. In fact, they might be even higher, if the owners share the investors' specific antipathy toward engaging in the armament industry. The burden of the lower prices at each stage of production, then, falls on the *purely specific* factors in the industry, those which *must* be devoted to this industry if they are to be in the production system at all. In the long run of the ERE, these will not be capital goods, since capital goods always need to be reproduced, and the equivalent resources can gradually or rapidly leave the industry, depending in each case on the durability of the capital good and the length of the process of its production. The specific factor may be labor, but this is not empirically likely, since labor is almost always a nonspecific factor that may shift to several occupations. It is therefore likely to be specific *land* factors that bear the brunt of the lower return.

The opposite will occur in the case of an industry that most investors specifically are very eager to engage in for one reason or another. In that case, they will accept a lower interest return in this production process than in others. The force of competition on the market will, once again, keep nonspecific factors at the same price from industry to industry, although the price might be lower if the factor-owners were also particularly eager to work in this industry. The higher prices at the various stages are therefore reaped by the owners of specific factors, generally land factors.

The rate of interest, then, always tends toward equality throughout its various submarkets and in its various forms. In the ERE, the rates will be uniformly equal throughout. This conclusion must be modified, however, to state that the rates of interest will differ in accordance with a "psychic" component, either positive or negative, depending on whether there is an acute dislike or liking among investors for a particular production process.[37] We may say that, in the case of a particular liking, the investors are "consuming" the enjoyment of investing in the particular process and paying the price of a lower return; in the case of a particular dislike, they are charging more for a particular disutility. It must be emphasized, however, that these differences in return do not occur if merely *one person* particularly likes or dislikes a certain field, but only if there is a significant aggregate of strong preferences in one direction or another. This type of consumption, positive or negative, is intertwined in the production process and occurs directly with production, and thus differs from ordinary consumption, which occurs at the end of the production process.

10. *Forces Affecting Time Preferences*

Praxeology can never furnish an ultimate explanation for a man's time preferences. These are psychologically determined by each person and must therefore be taken, in the final analysis, as data by economists. However, praxeological analysis can supply some truths about time preferences, using *ceteris paribus* assumptions. Thus, as we have seen above, each person has a time-preference schedule relating to his money stock. A lower money stock will cause a higher time-preference rate for any unit of money remaining in his possession, until finally his time-preference rate will rise to infinity when the money stock—or rather, the money for consumption—is low enough. Here, one element, a man's money stock, is varied and his value scale is otherwise assumed to remain constant. Hence, we can in this way gauge the effects of a change in one determinant, the money stock.

Actually, it is not his *money* stock that is relevant to his time preferences, but the *real* value of his money stock. In the ERE, of course, where the purchasing power of the money unit remains unchanged, the two are identical. *Ceteris paribus,* an increase in his real income—real additions to his money stock—will lower the time-preference rate on his schedule. Of course, historically, there is no reason why his time-preference *schedule* should remain unchanged. It is important to know, however, that, given an unchanged schedule, his relevant time-preference rate will fall.

There are other elements that enter into the determination of the time-preference schedules. Suppose, for example, that people were certain that the world would end on a definite date in the near future. What would happen to time preferences and to the rate of interest? Men would then stop providing for future needs and stop investing in all processes of production longer than the shortest. Future goods would become almost valueless compared to present goods, time preferences for present goods would zoom, and the pure interest rate would rise almost to infinity. On the other hand, if people all became immortal and healthy as a result of the discovery of some new drug, time preferences would tend to be very much lower, there would be a great increase in investment, and the pure rate of interest would fall sharply.

11. *The Time Structure of Interest Rates*

It is clear that the natural interest rates are highly flexible; they tend toward uniformity and are easily changed as entrepreneurial expectations change. In the real world the prices of the various factors and intermediate products, as well as of the final products, are subject to continual fluctuation, as are the prices of stock and the interest return on them. It is also clear that the interest rate on short-term loans is easily changed with changed conditions. As the natural interest rate changes, the new loans for short periods can easily conform to the change.

A difficulty seems to arise, however, in the case of *long-term* producers' loans. Here is an apparently clear-cut rigid element in the system, and one which can conform to the natural rate of interest in investments only after a great lag. After all, a twenty-year loan is contracted at an original interest rate that remains fixed for the duration; is this not a fixed element that cannot conform to changing conditions and valuations? This superficial view is incorrect. Long-term I. O. U.'s can also be bought and sold in a market. Most of these long-term debts are called *bonds*, and they are traded in a flourishing and flexible bond market. The fixed rate of interest at the beginning is unimportant. Thus, a 100-ounce long-term loan is contracted at 5% fixed interest, or 5 ounces per year. If the general interest rate rises, people will tend to sell their bonds, which have been yielding them only 5%, and invest their money elsewhere—either in whole firms, stocks of firms, or short-term loans. This increased willingness to sell bonds—an increased supply schedule—depresses the *price* of the bond until the interest *yield* to the buyer is the same as the general interest rate elsewhere. Thus, if the general interest rate goes up from 5% to 10%, the price of the bond will fall from 100 to 50, so that the fixed annual return of 5 will provide an interest yield of 10%. The important element in bond investment is not the original interest rate (the fixed return on the so-called "par value" of the bond), but the interest *yield* on the market price of the bond. A general lowering of the interest rate will, on the other hand, raise the bond prices above par and push yield below 5%. As the day of redemption of the bond draws near, the market price of the bond will, of course, rapidly approach the par value, until it finally sells at par, since the amount redeemed will be the original par value, or principal, of the loan.

It is clear that, in the ERE, the interest rates for all periods of time will be equal. The *tendency* toward such equality at any one time, however, has been disputed in the case of *expected future changes* in the interest rate. Although surprisingly little attention has been devoted to this subject, the prevailing theory is that, on the loan market, there will not be a tendency toward equalization if a change in interest rates is expected in the near future.[38] Suppose that the interest rate is now 5%, and it is expected to remain there. Then the interest rate on loans of all maturities will be the same, 5%. Suppose, however, that the interest rate is expected to increase steadily in the near future, say to increase each year by 1% until it will be 9% four years from now. In that case, since the short-run rate (say the rate of interest on loans lasting one year or less) is expected to increase over the next four-year period, then the present long-run rate for that period—e.g., the present rate for five-year loans—will be an average of the expected future short-run rates during this period. Thus, the present rate on four-year loans will be 5% plus 6% plus 7% plus 8% plus 9% divided by 5, equaling 7%. The long-run rate will be the average of short-run rates over the relevant period. Consequently, the long-run rates will be proportionately higher than short-run rates when the latter are expected to increase, and lower when the later are expected to be lower. (See Fig. 54.)

This, however, is a completely question-begging theory. Suppose that a rise in interest rates is expected; why should this be

simply confined to a rise in the *short-term rates?* Why should not
the expectation be equally applicable to long-term rates so that
they rise as well? [39] The theory rests on the quite untenable assumption that it sets out to prove, namely, that there is no tendency for short-term and long-term rates to be equal. The assumption that a change in the interest rate will take place only over
the short term is completely unproved and goes against our demonstration that the short-run and long-run rates tend to move to-

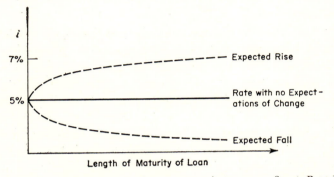

FIG. 54.   LONG-RUN INTEREST RATES CONCEIVED AS AVERAGES OF SHORT-RUN INTEREST
RATES

gether. Further, the theory rests on the implicit assumption that
individuals will be content to remain lenders in "shorts" at 5%
while their fellow investors reap 7% on the long market, simply
because they expect that eventually, if they stay in the short
market, they will earn an average of 7%. *What is there to prevent a present lender in shorts from selling his currently earning 5% loan, purchasing a 7% long, waiting for the presumed
rise in shorts above 7% after two years, and then re-entering the
short market, earning 8% or 9%?* If he does this, he will not
simply earn 7% as the foregoing diagram postulates (either directly in longs or in an average of 5%–9% in shorts); he will
earn 7% plus 7% plus 7% plus 8% plus 9%, or an annual
average of 7.6%. By striving to do so, he will set up an *irresistible* arbitrage movement from shorts to longs, with the rate
of interest in the former thereby rising from the sales of loans

on the market, and the rate of interest in longs falling, *until the rate of interest is uniform throughout the time structure.*

The same thing occurs in the case of an expectation of a future fall. Longs cannot remain in equilibrium below shorts for any length of time, since there will be a present movement from longs to shorts on the market, until the rates of interest for all time structures are equal and the arbitrage movement ceases.

The interest rate, then, always tends to be uniform throughout its time structure. What happens if the interest rate is expected to *change* in the near future? In that case, there will be a similar process as in the case of speculation in commodities. Speculators will bid up the interest rate in the expectation of an imminent rise or bid down the rate in expectation of a fall. Clearly, the earlier a rise or fall is expected to take place, the greater proportionately will be the effect on the speculators, and the greater impact it will have on current movement in the rate. In the case of a commodity, stocks would be withheld in expectation of a rise in demand and price, and then released, thereby effecting a more rapid transition to the price eventually established by underlying supply-and-demand forces. Similarly, in this case money will tend to be withheld from investments and held in cash balances until the rate reaches its expected higher level, or dislodged from cash balances and added to investment if the rate of interest is expected to be lower. This action will speed up the transition to the rate determined by the new alignment of basic time preferences. Just as speculative errors in regard to commodity prices cause losses and impel further change to the "real" underlying price, so speculative errors will be self-correcting here too and lead the rate of interest to the height determined by underlying time preferences.

The time-structure diagram of interest, then, will rather tend to be as depicted in Fig. 55.

The absurdity of separating the long-run and the short-run interest rates becomes evident when we realize that the basic interest rate is the natural rate of interest on investments, not interest on the producers' loan market. We have already seen the essential identity of the rate of earnings on the loan market with that on the stock market. If we consider the stock market, it becomes obvious that there is no distinction in rates between short-run and long-run investments. Different firms engage in stages of production of varying lengths; yet the stock market equates the rate of interest on all investments, obliterating the differences in time structure so thoroughly that it becomes difficult for many writers to grasp the very concept of period of production. But

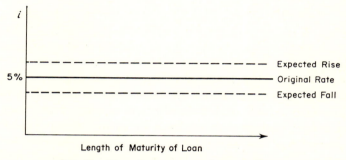

Fig. 55. Time Structure of Interest Rates

since the operations of the stock market and the loan market are essentially the same, it is obvious that there is no difference in causal explanation between short-run and long-run interest rates. Those writers who postulate an essential difference between the nature of long-run and short-run rates have been misled by a common penchant for considering the time market as confined exclusively to the loan market, when in fact the loan market is only a dependent one.[40]

In actual practice, it may well happen that either the short-run loan market or the long-run market may change first, with the other market following. Which market characteristically changes first is the outcome of the concrete conditions.[41]

APPENDIX: SCHUMPETER AND THE ZERO RATE OF INTEREST

The late Professor Joseph Schumpeter pioneered a theory of interest which holds that the rate of interest will be zero in the evenly rotating economy. It should be clear from the above discussion why the rate of interest (the *pure* rate of interest in the ERE) could never be zero. It is determined by individual time preferences, which are all positive. To maintain his position, Schumpeter was forced to assert, as does Frank Knight, that capital maintains itself permanently in the ERE. If there is no problem of maintenance, then there appears to be no necessity for the payment of interest in order to maintain the capital structure. This view, treated above, is apparently derived from the static state of J. B. Clark and seems to follow purely *by definition,* since the value of capital is maintained by definition in the ERE. But this, of course, is no answer whatever; the important question is: *How* is this constancy maintained? And the only answer can be that it is maintained by the decisions of capitalists induced by a rate of interest return. If the rate of interest paid were zero, complete capital consumption would ensue.[42]

The conclusive Mises-Robbins critique of Schumpeter's theory of the zero rate of interest, which we have tried to present above, has been attacked by two of Schumpeter's disciples.[43] First, they deny that constancy of capital is assumed by definition in Schumpeter's ERE; instead it is "deduced from the conditions of the system." What are these conditions? There is, first, the absence of uncertainty concerning the future. This, indeed, would seem to be the condition for any ERE. But Clemence and Doody add: "Neither is there time preference unless we introduce it as a special assumption, in which case it may be either positive or negative as we prefer, and there is nothing further to discuss." With such a view of time preference, there is indeed nothing to discuss. The whole basis for pure interest, requiring interest payments, is time preference, and if we casually assume that time preference is either nonexistent or has no discernible influence, then it follows very easily that the pure rate of interest is zero. The authors' "proof" simply consists of ignoring the powerful, universal fact of time preference.[44]

7

Production: General Pricing
of the Factors

1. *Imputation of the Discounted Marginal Value Product*

Up to this point we have been investigating the rate of interest as it would be determined in the evenly rotating economy, i.e., as it always *tends* to be determined in the real world. Now we shall investigate the pricing of the various factors of production in the same terms, i.e., as they tend to be in the real world, and as they would be in the evenly rotating economy.

Whenever we have touched on the pricing of productive factors we have signified the prices of their *unit services,* i.e., their *rents.* In order to set aside consideration of the pricing of the factors as "wholes," as embodiments of a series of future unit services, we have been assuming that no businessmen purchase factors (whether land, labor, or capital goods) outright, but only unit services of these factors. This assumption will be continued for the time being. Later on, we shall drop this restrictive assumption and consider the pricing of "whole factors."

In chapter 5 we saw that when all factors are specific there is no principle of pricing that we can offer. Practically, the only thing that economic analysis can say about the pricing of the productive factors in such a case is that voluntary bargaining among the factor-owners will settle the issue. As long as the factors are all purely specific, economic analysis can say little more about the determinants of their pricing. What conditions must apply, then, to enable us to be more definite about the pricing of factors?

The currently fashionable account of this subject hinges on the *fixity* or *variability* in the proportions of the combined factors used per unit of product. If the factors can be combined only in certain fixed proportions to produce a given quantity of product, it is alleged, then there can be no determinate price; if the proportions of the factors can be varied to produce a given result, then the pricing of each factor can be isolated and determined. Let us examine this contention. Suppose that a product worth 20 gold ounces is produced by three factors, each one purely specific to this production. Suppose that the proportions are variable, so that a product worth 20 gold ounces can be produced either by 4 units of factor A, 5 units of factor B, and 3 units of factor C, or by 6 units of A, 4 units of B, and 2 units of C. How will this help the economist to say anything more about the pricing of these factors than that it will be determined by bargaining? The prices will still be determined by bargaining, and it is obvious that the variability in the proportions of the factors does not aid us in any determination of the specific value or share of each particular product. Since each factor is purely specific, there is no way we can analytically ascertain how a price for a factor is obtained.

The fallacious emphasis on variability of proportion as the basis for factor pricing in the current literature is a result of the prevailing method of analysis. A typical single firm is considered, with its selling prices and *prices of factors given*. Then, the proportions of the factors are assumed to be variable. It can be shown, accordingly, that if the price of factor A increases compared to B, the firm will use less of A and more of B in producing its product. From this, demand curves for each factor are deduced, and the pricing of each factor established.

The fallacies of this approach are numerous. The chief error is that of basing a causal explanation of factor pricing on the *assumption of given factor prices*. On the contrary, we cannot explain factor prices while assuming them as given from the very beginning of the analysis.[1] It is then assumed that the price of a factor changes. But *how* can such a change take place? In the market there are no uncaused changes.

It is true that this is the way that the market looks to a typical firm. But concentration on a single firm and the reaction of its owner is not the appropriate route to the theory of production; on the contrary, it is likely to be misleading, as in this case. In the current literature, this preoccupation with the single firm rather than with the interrelatedness of firms in the economy has led to the erection of a vastly complicated and largely valueless edifice of production theory.

The entire discussion of variable and fixed proportions is really technological rather than economic, and this fact should have alerted those writers who rely on variability as the key to their explanation of pricing.[2] The one technological conclusion that we know purely from *praxeology* is the law of returns, derived at the beginning of chapter 1. According to the law of returns, there is an optimum of proportions of factors, given other factors, in the production of any given product. This optimum may be the *only* proportion at which the good can be produced, or it may be one of many proportions. The former is the case of fixed proportions, the latter of variable proportions. Both cases are subsumed under the more general law of returns, and we shall see that our analysis of factor pricing is based only on this praxeological law and not on more restrictive technological assumptions.

The key question, in fact, is not variability, but *specificity* of factors.[3] For determinate factor pricing to take place, there must be *nonspecific* factors, factors that are useful in several production processes. It is the prices of these nonspecific factors that are determinate. If, in any particular case, only one factor is specific, then its price is also determined: it is the residual difference between the sum of the prices of the nonspecific factors and the price of the common product. When there is more than one specific factor in each process, however, only the *cumulative* residual price is determined, and the price of each specific factor singly can be determined solely by bargaining.

To arrive at the principles of pricing, let us first leap to the conclusion and then trace the process of arriving at this conclusion. Every capitalist will attempt to employ a factor (or rather, the service of a factor) at the price that will be at least *less than its discounted marginal value product.* The *marginal value product* is the monetary revenue that may be attributed, or "imputed," to one service unit of the factor. It is the "marginal" value product, because the supply of the factor is in discrete units. This MVP (marginal value product) is *discounted* by the social rate of time preference, i.e., by the going rate of interest. Suppose, for example, that a unit of a factor (say a day's worth of a certain acre of land or a day's worth of the effort of a certain laborer) will, imputably, produce for the firm a product one year from now that will be sold for 20 gold ounces. The MVP of this factor is 20 ounces. But this is a future good. The *present value of the future good,* and it is this present value that is *now* being purchased, will be equal to the MVP discounted by the going rate of interest. If the rate of interest is 5%, then the discounted MVP will be equal to 19 ounces. To the employer—the capitalist —then, the maximum amount that the factor unit is now worth is 19 ounces. The capitalist will be willing to buy this factor at any price up to 19 ounces.

Now suppose that the capitalist owner or owners of one firm pay for this factor 15 ounces per unit. As we shall see in greater detail later on, this means that the capitalist earns a *pure profit* of 4 ounces per unit, since he reaps 19 ounces from the final sale. (He obtains 20 ounces on final sale, but 1 ounce is the result of his time preference and waiting and is not pure profit; 19 ounces is the *present value* of his final sale.) But, seeing this happen, other entrepreneurs will leap into the breach to reap these profits. These capitalists will have to bid the factor away from the first capitalist and thus pay more than 15 ounces, say 17 ounces. This process continues until the factor earns its full DMVP (discounted marginal value product), and no pure profits remain. The result is that in the ERE every isolable factor will earn its DMVP, and this will be its price. As a result, each factor will earn its DMVP, and the capitalist will earn the going rate of interest for purchasing future goods with his savings. In the ERE, as we have seen, all capitalists will earn the same going rate of interest, and no pure profit will then be reaped. The sale price of a good will be necessarily equal to the sum of the DMVP's of its factors plus the rate of interest return on the investment.

It is clear that if the marginal value of a specific unit of factor service can be isolated and determined, then the forces of competition on the market will result in making *its price equal to its DMVP in the ERE*. Any price higher than the discounted marginal value product of a factor service will not long be paid by a capitalist; any price lower will be raised by the competitive actions of entrepreneurs bidding away these factors through offers of higher prices. These actions will lead, in the former case to the disappearance of losses, in the latter, to the disappearance of pure profit, at which time the ERE is reached.

When a factor is isolable, i.e., if its service can be separated out in appraised value from other factors, then its price will always tend to be set equal to its DMVP. The factor is clearly not isolable, if, as mentioned in note 3 above, it must always be combined with some other particular factor in fixed proportions. If this happens, then a price can be given only to the cumulative product of the factors, and the individual price can be determined only through bargaining. Also, as we have stated, if the factors are all purely specific to the product, then, regardless of any variability in the proportions of their combination, the factors will not be isolable.

It is, then, the nonspecific factors that are directly isolable; a specific factor is isolable if it is the only specific factor in the combination, in which case its price is the difference between the price of the product and the sum of the prices of the nonspecific factors. But by what process does the market isolate and determine the share (the MVP of a certain unit of a factor) of income yielded from production?

Let us refer back to the basic law of utility. What will be the marginal value of a unit of any good? It will be equal to the individual's valuation of the end that must remain unattained should this unit be removed. If a man possesses 20 units of a good, and the uses served by the good are ranked 1 to 20 on his value scale (1 being the ordinal highest), then his loss of a unit—

regardless of which end the unit is supplying *at present*—will mean a loss of the use ranked twentieth in his scale. Therefore, the marginal utility of a unit of the good is ranked at 20 on the person's value scale. Any further unit to be acquired will satisfy the next highest of the ends *not yet being served,* i.e., at 21—a rank which will necessarily be *lower* than the ends already being served. The greater the supply of a good, then, the lower the value of its marginal utility.

A similar analysis is applicable to a producers' good as well. A unit of a producers' good will be valued in terms of the revenue that will be lost should one unit of the good be lost. This can be determined by an entrepreneur's knowledge of his "production function," i.e., the various ways in which factors can technologically be combined to yield certain products, and his estimate of the demand curve of the buyers of his product, i.e., the prices that they would be willing to pay for his product. Suppose, now, that a firm is combining factors in the following way:

$$4X + 10Y + 2Z \rightarrow 100 \text{ gold oz.}$$

4 units of X plus 10 units of Y plus 2 units of Z produce a product that can be sold for 100 gold ounces. Now suppose that the entrepreneur estimates that the following would happen if one unit of X were eliminated;

$$3X + 10Y + 2Z \rightarrow 80 \text{ gold oz.}$$

The loss of one unit of X, other factors remaining constant, has resulted in the loss of *20 gold ounces of gross revenue.* This, then, is the marginal value product of the unit at this position and with this use.[4]

This process is reversible as well. Thus, suppose the firm is at present producing in the latter proportions and reaping 80 gold ounces. If it adds a fourth unit of X to its combination, keeping other quantities constant, it earns 20 more gold ounces. So that here as well, the MVP of this unit is *20 gold ounces.*

This example has implicitly assumed a case of variable proportions. What if the proportions are necessarily fixed? In that case, the loss of a unit of X would require that proportionate quantities of Y, Z, etc., be disposed of. The combination of factors built on $3X$ would then be as follows:

$$3X + 7.5Y + 1.5Z \rightarrow 75 \text{ gold oz. (assuming no price change in the final product)}$$

With fixed proportions, then, the marginal value product of the varying factor would be greater, in this case 25 gold ounces.[5]

Let us for the moment ignore the variations in MVP *within* each production process and consider only variations in MVP among different processes. This is basic since, after all, it is necessary to have a factor usable in more than one production process before its MVP can be isolated. Inevitably, then, the MVP will differ from process to process, since the various production combinations of factors and prices of products will differ. For every factor, then, there is available a sheaf of possible investments in different production processes, each differing in MVP. The MVP's (or, strictly, the discounted MVP's), can be arrayed in descending order. For example, for factor X:

$$
\begin{aligned}
&25 \text{ oz.} \\
&24 \text{ oz.} \\
&22 \text{ oz.} \\
&21 \text{ oz.} \\
&20 \text{ oz.} \\
&19 \text{ oz.} \\
&18 \text{ oz.} \\
&\text{etc.}
\end{aligned}
$$

Suppose, that we begin in the economy with a zero supply of the factor, and then add one unit. Where will this one unit be employed? It is obvious that it will be employed in the use with the highest DMVP. The reason is that capitalists in the various production processes will compete with one another for the use of the factor. But the use in which the DMVP is 25 can bid away the unit of the factor from the other competitors, and it can do this finally only by paying 25 gold ounces for the unit. When the second unit of supply arrives in society, it goes to the second highest use, and it receives a price of 24 ounces, and a similar process occurs as new units of supply are added. *As new supply is added, the marginal value product of a unit declines.* Conversely, *if the supply of a factor decreases* (i.e., the total supply in the economy), *the marginal value product of a unit increases.* The same laws apply, of course, to the DMVP, since this is just the MVP discounted by a common factor, the market's pure rate of interest. As supply increases, then, more and more of the sheaf of available employments for the factor are used, and lower and lower MVP's are tapped.

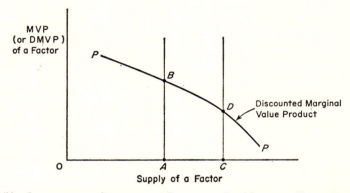

FIG. 56.   INFLUENCE OF SUPPLY OF A FACTOR ON ITS MARGINAL VALUE PRODUCT

Diagrammatically, we may present this situation as in Fig. 56.

The line *PP* is the curve of the marginal value product (or discounted MVP) of a factor. It is *always declining* as it moves to the right, because new units of supply always enter those uses that are most productive of revenue. On the horizontal axis is the quantity of supply of the factor. When the supply is *OA,* then the MVP is *AB.* When the supply is larger at *OC,* then the MVP is lower at *CD.*

Let us say that there are 30 units of factor *X* available in the economy, and that the MVP corresponding to such a supply is 10 ounces. The price of the thirtieth unit, then, will tend to be 10 ounces and will be 10 ounces in the ERE. This follows from the tendency of the price of a factor to be equal to its MVP. But now we must recall that there takes place the inexorable tendency in the market for the *price of all units of any good to be uniform throughout its market.* This must apply to a productive factor just as to any other good. Indeed, this result follows from the very basic law of utility that we have been considering. For, since factor units by definition are interchangeable, the value of one unit will be equal to the value of every other unit at any one time. The value of every unit of a good will be equal to the value of the lowest-ranking use now served by a unit. In the present case, every unit of the factor will be priced at 10 gold ounces.

Suppose, for example, that the owner of the factor unit serving the top-ranking use in our array should demand that he receive 24 ounces, instead of 10 ounces, as his price. In that case, the capitalist in that line of production can refuse to hire this factor and instead bid away the unit employed in the lowest-ranking use, say by paying for the latter 10.5 ounces. The only alternative left to the owner of the factor who had demanded 24 ounces is to replace the other factor in the lowest-ranking spot, at 10 ounces. Effectively, all factors will shift until the prices that they can attain will be uniform throughout the market for their services.

The price of *X*, then, is determined at 10 ounces. It is determined by the MVP (or rather DMVP) of the supply, which decreases as the supply increases, and *vice versa.* Let us assume that *Y* is also a nonspecific factor and that *Z* is a factor *specific* to the particular process considered above. Let us further assume that, by a similar process, the DMVP, and therefore the price, of *Y* is determined at 2 ounces.

At this point, we must reintroduce the concept of production *within* each line. We have been discussing MVP's of factors shifted from one use to another. In our example, a unit of *X* may have an MVP (or DMVP) of 20 ounces in a particular use; yet its price, as determined by the MVP of the lowest-ranking use for which it is employed, is 10 ounces. This means that, in this use, the capitalist is hiring a factor for 10 ounces which earns for him 20 ounces. Spurred on by this profit, he will hire more units of the factor until the MVP in this use will equal the MVP in the lowest-ranking use, i.e., the factor price, 10 ounces. The same process will occur in regard to each of the other uses. The tendency will always be, then (and this will always obtain in the ERE), *for the DMVP of any factor to be equal in each line of production.* We will see shortly why increased purchase of a factor even within each line will lower the MVP in that line.

Suppose, then, that the price of X and Y are 10 and 2 ounces respectively and that all the capitalists have so arranged their production as to equate the DMVP of each factor in each line with this price. Suppose, further, that the equilibrium point in this particular use is the combination:

$$3X + 10Y + 2Z \rightarrow 80 \text{ oz.}$$

Substituting the given prices of X and Y:

$$30 + 20 + 2Z \rightarrow 80 \text{ oz.}$$

$$2Z \rightarrow 30 \text{ oz.}$$

$$Z \rightarrow 15 \text{ oz.}$$

Therefore, $Z = 15$ oz.

The price of the specific factor Z, residual to the other factors, is thereby determined at 15 ounces.

It is obvious that the impact of a change in consumer demand on a specific factor will be far greater, in either direction, than it will be on the price of employment of a nonspecific factor.

It is now clear why the temptation in factor-price analysis is for the *firm* to consider that factor prices are given externally to itself and that it simply varies its production in accordance with these prices. However, from an analytic standpoint, it should be evident that the array of MVP's as a whole is the determining factor, and the lowest-ranking process in terms of MVP will, through the medium of factor prices, transmit its message, so to speak, to the various firms, each of which will use the factor to such an extent that its DMVP will be brought into alignment with its price. But the ultimate determining factor is the DMVP schedule, not the factor price. To make the distinction, we may term the full array of all MVP's for a factor, the *general DMVP schedule* of a factor, while the special array of DMVP's *within* any particular production process or stage, we may term the *particular DMVP schedule* of the factor. It is the *general* DMVP schedule that determines the price of the supply of the factor, and then the *particular* DMVP schedules within each production process are brought into alignment so that the DMVP's of the factor equal its price. Fig. 56 above was a *general* schedule. The particular MVP's are subarrays within the widest array of all the possible alternatives—the general MVP schedule.

In short, the prices of productive factors are determined as follows: Where a factor is isolable, its price will tend toward its discounted marginal value product and will equal its DMVP in the ERE. A factor will be isolable where it is nonspecific, i.e., is useful in more than one productive process, or where it is the *only* specific factor in a process. The nonspecific factor's price will be set equal to its DMVP as determined by its general DMVP schedule: the full possible array of DMVP's, given various units of supply of the factor in the economy. Since the most value-productive uses will be chosen first, and the least abandoned first, the curve of general MVP declines as the supply increases. The various particular MVP's in the various processes will be arranged so as to equal the factor price set by the general DMVP schedule. The specific factor's imputed DMVP is the residual difference between the price of the product and the sum of the prices of the nonspecific factors.

The marginal utility of a unit of a good is determined by a man's diminishing marginal utility schedule evaluating a certain supply or stock of that good. Similarly, the market's establishment of the price of a consumers' good is determined by the aggregate consumer demand schedules—diminishing—and their intersection with the given supply or stock of a good. We are now engaged in pursuing the problem still further and in finding the answer to two general questions: What determines the prices of factors of production on the market, and what determines the quantity of goods that will be produced? We have seen in this section that the price of a factor is determined by its diminish-

ing general (discounted) marginal value productivity curve inter-
secting with the given supply (stock) of the factor in the economy.

2. *Determination of the Discounted Marginal Value Product*

A. DISCOUNTING

If the DMVP schedules determine the prices of nonspecific
factor services, what determines the shape and position of the
DMVP schedules? In the first
place, by definition it is clear
that the DMVP schedule is the
MVP schedule for that factor
discounted. There is no mystery
about the *discounting;* as we
have stated, the MVP of the factor is discounted in accordance
with the going pure rate of interest on the market. The relation of the MVP schedule and
the DMVP schedule may be
diagrammed as in Fig. 57.

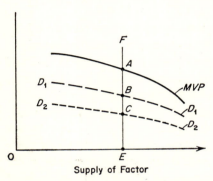

FIG. 57. EFFECT OF CHANGES IN THE RATE
OF INTEREST ON THE DISCOUNTED MAR-
GINAL VALUE PRODUCT AS SUPPLY OF THE
FACTOR VARIES

The supply of the factor is the
EF line at the given quantity
OE. The solid line is the MVP schedule at various supplies. The
MVP of the supply *OE* is *EA.* Now the broken line D_1D_1 is the
discounted marginal value product schedule at a certain rate of
interest. Since it is discounted, it is uniformly lower than the
MVP curve. In absolute terms, it is relatively lower at the left
of the diagram, because an equal percentage drop implies a
greater absolute drop where the amount is greater. The DMVP
for supply *OE* equals *EB. EB* will be the price of the factor in
the evenly rotating economy. Now suppose that the rate of interest in the economy rises, as a result, of course, of rises in time-
preference schedules. This means that the rate of discount for
every hypothetical MVP will be greater, and the absolute levels
lower. The new DMVP schedule is depicted as the dotted line

D_2D_2. The new price for the same supply of the factor is EC, a lower price than before.

One of the determinants of the DMVP schedule, then, is the rate of discount, and we have seen above that the rate of discount is determined by individual time preferences. The higher the rate of discount, the lower will tend to be the DMVP and, therefore, the lower the price of the factor; the lower the interest rate, the higher the DMVP and the price of the factor.

B. THE MARGINAL PHYSICAL PRODUCT

What, then, determines the position and shape of the MVP schedule? What is the marginal value product? It is the amount of revenue intake attributable to a unit of a factor. And this revenue depends on two elements: (1) the physical product produced and (2) the price of that product. If one hour of factor X is estimated by the market to produce a value of 20 gold ounces, this might be because one hour produces 20 units of the physical product, which are sold at a price of one gold ounce per unit. Or the same MVP might result from the production of 10 units of the product, sold at 2 gold ounces per unit, etc. In short, *the marginal value product of a factor service unit is equal to its marginal physical product times the price of that product.*[6]

Let us, then, investigate the determinants of the marginal physical product (MPP). In the first place, there can be no general schedule for the MPP as there is for the MVP, for the simple reason that *physical* units of various goods are not comparable. How can a dozen eggs, a pound of butter, and a house be compared in *physical* terms? Yet the same factor might be useful in the production of any of these goods. There can be an MPP schedule, therefore, only in *particular* terms, i.e., in terms of each particular production process in which the factor can be engaged. For each production process there will be for the factor a marginal physical production schedule of a certain shape. The MPP for a supply *in that process* is the amount of the physical product imputable to one unit of that factor, i.e., the amount of the product that will be lost if one unit of the factor is removed. If the supply of the factor in the process is increased by one unit, other factors remaining the same, then the MPP of the supply becomes the additional physical product that can be gained from the addition of the unit. The supply of the factor that is relevant for the MPP schedules is not the total supply in the society, but the supply *in each process,* since the MPP schedules are established for each process separately.

1) *The Law of Returns*

In order to investigate the MPP schedule further, let us recall the law of returns, set forth in chapter 1. According to the law of returns, an eternal truth of human action, if the quantity of one factor varies, and the quantities of other factors remain constant, there is a point at which the physical product per factor is at a maximum. Physical product per factor may be termed the *average physical product* (APP). The law further states that with either a lesser or a greater supply of the factor the APP must be lower. We may diagram a typical APP curve as in Fig. 58.

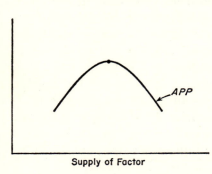

Fig. 58. Average Physical Product in Relation to the Supply of a Factor

2) *Marginal Physical Product and Average Physical Product*

What is the relationship between the APP and MPP? *The MPP is the amount of physical product that will be produced with the addition of one unit of a factor, other factors being given. The APP is the ratio of the total product to the total quantity of the variable factor, other factors being given.* To illustrate the meanings of APP and MPP, let us consider a hypothetical case in which all units of other factors are constant, and the number of units of one factor is variable. In Table 13 the first column lists the number of units of the variable factor, and the second column the total physical product produced when these varying units are combined with fixed units of the other factors. The third column is the APP = total product divided by the number of units of the factor, i.e., the average physical productivity of a unit of the factor. The fourth column is the MPP = the difference in total product yielded by adding one more unit of the variable factor, i.e., the total product of the current row minus the total product of the preceding row:

TABLE 13

UNITS OF VARIABLE FACTOR	TOTAL PRODUCT	AVERAGE PHYSICAL PRODUCT	MARGINAL PHYSICAL PRODUCT
0.........	0	0	0
1.........	3	3	3
2.........	8	4	5
3.........	15	5	7
4.........	22	5.2	7
5.........	27.5	5.5	5.5
6.........	30	5	2.5
7.........	28	4	−2

In the first place, it is quite clear that *no factor will ever be employed in the region where the MPP is negative.* In our example, this occurs where 7 units of the factor are being employed. 6 units of the factor, combined with given other factors, produced 30 units of the product. An addition of another unit results in a loss of two units of the product. The MPP of the factor when 7 units are employed is −2. Obviously, no factor will ever be employed in this region, and this holds true whether the factor-owner is also owner of the product, or a capitalist hires the factor to work on the product. It would be senseless and contrary to the principles of human action to expend either effort or money on added factors only to have the quantity of the total product decline.

In the tabulation, we follow the law of returns, in that the APP, beginning, of course, at zero with zero units of the factor, rises to a peak and then falls. We also observe the following from our chart: (1) *when the APP is rising* (with the exception of the

very first step where TP, APP and MPP are all equal) *MPP is
higher than APP:* (2) *when the APP is falling, MPP is lower than
APP;* (3) *at the point of maximum APP, MPP is equal to APP.*
We shall now prove, algebraically, that these three laws *always*
hold.[7]

Let F be any number of units of a variable factor, other factors being given, and P be the units of the total product yielded
by the combination. Then P/F is the Average Physical Product.
When we add ΔF more units of the factor, total product increases by ΔP. Marginal Physical Product corresponding to the
increase in the factor is $\Delta P/\Delta F$. The new Average Physical Product, corresponding to the greater supply of factors, is:

$$\frac{P + \Delta P}{F + \Delta F}$$

Now the new APP might be higher or lower than the previous one. Let us suppose that the new APP is higher and that
therefore we are in a region where the *APP is increasing.* This
means that:

$$\frac{P + \Delta P}{F + \Delta F} > \frac{P}{F} \qquad \text{> is the symbol for "is greater than."}$$

or $$\frac{P + \Delta P}{F + \Delta F} - \frac{P}{F} > 0$$

Combining terms:

$$\frac{FP + F\Delta P - PF - P\Delta F}{F(F + \Delta F)} > 0$$

Then, surely:

$$FP + F\Delta P - PF - P\Delta F > 0$$

$$F\Delta P - P\Delta F > 0$$

$$F\Delta P > P\Delta F$$

$$\therefore \frac{\Delta P}{\Delta F} > \frac{P}{F}$$

Thus, the MPP is greater than the *old* APP. Since it is greater, this means that there exists a positive number k such that:

$$\frac{\Delta P}{\Delta F} = \frac{kP}{F}$$

Now there is an algebraic rule according to which, if:

$$\frac{a}{b} = \frac{c}{d},$$

then

$$\frac{a}{b} = \frac{c+a}{d+b}$$

Therefore,

$$\frac{\Delta P}{\Delta F} = \frac{kP + \Delta P}{F + \Delta F}$$

Since k is positive,

$$\frac{kP + \Delta P}{F + \Delta F} > \frac{P + \Delta P}{F + \Delta F}$$

Therefore,

$$\boxed{\frac{\Delta P}{\Delta F} > \frac{P + \Delta P}{F + \Delta F}}$$

In short, the MPP is *also* greater than the *new* APP.

In other words, *if APP is increasing, then the marginal physical product is greater than the average physical product* in this region. This proves the first law above. Now, if we go back in our proof and substitute "less than" signs for "greater than" signs and carry out similar steps, we arrive at the opposite conclusion: *where APP is decreasing, the marginal physical product is lower than the average physical product.* This proves the second of our three laws about the relation between the marginal and the average physical product. But if MPP is greater than APP when the latter is rising, and is lower than APP when the latter is falling, then it follows that when *APP is at its maximum, MPP must be neither lower nor higher than, but equal to, APP.* And this proves the third law. We see that these characteristics of our table apply to all possible cases of production.

The diagram in Fig. 59 depicts a typical set of MPP and APP

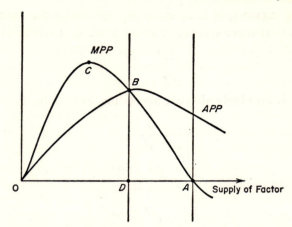

schedules. It shows the various relationships between APP and
MPP. Both curves begin from zero and are identical very close
to their origin. The APP curve rises until it reaches a peak at
B, then declines. The MPP curve rises faster, so that it is higher
than APP, reaches its peak earlier at *C*, then declines until it
intersects with APP at *B*. From then on, the MPP curve declines
faster than APP, until finally it crosses the horizontal axis and
becomes negative at some point *A*. No firm will operate beyond
the *OA* area.

Now let us explore further the area of *increasing APP,* between *O* and *D*. Let us take another hypothetical tabulation (Table 14), which will be simpler for our purpose.

TABLE 14

UNITS OF FACTOR	TOTAL PRODUCT	AVERAGE PHYSICAL PRODUCT
2...........	10	5
3...........	18	6
4..........	25	6.2

This is a segment of the increasing section of the average physical product schedule, with the peak being reached at 4 units and 6.2 APP. The question is: What is the likelihood that this region will be settled upon by a firm as the right input-output combination? Let us take the top line of the chart. Two units of the variable factor, plus a bundle of what we may call *U* units of all the other factors, yield 10 units of the product. On the other hand, at the maximum APP for the factor, 4 units of it, plus *U* units of other factors, yield 25 units of the product. We have seen above that it is a fundamental truth in nature that the same quantitative causes produce the same quantitative effects. Therefore, if we halve the quantities of all of the factors in the third line, we shall get half the product. In other words, 2 units of the factor combined with *U*/2—with half of the various units of each of the other factors—will yield 12.5 units of the product.

Consider this situation. From the top line we see that 2 units of the variable factor, plus *U* units of given factors, yield 10 units of the product. But, extrapolating from the bottom line, we see that 2 units of the variable factor, plus *U*/2 units of given factors, yield 12.5 units of the product. It is obvious that, as in the case of going beyond *OA,* any firm that allocated factors so as to be in the *OD* region would be making a most unwise decision. Obviously, no one would want to spend *more* in effort or money on factors (the "other" factors) and obtain *less* total output or, for that matter, the same total output. It is evident that if the producer remains in the *OD* region, he is in an area of *negative marginal physical productivity of the other factors.* He would be in a situation where he would obtain a greater total product by throwing away some of the other factors. In the same way, after *OA,* he would be in a position to gain greater total output if he threw away some of the present variable factor. *A region of increasing APP for one factor,* then, signifies a region of *negative MPP for other factors,* and *vice versa.* A producer, then, will never wish to allocate his factor in the *OD* region or in the region beyond *A.*

Neither will the producer set the factor so that its MPP is at the points *B* or *A*. Indeed, the variable factor will be set so that it has zero marginal productivity (at *A*) *only if it is a free good.* There is however, no such thing as a free good; there is only a condition of human welfare not subject to action, and therefore not an element in productivity schedules. Conversely, the APP is at *B,* its maximum for the variable factor, only when the *other* factors are free goods and therefore have zero marginal productivity at this point. Only if all the other factors were free and could be left out of account could the producer simply concentrate on maximizing the productivity of one factor alone. However, there can be no production with only one factor, as we saw in chapter 1.

The conclusion, therefore, is inescapable. A factor will always be employed in a production process in such a way that *it is in a region of declining APP and declining but positive MPP* —between points *D* and *A* on the chart. In every production process, therefore, every factor will be employed in a region of diminishing MPP and diminishing APP *so that additional units of the factor employed in the process will lower the MPP, and decreased units will raise it.*

C. MARGINAL VALUE PRODUCT

As we have seen, the MVP for any factor is its MPP multiplied by the selling price of its product. We have just concluded that every factor will be employed in its region of diminishing marginal physical product in each process of production. What will be the shape of the marginal *value* product schedule? As the supply of a factor increases, and other factors remain the same, it follows that the total physical output of the product is greater. A greater stock, given the consumers' demand curve, will lead to a lowering of the market price. The price of the product will then fall as the MPP diminishes and rise as the latter increases. It follows that the MVP curve of the factor will always be falling, and falling at a *more rapid* rate than the MPP curve. *For each specific production process, any factor will be employed in the region of diminishing MVP.*[8] This correlates with the previous conclusion, based on the law of utility, that the factor in general, among various production processes, will be employed in such a way that its MVP is diminishing. Therefore, its *general MVP* (between various uses and within each use) is diminishing, and its various *particular MVP's* are diminishing (within each use). Its DMVP is, therefore, diminishing as well.

The price of a unit of any factor will, as we have seen, be established in the market as equal to its discounted marginal value product. This will be the DMVP as determined by the general schedule including all the various uses to which it can be put. Now the producers will employ the factor in such a way *that its DMVP will be equalized among all the uses*. If the DMVP in one use is greater than in another, then employers in the former line of production will be in a position to bid more for the factor and will use more of it until (according to the principle of diminishing MVP) the DMVP of the expanding use diminishes to the point at which it equals the increasing DMVP in the contracting use. The price of the factor will be set as equal to the general DMVP, which in the ERE will be uniform throughout all the particular uses.

Thus, by looking at a factor in all of its interrelations, *we have been able to explain the pricing of its unit service without previously assuming the existence of the price itself.* To focus the analysis on the situation as it looks from the vantage point of the firm is to succumb to such an error, for the individual firm obviously finds a certain factor price given on the market. The price of a factor unit will be established by the market as equal to its marginal value product, discounted by the rate of interest for the length of time until the product is produced, provided that this valuation of the share of the factor is isolable. It is isolable if the factor is nonspecific or is a single residual specific factor in a process. The MVP in question is determined by the general MVP schedule covering the various uses of the factor and the supply of the factor available in the economy. The general MVP schedule of a factor diminishes as the supply of the factor increases; it is made up of particular MVP schedules for the various uses of the factor, which in turn are compounded of diminishing Marginal Physical Product schedules and declining product prices. Therefore, if the supply of the factor increases, the MVP schedule in the economy remaining the same, the MVP and hence the price of the factor will drop; and as the supply of the factor dwindles, *ceteris paribus,* the price of the factor will rise.

To the individual firm, the price of a factor established on the market is the signal of its discounted marginal value product elsewhere. This is the opportunity cost of the firm's using the product, since it equals the value product that is forgone through failure to use the factor unit elsewhere. In the ERE, where all factor prices equal discounted marginal value products, it follows that factor prices and (opportunity) "costs" will be equal.

Critics of the marginal productivity analysis have contended that in the "modern complex world" all factors co-operate in producing a product, and therefore it is impossible to establish any sort of imputation of part of the product to various co-operating factors. Hence, they assert, "distribution" of product to factors is separable from production and takes place arbitrarily according to bargaining theory. To be sure, no one denies that many factors do co-operate in producing goods. But the fact that most factors (and all labor factors) are nonspecific, and that there is very rarely more than one purely specific factor in a production process, enables the market to isolate value productivity and to tend to pay each factor in accordance with this marginal product. On the free market, therefore, the price of each factor is not determined by "arbitrary" bargaining, but tends to be set strictly in accordance with its discounted marginal value product. The importance of this market process becomes *greater* as the economy becomes more specialized and complex and the adjustments more delicate. The more uses develop for a factor, and the more types of factors arise, the more important is this market "imputation" process as compared to simple bargaining. For it is this process that causes the effective allocation of factors and the flow of production in accordance with the most urgent demands of the consumers (including the nonmonetary desires of the producers themselves). In the free market process, therefore, there is no separation between production and "distribution." There is no heap somewhere on which "products" are arbitrarily thrown and from which someone does or can arbitrarily "distribute" them among various people. On the contrary, individuals produce goods and sell them to consumers for money, which they in turn spend on consumption or on investment in order to increase future consumption. There is no separate "distribution"; there is only production and its corollary, exchange.

It should always be understood, even where it is not explicitly stated in the text for reasons of exposition, that the MVP schedules used to set prices are *discounted* MVP schedules, discounting the final MVP by the length of time remaining until the final consumers' product is produced. It is the DMVP's that are equalized throughout the various uses of the factor. The importance of this fact is that it explains the market allocation of non-specific factors among various productive *stages* of the same or of different goods. Thus, if the DMVP of a factor is 6 gold ounces, and if the factor is employed on a process practically instantaneous with consumption, its MVP will be 6. Suppose that the pure rate of interest is 5%. If the factor is at work on a process that will mature in final consumption five years from now, a DMVP of 6 signifies an MVP of 7.5; if it is at work on a ten-year process, a DMVP of 6 signifies an MVP of 10; etc. The more remote the time of operation is from the time when the final product is completed, the greater must be the difference allowed for the annual interest income earned by the capitalists who advance present goods and thereby make possible the entire length of the production process. The *amount* of the discount from the MVP is greater here because the higher stage is more remote than the others from final consumption. Therefore, in order for investment to take place in the higher stages, their MVP has to be far higher than the MVP in the shorter processes.[9]

3. *The Source of Factor Incomes*

Our analysis permits us now to resolve that time-honored controversy in economics: Which is the source of wages—capital or consumption? Or, as we should rephrase it, which is the source of original-factor incomes (for labor and land factors)? It is clear that the ultimate goal of the investment of capital is future consumption. In that sense, consumption is the necessary requisite without which there would be no capital. Furthermore, for each particular good, consumption dictates, through market demands, the prices of the various products and the shifting of (nonspecific) factors from one process to another. However, consumption by itself provides nothing. Savings and investment are needed in order to permit any consumption at all, since very little consumption could be obtained with no production processes or capital structure at all—perhaps only the direct picking of berries.[10]

In so far as labor or land factors produce and sell consumers' goods *immediately,* no capital is required for their payment. They are paid directly by consumption. This was true for Crusoe's berry-picking. It is also true in a highly capitalistic economy for labor (and land) in the final stages of the production process. In these final stages, which include pure labor incomes earned in the sale of personal services (of doctors, artists, lawyers, etc.) to consumers, the factors earn MVP directly without being discounted in advance. All the other labor and land factors participating in the production process are paid by saved capital in advance of the produced and consumed product.

We must conclude that in the dispute between the classical theory that wages are paid out of capital and the theory of Henry George, J. B. Clark, and others that wages are paid out of the annual product consumed, the former theory is correct in the overwhelming majority of cases, and that this majority becomes more preponderant the greater the stock of capital in the society.[11]

4. *Land and Capital Goods*

The price of the unit service of every factor, then, is equal to its discounted marginal value product. This is true of *all* factors, whether they be "original" (land and labor) or "produced" (capital goods). However, as we have seen, there is no *net* income to the owners of capital goods, since their prices contain the prices of the various factors that co-operate in their production. Essentially, then, *net* income accrues only to owners of land and labor factors and to capitalists for their "time" services. It is still true, however, that the pricing principle—equality to discounted MVP—applies whatever the factor, whether capital good or any other.

Let us revert to the diagram in Fig. 41. This time, let us assume for simplicity that we are dealing with one unit of one consumers' good, which sells for 100 ounces, and that *one unit* of each particular factor enters into its production. Thus, on Rank 1, 80 refers to one unit of a capital good. Let us consider the first rank first. Capitalists$_1$ purchase one capital good for 80 ounces and (we assume) one labor factor for 8 ounces and one land factor for 7 ounces. The joint MVP for the three factors is 100. Yet their total price is 95 ounces. The remainder is the *discount* accruing to the capitalists because of the time element. The sum of the discounted MVP's, then, is 95 ounces, and this is precisely what the owners of three factors received in total. The discounted MVP of the labor factor's service was 8, the DMVP of the land's service was 7, the DMVP of the capital good's service was 80. Thus, each factor obtains its DMVP as its received price. But what happens in the case of the capital good? It has been sold for 80, but it has had to be produced, and this production cost money to pay the income of the various factors. The price of the capital good, then, is reduced to, say, another land factor, paid 8 ounces; another labor factor paid 8 ounces, and a capital-goods factor paid 60 ounces. The prices, and therefore the incomes, of all these factors are discounted again to account for the time, and this discount is earned by Capitalists$_2$. The sum of these factor incomes is 76, and once again each factor service earns its DMVP.

Each capital-goods factor must be produced and must continue to be produced in the ERE. Since this is so, we see that the capital-goods factor, though obtaining its DMVP, does not earn it *net,* for *its* owner, in turn, must pay money to the factors that produce it. Ultimately, only land, labor, and time factors earn net incomes.

This type of analysis has been severely criticized on the following grounds:

This "Austrian" method of tracing everything back to land and labor (and time!) may be an interesting historical exercise, and we may grant that, if we trace back production and investment far enough, we shall ultimately reach the world of primitive men, who began to produce capital with their bare hands. But of what relevance is this for the modern, complex world around us, a world in which a huge amount of capital already exists and can be worked with? In the modern world there is no production without the aid of capital, and therefore the whole Austrian capital analysis is valueless for the modern economy.

There is no question about the fact that we are not interested in historical analysis, but rather in an economic analysis of the complex economy. In particular, acting man has no interest in the historical origin of his resources; he is acting in the *present* on behalf of a goal to be achieved *in the future*.[12] Praxeological analysis recognizes this and deals with the individual acting at present to satisfy ends of varying degrees of futurity (from instantaneous to remote).

It is true, too, that the presentation by the master of capital and production theory, Böhm-Bawerk, sowed confusion by giving an historical interpretation to the structure of production. This is particularly true of his concept of the "average period of production," which attempted to establish an average length of production processes operating at present, but stretching back to the beginning of time. In one of the weakest parts of his theory, Böhm-Bawerk conceded that "The boy who cuts a stick with his knife is, strictly speaking, only continuing the work of the miner who, centuries ago, thrust the first spade into the ground to sink the shaft from which the ore was brought to make the blade." [13] He then tried to salvage the relevance of the production structure by averaging periods of production and maintaining that the effect in the present product of the early centuries' work is so small (being so remote) as to be negligible.

Mises has succeeded, however, in refining the Austrian production theory so as to eliminate reliance on an almost infinitely high production structure and on the mythical concept of an "average period of production."

As Mises states:

> Acting man does not look at his condition with the eyes of an historian. He is not concerned with how the present situation originated. His only concern is to make the best use of the means available today for the best possible removal of future uneasiness . . . He has at his disposal a definite quantity of material factors of production. He does not ask whether these factors are nature-given or the product of production processes accomplished in the past. It does not matter for him how great a quantity of nature-given, i.e., original material factors of production and labor, was expended in their production and how much time these processes of production have absorbed. He values the available means exclusively from the aspect of the services they can render him in his endeavors to make future conditions more satisfactory. The period of production and the duration of serviceableness are for him categories in planning future action, not concepts of academic retrospection. . . . They play a role in so far as the actor has to choose between periods of production of different length. . . .
>
> [Böhm-Bawerk] . . . was not fully aware of the fact that the period of production is a praxeological category and that the role it plays in action consists entirely in the choices acting man makes between periods of production of different length. The length of time expended in the past for the production of capital goods available today does not count at all.[14]

But if the past is not taken into account, how can we use the production-structure analysis? How can it apply to an ERE if the structure would have to go back almost endlessly in time? If we base our approach on the present, must we not follow the Knightians in scrapping the production-structure analysis?

A particular point of contention is the dividing line between land and capital goods. The Knightians, in scoffing at the idea of tracing periods of production back through the centuries, scrap the *land* concept altogether and include land as simply a part of capital goods. This change, of course, completely alters production theory. The Knightians point correctly, for example, to the fact that present-day land has many varieties and amounts of past labor "mixed" with it: canals have been dug, forests cleared, basic improvements have been made in the soil, etc. They assert that practically nothing is pure "land" anymore and therefore that the concept has become an empty one.

As Mises has shown, however, we can revise Böhm-Bawerk's theory and still retain the vital distinction between land and capital goods. We do not have to throw out, as do the Knightians, the land baby with the average-period-of-production bathwater. We can, instead, reformulate the concept of "land." Up to this point we have simply assumed land to be the original, nature-given factors. Now we must modify this, in keeping with our focus on the present and the future rather than the past. Whether or not a piece of land is "originally" pure land is in fact economically immaterial, so long as whatever alterations have been made are permanent—or rather, so long as these alterations do not have to be reproduced or replaced.[15] Land that has been irrigated by canals or altered through the chopping down of forests has become a present, permanent *given*. Because it is a present given, not worn out in the process of production, and not needing to be replaced, it becomes a *land* factor under our definition. In the ERE, this factor will continue to give forth its natural powers unstinted and without further investment; it is therefore *land* in our analysis. Once this occurs, and the permanent are separated from the nonpermanent alterations, we see that the structure of production no longer stretches back infinitely in time, but comes to a close within a relatively brief span of time.[16] The capital goods are those which are continually wearing out in the process of production and which labor and land factors must work to replace. When we consider physical wearing out and replacement, then, it becomes evident that it would not take many years for the whole capital-goods structure to collapse if no work were done on maintenance and replacement, and this is true even in the modern, highly capitalist economy. Of course, the higher the degree of "capitalist" development and the more stages in production, the longer will it take for all the capital goods to wear out.[17]

The "permanence" with which we are dealing refers, of course, to the *physical* permanence of the goods, and *not* to the permanence of their value. *The latter depends on the shifting desires of consumers and could never be called permanent.* Thus, there might be a land factor uniquely and permanently suitable as a vineyard. It is *land* and remains so, therefore, indefinitely. If, at some time, the consumers should completely lose their taste for wine, and the land becomes valueless and no longer used, it is *still* a permanent factor, and therefore is land, although now submarginal. It should be noted that the "permanence" is relevant to present considerations of human action. A piece of land might give forth a permanent marginal (physical) product, without necessity of maintenance, and suddenly a volcano might erupt or a hurricane strike in the area, and the permanence could be destroyed. Such conceivable natural events, however, are not *ex ante* relevant to human action, and therefore from the point of view of action this land is rightly considered as "permanent," until the natural changes occur.[18,19]

The concept of "land" as used throughout this book, then, is entirely different from the popular concept of land. Let us, in this section, distinguish between the two by calling the former *economic land* and the latter *geographic land*. The economic concept includes *all* nature-given sources of value: what is usually known as natural resources, land, water, and air in so far as they are not free goods. On the other hand, a large part of the value of what is generally considered "land"—i.e., that part that has to be maintained with the use of labor—is really a capital good.

That agricultural land is an example of the latter may surprise the reader who is likely to think of it as permanently productive. This is completely wrong; the marginal physical productivity of (geographic) land varies greatly in accordance with the amount of labor that is devoted to maintaining or improving the soil, as against such use or nonuse of the soil as leads to erosion and a lower MPP. The basic soil (and here we are referring to the soil that would remain *now* if maintenance were suspended, *not* to the soil as it was in the dim past before cultivation) is the *land element,* while the final product—which is popularly known as agricultural land—is usually a capital good containing this land element.

And Van Sickle and Rogge say about the soil:

Land, as the top 12 to 18 inches from which grains, vegetables, grasses, and trees draw almost their entire nourishment, is highly destructible. Top soil can be washed or blown away (eroded), or its organic and mineral content can be dissolved and drawn down out of reach of plant life (leached) in a relatively few years, unless great care is exercised in its use. It can also be rebuilt by careful husbandry. Hence it can be said of all soils . . . that their maintenance requires saving.[20]

The indestructibility of land is much more clearly exemplified in what is commonly called "urban land." For land in urban areas (and this includes suburban land, land for factories, etc.) clearly evinces one of its most fundamentally indestructible features: *its physical space*—its part of the surface of the earth. For the surface area of the earth is, except in rare cases, eternally fixed, as is the geographic position of each piece of geographic land on the surface. This eternally fixed, permanent, *positional* aspect of geographic land is called the *site* aspect of the land, or as Mises aptly puts it, "the land as standing room." Since it is permanent and nonreproducible, it very clearly comes under the category of economic land. The permanence, once again, refers to its physical spatial aspect; its site *values*, of course, are always subject to change.[21] Midtown Manhattan is on the same site—the same geographical location—now as it was in the 1600's, although the monetary values accruing to it have changed.

Suppose that a piece of currently unused land can be used for various agricultural purposes or for urban purposes. In that case, a choice will be made according to its alternative values as nonreplaceable economic land: between its discounted MVP as a result of the fertility of its basic soil and its discounted MVP as an urban site. And if a decision must be made whether land *now* used in agriculture and being maintained for that purpose should remain in agriculture or be used as a site for building, the principles of choice are the same. The marginal value return to the agricultural or urban land is broken down by the owner of the land—the "landlord"—into the interest return on the capital maintenance and improvement and the discounted marginal value return to the basic economic land.

"Basic land" (or "ground land") in this treatise refers to the *soil without maintenance,* in the case of agriculture, or the *pure site without depreciating superstructure,* in the case of urban land. The basic land, therefore, whether it be soil or site, earns for its owner an ultimate unit price, or rent, equaling its DMVP. Working on this basic land, labor and investment create a finished capital good. This capital good, like all capital goods, also earns unit rents equal to its DMVP. However, this earning is broken down (and relevantly so in the *current* market, not as an historical exercise) into basic land rent and interest return on the capital invested (as well, of course, as returns to labor that works on the basic land, i.e., labor's wage or "rent-price," equaling its DMVP). This capital-good land we have variously termed "geographic land," "land in the popular sense," "final land," "finished land." When we speak simply of "land," on the other hand, we shall always be referring to the true economic land—the currently nature-given factor.

5. *Capitalization and Rent*

The subject of "rent" is one of the most confused in the entire economic literature. We must, therefore, reiterate the meaning of rent as set forth above. We are using "rent" *to mean the unit price of the services of any good.* It is important to banish any preconceptions that apply the concept of rent to land only. Perhaps the best guide is to keep in mind the well-known practice of "renting out." Rent, then, is the same as *hire:* it is the sale and purchase of the *unit services* of any good.[22] It therefore applies as well to prices of labor services (called "wages") as it does to land or to any other factor. The rent concept applies to all goods, whether durable or nondurable. In the case of a completely nondurable good, which vanishes fully when first used, its "unit" of service is simply identical in size with the "whole" good itself. In regard to a durable good, of course, the rent concept is more interesting, since the price of the unit service is distinguishable from the price of the "good as a whole." So far, in this work, we have been assuming that no durable producers' goods are ever bought outright, that only their *unit services* are exchanged on the market. Therefore, our entire discussion of pricing has dealt with rental pricing. It is obvious that *the rents are the fundamental prices*. The marginal utility analysis has taught us that men value goods in *units* and not as wholes; the *unit price* (or "rent") is, then, the fundamental price on the market.

In chapter 4 we analyzed rental pricing and the price of the "good as a whole" for durable consumers' goods. The principle is precisely the same for producers' goods. The rental value of the unit service is the basic one, the one ultimately determined on the market by individual utility scales. The price of the "whole good," also known as *the capital value of the good,* is equal to the sum of the expected future rents discounted by what we then vaguely called a time-preference factor and which we now know is the *rate of interest*. The capital value, or price of the good as a whole, then, is completely dependent on the rental prices of the good, its physical durability, and the rate of interest.[23] Obviously, the concept of "capital value" of a good has meaning only when that good is durable and does not vanish instantly upon use. If it did vanish, then there would only be pure rent, without separate valuations for the good as a whole. When we use the term "good as a whole," we are not referring to the aggregate supply of the whole good in the economy. We are referring, e.g., not to the total supply of housing of a certain type, but to *one* house, which can be rented out over a period of time. We are dealing with *units of "whole goods,"* and these units, being durable, are necessarily larger than their constituent unit services, which can be rented out over a period of time.

The principle of the determination of "capital values," i.e., prices of "whole goods," is known as *capitalization,* or the capitalizing of rents. This principle applies to *all* goods, not simply capital goods, and we must not be misled by similarity of terminology. Thus, capitalization applies to durable consumers' goods, such as houses, TV sets, etc. It also applies to all factors of production, including basic land. The rental price, or rent, of a factor of production is equal, as we have seen, to its discounted marginal value product. *The capital value of a "whole factor" will be equal to the sum of its future rents, or the sum of its DMVP's.*[24] This capital value will be the price for which the "whole good" will exchange on the market. It is at this capital value that a unit of a "whole good" such as a house, a piano, a machine, an acre of land, etc., will sell on the market. There is clearly no sense to capitalization if there is no market, or price, for the "whole good." The capital value is the appraised value set by the market on the basis of rents, durability, and the interest rate.

The process of capitalization can encompass many units of a "whole good," as well as one unit. Let us consider the example of chapter 4, section 7, and generalize from it to apply, not only to houses, but to all durable producers' goods. The good is a ten-year good; expected future rents are 10 gold ounces per year (determined by consumer utilities for consumers' goods, or by MVP's for producers' goods). The rate of interest is 10% per annum. The present capital value of this good is 59.4 gold ounces. But this "whole good" is itself a unit of a larger supply; one of many houses, machines, plants, etc. At any rate, since all units of a good have equal value, the capital value of two such houses, or two such machines, etc., added together equals precisely twice the amount of one, or 118.8 ounces. Since we are adding rents or DMVP's in money terms, we may keep adding them to determine capital values of larger aggregates of durable goods. As a matter of fact, in adding capital values, *we do not need to confine ourselves to the same good.* All we need do is to add the capital values in whatever bundle of durable goods we are interested in appraising. Thus, suppose a firm, Jones Construction Company, wishes to sell all its assets on the market. These assets, necessarily durable, consist of the following:

3 machines. Each machine has a capital value (based on the sum of the DMVP's) of 10 ounces. Therefore, total capital value is *30 ounces.*

1 building, with a capital value of *40 ounces*.

5 acres of land. Each acre has a capital value of 10 ounces. Total is *40 ounces*.

Total capital value of these assets: *110 ounces*.

But we must always remember, in adding capital values, that these are relevant only in so far as they are expressed in market price or potential market price. Many writers have fallen into the trap of assuming that they can, in a similar way, add up the entire capital value of the nation or world and arrive at a meaningful figure. Estimates of National Capital or World Capital, however, are completely meaningless. The world, or country, cannot sell all its capital on the market. Therefore, such statistical exercises are pointless. They are without possible reference to the very goal of capitalization: correct estimation of potential market price.

As we have indicated, capitalization applies to *all* factors of production, or rather, to all factors where there are markets for the whole goods that embody them. We may call these markets *capital markets*. They are the markets for exchange of ownership, total or partial, of durable producers' goods. Let us take the case of capital goods. The rent of a capital good is equal to its DMVP. The capitalized value of the capital good is the sum of the future DMVP's, or the discounted sum of the future MVP's. This is the *present* value of the good, and this is what the good will sell for on the capital market.

The process of capitalization, because it permeates all sectors of the economy, and because it is flexible enough to include different types of assets—such as the total capital assets of a firm— is a very important one in the economy. Prices of shares of the ownership of this capital will be set at their proportionate fraction of the total capital value of the assets. In this way, given the *MVP's, durability,* and the *rate of interest,* all the prices on the capital market are determined, and these will be the prices in the ERE. This is the way in which the prices of individual capital goods (machines, buildings, etc.) will be set on the market, and this is the way in which these values will be summed up to set the price of a bundle of capital assets, similar and dissimilar. Share prices on the stock market will be set according to the proportion that they bear to the capitalized value of the firm's total assets.

We have stated that *all* factors that can be bought and sold as "whole goods" on the market are capitalized. This includes capital goods, ground land, and durable consumers' goods. It is clear that capital goods and durable consumers' goods can be and are capitalized. But what of ground land? How can this be capitalized?

We have seen in detail above that the ultimate earnings of factors go to the owners of labor and of ground land and, as interest, to capitalists. If land can be capitalized, does this not mean that land and capital goods are "really the same thing" after all? The answer to the latter question is No.[25] It is still emphatically true that the earnings of basic land factors are ultimate and irreducible, as are labor earnings, while capital goods have to be constantly produced and reproduced, and therefore their earnings are always reducible to the earnings of ground land, labor, and time.

Basic land can be capitalized for one simple reason: it can be bought and sold "as a whole" on the market. (This cannot be done for labor, except under a system of slavery, which, of course, cannot occur on the purely free market.) Since this can be and is being done, the problem arises how the prices in these exchanges are determined. These prices are the capital values of ground land.

A major characteristic of land as compared to capital goods is that its series of future rents is generally *infinite*, since, whether as basic soil or site, it is physically indestructible. In the ERE, the series of future rents will, of course, always be the same. The very fact that any land is ever bought and sold, by the way, is a demonstration of the universality of time preference. If there were no time preference for the present, then an infinite series of future rents could never be capitalized. A piece of land would have to have an infinite present price and therefore could never be sold. The fact that lands *do* have prices is an indication that there is always a time preference and that future rents are discounted to reduce to a present value.

As in the case of any other good, the capital value of land is equal to the sum of its discounted future rents. For example, it can be demonstrated mathematically that if we have a constant rent expected to be earned in perpetuity, the capital value of the asset will equal the annual rent divided by the rate of interest.[26] Now it is obvious that on such land, the investor annually obtains the market rate of interest. If, in other words, annual rents will be 20, and the rate of interest is 5%, the asset will sell for 20/.05, or 1,000. The investor who purchases the asset for 1,000 ounces will earn 20 ounces a year from it, or 5%, the market rate of interest.

Ground land, then, is "capitalized" just as are capital goods, shares in capital-owning firms, and durable consumers' goods. All these owners will tend to receive the same rate of interest return, and all *will* receive the same rate of return in the ERE. In short, all owned assets will be capitalized. In the ERE, of course, the capital values of all assets will remain constant; they will also be equal to the discounted sum of the MVP's of their unit rents.

Above, we saw that a key distinction between land and capital goods is that the owners of the former sell future goods for present money, whereas the owners of the latter *advance* present money, buy future goods, and later sell their product when it is less distantly future. This is still true. But then we must ask the question: How does the landowner come to own this land? The answer is (excepting his or his ancestors' finding unused land and putting it to use) that he must have bought it from someone else. If he did so, then, in the ERE, he must have bought it *at its capitalized value.* If he buys the piece of land at a price of 1,000 ounces, and receives 20 ounces per annum in rent, then he earns *interest,* and *only* interest. He sells future goods (land service) in the production process, but *he too first bought the whole land with money.* Therefore, he too is a "capitalist-investor" earning interest.

"Pure rent," i.e., rent that is *not* simply a return on previous investment and is therefore not capitalized, *seems,* therefore, to be earned only by those who have *found* unused land themselves (or inherited it from the finders). But even *they* do not earn pure rent. Suppose that a man finds land, unowned and worth zero, and then fences it, etc., until it is now able to yield a perpetual rental of 20 ounces per annum. Could we not say that *he* earns pure rent, since he did not buy the land, capitalized, from someone else? But this would overlook one of the most important features of economic life: *implicit earnings.* Even if this man did not buy the land, the land is *now* worth a certain capital value, the one it *could obtain* on the market. This capital value is, say, 1,000. Therefore, the man could sell the land for 1,000 at any time. *His forgone opportunity cost of owning the land and renting out its services is sale of the land for 1,000 ounces.* It is true that he earns 20 ounces per year, but this is only at the sacrifice of not selling the whole land for 1,000 ounces. His land, therefore, is really as much capitalized as land that has been bought on the market.

We must therefore conclude that *no one* receives pure rent except laborers in the form of wages, that the *only* incomes in the productive ERE economy are *wages* (the term for the prices and incomes of labor factors) and *interest.* But there is still a crucial distinction between land and capital goods. For we see that a fundamental, irreducible element is the *capital value of land.* The capital value of capital goods still reduces to wages and the capital value of land. In a *changing* economy, there is another source of income: *increases in the capital value of ground land.* Typical was the man who found unused land and then sold its services. Originally, the capital value of the land was zero; it was worthless. Now the land has become valuable because it earns rents. As a result, the capital value has risen to 1,000 ounces. His income, or gain, consisted of the *rise* of 1,000 ounces in capital value. This, of course, cannot take place in the ERE. In the ERE, all capital values must remain constant; here, we see that a source of monetary gain is a *rise* in the capital value of land, a rise resulting from increases in expected rental yields of land.[27] If the economy becomes an ERE after this particular change from 0 to 1,000, then this income was a "one-shot" affair, rather than a con-

tinuing and recurring item. The capital value of the land rose
from 0 to 1,000, and the owner can reap this income at any time.
However, after this has been reaped once, it is never reaped again.
If he sells the land for 1,000, the next buyer receives no gain
from the increase in capital value; he receives only market interest. Only interest and wages accrue continuously. As long as
the ERE continues, there will be no further gains or losses in
capital value.[28]

6. *The Depletion of Natural Resources*

One category has been purposely omitted so far from the
discussion of land factors. At first, we defined land as the *original, nature-given factor.* Then we said that land which had been
improved by human hands but which is now permanently given
must also be considered as *land.* Land, then, became the cat-
allactically permanent, nonreproducible resource, while capital
goods are those that are nonpermanent and therefore must be
produced again in order to be replaced. But there is one type
of resource that is nonreplaceable but also nonpermanent: the
natural resource that is being depleted, such as a copper or a dia-
mond mine. Here the factor is definitely original and nature-
given; it cannot be produced by man. On the other hand, it is
not permanent, but subject to *depletion* because any use of it
leaves an absolutely smaller amount for use in the future. It is
original, but nonpermanent. Shall it be classed as land or as a
capital good?

The crucial test of our classificatory procedure is to ask: Must
labor and land factors work in order to reproduce the good? In
the case of permanent factors this is not necessary, since they do
not wear out. But in this case, we must answer in the negative
also, for these goods, though nonpermanent, *cannot* be reproduced by man despite their depletion. Therefore, the natural resource comes as a special division under the "land" category.[29]

Table 15, adapted from one by Professor Hayek, reveals our
classification of various resources as either land or capital goods: [30]

TABLE 15

RESOURCES	PERMANENT	NONPERMANENT (CONSUMABLE)
Original (nonproducible)	Land	Land
Produced (producible)	Land	Capital Goods

Hayek criticizes the criterion of *reproducibility* for classifying a capital good. He declares: "The point that is relevant . . . is not that certain existing resources *can* be replaced by others which are in some technological sense similar to them, but that they have to be replaced by something, whether similar or not, if the income stream is not to decline." [31] But this is confusing *value* with *physical* considerations. We are attempting to classify *physical* goods here, not to discuss their possible values, which will fluctuate continually. The point is that the resources subject to depletion *cannot* be replaced, much as the owner would like to do so. They therefore earn a *net rent*. Hayek also raises the question whether a stream is "land" if a new stream can be created by collecting rain water. Here again, Hayek misconceives the issue as one of maintaining a "constant income stream" instead of classifying a physical concrete good. The stream is land because it does not *need* to be physically replaced. It is obvious that Hayek's criticism is valid against Kaldor's definition. Kaldor defined capital as a reproducible resource which it is *economically* profitable to produce. In that case, obsolete machines would no longer be capital goods. (Would they be "land"?) The definition should be: *physically* reproducible resources. Hayek's criticism that then the possibility of growing artificial fruit, etc., would make all land "capital" again misconceives the problem, which is one of the physical *need and possibility* of reproducing the agent. Since the basic *land—not* its fruit—needs no reproduction, it is excluded from the capital-good category.

The fact that the natural resources *cannot* be reproduced means that they earn a *net rent* and that their rent is not absorbed by land and labor factors that go into their production. Of course, from the net rents they earn the usual interest rate of the society for their owners, interest earnings being related to their capital value. Increases in capital values of natural resources go ultimately to the resource-owner himself and are not absorbed in gains by other land and labor factors.

There is no problem in capitalizing a resource that is subject to depletion, since, as we have seen, capitalization can take place for either a finite or an infinite series of future rental incomes.

There is, however, one striking problem that pervades any analysis of the resource subject to depletion and that distinguishes it from all other types of goods. This is the fact that there can be *no* use for such a resource in an evenly rotating economy. For the basis of the ERE is that all economic quantities continue indefinitely in an endless round. But this cannot happen in the case of a resource that is subject to depletion, for whenever it is used, the total stock of that good in the economy decreases. The situation at the next moment, then, cannot be the same as before. This is but one example of the insuperable difficulties encountered whenever the ERE is used, not as an auxiliary construction in analysis, but as some sort of ideal that the free economy must be forced to emulate.

There can be a reserve demand for a depletable resource, just as there is speculative reserve demand for any other stock of goods on the market. This speculation is not simple wickedness, however; it has a definite function, namely, that of allocating the scarce depletable resource to those uses *at those times* when consumer demand for them will be greatest. The speculator, waiting to use the resources until a future date, benefits consumers by shifting their use to a time when they will be more in demand than at present. As in the case of ground land, the permanent resource belongs to the first finder and first user, and often some of these initial capital gains are absorbed by interest on the capital originally invested in the business of resource-finding. The absorption can take place only in so far as the finding of new resources is a regular, continuing business. But this business, which by definition could not exist in the ERE, can never be completely regularized.

Minerals such as coal and oil are clearly prime examples of depletable resources. What about such natural resources as forests? A forest, although growing by natural processes, can be "produced" by man if measures are taken to maintain and grow more trees, etc. Therefore, forests would have to be classified as capital goods rather than depletable resources.

One of the frequent attacks on the behavior of the free market is based on the Georgist bugbear of natural resources held off the market for speculative purposes. We have dealt with this alleged problem above. Another, and diametrically opposite, attack is the common one that the free market wastes resources, especially depletable resources. Future generations are allegedly robbed by the greed of the present. Such reasoning would lead to the paradoxical conclusion that *none* of the resource be consumed at all. For whenever, at any time, a man consumes a depletable resource (here we use "consumes" in a broader sense to include "uses up" in production), he is leaving less of a stock for himself or his descendants to draw upon. It is a fact of life that *whenever* any amount of a depletable resource is used up, less is left for the future, and therefore *any* such consumption could just as well be called "robbery of the future," if one chooses to define robbery in such unusual terms.[32] Once we grant *any* amount of use to the depletable resource, we have to discard the robbery-of-the-future argument and accept the individual preferences of the market. There is then no more reason to assume that the market will use the resources too fast than to assume the opposite. The market will tend to use resources at precisely the rate that the consumers desire.[33]

Having developed, in Volume I, our basic analysis of the economics of the isolated individual, barter, and indirect exchange, we shall now proceed, in Volume II, to develop the analysis further by dealing with "dynamic" problems of a changing economy, particular types of factors, money and its value, and monopoly and competition, and discussing, in necessarily more summary fashion, the consequences of violent intervention in the free market.

For purposes of simplification, we have described *marginal value product* (MVP) as equal to *marginal physical product* (MPP) times *price*. Since we have seen that a factor must be used in the region of declining MPP, and since an increased supply of a factor leads to a fall in price, the conclusion of the analysis was that every factor works in an area where increased supply leads to a decline in MVP, and hence in DMVP. The assumption made in the first sentence, however, is not strictly correct.

Let us, then, find out what *is* the multiple of MPP that will yield an MVP. MVP is equal to an increase in revenue acquired from the addition of a unit, or lost from the loss of a unit, of a factor. MVP will then equal the difference in revenue from one position to another, i.e., the change in position resulting from an increase or decrease of a unit of a factor. Then, *MVP equals R_2 minus R_1*, where R is the gross revenue from the sale of a product, and a higher subscript signifies that *more* of a factor has been used in production. The *MPP* of this increase in a factor is $P_2 - P_1$, where P is the quantity of product produced, a higher subscript again meaning that more of a factor has been used.

So: $$\text{MVP} = R_2 - R_1 \quad \text{by definition.}$$

$$\text{MPP} = P_2 - P_1 \quad \text{by definition.}$$

Revenue is acquired by sale of the product; therefore, for any given point on the demand curve, total revenue equals the quantity produced and sold, multiplied by the price of the product.

Therefore, $R = P \cdot p$, where p is the price of the product.

So: $$R_2 = P_2 \cdot p_2$$

$$R_1 = P_1 \cdot p_1$$

Now, since the factors are economic goods, any increase in the use of a factor, other factors remaining constant, must *increase* the quantity produced. It would obviously be pointless for an entrepreneur to employ more factors which would not increase the product. Therefore, $P_2 > P_1$.

On the other hand, the price of the product falls as the supply increases, so that:

$$p_2 < p_1$$

Now, we are trying to find out what multiplied by MPP yields MVP. This unknown will be equal to:

$$\frac{MVP}{MPP} = \frac{R_2 - R_1}{P_2 - P_1}$$

This may be called the *marginal revenue,* which is the change in revenue divided by the change in output.

It is obvious that this figure, which we may call MR, will not equal either p_2 or p_1, or any average of the two. Simple multiplication of the denominator by either of the p's or both will reveal that this does not amount to the numerator. What *is* the relation between MR and price?

A price is the *average revenue,* i.e., it equals the total revenue divided by the quantity produced and sold. In short,

$$p = \frac{R}{P}$$

But above, in the discussion of marginal and average product, we saw the mathematical relationship between "average" and "marginal," and this holds for revenue as well as for productivity: namely, that in the range where the average is increasing, marginal is greater than average; in the range where average is decreasing, marginal is less than average. But we have established early in this book that the demand curve—i.e., the price, or average revenue curve—is always *falling* as the quantity increases. Therefore, the marginal revenue curve is falling also and is always below average revenue, or price. Let us, however, cement the proof by demonstrating that, for any two positions, p_2 is greater than MR. Since p_2 is smaller than p_1, as price falls when supply increases, the proposition that MR is less than both prices will be proved.

First, we know that $p_2 < p_1$
which means that

$$\frac{R_2}{P_2} < \frac{R_1}{P_1}$$

Now, we may take point 1 as the starting point and then consider the change to point 2, so that:

$$\frac{R + \Delta R}{P + \Delta P} < \frac{R}{P}$$

thus translating into the same symbols we used in the productivity proof above.

Now this means that

$$\frac{R}{P} - \frac{R + \Delta R}{P + \Delta P} > 0$$

Combining the two fractions, and then multiplying across, we get

$$R\Delta P - P\Delta R > 0$$

Or

$$R\Delta P > P\Delta R$$

So that

$$\frac{R}{P} > \frac{\Delta R}{\Delta P}$$

(We have here proved that MR is less than p_1, the higher of the two prices.)

Now this means that there is some unknown, constant positive *fraction* $1/k$ which, multiplied by the larger, will yield the smaller ratio (MR) in the last inequality. Thus

$$\frac{R}{kP} = \frac{\Delta R}{\Delta P}$$

Now, by algebra,

$$\frac{\Delta R}{\Delta P} = \frac{R + \Delta R}{kP + \Delta P}$$

And since k is a positive number,

$$\frac{R + \Delta R}{P + \Delta P} > \frac{R + \Delta R}{kP + \Delta P}$$

But this establishes that

$$\frac{R + \Delta R}{P + \Delta P} > \frac{\Delta R}{\Delta P}$$

i.e., *that MR is less than p_2.* Q.E.D.

Hence, when we consider that, strictly, *MR*, and not price, should be multiplied by MPP to arrive at MVP, we find that our conclusion— that production always takes place in the zone of a falling MVP curve—is *strengthened* rather than weakened. MVP falls even more rapidly in relation to MPP than we had been supposing. Furthermore, our analysis is not greatly modified, because no new basic deter- minants—beyond MPP and prices set by the consumer demand curve— have been introduced in our corrective analysis. In view of all this, we may continue to treat MVP as equaling MPP times price as a legitimate, simplified approximation to the actual result.[34]

APPENDIX B: PROFESSOR ROLPH AND THE DISCOUNTED MARGINAL PRODUCTIVITY THEORY

Of current schools of economic thought, the most fashionable have been the Econometric, the Keynesian, the Institutionalist, and the Neo-Classic. "Neo-Classic" refers to the pattern set by the major economists of the late nineteenth century. The dominant neoclassical strain at present is to be found in the system of Professor Frank Knight, of which the most characteristic feature is an attack on the whole concept of time preference. Denying time preference, and basing interest return solely on an alleged "productivity" of capital, the Knightians attack the doctrine of the *discounted* MVP and instead advocate a pure MVP theory. The clearest exposition of this approach is to be found in an article by a follower of Knight's, Professor Earl Rolph.[35]

Rolph defines "product" as any *immediate* results of "present valu- able activities." These include work on goods that will be consumed only in the future. Thus, "workmen and equipment beginning the construction of a building may have only a few stakes in the ground to show for their work the first day, but this and not the completed structure is their immediate product. Thus, the doctrine that a fac- tor receives the value of its marginal product refers to this immediate product. The simultaneity of production and product does not re- quire any simplifying assumptions. It is a direct appeal to the obvious. Every activity has its immediate results."

Obviously, no one denies that people work on goods and move capital a little further along. But is the immediate result of this a *product* in any meaningful sense? It should be clear that the product is the end product—the good sold to the consumer. The whole purpose of the production system is to lead to final consumption. All the intermediate purchases are based on the expectation of final purchase by the consumer and would not take place otherwise. Every activity may have its immediate "results," but they are not results that would command any monetary income from anyone if the owners of the factors themselves were joint owners of all they produced until the final consumption stage. In that case, it would be obvious that they do not get paid immediately; hence, their product is not immediate. The only reason that they *are* paid immediately (and even here there is not strict immediacy) on the market is that capitalists *advance* present goods in exchange for those *future* goods for which they expect a premium, or interest return. Thus, the owners of the factors are paid the *discounted* value of their marginal product.

The Knight-Rolph approach, in addition, is a retreat to a real-cost theory of value. It assumes that present efforts will somehow always bring present results. But when? In "present valuable activities." But how do these activities *become* valuable? Only if their *future product* is sold, as expected, to consumers. Suppose, however, that people work for years on a certain good and are paid by capitalists, and then the final product is not bought by consumers. The capitalists absorb monetary losses. Where was the immediate payment according to marginal product? The payment was only an investment in future goods by capitalists.

Rolph then turns to another allegedly heinous error of the discount approach, namely, the "doctrine of *nonco-ordination of factors*." This means that some factors, in their payment, receive the *discounted* value of their product and some do not. Rolph, however, is laboring under a misapprehension; there is no assumption of nonco-ordination in any sound discounting theory. As we have stated above, *all* factors —labor, land, and capital goods—receive their discounted marginal value product. The difference in regard to the owners of capital goods is that, in the ultimate analysis, they do not receive any *independent* payment, since capital goods are resolved into the factors that produced them, ultimately land and labor factors, and to interest for the time involved in the advance of payment by the capitalists.[36] Rolph believes that nonco-ordination is involved because owners of land and labor factors "receive a discounted share," and capital "receives an undiscounted share." But this is a faulty way of stating the conclusion. Owners of land and labor factors receive a discounted share, but owners of capital (money capital) receive *the discount*.

The remainder of Rolph's article is largely devoted to an attempt to prove that no time lag is involved in payments to owners of factors. Rolph assumes the existence of "production centers" within every firm, which, broken down into virtually instantaneous steps, produce and then implicitly receive payment instantaneously. This tortured and unreal construction misses the entire point. Even if there were atomized "production centers," the point is that some person or persons will have to make advances of present money along the route, in whatever order, until the final product is sold to the consumers. Let Rolph picture a production system, atomized or integrated as the case may be, with no one making the advances of present goods (money capital) that he denies exist. And as the laborers and landowners work on the intermediate products for years without pay, until the finished product is ready for the consumer, let Rolph exhort them not to worry, since they have been implicitly paid simultaneously as they worked. For this is the logical implication of the Knight-Rolph position.[87]

Notes

NOTES TO CHAPTER 1

1. For further reading on this topic, the best source is the epochal work of Ludwig von Mises, *Human Action* (New Haven: Yale University Press, 1949), pp. 1–143, and *passim*.

2. Cf. *ibid.,* p. 11; F. A. Hayek, "The Facts of the Social Sciences," *Individualism and Economic Order* (Chicago: University of Chicago Press, 1948), pp. 57–76; Hayek, *The Counter-Revolution of Science* (Glencoe, Ill.: The Free Press, 1952), pp. 25–35; and Edith T. Penrose, "Biological Analogies in the Theory of the Firm," *American Economic Review,* December, 1952, pp. 804–19 especially pp. 818–19.

3. Cf. Aristotle, *Ethica Nicomachea,* Bk. I, especially ch. vii.

4. This chapter consists solely of a development of the logical implications of the existence of human action. Future chapters—the further parts of the structure—are developed with the help of a very small number of subsidiary assumptions. Cf. Appendix below and Murray N. Rothbard, "Praxeology: Reply to Mr. Schuller," *American Economic Review,* December, 1951, pp. 943–46; and "In Defense of 'Extreme Apriorism,'" *Southern Economic Journal,* January, 1957, pp. 314–20.

5. There is no need to enter here into the difficult problem of animal behavior, from the lower organisms to the higher primates, which might be considered as on a borderline between purely reflexive and motivated behavior. At any rate, men can *understand* (as distinguished from merely observe) such behavior only in so far as they can impute to the animals motives that they can understand.

6. To say that only individuals act is not to deny that they are influenced in their desires and actions by the acts of other individuals, who might be fellow members of various societies or groups. We do not at all assume, as some critics of economics have charged, that individuals are "atoms" isolated from one another.

7. Cf. F. A. Hayek, *The Counter-Revolution of Science,* p. 34. Also cf. Mises, *Human Action,* p. 42.

8. Cf. Talcott Parsons, *The Structure of Social Action* (Glencoe, Ill.: The Free Press, 1949), pp. 44 ff.

9. Some writers have unfoundedly believed that praxeology and economics assume that all action is cool, calculating, and deliberate.

10. The common distinction between "economic goods" and "free goods" (such as air) is erroneous. As explained above, air is not a means, but a general condition of human welfare, and is not the object of action.

11. The term "land" is likely to be misleading in this connection because it is not used in the popular sense of the word. It includes such *natural* resources as water, oil, and minerals.

12. We shall not deal at this point with the complications involved in the original learning of any recipe by the actor, which is the object of human action.

13. Cf. Carl Menger, *Principles of Economics* (Glencoe, Ill.: The Free Press, 1950), pp. 51–67.

14. For each actor, then, the period of production is equivalent to his *waiting time*—the time that he must expect to wait for his end after the commencement of his action.

15. *Time preference* may be called the preference for *present satisfaction* over *future satisfaction* or *present good* over *future good*, provided it is remembered that it is the *same* satisfaction (or "good") that is being compared over the periods of time. Thus, a common type of objection to the assertion of universal time preference is that, in the winter time, a man will prefer the delivery of ice the next summer (future) to delivery of ice in the present. This, however, confuses the concept "good" with the material properties of a thing, whereas it actually refers to subjective satisfactions. Since ice-in-the-summer provides different (and greater) satisfactions than ice-in-the-winter, they are *not* the same, but *different* goods. In this case, it is different satisfactions that are being compared, despite the fact that the *physical* property of the thing may be the same.

16 It has become the custom to designate consumer goods with a longer duration of serviceableness as *durable goods*, and those of shorter duration as *nondurable goods*. Obviously, however, there are innumerable degrees of durability, and such a separation can only be unscientific and arbitrary.

17. Accordingly, the numbers by which ends are ranked on value scales are *ordinal*, not *cardinal*, numbers. Ordinal numbers are only ranked; they cannot be subject to the processes of measurement. Thus, in the above example, all we can say is that going to a concert is valued more than playing bridge, and either of these more than watching the game. We cannot say that going to a concert is valued "twice as much" as watching the game; the numbers 2 and 4 cannot be subject to processes of addition, multiplication, etc.

18. An example of suffering a loss as a result of an erroneous action would be going to the concert and finding that it was not at all enjoyable. The actor then realizes that he would have been much happier continuing to watch the game or playing bridge.

19. A large part of this book is occupied with the problem of how this process of value imputation can be accomplished in a modern, complex economy.

20. This is the solution of a problem that plagued writers in the economic field for many years: the source of the value of goods.

21. Cf. Ludwig von Mises, *The Theory of Money and Credit* (New Haven: Yale University Press, 1953), p. 46.

22. Also cf. T. N. Carver, *The Distribution of Wealth* (New York: Macmillan & Co., 1904), pp. 4–12. See below for a further discussion of the influences on man's valuation of specific units resulting from the size of the available stock.

23. This would not be true only if the "good" were not a means, but a general condition of human welfare, in which case one less unit of supply would make no difference for human action. But in that case it would not be a *good*, subject to the economizing of human action.
24. On the whole subject of marginal utility, *see* Eugen Von Böhm-Bawerk, *The Positive Theory of Capital* (New York: G. E. Stechert & Co., 1930), pp. 138–65, especially pp. 146–55.
25. For algebraic proof, *see* George J. Stigler, *The Theory of Price* (New York: Macmillan & Co., 1946), pp. 44–45.
26. For further reading on this subject, *see* Böhm-Bawerk, *op. cit.*, pp. 170–88; and F. A. Hayek, *The Counter-Revolution of Science*, pp. 32–33.
27. This is the first proposition in this chapter that has not been deduced from the axiom of action. It is a subsidiary assumption, based on empirical observation of actual human behavior. It is not deducible from human action because its contrary is conceivable, although not generally existing. On the other hand, the assumptions above of quantitative relations of cause and effect were logically implicit in the action axiom, since knowledge of definite cause-and-effect relations is necessary to any decision to act.
28. Cf. Mises, *Human Action*, p. 131.
29. *Ibid.*, p. 132.
30. Leisure is the amount of time not spent in labor, and play may be considered as one of the forms that leisure may take in yielding satisfaction. On labor and play, cf. Frank A. Fetter, *Economic Principles* (New York: The Century Co., 1915), pp. 171–77, 191, 197–206.
31. Cf. L. Albert Hahn, *Common Sense Economics* (New York: Abelard-Schuman Co., 1956), pp. 1 ff.
32. In this sense, the stick might be called a "labor-saving device," although the terminology is misleading. It is "labor-saving" only to the extent that the actor chooses to take the increased productivity in the form of leisure.
33. It is necessary to emphasize that independent acts of saving are necessary for replacement of goods, since many writers (e.g., J. B. Clark, Frank H. Knight) tend to assume that, once produced, capital, in some mystical way, reproduces itself without further need for acts of saving.
34. Cf. Frederic Benham, *Economics* (New York: Pitman Publishing Co., 1941), p. 162.
35. Böhm-Bawerk, *op. cit.*, pp. 95–96. *Also see* Mises, *Human Action*, pp. 480–90, and pp. 476–514.
36. This uncertainty is a subjective feeling ("hunch" or estimate) and cannot be measured in any way. The efforts of many popular writers to apply mathematical "probability theory" to the uncertainty of future historical events are completely vain. Cf. Mises, *Human Action*, pp. 105–18.
37. That such a range of investment decisions enabling him to achieve greater future output must always be open to him is a fundamental truth derived from the assumption of human action. If they were not open to him, it would mean that man could not (or rather, believed that he could not) act to improve his lot, and therefore there would be no possi-

bility of action. Since we cannot even conceive of human existence without action, it follows that "investment opportunities" are always available.
38. On the "unused capacity" bogey, *see* Benham, *op. cit.,* pp. 147–49.
39. Cf. Böhm-Bawerk, *op. cit.,* pp. 238–44.
40. Plain saving is not to be confused with an earlier example, when Crusoe saved stocks of consumers' goods to be consumed while devoting his labor to the production of capital.
41. See note 15 above.
42. The period of production will be equal to the time difference between the act of saving and the act of future consumption, as in all other cases of investment.
43. See page 16 above.
44. Cf. G. J. Schuller, "Rejoinder," *American Economic Review,* March, 1951, p. 188. For a reply, *see* Murray N. Rothbard, "Toward a Reconstruction of Utility and Welfare Economics" in M. Sennholz, ed., *On Freedom and Free Enterprise,* Essays in Honor of Ludwig von Mises (Princeton, N. J.: D. Van Nostrand Co., 1956), p. 227. *Also see* Boris Ischboldin, "A Critique of Econometrics," *Review of Social Economy,* September, 1960, pp. 110–27; and Vladimir Niksa, "The Role of Quantitative Thinking in Modern Economic Theory," *Review of Social Economy,* September, 1959, pp. 151–73.
45. Cf. René Poirier, "Sur Logique" in André Lalande, *Vocabulaire technique et critique de la philosophie* (Paris: Presses Universitaires de France, 1951), pp. 574–75.

NOTES TO CHAPTER 2

1. For a discussion of the transformation from murder to slavery, cf. Franz Oppenheimer, *The State* (New York: Vanguard Press, 1914, reprinted 1928), pp. 55–70 and *passim.*
2. It is true that man, being what he is, cannot absolutely guarantee lifelong service to another under a voluntary arrangement. Thus, Jackson, at present, might agree to labor under Crusoe's direction for life, in return for food, clothing, etc., but he cannot guarantee that he will not change his mind at some point in the future and decide to leave. In this sense, a man's own person and will is "inalienable," i.e., cannot be given up to someone else for any future period.
3. Such an arrangement is *not* a *guarantee* of "security" of provisions, since no one can guarantee a steady supply of such goods. It simply means that A *believes* that B is better able to furnish a supply of these goods than he is himself.
4. Cf. Mises, *Human Action,* pp. 196–99, and, for a comparison of slaves and animals, *ibid.,* pp. 624–30.
5. There is, of course, no judgment at this point concerning whether the establishment of a society or such a society is a good, bad, or indifferent development.

6. This system has sometimes been called "compulsory co-operation," but we prefer to restrict the term "co-operation" to the result of voluntary choices.

7. For an analysis of exchange, *see* Menger, *op. cit.,* pp. 175–90. For a vivid discussion of exchange, *see* Frédéric Bastiat, *Harmonies of Political Economy* (Santa Ana, Calif.: The Register Publishing Co., 1944), I, 96–130.

8. Strictly, the law of marginal utility is also applicable to the case where the supply is only one unit, and we can say that, in the example above, exchange will take place if, for A, the marginal utility of good Y is greater than the marginal utility of good X, and vice versa for B.

9. On use-value and exchange-value, *see* Menger, *op. cit.,* pp. 226–35.

10. Analytically, receiving a factor from someone as a gift simply pushes the problem back another stage. At some point, the actor must have appropriated it from the realm of unused factors, as Crusoe appropriated the unused land on the island.

11. On self-ownership and the acquisition of property, cf. the classic discussion of John Locke, "An Essay Concerning the True Original Extent and End of Civil Government, Second Treatise" in Ernest Barker, ed., *Social Contract* (London: Oxford University Press, 1948), pp. 15–30.

12. The problem of self-ownership is complicated by the question of *children.* Children cannot be considered self-owners, because they are not yet in possession of the powers of reason necessary to direct their actions. The fact that children are under the hegemonic authority of their parents until they are old enough to become self-owning beings is therefore not contrary to our assumption of a purely free market. Since children are not capable of self-ownership, authority over them will rest in some individuals; on an unhampered market, it would rest in their *producers,* the parents. On the other hand, the property of the parents in this unique case is not exclusive; the parents may not injure the children at will. Children, not long after birth, begin to acquire the powers of reasoning human beings and embody the potential development of full self-owners. Therefore the child will, on the free market, be defended from violent actions in the same way as an adult. On children, see *ibid.,* pp. 30–38.

13. For more on invasive and noninvasive acts in a free market, see section 13 below.

14. It is possible that Crusoe and Jackson, for the mutual fun of it, might pass fifty berries back and forth between them. This, however, would not be genuine exchange, but joint participation in an enjoyable consumers' good—a game or play.

15. Basically, class (*b*) is resolvable into differences in classes (*a*) and (*c*), which account for their production.

16. Mises, *Human Action,* pp. 157 ff. On the pervasiveness of variation, also cf. F. A. Harper, *Liberty, A Path to Its Recovery* (Irvington-on-Hudson, N. Y.: Foundation for Economic Education, 1949), pp. 65–77, 139–41.

17. Kenneth E. Boulding, *Economic Analysis* (1st ed., New York: Harper & Bros., 1941), p. 30; also *ibid.,* pp. 22–32.

18. Those critics of Adam Smith and other economists who accuse the latter of "assuming" that God or Nature directs the market process by an "invisible hand" for the benefit of all participants completely miss the mark. The fact that the market provides for the welfare of each individual participating in it is a *conclusion* based on scientific analysis, not an assumption upon which the analysis is based. The "invisible hand" was simply a metaphor used in commenting on this process and its results. Cf. William D. Grampp, "Adam Smith and the Economic Man," *Journal of Political Economy,* August, 1948, pp. 315–36, especially pp. 319–20.
19. See Mises, *Human Action,* pp. 157–58.
20. Such specialization of stages requires the adoption of *indirect exchange,* discussed in the following chapters.
21. Cf. Mises, *ibid.,* pp. 204–06, and Menger, *op. cit.,* pp. 192–94, 305–06.
22. Cf. Böhm-Bawerk, pp. 195–222. Also cf. Fetter, *op. cit.,* pp. 42–72; and Menger, *op. cit.,* pp. 191–97.
23. Of course, given other value scales, the final prices might be determinate at our point, or within a narrow range. Thus, if Smith's maximum buying price is 87, and Johnson's minimum selling price is 87, the price will be uniquely determined at 87.
24. Auction sales are examples of markets for one unit of a good with one seller and many buyers. Cf. Boulding, *op. cit.,* pp. 41–43.
25. It is possible that the equilibrium point will not be uniquely determined at one definite price. Thus, the pattern of supply and demand schedules might be as follows:

P	S	D
89	5	6
90	6	5

The inequality is the narrowest possible, but there is no one point of equality. In that case, if the units are further divisible, then the price will be set to clear the market at a point in between, say 89.5 barrels of fish per horse. If both goods being exchanged are indivisible further, however, such as cows against horses, then the equilibrium price will be either 89 or 90, and this will be the closest approach to equilibrium rather than equilibrium itself.
26. Cf. Benham, *op. cit.,* pp. 60–63.
27. The attention of some writers to the elasticity of supply stems from an erroneous approach to the entire analysis of utility, supply, and demand. They assume that it is possible to treat human action in terms of "infinitely small" differences, and therefore to apply the mathematically elegant concepts of the calculus, etc., to economic problems. Such a treatment is fallacious and misleading, however, since human action must treat all matters only in terms of discrete steps. If, for example, the utility of X is so little smaller than the utility of Y that it can be regarded as identical or negligibly different, then human action will treat them as such, i.e., as the same good. Because it is conceptually impossible to measure utility, even the drawing of continuous utility curves is

pernicious. In the supply and demand schedules, it is not harmful to draw continuous curves for the sake of clarity, but the mathematical concepts of continuity and the calculus are not applicable. As a result, the seemingly precise concept of "elasticity at a point" (percentage increase in demand divided by a "negligibly small" percentage decrease in price) is completely out of order. It is this mistaken substitution of mathematical elegance for the realities of human action that lends a seeming importance to the concept of "elasticity of supply," comparable to the concept of elasticity of demand.

28. On the total demand-stock analysis, *see* Philip H. Wicksteed, *The Common Sense of Political Economy and Selected Papers* (London: Routledge and Kegan Paul, 1933), I, 213–38; II, 493–526 and 784–88. *Also see* Boulding, *op. cit.,* pp. 51–80.

29. This situation is not likely to arise in the case of the *market equilibria* described above. Generally, a market tends quickly to "clear itself" by establishing its equilibrium price, after which a certain number of exchanges take place, leading toward what has been termed the *plain state of rest*—the condition after the various exchanges have taken place. These equilibrium market prices, however (as will be seen in later chapters), in turn tend to move toward certain long-run equilibria, in accordance with the demand schedule and the effect on the size of stock produced. The supply curve involved in this *final state of rest* involves the ultimate decisions in producing a commodity and differs from the market supply curve. In the movements toward this "final state," conditions, such as the demand curve, always change in the interim, thus setting a new final state as the goal of market prices. The final state is never reached. *See* Mises, *Human Action,* pp. 245 ff.

30. The *addition* of supply schedules is a simple process to conceive: if at a price X, the class (a) sellers will supply T tons of a good and the class (b) sellers will supply T' tons, the total market supply for that price is T + T' tons. The same process applies to each hypothetical price.

31. Strictly, of course, costs of storage will have to be considered in their calculations.

32. On the importance of services, *see* Arthur Latham Perry, *Political Economy* (21st ed., New York: Charles Scribner's Sons, 1892), pp. 124–39.

33. This is not to deny, of course, that the existence of *several* violinists of different quality will affect the consumer's evaluations of each one.

34. If he has taken the property of another by means of such an agreement, he will, on the free market, have to return the property. Thus, if A has agreed to work for life for B in exchange for 10,000 grams of gold, he will have to return the proportionate amount of property if he terminates the arrangement and ceases the work.

35. In other words, he cannot make enforceable contracts binding his future personal actions. (On contract enforcement in an unhampered market, see section 13 below.) This applies also to *marriage contracts.* Since human self-ownership cannot be alienated, a man or a woman, on a free market, could not be compelled to continue in marriage if he or she no

longer desired to do so. This is regardless of any previous agreement. Thus, a marriage contract, like an individual labor contract, is, on an unhampered market, terminable at the will of *either one* of the parties.

36. In a credit transaction, it is not necessary for the present and the future goods exchanged to be the same commodity. Thus, a man can sell wheat now in exchange for a certain amount of corn at a future date. The example in the text, however, highlights the importance of time preference and is also more likely to occur in practice.

37. Léon Wolowski and Émile Levasseur, "Property," *Lalor's Cyclopedia of Political Science, etc.* (Chicago: M. B. Cary & Co., 1884), III, 392.

38. See the vivid discussion by Edmond About, *Handbook of Social Economy* (London: Strahan & Co., 1872), pp. 19–30. Even urban sites embody much past labor. Cf. Herbert B. Dorau and Albert G. Hinman, *Urban Land Economics* (New York: Macmillan & Co., 1928), pp. 205–13.

39. If a channel has to be a certain number of wave lengths in width in order to permit clear transmission, then the property would accrue to the first user, in terms of such width.

40. Professor Coase has demonstrated that Federal ownership of airwaves was arrogated, in the 1920's, not so much to alleviate a preceding "chaos," as to forestall this very acquisition of private property rights in air waves, which the courts were in the process of establishing according to common law principles. Ronald H. Coase, "The Federal Communications Commission," *The Journal of Law and Economics,* October, 1959, pp. 5, 30–32.

41. It is rapidly becoming evident that air lanes for planes *are* becoming scarce and, in a free society, would be owned by first users—thus obviating a great many plane crashes.

42. *Flowing* water should be owned in proportion to its rate of use by the first user—i.e., by the "appropriation" rather than the "riparian" method of ownership. However, the appropriator would then have absolute control over his property, might transfer his share, etc., something which cannot be done in those areas, e.g., states in the West, where an approach to appropriation ownership now predominates. *See* Murray N. Rothbard, "Concerning Water," *The Freeman,* March, 1956, pp. 61–64. Also see the excellent article by Professor Jerome W. Milliman, "Water Law and Private Decision-Making: A Critique," *The Journal of Law and Economics,* October, 1959; pp. 41–63; Milliman, "Commonality, the Price System, and Use of Water Supplies," *Southern Economic Journal,* April, 1956, pp. 426–37.

43. On Ingalls and his doctrines, *see* James J. Martin, *Men Against the State* (DeKalb, Ill.; Adrian Allen Associates, 1953), pp. 142–52, 220 ff., 246 ff. Also cf. Benjamin R. Tucker, *Instead of a Book* (2nd ed., New York: B. R. Tucker, 1897), pp. 299–357, for the views of Ingalls' most able disciple. Despite the underlying similarity and their many economic errors, the Ingalls-Tucker group launched some interesting and effective critiques of the Georgist position. These take on value in the light of the excessive kindness often accorded to Georgist doctrines by economists.

44. This is true *even* if the actor had previously agreed in a contract that he would pay damages. For this is still merely a promise; he has not implicitly seized someone else's property. The object of an enforcing agency in a free society is not to uphold promise-keeping by force, but to redress any invasions of person and property.

45. Sir Frederick Pollock thus describes original English contract law: "Money debts, it is true, were recoverable from an early time. But this was not because the debtor had promised to repay the loan; it was because the money was deemed still to belong to the creditor, as if the identical coins were merely in the debtor's custody. The creditor sued to recover money . . . in exactly the same form which he would have used to demand possession of land . . . and down to Blackstone's time the creditor was said to have a property in the debt—property which the debtor had granted him. Giving credit, in this way of thinking, is not reliance on the right to call thereafter for an act . . . to be performed by the debtor, but merely suspension of the immediate right to possess one's own particular money, as the owner of a house lot suspends his right to occupy it . . . The foundation of the plaintiff's right was not bargain or promise, but the unjust detention by the defendant of the plaintiff's money or goods." Sir Frederick Pollock, "Contract," *Encyclopaedia Britannica* (14th ed.; London, 1929), VI, 339–40.

46. "In Rome one could recover stolen goods, or damages for their loss, by what we should call a civil process, without in the least affecting the relation between the thief and the public by reason of the theft. Restitution first and punishment afterwards was the rule." Wordsworth Donisthorpe, *Law in A Free State* (London: Macmillan & Co., 1895), p. 135.

47. This reason for the unenforceability of a cartel agreement in a free society has no relation to any common-law hostility to agreements allegedly "in restraint of trade." However, it is very similar to the English common-law doctrine finally worked out in the *Mogul Steamship Case* (1892). *See* William L. Letwin, "The English Common Law Concerning Monopolies," *University of Chicago Law Review*, Spring, 1954, pp. 382 ff.

48. *Noise* is also an invasive act against another, a transmission of sound waves assaulting the eardrums of others. On "external diseconomies," the only good discussion by an economist is the excellent one in Mises, *Human Action*, pp. 650–53. For an appreciation of the distinction between judicial and administrative action in a free society, as well as a fine grasp of property rights and governmental enforcement, see the classic discussion of adulteration in Donisthorpe, *op. cit.*, pp. 132–58.

49. Similarly, *blackmail* would not be illegal in the free society. For blackmail is the receipt of money in exchange for the service of not publicizing certain information about the other person. No violence or threat of violence to person or property is involved.

50. Auberon Herbert, in A. Herbert and J. H. Levy, *Taxation and Anarchism* (London: The Personal Rights Assn., 1912), pp. 24, 36–39; and in "A Cabinet Minister's Vade Mecum" in Michael Goodwin, ed., *Nineteenth-Century Opinion* (London: Penguin Books, 1951), pp. 206–07.

NOTES TO CHAPTER 3

1. See, for example chapter 1 above, page 50.
2. For a vivid and accurate contrast between man's condition in a market society and that in a primitive society, *see* About, *op. cit.,* pp. 5–17.
3. For further analysis of this process of the emergence of common media, *see* Mises, *The Theory of Money and Credit,* pp. 30–33, and *Human Action,* pp. 402–04. *Also see* Menger, *op. cit.,* pp. 257–63. For an historical description, *see* J. Laurence Laughlin, *Money, Credit, and Prices* (Chicago: University of Chicago Press, 1931), I, 3–15, 28–31.
4. Cf. Adam Smith, *The Wealth of Nations* (New York: Modern Library, 1937), pp. 22–24; Menger, *op. cit.,* pp. 263–71; Laughlin, *op. cit.,* pp. 15–23, 38–43.
5. On the significance of money for civilized society, cf. Wicksteed, *op. cit.,* I, 140 ff.
6. Later sections will deal further with the receipt of money income in the production process. Here it must be noted that since the owner and seller of capital goods must pay for the land, labor, and capital goods in *their* production, in the last analysis the owner of capital receives income only as a holder of goods over a period of *time.*
7. The names of the units can be, and have been, anything conceivable, dependent on custom, language, etc. Such names as dollars, francs, marks, shekels, are examples. The "dollar" originated as the generally applied name of ounce weights of silver coined by the Count of Schlick in Bohemia. The Count, who lived in Joachim's valley (or Joachims*thal*) began coining ounces of silver in 1518, and their uniformity and fineness earned a reputation throughout Europe. They became known as Joachimsthalers, finally abbreviated to *thalers.* The name "dollar" is derived from "thaler." Cf. Charles A. Conant, *The Principles of Money and Banking* (New York: Harper & Bros., 1905), I, 135–40; Menger, *op. cit.,* p. 283.
8. Gold, for example, has been traded as money in the raw form of nuggets, as gold dust in sacks, or as jewelry and other ornaments. One interesting example of a money shape was the iron money of central Africa. Iron was a valuable commodity, in use as hoes. The money form was made to be divisible into two parts, easily shaped into hoes. *See* Laughlin, *op. cit.,* p. 40.
9. This is also true if the income is gradual and the expenditure is in discrete sums, or for any other pattern of money income and expenditures.
10. This section is limited to a discussion of expenditures on consumers' goods. A later section will discuss producers' expenditures on producers' goods. It will be seen, however, that even unwelcome losses from cash balances suffered by producers are purely the result of voluntary action that, in a later period, proved erroneous.
11. The assertion has also been made that a person who spends most or all of his income on food and clothing *must* also have an "unfavorable bal-

ance of trade," since his money expenditures *must* be at a certain minimum amount. However, if the man has spent all his cash balance, he can no longer continue to have an "unfavorable balance," regardless of what goods he buys or what his standard of living is.

12. Producers could also borrow the saved funds of others, but the whole process of lending and borrowing is omitted in this section in order to clarify the analysis. Loans will be analyzed in a later chapter.

13. It was partly confusion between the *total* action of the individual and his action as a businessman that led writers to extrapolate from the behavior of the businessman and conclude that "nations" are "better off" if "they" export more than "they" import.

14. The terms "nonexchangeable" (or "unexchangeable") and "exchangeable" goods are far superior to the terms "ideal" and "material." The latter classification errs on two counts, aside from failing to convey the essential difference between the two types of goods. In the first place, as has been stated above, many exchangeable goods are intangible services rather than tangible, "material" things. Secondly, many of the nonexchangeable goods valued by some persons would hardly be considered "ideal" by others, so that a less colored term is necessary.

15. The belief of the classical economists, notably John Stuart Mill, as well as their critics, that economics must postulate a mythical "economic man," who is interested only in acquiring money income, is thus a completely erroneous one.

16. Of course, the concrete result differs with the individual and with the *unit of time* selected for consideration. In terms of income per hour, the point at which labor stops may come fairly quickly; in terms of income per year, it may never come. Regardless of his money income per hour, in other words, he is likely to stop work after a certain number of hours worked, whereas he is likely to take a year off from work only if his annual income is substantial.

NOTES TO CHAPTER 4

1. The exceptions are direct exchanges that might be made between two goods on the basis of their hypothetical exchange ratios on the market. These exchanges, however, are relatively isolated and unimportant and depend on the money prices of the two goods.

2. Many writers interpret the "purchasing power of the monetary unit" as being some sort of "price level," a measurable entity consisting of some sort of average of "all goods combined." The major classical economists did not take this fallacious position: "When they speak of the value of money or of the level of prices without explicit qualification, they mean the array of prices, of both commodities and services, in all its particularity and without conscious implication of any kind of statistical average." Jacob Viner, *Studies in the Theory of International Trade* (New York: Harper & Bros., 1937), p. 314. Also cf. Joseph A. Schumpeter, *History of Economic Analysis* (New York: Oxford University Press, 1954), p. 1094.

3. The tabulations in the text are simplified for convenience and are not strictly correct. For suppose that the man had already paid 6 gold grains for 1 ounce of butter. When he decides on a purchase of another pound of butter, his ranking for *all* the units of money rise, since he now has a lower stock of money than he had before. Our tabulations, therefore, do not fully portray the rise in the marginal utility of money as money is spent. However, the correction *reinforces,* rather than modifies, our conclusion that the maximum demand-price falls as quantity increases, for we see that it will fall still further than we have depicted.

4. On market-supply schedules, cf. Friedrich von Wieser, *Social Economics* (London: George Allen & Unwin, 1927), pp. 179–84.

5. The reader is referred to the section on "Stock and the Total Demand to Hold" in chapter 2, pp. 118–23 above.

6. If there is no reservation-demand schedule on the part of the sellers, then the total demand to hold is *identical* with the regular demand schedule.

7. The proof that the two sets of curves always yield the same equilibrium price is as follows: Let, at any price, the quantity demanded = D, the quantity supplied = S, the quantity of existing stock = K, the quantity of reserved demand = R, and the total demand to hold = T. The following are always true, by definition:

$$S = K - R$$

$$T = D + R$$

Now, at the equilibrium price, where S and D intersect, S is obviously equal to D. But if $S = D$, then $T = K - R + R$, or $T = K$.

8. Of course, this equilibrium price might be a *zone* rather than a single price in those cases where there is a zone between the valuations of the marginal buyer and those of the marginal seller. See the analysis of one buyer and one seller in chapter 2, above, pp. 91–93. In such rare cases, where there generally must be very few buyers and very few sellers, there is a zone within which the market is cleared at any point, and there is room for "bargaining skill" to maneuver. In the extensive markets of the money economy, however, even one buyer and one seller are likely to have one determinate price or a very narrow zone between their maximum buying- and minimum selling-prices.

9. See chapter 2 above, pp. 112–17.

10. This and the analysis of chapter 2 refute the charge made by some writers that speculation is "self-justifying," that it distorts the effects of the underlying supply and demand factors, by tending to establish pseudoequilibrium prices on the market. The truth is the reverse; speculative errors in estimating underlying factors are self-correcting, and anticipation tends to establish the true equilibrium market-price more rapidly.

11. Compare this analysis with the analysis of direct exchange, chapter 2 above, p. 139.

12. See chapter 2 above, pp. 123–24.

13. We might, in some situations, make such comparisons as historians, using imprecise judgment. We cannot, however, do so as praxeologists or economists.

14. For more on these matters, *see* Rothbard, "Toward a Reconstruction, etc." *op. cit.,* pp. 224–43. *Also see* Mises, *Theory of Money and Credit,* pp. 38–47.

15. It is interesting that those who attempt to measure consumers' surplus explicitly rule out consideration of *all* goods or of any good that looms "large" in the consumers' budget. Such a course is convenient, but illogical, and glosses over fundamental difficulties in the analysis. It is, however, typical of the Marshallian tradition in economics. For an explicit statement by a leading present-day Marshallian, *see* D. H. Robertson, *Utility and All That* (London: George Allen & Unwin, 1952), p. 16.

16. See chapter 2 above, p. 139.

17. For a further discussion of this point, see Appendix A below, on "The Diminishing Marginal Utility of Money."

18. It is true that "he who considers acquiring or giving away money is, of course, first of all interested in its future purchasing power and the future structure of prices. But he cannot form a judgment about the future purchasing power of money otherwise than by looking at its configuration in the immediate past." Mises, *Human Action,* p. 407.

19. *See* Mises, *Theory of Money and Credit,* pp. 97–123, and *Human Action,* pp. 405–08. *Also see* Schumpeter, *op. cit.,* p. 1090. This problem obstructed the development of economic science until Mises provided the solution. Failure to solve it led many economists to despair of ever constructing a satisfactory economic analysis of money prices. They were led to abandon fundamental analysis of money prices and to separate completely the prices of goods from their money components. In this fallacious course, they assumed that individual prices are determined wholly as in barter, without money components, while the supply of and the demand for money determined an imaginary figment called the "general price level." Economists began to specialize separately in the "theory of price," which completely abstracted from money in its real functions, and a "theory of money," which abstracted from individual prices and dealt solely with a mythical "price level." The former were solely preoccupied with a particular price and its determinants; the latter solely with the "economy as a whole" without relation to the individual components—called "microeconomics" and "macroeconomics" respectively. Actually, such fallacious premises led inevitably to erroneous conclusions. It is certainly legitimate and necessary for economics, in working out an analysis of reality, to isolate different segments for concentration as the analysis proceeds; but it is not legitimate to falsify reality in this separation, so that the final analysis does not present a correct picture of the individual parts and their interrelations.

20. As we regress in time and approach the original days of barter, the exchange use in the demand for gold becomes relatively weaker as compared to the direct use of gold, until finally, on the last day of barter, it dies out altogether, the time component dying out with it.

21. It should be noted that the crucial stopping point of the regression is *not* the cessation of the use of gold as "money," but the cessation of its use as a *medium of exchange*. It is clear that the concept of a "general" medium of exchange (money) is not important here. As long as gold is used as a medium of exchange, gold prices will continue to have temporal components. It is true, of course, that for a commodity used as a *limited* medium of exchange only a limited array of prices has to be taken into account in considering its utility.

22. Professor Patinkin criticizes Mises for allegedly basing the regression theorem on the view that the marginal utility of money refers to the marginal utility of the goods for which money is exchanged rather than the marginal utility of holding money, and charges Mises with inconsistently holding the latter view in parts of his *Theory of Money and Credit*. In fact, Mises' concept of the marginal utility of money *does* refer to the utility of *holding* money, and Mises' point about the regression theorem is a different one, namely, that the marginal utility-to-hold is in itself based on the prior fact that money can exchange for goods, i.e., on the prior money prices of goods. Hence, it becomes necessary to break out of this circularity—by means of the regression theorem. In short, the prices of goods have to exist *in order* to have a marginal utility of money to hold.

    In his own theory, Patinkin very feebly tries to justify circularity, by saying that in analyzing the market (market "experiment") he begins with utility, and in analyzing utility he begins with prices (individual "experiment"), but the fact remains that he is caught inextricably in a circular trap, which a methodology of cause-and-effect (in contrast to a mathematical type of mutual determination) would quickly reveal. Don Patinkin, *Money, Interest, and Prices* (Evanston, Ill.: Row, Peterson & Co., 1956), pp. 71–72, 414.

23. As Wicksteed states: "Efforts are regulated by anticipated values, but values are not controlled by antecedent efforts," and "The value of what you have got is not affected by the value of what you have relinquished or forgone in order to get it. But the measure of the advantages you are willing to forgo in order to get a thing is determined by the value that you expect it to have when you have got it." Wicksteed, *op. cit.*, I, 88–93.

24. We shall see below, in chapter 11, that money is unique in not conferring any general benefit through an increase in the supply once money has been established on the market.

25. "Planning" does not necessarily mean that the man has pondered long and hard over a decision and subsequent action. He might have made his decision almost instantaneously. Yet this is still planned action. Since all action is purposive rather than reflexive, there must always, before an action, have been a decision to act as well as valuations. Therefore, there is always planning.

26. Economics "must at any rate include and imply a study of the way in which members of . . . society will spontaneously administer their own

resources and the relations into which they will spontaneously enter with each other." Wicksteed, *op. cit.*, I, 15–16.

27. Wicksteed, *op. cit.*, I, 21–22.
28. The exception is those cases in which the demand curve for the good is directly vertical, and there will then be no effect on the complementary good.
29. We omit at this point analysis of the case in which the increase in demand results from decreases of cash balance and/or decreases in investment.
30. Strictly, this is not correct, and the important qualification will be added below. Since, as a result of time preference, present services are worth more than the same ones in the future, and those in the near future more than those in the far future, the price of *B* will be *less* than twice the price of *A*.
31. It needs to be kept in mind that, strictly, there is no such thing as a "present" price established by the market. When a man considers the price of a good, he is considering that price agreed upon in the last recorded transaction in the market. The "present" price is always in reality the historically recorded price of the most immediate past (say, a half-hour ago). What always interests the actor is what various prices will be at various times in the future.
32. On the different uses of the term "value," see Appendix B, "On Value," below.
33. The concept of monetary profit and loss and their relation to capitalization will be explored below.
34. Cf. Fetter, *op. cit.*, pp. 158–60.
35. For a discussion of the value of durable goods, see the brilliant treatment in Böhm-Bawerk, *Positive Theory, etc.*, pp. 339–57; Fetter, *op. cit.*, pp. 111–21; and Wicksteed, *op. cit.*, I, 101–11.
36. We are omitting possible shifts in rank resulting from the increasing utility of money, which would only complicate matters unduly.
37. W. Stanley Jevons, *The Theory of Political Economy* (3rd ed.; London: Macmillan & Co., 1888), pp. 59–60.
38. See Appendix A below, "The Diminishing Marginal Utility of Money," and Rothbard, "Toward a Reconstruction, etc.," *loc. cit.*
39. Mises, *Human Action*, p. 102. Dr. Bernardelli justly says: "If someone asks me *in abstracto* whether my love for my country is greater than my desire for freedom, I am somewhat at a loss how to answer, but actually having to make a choice between a trip in my country and the danger of losing my freedom, the order of intensities of my desire becomes only too determinate." Harro F. Bernardelli, "What has Philosophy to Contribute to the Social Sciences, and to Economics in Particular?" *Economica*, November, 1936, p. 451. Also see our discussion of "consumer surplus" in section 4 above.
40. Schumpeter, *op. cit.*, pp. 94 n. and 1064.
41. See chapter 1, p. 64.
42. Cf. the excellent discussion of the sizes of units in Wicksteed, *op. cit.*, I, 96–101, and 84.

43. Mises, *Theory of Money and Credit,* pp. 46–47. *Also see* Harro F. Ber- nardelli, "The End of the Marginal Utility Theory?" *Economica,* May, 1938, pp. 205–07; and Bernardelli, "A Reply to Mr. Samuelson's Note," *Economica,* February, 1939, pp. 88–89.

44. It must always be kept in mind that "total" and "marginal" do not have the same meaning, or mutual relation, as they do in the calculus. "Total" is here another form of "marginal." Failure to realize this has plagued economics since the days of Jevons and Walras.

45. For further analysis of the determination of the purchasing power of money and of the demand for and the supply of money, see chapter 11 below on "Money and Its Purchasing Power."

46. On appraisement and valuation, cf. Mises, *Human Action,* pp. 328–30.

NOTES TO CHAPTER 5

1. Another difference is one we have already discussed: that mathematics, particularly the calculus, rests in large part on assumptions of infinitely small steps. Such assumptions may be perfectly legitimate in a field where behavior of unmotivated matter is under study. But *human action* disregards infinitely small steps precisely because they *are* infinitely small and therefore have no relevance to human beings. Hence, the action under study in economics must always occur in finite, discrete steps. It is therefore incorrect to say that such an assumption may just as well be made in the study of human action as in the study of physical par- ticles. In human action, we may describe such assumptions as being not simply unrealistic, but *antirealistic.*

2. The mathematical economists, or "econometricians," have been trying without success for years to analyze the path of equilibrium as well as the equilibrium conditions themselves. The econometrician F. Zeuthen recently admitted that such attempts cannot succeed. All that mathe- matics can describe is the final equilibrium point. See the remarks of F. Zeuthen at the 16th European meeting of the Econometric Society, in *Econometrica,* April, 1955, pp. 199–200.

3. For a brilliant critique of the use of mathematics in economics, *see* Mises, *Human Action,* pp. 251, 347–54, 697–99, 706–11. *Also see* Mises, "Comments about the Mathematical Treatment of Economic Problems," *Studium Generale,* VI, 2 (1953), (Springer Verlag: unpublished trans- lation by Helena Ratzka); Niksa, *loc. cit.;* Ischboldin, *loc. cit.;* Paul Pain- levé, "The Place of Mathematical Reasoning in Economics" in Louise Sommer, ed., *Essays in European Economic Thought* (Princeton: D. Van Nostrand, 1960), pp. 120–32; and Wieser, *op. cit.,* pp. 51 ff. For a dis- cussion of the logical method of economics, see *Human Action* and the neglected work, J. E. Cairnes, *The Character and Logical Method of Political Economy* (2nd ed.; London: Macmillan & Co., 1888). *Also see* Marian Bowley, *Nassau Senior and Classical Economics* (New York: Augustus M. Kelley, 1949), pp. 55–65. If any mathematics has been used in this treatise, it has been only along the lines charted by Cairnes: "I have no desire to deny that it may be possible to employ geometrical

diagrams or mathematical formulae for the purpose of exhibiting economic doctrines *reached by other paths.* . . . What I venture to deny is the doctrine which Professor Jevons and others have advanced—that economic knowledge can be extended by such means; that Mathematics can be applied to the development of economic truth, as it has been applied to the development of mechanical and physical truth; and unless it can be shown either that mental feelings admit of being expressed in precise quantitative forms, or, on the other hand, that economic phenomena do not depend on mental feelings, I am unable to see how this conclusion can be avoided." Cairnes, *op. cit.,* pp. iv–v.

4. George J. Stigler, *Production and Distribution Theories* (New York: Macmillan & Co., 1946), p. 181. For Carl Menger's attack on the concept of mutual determination and his critique of mathematical economics in general, *see* T. W. Hutchison, *A Review of Economic Doctrines, 1870–1929* (Oxford: The Clarendon Press, 1953), pp. 147–48, and the interesting article by Emil Kauder, "Intellectual and Political Roots of the Older Austrian School," *Zeitschrift für Nationalökonomie,* XVII, 4 (1958), 412 ff.

5. Stigler appends a footnote to the above paragraph, which is meant as the *coup de grace* to Böhm-Bawerk: "Böhm-Bawerk was not trained in mathematics," Stigler, *op. cit.* Mathematics, it must be realized, is only the servant of logic and reason, and not their master. "Training" in mathematics is no more necessary to the realization of its uselessness for and inapplicability to the sciences of human action than, for example, "training" in agricultural techniques is essential to knowing that they are not applicable on board an ocean liner. Indeed, training in mathematics, without adequate attention to the epistemology of the sciences of human action, is likely to yield unfortunate results when applied to the latter, as this example demonstrates. Böhm-Bawerk's greatness as an economist needs no defense at this date. For a sensitive tribute to Böhm-Bawerk, *see* Joseph A. Schumpeter, "Eugen von Böhm-Bawerk, 1851–1914" in *Ten Great Economists* (New York: Oxford University Press, 1951), pp. 143–90. For a purely assertive and unsupported depreciation of Böhm-Bawerk's stature as an economist, *see* Howard S. Ellis' review of Schumpeter's book in the *Journal of Political Economy,* October, 1952, p. 434.

6. The literature in economics has been immeasurably confused by writers on production theory who deal with problems in terms of technology rather than valuation. For an excellent article on this problem, cf. Lionel Robbins, "Remarks upon Certain Aspects of the Theory of Costs," *Economic Journal,* March, 1934, pp. 1–18.

7. We must hasten to add that this does *not* signify adoption of the old classical fallacy that treated each of these groups of factors as homogeneous. Clearly, they are heterogeneous and for pricing purposes and in human action are treated as such. Only the same good, homogeneous for human valuation, is treated as a common "factor," and all factors are treated alike—for their contribution to revenue—by producers. The categories "land, labor, and capital goods" are essential, however, for a

deeper analysis of production problems, in particular the analysis of various income returns and of the relation of time to production.

8. It must be understood that "factors of production" include *every* service that advances the product toward the stage of consumption. Thus, such services as "marketing costs," advertising, etc., are just as legitimately productive services as any other factors. The fallacy in the spurious distinction between "production costs" and "selling costs" has been definitely demonstrated by Mises, *Human Action,* p. 319.

9. On the structure of production, *see* Wieser, *op. cit.,* pp. 47 ff.

10. In practice, one or more persons can be the owners of any of the factors. Thus, the original factors might also be jointly owned by several persons. This would not affect our analysis. The only change would be that the joint owners of a factor would have to allocate the factor's income according to voluntary contract. But the type of allocation would remain the same.

11. Actually, this case cannot occur, since labor, as we shall see below, is always a nonspecific factor.

12. It is therefore our contention that the term "consumers' sovereignty" is highly inapt and that "individual sovereignty" would be a more appropriate term for describing the free market system. For an analysis of the concept of "consumers' sovereignty," see chapter 10 below.

13. Cf. the excellent discussion of cost by G. F. Thirlby, "The Subjective Theory of Value and Accounting 'Cost,'" *Economica,* February, 1946, pp. 33 f.; and especially Thirlby, "Economists' Cost Rules and Equilibrium Theory," *Economica,* May, 1960, pp. 148–53.

14. As Thirlby says, "Cost is ephemeral. The cost involved in a particular decision loses its significance with the making of a decision because the decision displaces the alternative course of action." Thirlby, "Subjective Theory of Value," *op. cit.,* p. 34. And Jevons: *"Labor once spent has no influence on the future value of any article:* it is gone and lost for ever. In commerce bygones are forever bygones and we are always starting clear at each moment, judging the values of things with a view to future utility. Industry is essentially prospective, not retrospective." Jevons, *op. cit.,* p. 164.

15. There will undoubtedly be exceptions, such as cases where the owner obtains enjoyment from the land or capital good from its lying idle— such as the esthetic enjoyment of using it as an uncultivated forest. These alternatives are then also costs, when a decision is made on the use of the land.

16. It is unfortunate that these truths, substantially set forth by the "Austrian School of economics" (which included some Englishmen and Americans) close to three-quarters of a century ago, should have been almost entirely obscured by the fashinable eclectic doctrine that "real costs" and utility are somehow co-ordinate in price determination, with "costs" being "really" more important "in the long run." How often has Alfred Marshall's homely analogy of utility and cost being "two blades of a scissors" been invoked as a substitute for analysis! Emil Kauder has supplied an interesting interpretation of the reason for the failure of

British thought to adopt the nascent subjective value approach in previous centuries. He attributes the emphasis on labor and real cost, as contrasted to subjective utility and happiness, to the Calvinist background of the British classicists, typified by Smith and Locke. Of particular interest here is his citation of the strongly Evangelical background of Marshall. Implicit in his treatment is the view that the second major reason for the classicists' failure to follow subjectivist leads was their search for an invariable measurement of value. This search embodied the "scientistic" desire to imitate the methods of the natural sciences. Emil Kauder, "The Retarded Acceptance of the Marginal Utility Theory," *Quarterly Journal of Economics*, November, 1953, pp. 564–75.

17. The term "pure rate of interest" corresponds to Mises' term "originary rate of interest." See *Human Action, passim.*

18. Here the reader is referred to one of the great works in the history of economic thought, Eugen von Böhm-Bawerk's *Capital and Interest* (New York: Brentano's, 1922), where the correct theory of interest is outlined; in particular, the various false theories of interest are brilliantly dissected. This is not to say that the present author endorses all of Böhm-Bawerk's theory of interest as presented in his *Positive Theory of Capital.*

19. Strictly, this assumption is incorrect, and we make it in this section only for purposes of simplicity. For interest may be an opportunity cost for an individual investor, but it is *not* a *money* cost, nor is it an opportunity cost for the aggregate of capitalists. For the implications of this widely held error in economic literature, *see* André Gabor and I. F. Pearce, "The Place of Money Capital in the Theory of Production," *Quarterly Journal of Economics*, November, 1958, pp. 537–57; and Gabor and Pearce, "A New Approach to the Theory of the Firm," *Oxford Economic Papers*, October, 1952, pp. 252–65.

20. Cf. Menger, *op. cit.*, pp. 149 ff.

21. The very interesting researches by Emil Kauder indicate that the essentials of the Austrian marginal utility theory (the basis of the view that price determines cost and not *vice versa* or mutually) had already been formulated by French and Italian economists of the seventeenth and eighteenth centuries and that the English classical school shunted economics onto a very wrong road, a road from which economics was extricated only by the Austrians. *See* Emil Kauder, "Genesis of the Marginal Utility Theory," *Economic Journal*, September, 1953, pp. 638–50; and Kauder, "The Retarded Acceptance of the Marginal Utility Theory," *loc. cit.*

22. Alfred Marshall, *Principles of Economics* (8th ed.; London: Macmillan & Co., 1920), pp. 349 ff.

23. This analogy, though not used in this context, was often used by classical economists as applied to prices and "the price level," an application equally erroneous.

24. On this error in Marshall, *see* F. A. Hayek, *The Pure Theory of Capital* (Chicago: University of Chicago Press, 1941), pp. 21, 27–28. Marshall is

here committing the famous fallacy of "conceptual realism," in which theoretical constructs are mistaken for actually existing entities. For other examples, cf. Leland B. Yeager, "Some Questions on Growth Economics," *American Economic Review*, March, 1954, p. 62.

25. Marshall, *op. cit.*, pp. 338 ff.

26. We must hasten to point out that this is by no means the same criticism as the neo-Keynesian charge that economists must deal in broad aggregates, and not with individual cases. The latter approach is even worse, since it begins with "wholes" that have no basis in reality whatever. What we are advocating is a theory that deals with all the individuals as they interact in the economy. Furthermore, this is the "Austrian," and not the Walrasian approach, which has recently come into favor. The latter deals with interrelations of individuals ("the general equilibrium approach") but only in the ERE and with mathematical abstractions in the ERE.

27. Little of value has been said about bargaining since Böhm-Bawerk. *See* Böhm-Bawerk, *Positive Theory*, pp. 198–99. This can be seen in J. Pen's "A General Theory of Bargaining," *American Economic Review*, March, 1952, pp. 24 ff. Pen's own theory is of little worth because it rests explicitly on an assumption of the measurability of utility. *Ibid.*, p. 34 n.

28. Contrast the discussion in most textbooks, where bargaining occupies an important place in explanation of market pricing *only* in the discussion of labor incomes.

29. See Mises, *Human Action*, p. 336.

30. Any zone of indeterminacy in pricing must consist of the coincidence of an absolutely vertical supply curve with an absolutely vertical market demand curve for the good or service, so that the equilibrium price is in a zone rather than at a point. As Hutt states, "It depends entirely upon the fortuitous coincidence of . . . an unusual and highly improbable demand curve with an absolutely rigid supply curve." W. H. Hutt, *The Theory of Collective Bargaining* (Glencoe, Ill.: The Free Press, 1954), pp. 90, and 79–109.

NOTES TO CHAPTER 6

1. The discussion in this chapter deals with the *pure* rate of interest, as determined by time preference. On the role of the purchasing-power component in the market rate of interest, cf. chapter 11 on money, below.

2. On production theory and stages of production, see the important works of F. A. Hayek, particularly *Prices and Production* (2nd ed.; London: Routledge and Kegan Paul, 1935); and *Profits, Interest, and Investment* (London: Routledge and Kegan Paul, 1939).

3. Cf. Böhm-Bawerk, *Positive Theory*, pp. 304–05, 320.

4. In the ERE of our example, the *pure* rate of interest is *the* rate of interest, since, as we shall see, deviations from the pure rate are due solely to uncertainty.

5. In the reams of commentary on J. M. Keynes' *General Theory*, no one has noticed the very revealing passage in which Keynes criticizes Mises'

discussion of this point. Keynes asserted that Mises' "peculiar" new theory of interest "confused" the "marginal efficiency of capital" (the net rate of return on an investment) with the rate of interest. The point is that the "marginal efficiency of capital" *is indeed* the rate of interest! It is a price on the time market. It was precisely this "natural" rate, rather than the loan rate, that had been a central problem of interest theory for many years. The essentials of this doctrine were set forth by Böhm-Bawerk in *Capital and Interest* and should therefore not have been surprising to Keynes. *See* John Maynard Keynes, *The General Theory of Employment, Interest and Money* (New York: Harcourt, Brace & Co., 1936), pp. 192–93. It is precisely this preoccupation with the relatively unimportant problems of the loan market that constitutes one of the greatest defects of the Keynesian theory of interest.

6. As Böhm-Bawerk declared: "Interest . . . may be obtained from any capital, no matter what be the kind of goods of which the capital consists: from goods that are barren as well as from those that are naturally fruitful; from perishable as well as from durable goods; from goods that can be replaced and from goods that cannot be replaced; from money as well as from commodities." Böhm-Bawerk, *Capital and Interest*, p. 1.

7. Cf. Mises, *Human Action*, pp. 521–42.

8. This is a highly simplified portrayal of the value scale. For purposes of exposition, we have omitted the fact that the *second* unit of 13 added future ounces will be worth less than the first, the third unit of 13 less than the second, etc. Thus, in actuality, the demand schedule of future goods will be lower than portrayed here. However, the essentials of the analysis are unaffected, since we can assume a demand schedule of any size that we wish. The only significant conclusion is that the demand curve is shaped so that an individual demands more future goods as the market rate of interest rises, and this conclusion holds for the actual as well as for our simplified version.

9. The reader may drop the parentheses around the future moneys at the lower end of the value scale, for Robinson is considering supplying them as well as demanding them.

10. In the same way, though we cannot compare utilities, we can compare (if we know them) individual *demand* schedules for goods.

11. It is not valid to object that some might prefer to *use* the money in the future rather than in the present. That is not the issue here, which is one of *availability* for use. If a man wants to "save" money for some future use, he may "hoard" it rather than spend it on a future good, and thus have it always available. We have abstracted from hoarding, which will be dealt with in the chapter on money; it would have no place, anyway, in the evenly rotating world of certainty.

12. The importance of time preference was first seen by Böhm-Bawerk in his *Capital and Interest*. The *sole* importance of time preference has been grasped by extremely few economists, notably by Frank A. Fetter and Ludwig von Mises. See Fetter, *Economic Principles*, pp. 235–316; id., "Interest Theories, Old and New," *American Economic Review*, March, 1914, pp. 68–92; and Mises, *Human Action*, pp. 476–534.

13. The fact that consumers may physically consume all or part of these goods at a later date does not affect this conclusion, because any further consumption takes place outside the money nexus, and it is the latter that we are analyzing.

14. No important complication arises from the greater degree of futurity of the higher-order factors. As we have indicated above, a *more* distantly future good will simply be discounted by the market by a greater amount, though at the same rate per annum. The interest *rate*, i.e., the discount rate of future goods per unit of time, remains the same regardless of the degree of futurity of the good. This fact serves to resolve one problem mentioned above—vertical integration by firms over one or more stages. If the equilibrium rate of interest is 5% per year, then a one-stage producer will earn 5% on his investment, while a producer who advances present goods over three stages—for three years—will earn 15%, i.e., 5% per annum.

15. Very recently, greater realism has been introduced into social accounting by considering intercapitalist "money flows."

16. Problems of hoarding and dishoarding from the cash balance will be treated in chapter 11 on money and are prescinded from the present analysis.

17. Cf. Knut Wicksell, *Lectures on Political Economy* (London: Routledge and Kegan Paul, 1934), I, 189–91.

18. For more on the relations between the interest rate, i.e., the price spreads or margins, and the proportions invested and consumed, see below.

19. On gross and net product, *see* Milton Gilbert and George Jaszi, "National Product and Income Statistics as an Aid in Economic Problems" in W. Fellner and B. F. Haley, eds., *Readings in the Theory of Income Distribution* (Philadelphia: Blakiston, 1946), pp. 44–57; and Simon Kuznets, *National Income, A Summary of Findings* (New York: National Bureau of Economic Research, 1946), pp. 111–21, and especially p. 120.

20. If permanence is attributed to the mythical entity, the aggregate value of capital, it becomes an independent factor of production, along with labor, and earns interest.

21. The fallacy of the "net" approach to capital is at least as old as Adam Smith and continues down to the present. *See* Hayek, *Prices and Production,* pp. 37–49. This book is an excellent contribution to the analysis of the production structure, gross savings and consumption, and its application to the business cycle, based on the production and business cycle theories of Böhm-Bawerk and Mises respectively. *Also see* Hayek, "The Mythology of Capital" in *Readings in the Theory of Income Distribution,* pp. 355–83; *id., Profits, Interest, and Investment, passim.*

22. For a critique of the analogous views of J. B. Clark, *see* Frank A. Fetter, "Recent Discussions of the Capital Concept," *Quarterly Journal of Economics,* November, 1900, pp. 1–14. Fetter succinctly criticizes Clark's failure to explain interest on consumption goods, his assumption of a permanent capital fund, and his assumption of "synchronization" in production.

23. Cf. Böhm-Bawerk, *Positive Theory*, pp. 299–322, 329–38.
24. The rate of interest, however, will make a great deal of difference in so far as he is an owner and seller of a durable good. Land is, of course, durable almost by definition—in fact, generally permanent. So far, we have been dealing only with the sale of factor *services,* i.e., the "hire" or "rent" of the factor, and abstracting from the sale or valuation of durable factors, which embody future services. Durable land, as we shall see, is "capitalized," i.e., the value of the factor as a whole is the discounted sum of its future MVP's, and there the interest rate will make a significant difference. The price of durable land, however, is irrelevant to the supply schedule of land *services* in demand for present money.
25. Strictly, of course, the slope would not be constant, since the return is in equal *percentages,* not in equal absolute amounts. Slopes are treated as constant here, however, for the sake of simplicity in presenting the analysis.
26. This Marxian error stemmed from a very similar error introduced into economics by Adam Smith. Cf. Ronald L. Meek, "Adam Smith and the Classical Concept of Profit," *Scottish Journal of Political Economy,* June, 1954, pp. 138–53.
27. For brilliant dissections of various forms of the "productivity" theory of interest (the neoclassical view that investment earns an interest return because capital goods are *value*-productive), see the following articles by Frank A. Fetter: "The Roundabout Process of the Interest Theory," *Quarterly Journal of Economics,* 1902, pp. 163–80, where Böhm-Bawerk's highly unfortunate lapse into a productivity theory of interest is refuted; "Interest Theories Old and New," *op. cit.,* pp. 68–92, which presents an extensive development of time-preference theory, coupled with a critique of Irving Fisher's concessions to the productivity doctrine; *also see* "Capitalization Versus Productivity, Rejoinder," *American Economic Review,* 1914, pp. 856–59, and "Davenport's Competitive Economics," *Journal of Political Economy,* 1914, pp. 555–62. Fetter's only mistake in interest theory was to deny Fisher's assertion that time preference (or, as Fisher called it, "impatience") is a universal and *necessary* fact of human action. For a demonstration of this important truth, *see* Mises, *Human Action,* pp. 480 ff.
28. On Keynes' failure to perceive this point, see page 454 of this chapter, note 5 above.
29. The shares of stock, or the units of property rights, "have the characteristic of fungibility; one unit is exactly the same as another. . . . We have a mathematical division of the one set of rights. This fungible quality makes possible organized commodity and security markets or exchanges. . . . With these fungible units of . . . property rights we have a possible acceleration of changes of ownership and in membership of the groups. . . . If a course of market dealings arises, the unit of property has a swift cash conversion value. Its owner may readily resume the cash power to command the uses of wealth." Hastings Lyon, *Corporations and their Financing* (Boston: D. C. Heath, 1936), p. 11.

Thus, *shares* of property as well as total property have become readily marketable.

30. The literature on the so-called "co-operative movement" is of remarkably poor quality. The best source is *Co-operatives in the Petroleum Industry,* ed. by K. E. Ettinger (New York: Petroleum Industry Research Foundation, 1947), especially Pt. I, Ludwig von Mises, "Observations on the Co-operative Movement."

31. *See* Mises, *Human Action,* pp. 301–05, 703–05.

32. The proxy fights of recent years simply give dramatic evidence of this control.

33. Edgar M. Hoover, "Some Institutional Factors in Business Decisions," *American Economic Review, Papers and Proceedings,* May, 1954, p. 203.

34. For example, *see* Gerhard Colm, "The Corporation and the Corporation Income Tax in the American Economy," *American Economic Review, Papers and Proceedings,* May, 1954, p. 488.

35. As Frank Fetter brilliantly stated: "Contract [interest] is based on and tends to conform to economic interest [i.e., the 'natural interest' price differential between stages]. . . . It is economic interest that we seek to explain logically through the economic nature of the goods. Contract interest is a secondary problem—a business and legal problem—as to who shall have the benefit of the income arising with the possession of the goods. It is closely connected with the question of ownership." Fetter, "Recent Discussions of the Capital Concept," *op. cit.,* pp. 24–25.

36. "The creditor is always a virtual partner of the debtor or a virtual owner of the pledged and mortgaged property." Mises, *Human Action,* p. 536. *Also see* Fetter, "Recent Discussions of the Capital Concept," *op. cit.,* p. 43.

37. Similar psychic components may occur in the consumers' loan market—for example, if there is general strong liking or dislike for a certain borrower.

38. Thus, cf. Friedrich A. Lutz, "The Structure of Interest Rates" in *Readings in the Theory of Income Distribution,* pp. 499–532.

39. Since the writing of this text, Professor Luckett has published a critique of Lutz similar in part. *See* Dudley G. Luckett, "Professor Lutz and the Structure of Interest Rates," *Quarterly Journal of Economics,* February, 1959, pp. 131–44. *Also see* J. M. Culbertson, "The Term Structure of Interest Rates," *ibid.,* November, 1957, pp. 485–517.

40. It is remarkable that in his empirical study of the time structure of interest rates, Charls Walker found an irresistible tendency of interest rates to equalize, but was forced to multiply his assumptions in order to try to demonstrate that this was a proof of the theory that interest rates do not necessarily equalize. Charls E. Walker, "Federal Reserve Policy and the Structure of Interest Rates on Government Securities," *Quarterly Journal of Economics,* February, 1954, pp. 19–42. Walker's article has considerable merit in demonstrating the impossibilities of governmental maintenance of a differential interest pattern in the face of the market's drive to equality. Cf. Luckett, *op. cit.,* p. 143 n.

41. *See* Mises, *Human Action,* p. 541.

42. *See* Mises, *Human Action,* pp. 527–29. *Also see* Lionel Robbins, "On a Certain Ambiguity in the Conception of Stationary Equilibrium," in Richard V. Clemence, ed., *Readings in Economic Analysis* (Cambridge: Addison-Wesley Press, 1950), I, 176 ff.

43. Richard V. Clemence and Francis S. Doody, *The Schumpeterian System* (Cambridge: Addison-Wesley Press, 1950), pp. 28–30.

44. As has been the case with all theorists who have attempted to deny time preference, Clemence and Doody hastily brush *consumers' loans* aside. As Frank A. Fetter pointed out years ago, only time preference can integrate interest on consumers' as well as on producers' loans into a single unified explanation. Consumers' loans are clearly unrelated to "productivity" explanations of interest and are obviously due to time preference. Cf. Clemence and Doody, *op. cit.,* p. 29 n.

NOTES TO CHAPTER 7

1. The mathematical bent toward replacing the concepts of cause and effect by mutual determination has contributed to the willingness to engage in circular reasoning. *See* Rothbard, "Toward a Reconstruction of Utility and Welfare Economics," *op. cit.,* p. 236; and Kauder, "Intellectual and Political Roots of the Older Austrian School," *loc. cit.*

2. Clearly, the longer the period of time, the more variable will factor proportions tend to be. Technologically, varying amounts of time are needed to rearrange the various factors.

3. This justifies the conclusion of Mises, *Human Action,* p. 336, as compared, for example, with the analysis in George J. Stigler's *Production and Distribution Theories.* Mises adds the important proviso that if the factors have the same fixed proportions in *all* the processes for which they are nonspecific, then here too only bargaining can determine their prices.

4. Strictly, we should be dealing with *discounted* MVP's here, but treating just MVP's at this stage merely simplifies matters.

5. We are here postulating that equal quantities of factors produce equal quantities of results. The famous question whether this condition actually holds (sometimes phrased in pretentious mathematical language as whether the "production function is linear and homogeneous") is easily resolved if we realize that the proposition: equal causes produce equal results, is the major technological axiom in nature. Any cases that appear to confute this rule only do so in appearance; in reality, supposed exceptions always involve some "indivisibility" where one factor, in effect, cannot change proportionately with other factors.

6. This is not strictly true, but the technical error in the statement does not affect the causal analysis in the text. In fact, this argument is strengthened, for MVP actually equals MPP × "marginal revenue," and marginal revenue is always less than, or equal to, price. See Appendix A below, "Marginal Physical and Marginal Value Product."

7. It might be asked why we now employ mathematics after our strictures against the mathematical method in economics. The reason is that, in

this particular problem, we are dealing with a purely *technological* question. We are not dealing with human decisions here, but with the necessary technological conditions of the world as given to human factors. In this external world, given quantities of cause yield given quantities of effect, and it is this sphere, very limited in the over-all praxeological picture, that, like the natural sciences in general, is peculiarly susceptible to mathematical methods. The relationship between average and marginal is an obviously *algebraic,* rather than an ends-means, relation. Cf. the algebraic proof in Stigler, *Theory of Price,* pp. 44 ff.

8. This law applies to all factors, specific and nonspecific.
9. See the excellent discussion in Böhm-Bawerk, *Positive Theory of Capital,* pp. 304–12. For a further discussion of DMVP as against MVP, see Appendix B below, "Professor Rolph and the Discounted Marginal Productivity Theory."
10. *See* Wicksell, *op. cit.,* I, 108.
11. See the excellent analysis in Wicksell, *op. cit.,* I, 189–91, 193–95.
12. This was realized by Carl Menger. *See* F. A. Hayek, "Carl Menger" in Henry W. Spiegel, ed., *The Development of Economic Thought* (New York: John Wiley, 1952), pp. 530 ff.
13. Böhm-Bawerk, *Positive Theory of Capital,* p. 88.
14. Mises, *Human Action,* pp. 477, 485 f. *Also see* Menger, *op. cit.,* pp. 166–67.
15. "Nonreplaceable" as a criterion for *land,* in contrast to *capital goods,* is *not* equivalent to "permanent." "Permanent" is a subdivision of "nonreplaceable." It is clear that permanent improvements do not have to be replaced. However, *depletable* natural resources, such as coal, ores, etc., are not permanent, but are also nonreplaceable. The key question is whether a resource has to be *produced,* in which case it earns only *gross* rents. If it does not or cannot, it earns *net* rents as well. Resources that are being depleted obviously *cannot* be replaced and are therefore *land,* not capital goods. See the section on depletable resources below.
16. We may use "permanent" and "nonpermanent" in this section, because resources that are being depleted obviously cannot be included in any evenly rotating equilibrium. For more on depletable resources, see below. With depletable resources left aside, "permanent" becomes identical with "nonreproducible."
17. Cf. Wicksell, *op. cit.,* I, 186, and *passim;* and Hayek, *Pure Theory of Capital,* pp. 54–58.
18. Neither is there any relation between the present issue of permanence or nonpermanence and the cosmological question of the permanence of matter and energy. *See* Mises, *Human Action,* p. 634.
19. Stigler charges that the various distinctions between land and capital goods based on permanence or origin, such as are discussed herein, are physical rather than economic. These strictures miss the point. No one denies that these homogeneous factors can change greatly in *value* over time. But whether or not a given factor is original or improved, or permanent or needing to be maintained, *is* a physical question, and one that is very relevant to economic analysis. Certainly, the Knightian argu-

ment that all land is capital goods, because no land is original, is also an argument in the *physical* realm. Stigler, *Production and Distribution Theories*, p. 274.

20. John V. Van Sickle and Benjamin A. Rogge, *Introduction to Economics* (New York: D. Van Nostrand, 1954), p. 141.

21. But while the position is permanent, even the land itself was necessarily altered by man to prepare it for urban use. See chapter 2 above.

22. This concept of rent is based on the original contribution of Frank A. Fetter. Cf. Fetter, *Economic Principles*, pp. 143–70. Fetter's conception has, unfortunately, had little influence on economic thought. It is not only in accord with common usage; it provides a unifying principle, enabling a coherent explanation of the price determination of unit services and of the whole goods that embody them. Without the rental-price concept, it is difficult to distinguish between the pricing of unit services and of whole goods.

   Fetter used the rental concept to apply only to the services of durable goods, but it is clear that it can be extended to cover cases of non-durable goods where the unit service *is* the whole good.

23. See chapter 4 above. On capitalization, *see* Fetter, *Economic Principles*, pp. 262–84, 308–13; Böhm-Bawerk, *Positive Theory*, pp. 339–57.

24. It is often more convenient to define *rent* as equal to the MVP, rather than the DMVP. In that case, the capital value of the whole factor is equal to the *discounted* sum of its future rents.

25. Fetter's main error in capital theory was his belief that capitalization meant the scrapping of any distinction between capital goods and land.

26. Cf. Boulding, *Economic Analysis*, pp. 711–12.

27. In the *long run*, increases in the capital value of *capital goods* are unimportant, since they resolve into increases in wages and increases in the capital value of ground land.

28. The problem of gains from changes in capital values will be treated further below.

29. Cf. Fred R. Fairchild, Edgar S. Furniss, and Norman S. Buck, *Elementary Economics* (New York: Macmillan & Co., 1926), II, 147.

30. Hayek, *Pure Theory of Capital*, p. 58 n.

31. *Ibid.*, p. 92.

32. Unusual terms because robbery has been distinctively defined as seizure of *someone else's* property without his consent, not the use of one's *own* property.

33. As Stigler says in discussing the charge of "wasted" resources on the market, "It is an interesting problem to define 'wasteful' sensibly without making the word synonymous with 'unprofitable.'" Stigler, *Theory of Price*, p. 332 n. For a discussion of natural resources and a critique of the doctrines of "conservation," *see* Anthony Scott, *Natural Resources: The Economics of Conservation* (Toronto: University of Toronto Press, 1955).

34. A curious notion has arisen that considering *MR*, instead of price, as the multiplier somehow vitiates the optimum satisfaction of consumer

desires on the market. There is no genuine warrant for such an assumption.

35. Earl Rolph, "The Discounted Marginal Productivity Doctrine" in *Readings in Theory of Income Distribution,* pp. 278–93.

36. Rolph ascribes this error to Knut Wicksell, but such a confusion is not attributable to Wicksell, who engages in a brilliant discussion of capital and the production structure and the role of time in production. Wicksell demonstrates correctly that labor and land are the only ultimate factors, and that therefore the marginal productivity of capital goods is reducible to the marginal productivity of labor and land factors, so that money capital earns the interest (or discount) differential.

Wicksell's discussion of these and related issues is of basic importance. He recognized, for example, that capital goods are fully and basically co-ordinate with land and labor factors *only from the point of view of the individual firm,* but not when we consider the total market in all of its interrelations. Current economic theorizing is, to its detriment, even more preoccupied than writers of his day with the study of an isolated firm instead of the interrelated market. Wicksell, *Lectures,* I, 148–54, 185–95.

37. Rolph ends his article. consistently, with a dismissal of any time-preference influences on interest, which he explains in Knightian vein by the "cost" of producing new capital goods.